An American Color

RACE IN THE ATLANTIC WORLD, 1700–1900

SERIES EDITORS

Richard S. Newman, *Rochester Institute of Technology*
Patrick Rael, *Bowdoin College*
Manisha Sinha, *University of Connecticut*

ADVISORY BOARD

Edward Baptist, *Cornell University*
Christopher Brown, *Columbia University*
Vincent Carretta, *University of Maryland*
Laurent Dubois, *Duke University*
Erica Armstrong Dunbar, *Rutgers University*
Douglas Egerton, *LeMoyne College*
Leslie Harris, *Northwestern University*
Joanne Pope Melish, *University of Kentucky*
Sue Peabody, *Washington State University, Vancouver*
Erik Seeman, *State University of New York, Buffalo*
John Stauffer, *Harvard University*

An American Color

RACE AND IDENTITY
IN NEW ORLEANS AND
THE ATLANTIC WORLD

Andrew N. Wegmann

The University of Georgia Press
ATHENS

© 2022 by the University of Georgia Press
Athens, Georgia 30602
www.ugapress.org
All rights reserved
Set in 10.5/13.5 Adobe Caslon Pro Regular
by Kaelin Chappell Broaddus

Most University of Georgia Press titles are
available from popular e-book vendors.

Printed digitally

Library of Congress Cataloging-in-Publication Data

Names: Wegmann, Andrew N., author.
Title: An American color : race and identity in New Orleans and the
    Atlantic world / Andrew N. Wegmann.
Other titles: Race in the Atlantic world, 1700–1900.
Description: Athens : The University of Georgia Press, 2022. |
    Series: Race in the Atlantic world, 1700–1900 | Includes
    bibliographical references and index.
Identifiers: LCCN 2021031921 | ISBN 9780820360768 (hardback) |
    ISBN 9780820360782 (paperback) | ISBN 9780820360775 (ebook)
Subjects: LCSH: African Americans—History—To 1863. | Racially
    mixed people—Louisiana—New Orleans—History. | Racially
    mixed people—United States—History. | New Orleans (La.)—
    History—19th century. | United States—Race relations—History—
    19th century.
Classification: LCC E185.18 .W44 2022 | DDC 305.8009763/35—dc23
LC record available at https://lccn.loc.gov/2021031921

To my parents,
Julie-Ann and Richard Wegmann,
who took me to see the world, allowed me to experience an impossible sense of love and compassion, and gave me the only life I would ever want. This is for them, many years later, for the love, hope, and happiness I will never be able to repay.

And to
Edna Williams and Gerry Rault,
for giving me so much in such different ways.

CONTENTS

Acknowledgments ix
Note on Language xv

Introduction 1
CHAPTER 1. *Genèse Française*: The French 10
CHAPTER 2. The Vitriolic Blood of a Negro: The Spanish 32
CHAPTER 3. A Sensible Equivalent to the Original Blood: The Americans 60
CHAPTER 4. A Fire of Color and Class: The South 88
CHAPTER 5. "A Call Back to the Original": The Atlantic 118

Notes 147
Bibliography 201
Index 233

ACKNOWLEDGMENTS

I have waited to write these words, more than any of the others, for a very long time. I have written sections like this before, but never has one felt so difficult and foreboding. It is getting late, at least right now, and I am at a loss. This book has been my life for longer than most things. It has seen several homes, many mindsets, and more than a few bouts of hopelessness and wonder. More important than that, though, it has brought a new world to me, a community of people with whom I have grown alongside this book. Most of them appear below, but there are numberless others who have, perhaps without them or me knowing it, given life to this book in ways I could never express or explain—small chats at coffee shops, their very presence in an archive, longer chats at Parkview Tavern, The Chimes, Highland Coffees, Louie's, or anywhere else I've been over the years and lives it has taken me to finish this work. I appreciate them first, but perhaps not foremost.

Beyond most every person in my life, my parents, Julie-Ann and Richard Wegmann, mean the most—and not only because they gave me, literally, the opportunity to write these words, have these thoughts, and breathe the air I breathe. It goes much further with them. Although this is my only life, it is, as I wrote in the dedication, the only one I could ever want. In their own strange and brilliant ways, they taught me how to think, how to smile and mean it, how to love like nothing else matters in the world. It was unshakable, and still is. They drove me around the world, let me see what I could never imagine, and, from a very early age, taught me to open my eyes, listen for a second, and take a deep breath, even when I didn't know that I wanted to. There is a reason most of my memories appear in the daylight.

My mother is goodness. She is love. She is light. Her life, and all that has made it, gives me a sense of hope and optimism that makes streams of waves. I don't think I know the kind of love she feels. It is a special love, a love that settles and expands throughout a room, or a home, or a city. It is everything I have ever wanted, and it is all I have ever received.

My father worked too hard to make my life easy. He will say, "That's what you do when you love someone." But I could never possibly deserve the kindness, empathy, and generosity he has given me. He taught me humility and altruism, dedication and passion, and his honest interest in my work has been both surprising and inexplicably meaningful. Everything I wrote, I wrote with him in mind; and in many ways, that is what got me to writing this.

My brother, Matt, is an interesting story. As an academic himself and the most New Orleanian of New Orleanians, he always understood when it was time for a beer and a complaint, a sit-down on the porch, watching the cars drive by and talking about how good it was just being there. He saw me through the darkness and brought me up to breathe. He has always stood as that sentinel in the distance, that sense of home that makes each step count, even when strength is gone. He brings passion to each movement, joy to each word. He is unbridled dedication. He is the perfect kind of crazy. He is what I need when I need it. He is fire. He is wisdom. It is perfect.

I like to talk. I like to write. But now, when thinking of my wife, Maia, words turn to feeling. I never thought the world could handle a person like her—someone so brilliant and beautiful and kind and bright. Her love and life extend beyond what I thought possible before I met her that January night in the parking lot in which, two years later, I would ask her to marry me. She has given me a sense of comfort and home that shouldn't be possible outside of family; but that is what makes it so real. She doesn't *need* to do anything she does for me. But she does, every day, with heart. She has taught me what it means to love. She has taught me to appreciate the sun, and light, and laughter, and joy. She is my joy. She is each smile and song and ray of sunlight. She is everything I've ever wanted in a partner, in a wife, in a friend. I am glad to know that I have lived and will always live a life of happiness with her. Without that, I would not have finished this project. I would not have cared enough. But I did, and I do, and I love it because of her.

Geoff Cunningham, Terry Wagner, and Spencer McBride grew up with me, in a way. Geoff and his wife, Jaina, brought me to Manzanita Beach, where I came alive again. In many ways, those two saved me, and I can never thank them enough for it. With Terry, I danced into the night. With Spencer, I shared hotel rooms, archives, an academic lineage, and some of the most interesting conversations of my life. The respect I have for him is endless, both as a scholar and a dear friend. Adam Pratt has become a confidante and friend over the past few years. I'm not sure that how similar we are is good for the world, but I know that it has added a great deal to my life and the joy I find in it. He and his wife, Shelli, are gifts, and I look up to them very much.

As he knows, I can do this all *day*! Jay Gitlin has become family in a number of ways. His energetic support, invitations to places in which I never dreamed I belonged, and passion for stories and conversation and bringing great minds together continuously remind me that there is good in the world and that I am part of a broad, caring, and interesting community. From laughs in St. Louis to jambalaya in Davenport to the guestbook in old Calhoun, Jay has made every bit of this journey more meaningful. He is pure gold.

I have the great fortune of benefitting from a friend group, thrown about the Atlantic world, of varied and wild genius. Perhaps more than anyone else, the talispeople of that group are the wise, insane, brilliant, caring, supportive, fervent, engaging, and kind Whitney Stewart and Ben Wright. They have become life mates of me and my wife. We travel together, celebrate together, and talk long into the night. Their shared critical wit, piercing questions, and creative genius are mysteries of mankind. They are bespoke, for sure.

Professionally, I have accrued a list of people deserving thanks that would fill the pages of several volumes. To save the press money and myself time, I cannot list them all here. As with any work of history, the custodians of numerous archives helped me find the seemingly unfindable. First and foremost, I must thank the inimitable Greg Osborn at New Orleans Public Library–Main Branch. His encyclopedic knowledge of the Creoles of color led me to countless sources I would never have found on my own. Over the process of researching this work, over lunches at Tulane's commissary, drinks in the Marigny after work, and hours and hours of conversation, Greg became a good friend and ample guide. I thank him for his kindness, generosity, and genuine interest in my work. Also at NOPL, Irene Wainwright helped me with sincerity and dedication, as did the brilliant, bizarre, and always entertaining Yvonne Loiselle. Harlan Green at the College of Charleston Special Collections led me through the nuances of the Brown Fellowship Society, while Deborah Wright at the Avery Research Center provided fascinating conversation and let me see more collections than I could ever imagine.

I also must thank the staffs at the South Carolina Historical Society and the Charleston County Public Library for their help in untangling the lives of the Brown Elite. Edward Gaynor at the Library of Virginia first showed me around, then tirelessly worked to find some of the most valuable collections I used in this study. Frances Pollard, Nelson Lankford, and especially Jim McClure made my time at the Virginia Historical Society one of the most productive and enjoyable of my life. They also provided me with an Andrew W. Mellon Fellowship, which allowed me to spend an enormous amount of time at their facility free of stress and financial want. I appreciate that a great deal. I also appreciate the help of the nameless woman at Virginia State University, on the fourth floor of what otherwise appeared to be an abandoned building, who brought Joseph Jenkins Roberts, American, to life for me. That collection, beyond any other, was the most interesting I have ever seen, and I stumbled on it largely because of her. Before I could thank her, though, she disappeared into the hall, never to return. So here it is, many years later: Thank you so very, very much.

Bertrand Van Ruymbeke started as a name on books and in emails, but he became a friend and mentor. His passion for United States history and interest in my perspective has brought to me a new intellectual world. He has welcomed and invited me to France countless times to share my work, meet other scholars, and become part of a transatlantic community of thinkers and writers who have collectively given me nothing short of a new life. The acceptance Bertrand has shown me and the genuine friendship that has developed as a result defy any words I can write here. It has all meant the entire world to me. Also in France, Gilles Havard is the greatest, and so are his leather jacket and love for Elvis. Allan Potofsky, my favorite ex-pat, is always up for a good conversation and a hint of wisdom, even over beers in the Seventeenth. Elodie Peyrol, Anne-Claire Faucquez, Marie Lecouvrey, Céline Ugolini, who shares my love for New Orleans, Jean Hébrard, Iris de Rode, and David Chaunu have all lent their steady and helpful hands to this work and my life in writing it. In the UK, Trevor Burnard, Emma Hart, now at the McNeil Center, Richard Follett (COYW!), Mark and Tans Whitehead, Andy James, and the great Malcolm Bromham have all, through some combination of friendship, Fulham, and human relief, made their mark herein, and I thank them all for it.

On this end of things, Robert Englebert spent several years working with me, and I have no idea how he survived. Randy Sparks has become a dear friend and has provided an endless supply of support and advice. To repay him would take a lifetime or more. At LSU, Aaron Sheehan-Dean, Suzanne Marchand, Victor Stater, the great Gibril Cole, Kodi Roberts, David Lindenfeld, Carolyn Herbst Lewis, and Gaines Foster all deserve far more than I can give. At Loyola, Mark Fernandez first convinced me of the merits of this project in its current form. Justin Nystrom, David Moore, Eric Hardy, Ashley Howard, Rian Thum, David Lilly, and Nicole Eggers welcomed me into their department with warmth and unending support. At Delta State, Chuck Westmoreland, Tom Laub, and Brian Becker had the ultimate faith in me, not only hiring me but also allowing me to make this wild ride into a career. Dana Rasch, Leslie Green-Pimentel, Ren, William Ash-Houchen, Judith Coleman, Steven Cowser, Lauren Coker-Durso, Shalondo Jones (aka Olive Johnson), Garry Jennings, and David Baylis have likewise made DSU an unexpected and more than welcomed home.

Elsewhere, across the vast expanse of academia and the scholarly realm, Laurent Dubois, Drew McKevitt, Emily Conroy-Krutz, Martha Jones, Manisha Singh, Patrick Rael, Richard Newman, Kirt Von Daacke, Lo Faber, Julia Gaffield, Peter Onuf, Peter Kastor, Owen Stanwood, Ryan Brasseaux, Larry Tise, Matt Spooner, Paul Polgar, Ben Park, Tony Bourdain, Gautham Rao, Lou Roper, Julie Winch, Marie Stango, Warren Milteer, Libby Neidenbach, Stephen Berry, James Brooks, Brett Rushforth, Leslie Choquette, Chris Childers, Mike Robinson, Chris Willoughby, Urmi Engineer Willoughby, Adam Rothman, David Head, John Marks, Jennifer Spear, Emily Suzanne Clark, Tom Ward, Tom Hoffman, the late Fr. David Borbridge, John Welch, Pat Harrison, Fr. Mark Lewis, Ben Mackin (and Simon and Rosie, naturally), Francis Grant, Jeff "Ryan O'Patrick" O'Bryon, and Joseph Dunn can find their voices in this book in one form or another.

Andy Burstein knocked me down and helped me up until I learned to stand on my own. Nancy Isenberg made sure I never stayed down too long. Together, they convinced me, for the first time in my life, that I could do something like this. The kindness and support they showed me was unique and unsung, more a sharp wind than a warm sun. I'm not sure if I will ever be able to express how much they mean to me, but I hope this book will serve as a modest first attempt.

Walter Biggins, a beloved friend, talented editor, and incomparable man of letters, saw the potential and value of this project from the very beginning and eventually convinced me to submit it to UGA Press, where he was then an acquisitions editor. Having since moved up the ranks at UGA and then on to Penn, Walter has remained a sounding board, advocating for and brainstorming about this book with me at every stage. His faith in me has remained unflinching for years now, and he has become among my most trusted companions. There is no one in the world I would rather talk to for hours on end, my friend. Nate Holly, the noble soul who picked up this project after Walter moved to Penn, has shown the same dedication and honesty as his predecessor. He, too, has been a wonder.

The music has been playing for a while, but before I depart, Maia, Padraig, Sophie, Jeanne d'Arc, and Malta, this and everything I have ever done is for you and always will be. I love you all more than the wind and the trees. I know you will always stop somewhere, waiting for me.

NOTE ON LANGUAGE

The terminology of race within the Atlantic realm, and indeed within United States history as a whole, is fraught with uncertainty and active debate, perhaps no more than in the first quarter of the twenty-first century. A renewed discourse on the place of race and the inequalities still attached to it and its legacy has publicly forced American society—and many other white-dominated societies—to engage the complexities of race and the language used to enact and justify the privileges, acts of violence, and images of self and Others derived from the long history of race creation in the Atlantic and European colonial worlds.

A growing academic and social discourse has taken up the issue of how language is and can be used to describe the past and the present it creates. Central to this, at least as far as the content of this book is concerned, are the shortcomings of an antiquated binary racial code reducing complex and diverse communities into "b/Black" and "white" with little room in between. Throughout this book, I have chosen to use the weighted, somewhat controversial term "colored" to describe those people of color who consciously or clearly did not identify as "black" or directly of African descent within the colonial Atlantic world and the early United States, even if those same people would today fall within the social bounds of Blackness. I have not made this decision lightly or with an eye to minimize the importance of that word in the aggregation of people of color during more recent eras of social and political oppression. I did so in an attempt to represent the identities of the people discussed here more fully within their historical archive and the context that gave it meaning and life. In many cases, law painted these people as wholly one or the other, but they often identified with and lived their lives according to cultural roots that complicated and often betrayed the legal and social archetypes attached to such simplified terms. In several instances, members of this community, which tended as a whole to be remarkably conscious of its collective racial identity, used the term "colored" to describe their specific relationships to "Negroes," "blacks," and others more publicly associated with African ancestry in the slave societies of the Atlantic South. As a result, I use this term purely as used within its historical context to identify members of a community who fell outside the legal binaries of race and status at work in the nineteenth-century Atlantic world and who did not fit the more well-defined racial hierarchy of the Spanish Sistema de Castas and its early Atlantic derivatives.

Meaning, of course, changed and does change. In each chapter below, the complexity of the language used to describe, define, and reinforce human differences grows with that available to the subjects under study. I have avoided, to the best of my ability, using terms out of place or time. For example, the term "free black" was more an exception than a rule until it was introduced by academics in the 1960s and 1970s. There are very few consistent references in the historical record to "free blacks" anywhere in the Atlantic world and especially the United States prior to the twentieth century. Indeed, the term "blacks," when it was used at all, most often referred to slaves, while "Negroes" (and "free Negroes") referred either to people of obvious African descent generally, or to free people of obvious African descent. As a result, I consciously avoid using "free blacks" as a descriptor unless absolutely necessary or in a direct quote. The same goes for more specific terms as well. Unless an individual either self-identified or was identified repeatedly in the record using a specific designation—such as "mulatto," "quadroon," or other terms with particular definitions and contextual meanings—I use "colored" as a catchall in an effort to avoid mischaracterizing the past and placing meaning where I have no authority to place it. It is not my intention to ignore the more recent historical, emotional, and cultural weight of language still used to repress and otherize people today. It is only my intention to do justice to the complexity of race formation and identity in the past, where language itself so often seems unsettled and fluid.

An American Color

INTRODUCTION

"Six hundred of the Lincolnites were slain," he wrote, "and only fifty of our brave Southerners were killed." Jean Blandin, a mixed-race cigarmaker born and raised in New Orleans, was detailing a report he had heard of the Battle of Hampton, Virginia, to his friend, Henry Vasserot, on May 29, 1861, just a few months into the American Civil War. "Hurrah! for our brave Louisianans and may God bless them and [the] whole Southern Confederate army," he continued. "For we Southerners can stand any army the Northerners may send. We will give them the best licking they ever had since they known themselves. Receive this, my dear friend, from the heart of a Creole, and who is proud to be a Southern man." But it was not simply Southern pride that drove Blandin, a native French speaker, to write his friend. "It is not for liberty that we are about to spill our blood in struggling," he wrote, "but our right—our right to protect our home and each other and make men of us."[1]

Jean Blandin was part of a community many decades in the making. And he made sure to mention it to his friend. His reference to being "a Creole" stands among the first of its kind within his community, yet it also shows that it was well entrenched in the vernacular of his place and time. His use of "Creole" to describe himself tells us a lot about what he meant by the term. It did not, by itself, make him a "Southern man," as he made sure to mention the two designations separately, as though there could be some doubt within Vasserot's mind unless Blandin claimed outright his pride in being both a Southerner *and* a Creole. The term, by the 1860s, represented the foundation on which Blandin's stated "right" was built—the community, the "home," and the legitimacy that he sought to protect from "Lincolnites," Northerners, and any other invasive force threatening to change what his "brave Louisianans" had worked to create.

Whether or not he knew the history behind the word and the implications of his statements, Jean Blandin stood at one of the most important moments in the history of his people. Francophone natives of New Orleans, Blandin's Creoles were stuck at a crossroads. They were a solidly middle-class group by the 1860s, almost universally educated, literate, and property owning; they ran their own businesses, operated skilled workshops, and spent money on fine clothing, wine, homes, and slaves. They were proud of themselves, their families, their shared culture, and their bloodlines. As a result, they tended to isolate themselves from others deemed "foreign" and "strange."[2]

The Civil War created a problem. The vast majority of this middle-class francophone community came from mixed-race families and had lived in a racialized slave society—often as enslavers rather than enslaved—for their entire lives. As Blandin explained, it was not liberty that drove them toward their struggle. In most cases, their families had had that for generations, in some cases as far back as the 1750s. Using their ambiguous ancestry, light skin color, culture, and social reputations, by the 1860s these men and women had created a social identity that defied the standard narrative of free people of color in the antebellum South. They were part of society, granted privileges by the white establishment that functioned as rights, and they were celebrated for their dedication to and history in their collective home. The North, it would seem, rather than the Confederate South, was to them the strange invader, the foreign influence they feared threatened to universalize freedom and liberty, raze the city, and devalue the reputations and social foundations constructed by this community over many generations.

The definition of "Creole," then, is more a story than a sentence. It cannot fit in a single descriptor, stereotype, or individual. There is no model for it. At times the word described locally born slaves in the Caribbean, Gulf Coast, and even as far north as Virginia.[3] Elsewhere it simply described local people, both white and of color, who could claim some connection to the current or former colonial nation, whether by culture, blood, or assimilation.[4] In still other places and times, the word came to describe a people all their own, made native by the meeting of colonial influences and local practices, describing a process of naturalization and syncretism rather than birth, death, and external designations of culture.[5]

It is not the purpose of this study to define the term "Creole," however. It is, rather, to uncover the story of Blandin's Creoles—the mixed-race, francophone middle class of New Orleans and the surrounding area before the Civil War. But the study goes much further than just an extended, narrative, local definition of a largely indefinable term and people. It shows how the people who became the New Orleans Creoles of color—the *gens de couleur libre*, as they were often called—worked endlessly, over three colonial and territorial regimes and nearly 150 years, to define themselves according to the ever-changing cultural, social, and racial landscapes placed before them.

Beginning with the French founding of New Orleans in 1718 and concluding with the outbreak of the American Civil War in 1861, this study explores how these people, who first appear in the 1730s, became a self-conscious, identifiable community in an Atlantic world constantly in flux. It traces the impact of racial science, from the French Enlightenment to the American School of Ethnography, on colonial, territorial, and state law, and how personal reputation and identity interacted with, and often defied, the legal and social definitions repeatedly placed on this ambiguous class of "*mulâtres*," "Negroes," "coloreds," and "quadroons" with each change in regime, political ideology, and scientific trend.[6] It is a study of how people of mixed race, education, and familial and cultural pride fit into a sequence of systems that tried first to define them, then place them in society, then cut them out. It is a study of more than just race and law. It is a study of humanity in the Atlantic world, a study of how a people on the French colonial frontier in the mid-eighteenth century became unlikely parts of a vast political, social, and racial United States by the time slavery split the nation in two.

It is in this way that *An American Color* breaks new ground in the understanding of free people of color in the United States. Often referring to "free blacks" or "free Negroes," scholars have, for the past forty years, both complicated and simplified a massive antebellum population. With the release of Ira Berlin's *Slaves without Masters* in 1974, the academy first saw the "free Negro" as a diverse group. In a sweeping study that covered nearly every section of the South, Berlin explored the diversity of skin pigmentation, social standing, and skill within the South's "free Negro caste." He introduced, for the first time in any major work, the idea of the "tripartite" racial system, allowing free people of color to exist actively between the white population above and the enslaved black population below. He showed us that race did not technically define one's status in the antebellum United States, as free people of color could and often did own slaves, look down on darker-skinned chattel, and use white society as the model of social and political acceptance in American society. All of this was nothing short of revolutionary for its time.

But Berlin's work also limited future study in a way that many scholars have yet to realize—indeed, *Slaves without Masters* remains the most cited monograph in its field.[7] Not only did it assert, as its title suggests, that free people of color, or "free Negroes," in the South lived under the constant supervision, oppression, and restriction of the white political caste, "making their lives nearly indistinguishable from those of slaves," it also took Louisiana and its francophone, mixed-race community out of the standard narrative of American history, where it has remained for more than forty years.[8]

Seen as the northernmost city in the "circum-Caribbean," New Orleans, its culture, and the free colored population it produced have received very little interest from historians of United States history since *Slaves without Masters*. Focusing on its French and Spanish legal and social traditions, historians have set out to paint Louisiana and its cosmopolitan port at New Orleans as foreign, vibrant, independent, and unique—a mix of cultures unseen elsewhere in the continental United States. A flood of monographs and articles over the past fifteen years has reinforced this image of a New Orleans disconnected and isolated from other American cities and cultural hubs, each one celebrating the singular identity, social structure, and racial makeup of this "Caribbean Babel."[9]

Jean Blandin's Creoles and their forefathers seem lost in the flood. Although a number of works have highlighted the experiences of free people of color in New Orleans and Louisiana over the French, Spanish, and early American periods (circa 1718–1812), very few studies have reached beyond regional history and looked outside of New Orleans and the Caribbean for similarities farther north and more classically "American."[10] As a result, the free people of color in New Orleans, the community that would eventually become the famed Creoles of color, appear as strange products of a unique history, unfit for acceptance into the American canon, and incomparable in the known world.

The accepted narrative holds that free people of color in Louisiana and New Orleans first appeared in any meaningful number during the Spanish period (1769–1803), when lax manumission laws provided a conduit for internal growth. The French, who founded the city and served as the original colonial masters, established a status-based system devoid of racial designation, universalizing the notion of enslavement with the term *nègre*—Negro, Black—and thus ignoring race as a stand-alone concept. Under the Spanish, it is said, free people of color gained consciousness through official support of manumission and, most importantly, service in the colonial militia. Both "avenues of freedom" spurred the development of a corporate identity within a certain section of the free colored community in Spanish Louisiana—namely, those with mixed ancestry, free birth, and a claim to military service. And because the colonial government recognized both manumission and the colored militia, a "three-caste" social system developed, placing these ambitious, mixed-race people in the middle of two drastically different worlds.

This book places this local history in the wider context of the North American continent and the Atlantic world—the space within which these people actually lived. In so doing, it shows that New Orleans and its free colored population did not develop in a cultural, legal, or intellectual vacuum. Like elsewhere in North and Central America, the ideas of race and status in the eighteenth and nineteenth centuries were fluid and negotiable in New Orleans. If we look at developments in Enlightenment racial science, especially as it concerned phenotype and racial origin, we can recognize that status in French Louisiana, for example, simply overshadowed, but did not replace, the idea of race. Language was important. French colonial officials rarely mentioned race outside of status in Louisiana because the notion of blackness had always existed in tandem with enslavement, not because the idea of African blood relegated all individuals to the level of slaves. A word for a free person of African descent, and especially someone of mixed ancestry, did not officially exist in the French colonial lexicon until 1724, and even then, word traveled slowly.

It was indeed under the Spanish that free people of color emerged as a thoroughly identifiable entity, but it was not simply because of manumission law and the militia. Again, Louisiana did not exist in a vacuum. The Sistema de Castas, a royal initiative undertaken by King Charles I to regulate and classify the free population of the Spanish world, created a racial language the French did not have. It allowed colonial officials and thinkers to engage racial mixture and classify individuals based on ancestry, purity of blood, and color rather than relying on the generalized, status-laden terms used by the French a half century before. This system, implemented in Louisiana by Alexander O'Reilly in 1769, predated both manumission laws and the colonial militia, gave rise to the idea that race was largely detached from status, and established an official racial hierarchy in Louisiana, stretching from the pure *negro* to the "nearly white" *octavón* to the pure European. The militia helped, as did manumission. But the Sistema de Castas—called O'Reilly's Code in Louisiana—set the stage and provided the material from which a self-conscious, mixed-race community could form.

With the Louisiana Purchase, free people of color in New Orleans and the surrounding area all but disappear from scholarship. Although several recent works have shed some light on the territorial period (1803–12), the consensus holds that the francophone, mixed-race *gens de couleur* of New Orleans disappeared into the massive, unwanted influx of Saint Domingue refugees arriving in New Orleans between 1802 and 1811, and slowly broke under the weight of "Americanization" following the War of 1812 and the Battle of New Orleans.[11] But again, the accepted narrative ignores the larger context within which this self-conscious, organized, and proud community lived.

Most studies, having adopted the "slaves without masters" model, paint an image of fearful Americans actively challenging the continuation of French cultural practices in the former colony and pushing the strange, foreign, racially ambiguous people of the city beneath a wave of cultural and racial "Americanization."[12] Arnold R. Hirsch and Joseph Logsdon, whose pioneering scholarship brought New Orleans and the United States together for the first time, argued in 1992, for example, that American interests in early nineteenth-century New Orleans "were intent upon seizing control of the city and directing its destiny," casting racial ambiguity in strict terms of black versus white and rejecting the notion that one could be both French and American culturally. Joseph Tregle, who likewise laid the groundwork for many important reinterpretations of antebellum New Orleans, went so far as to describe the process as an "ethnic rivalry" between "hardened orthodoxies," one fluid and cognizant of multiple racial forms, the other reductionist and bound to legal and social standards of white freedom and black slavery.[13]

This conflict was real. Indeed, as this book shows, the development of conscious, rooted, mixed-race identities in New Orleans and along the southern Atlantic coast of the United States was no straight line. The slave systems of the British North American colonies and the early United States produced social environments drastically different from those found in other colonized parts of the New World, particularly under the French and Spanish along the Gulf Coast and throughout the Caribbean. The places discussed here, then, particularly in relation to New Orleans and its unique racial and social development, are not intended to stand as mirror images or examples of exacting processes of racial formation taking shape across a broad expanse. New Orleans was not part of British North America, as were Richmond, Charleston, and Petersburg. More a part of the Caribbean than anything else, New Orleans was a late initiate into the continental North American realm, by then long dominated by forces seemingly foreign and external to those which combined to lay the foundation of the city, its culture, and its people. But in the same vein as Cécile Vidal's remarkable recent work on race and slavery in French colonial New Orleans, this book argues that differences in colonial origin, language, religion, and even systems of racial identity should not necessarily be seen as evidence of static, "antithetical models" of development and analysis. Indeed, processes of racial identity formation and the social prejudices and practices that fueled and formed around them, as Vidal aptly put it in a similar but slightly more restricted context, "never ceased to evolve with changing local and extralocal circumstances." They were and are "contingent and pliable" processes, rarely "absolute and monolithic."[14]

But much of the scholarship on the conflict over "Americanization" in New Orleans—this meeting of divergent social, cultural, and racial environments across North America—focuses mainly on laws specific to Louisiana and New Orleans without looking at necessary contingent factors: the actual implementation and enforcement of those laws, for example, or what transplanted American officials and merchants in New Orleans reported back to Washington at the time and vice versa. Such studies, then, describe a hard-fought but ultimately unsuccessful battle to keep New Orleans culturally French and racially fluid in the face of rigid, uncompromising American legal and social standards of identity and acceptance.[15]

This study, for the first time, places New Orleans and its foreign, bizarre, frightening "mulattoes and quadroons" into the narrative of American racial identity and relations during the first half of the nineteenth century. It shows that although their origins, language, and social histories differed from those of similarly complected, educated, and reputable people of color elsewhere in the nation, the New Orleans free people of color experienced life, identified themselves, and functioned in society in surprisingly similar ways to people of mixed race as far north as Charleston, South Carolina, and Richmond, Virginia, while likewise remaining true to their shared, largely local interpretations of who they were and whence they came.

Such similarities were not always found in the most obvious places, nor were they always public and acknowledged in real time. Indeed, as far as public recognition is concerned, society as a whole often ignored or outright rejected them. That did not necessarily snuff out or veil the practice, however. It simply altered its public face. Although the word "quadroon," for example, did not actively exist in the Anglo-American racial vocabulary until the 1880s, the concept of a person with more white blood than black certainly did. Indeed, in 1815 Thomas Jefferson created his own racial arithmetic to make it clear. Race and racial mixture were no different in the United States than in Louisiana, the French Caribbean, or New Spain, at least as far as the recognition of possibilities was concerned. It was what each of those societies did with that recognition that changed from time to time. But an educated, mixed-race class of people existed in the United States long before the Louisiana Purchase, and the free colored "elite" of New Orleans—the future Creoles of color—became an active part of it afterward. Of course there were growing pains and misunderstandings, but, as this study shows, the only things that differentiated colored Orleanians like Jean Louis Dolliole and François Boisdoré from Virginians like Charles Forgason, Joseph Jenkins Roberts, and Beverly Yates were local history and memory, the historical and cultural direction from which each had arrived at a shared sense of belonging or lack thereof. Their experiences as educated, mixed-race, and, later, middle-class men in a slave society remained largely the same for more than five decades, even if seeking the fruits of that common experience, in the end, led some to abandon their native land and others to reach deeper into the soil. Over time, they came to identify with the same concepts of self, legitimacy, power, and race; they just used different languages and histories to do so.

Central to this book, then, is the idea of racial mixture and the social and cultural value of ambiguity. The idea of the Creole of color, of a middle-class, educated, freeborn community in a southern city, proceeds from the idea of the "mulatto." Over the course of the eighteenth and nineteenth centuries, and even before, the mulatto—variously called *mulâtre*, *mulato*, and *pardo*, depending on the region and the time—symbolized a known but largely unwanted departure from the standard racial system. Not only did it publicize the existence of interracial sex, miscegenation, and "amalgamation," it also called into question the very notion of freedom, blood, and status. From the Enlightenment to the 1850s, thinkers across the Atlantic worked to find a place for the mulatto in both society and intellectual discourse. And what they found, published, and promoted affected legal and social practice more than any scholar has yet to consider.[16]

The emergence of the *mulâtre/mulato* in Saint Domingue, New Spain, and finally eighteenth-century Louisiana ran parallel to the recognition of the mulatto in British North America. And although the paths by which both concepts emerged differ, their etymological and intellectual genealogies remain the same. This is evident in New Orleans as it moved from French to Spanish to American ideological and intellectual authority. In all three, the very existence of a mixed race, an "amalgam" of two polar racial varieties, led to a basic divergence of social practice and legal precedent. Society worked faster than law. While American state legislatures and ethnographers worked to define the "mulatto" and other "mixed breeds" in the legal and biological realms, society adapted. It created space for such people to prove their social and cultural worth through face-to-face interaction and the creation of a public self. Because they were mixed-race, brown-skinned, educated, and could prove their connection to both white society and white blood, the idea of blackness and the "stains" and "degenerations" African blood caused in the body evaporated on a personal level, once individuals proved themselves as such.

Society and law thus worked with different tools. To the former, mulattoes and other mixed-race people had proof of their whiteness—freedom, light skin, and a self-conscious identity as something other than a "Negro" or a slave. To the latter, the mulatto simply stood in the way of an organized racial system, calling into question the ideas of slavery, freedom, racial purity, and Christian morality. In law, it was their black blood that counted more than the white. It was easier for a legislature to restrict the rights of someone with Negro blood than it was to restrict the rights of someone with even a hint of white blood. Whiteness created privilege, freedom, citizenship, and legitimacy. If allowed to lay claim to their whiteness, mulattoes could justifiably claim citizenship, legitimacy, and liberty—things they experienced in everyday life, but could not protect in court, at the ballot box, or, in most cases, on the battlefield.

In spite of this, though, the Creoles developed, organized, and survived, eventually to be found in Jean Blandin's letter. And they did not do it alone. Educated, reputable people of mixed race across the South worked constantly to establish their own legitimacy, both communal and individual, in both society and law. These men and women had something others of their supposed "caste" did not. They had a recognizable claim to a place in the system, an identity that formed from the fact that they were not slaves, "Negroes," or "blacks." They were "Creole," "mulatto," and "Brown." They spoke different languages, prayed in different churches, and had differing ideas of nationality and home. But they shared the most important aspect of experience and belonging. They shared a sense of self.

CHAPTER 1

Genèse Française
THE FRENCH

In 1765, Louis Dolliole and his brother, Jean-François, both natives of La Sène-en-Provence, France, decided to leave their native country for the growing frontier town of New Orleans, then still under French control. Born in 1740, Louis was a builder and architect, designing some of the first modern family-style homes in Provence.[1] Arriving in New Orleans in the fall of 1765, Dolliole immediately entered into the construction business with his brother, a skilled carpenter.[2] Louis fit right in. By the mid-1770s, he owned at least eight slaves, all African-born "Negroes."[3] Between 1779 and 1790, he fathered four children—Jean Louis, Rosette (alias Madeleine), Marie Françoise, and Joseph. He lived on Bayou Road, just north of the city. He was unmarried and Catholic.[4]

The four Dolliole children, the first of their name born in New Orleans, were not like their father. They were colored, universally listed in censuses and successions as "mulattoes."[5] But in reality they were lighter still. A legacy of the 1724 Code Noir and the "lightening" of the free population under the French, their mother, Geneviève, was a "mulatress," born free in New Orleans in 1747 to a Frenchman named Azémare and his recently manumitted Negro slave.[6] Technically speaking, the four Dolliole children were quadroons, claiming just one-quarter African ancestry. Born during the 1770s and 1780s to an interracial couple of French origin, the Dollioles differed little from the standard of their generation and clan—those who would make up the established colored Creole social circle nearly a half century later.

Rosette Dolliole died before reaching adulthood sometime in the 1790s, but Marie Françoise, her sister, survived until at least the 1840s. She lived a more quiet life than her surviving siblings. Born sometime between 1780 and 1789, she disappears from the historical record until 1834. On August 24 of that year, having returned from a sojourn in Iberville Parish, she admitted to the Parish Court of Orleans that she was the "natural mother" of the child Jean Baptiste, then working for his "natural father," Pierre Deverges, a wealthy white gardener.[7] She again appeared in the 1843 city directory. She lived on the corner of Bagatelle and Greatmen Streets in the faubourg (neighborhood) Marigny, just a few blocks from her brothers. She lived alone and was "head of household."[8] She must have died shortly thereafter, as she never again appeared in any record in Orleans Parish. As for her son, history has remained silent. He never again lived with his father, and his mother never appeared in the census.[9] Perhaps he moved to Iberville Parish or left the state. As the son of a quadroon woman and a white man, he may have gone by a different name and blended into white society, forgetting his "black" roots altogether.

By the turn of the eighteenth century, Louis and Geneviève's two sons, Jean Louis and Joseph, had established themselves firmly within the New Orleans social and commercial scenes. Jean Louis, a member of the Spanish *pardo* militia, made up of only light-skinned free men, and a successful commercial trader, frequently did business with his brother, Joseph, then a prominent builder and amateur architect.[10] In fact, they worked together their entire lives, lending each other money, exchanging property, and running in the same social circles.[11] They included among their friends, colleagues, and clients some of the most influential white men in town and by the 1850s owned several dozen pieces of property and a handful of homes across the city.[12] By then they had both married free women of color, producing between them at least six children.[13] The last Dolliole daughter, born to Jean Louis and his second wife, Marie Eugénie Bodin, in November 1831, was named Geneviève Hermina Dolliole, after the woman who set the mixed-race family in motion.[14]

The Dolliole family stands out because of the actions of this early female progenitor, Geneviève Dolliole (née Azémare). Certainly not unique in early colonial New Orleans, Geneviève took it upon herself to establish her kin firmly in the developing society around her. She strategically used her body—as well as a knowledge of where metropolitan colonial law and local social practice intersected—to forge a familial, and perhaps quite meaningful, relationship with Louis Dolliole, a white man with whom she remained romantically involved until his death in 1822.¹⁵ As a sign of his affection for Geneviève as well as their children, Louis granted his entire estate, worth nearly $4,000, to "*ma femme, Geneviève, dit [alias] Mamie,*" as well as $300 to each of their three remaining children and $200 to each grandchild.¹⁶ With numerous white nieces and nephews, Louis did not have to bequeath anything to Geneviève or his children with her. He did it because he felt at least some obligation to look after his lifelong partner following his death, and Geneviève played a major part in the development of that feeling.

Most scholars who have looked at the early New Orleans social order have done so from the perspective of the men who engaged in interracial relations with free women of color. As Jennifer M. Spear rightly points out, "By forming families with women of color, Euro-Louisianan men undermined efforts that sought to define those women as unsuitable marriage partners for them."¹⁷ Although this is certainly true, one must not overlook the intent of the women in seeking a valid place in the nascent colonial social order. As Geneviève Dolliole and women like her exemplify, free women of color during the colonial period utilized sex and race to carve out the niche in the socioracial order occupied by a colored Creole elite several generations later. As this chapter shows, the concepts of race and social value developed in New Orleans at a local level, parallel to and intermingled with Continental notions of human difference and biological racial "science."

This is not to say that New Orleans moved more strongly in either direction. In many ways, the mores of New Orleans society, especially regarding the concepts of race and social order, fell in line with plans and racial "science" coming out of the Old World, at least at the legislative level separated from everyday life. But in social intercourse, race and the value New Orleans society attached to it developed along lines seen only in the colonial world and largely defied the "science" of the time.¹⁸ The story and context of Geneviève Dolliole's meaningful and lifelong relationship with Louis Dolliole, and the emergence of a budding middle-class colored Creole community from the roots of that and other similar relationships by the turn of the century, evince this process. As generations of native-born, mixed-race "creoles" came to see themselves as distinct from slaves and unmixed free "*nègres*," whites' notions of social order and racial designation became more concrete and refined. In essence, race, class, and status on the ground were fluid and undeveloped in early New Orleans, defined in different ways at different times by developments both local and Atlantic. By looking at the span of French colonial New Orleans (1718–69), one can observe this process and understand how the concept of race evolved from an inchoate notion of difference to a color-conscious paradigm by the start of the Spanish period (1769–1803), when the Dolliole family took root.

Origins of "Blackness" in an Atlantic Context

From the very beginning, New Orleans was black, but for quite some time, no one took notice. Founded in 1718 by the Canadian-born French nobleman Jean-Baptiste Le Moyne, Sieur de Bienville, New Orleans was originally home to a dissolute band of beggars, deserters, soldiers, vagabonds, and criminals. Bienville established the original settlement on a short natural levee on the east bank of an extreme bend in the Mississippi River, some ninety-five miles north of the river's mouth, or "Head of Pass." Surrounded by swamp, marsh, and low, mosquito-infested wetlands, the frontier settlement did not attract the most well-rounded citizens. In fact, for a time, it attracted no citizens at all. Known for "excessive stubbornness" and unused to the wet, subtropical climate of the Gulf Coast, most of the original group of male settlers, numbering no more than 122, died off within the first year, leaving the survivors as the outpost's only permanent inhabitants for months, with nary a word from any direction on reinforcements or supplies.[19]

The French Crown, and the newly chartered Company of the Indies, refused to let New Orleans sink forever into the surrounding swamp. The location of the settlement held too much value. Sitting just north of the mouth of the Mississippi River, New Orleans offered European investors the opportunity to control the entire inland trade of the North American continent. It could also serve as a buffer between the more heavily developed French settlements at Biloxi, Mobile, and Pensacola and the constantly encroaching Spanish colony of New Spain along the Río de Sabinas, just 216 miles west of the settlement.[20] So in 1719, the Company of the Indies, with the help of King Louis XV, set out to find willing—and unwilling—settlers for the drowning village.

Recognizing that most voluntary settlers would resist the hitherto unknown labor of levee building and swamp filling in a hot, malarial environment, the company resorted to deportation, indentured servitude, and slave importation to fill its nascent colony. Manipulating vagrancy and debtors' laws to pick and choose the appropriate mix of people, the Company of the Indies sent 416 homeless debtors, along with thirty marriageable women, to the colony in early 1719. By midsummer, the number of women deported to New Orleans had risen to 220. "Most of these women," historian Gwendolyn Midlo Hall explains, "were in their thirties and had been accused of theft, debauchery, prostitution, repeated lies, blasphemy, irreligion, and assassination." Some were even sent away "at the request of their families."[21] Yet they were meant to assume positive, maternal roles for the men and children of the colony.

A certain ambiguity resulted. Although King Louis XV held his Catholic faith close to heart, marriage, piety, and proper sexual conduct were not conducive to population growth on the North American frontier. Prostitutes, liars, and impious women would provide more children in less time than the righteous Catholic wives of the Continental metropole. In essence, the Company of the Indies and the French Crown allowed for the development of what anthropologist Shannon Dawdy calls a "rogue colonialism" in New Orleans. The people forced to settle there were not expected to follow the standard morality enforced in France. Rather, the mother country allowed the settlers to "push colonial frontiers in their own self-interest" and create their own society "one step removed from national fealty."[22] Rooted in enlightened absolutism, a political movement of the early French Enlightenment promoting rationality and experimentation with personal freedoms on a society-wide scale, the "rogue colonialism" promoted by the Company of the Indies and its governor, Bienville, targeted only that portion of the population intended for cultural and social development—that is, free deportees and volunteers. Numbering 2,493 by the end of 1721, this group amounted to less than one-third of all arrivals during the first three years of settlement.[23]

The majority of people who ended up in lower Louisiana and New Orleans during the colony's first half-decade were laborers, some free and some not. It is from this group that the first Africans arrived in the area. Between 1719 and 1721, the Company of the Indies, in business with Dutch and Portuguese slavers, imported 1,901 enslaved workers from the west coast of Africa to Louisiana.[24] The first of this lot arrived in 1719 in the slavers *Aurore* and *Duc du Maine*. On June 6 of that year, the two French-owned slave ships unloaded a cargo of 201 Beninois nègres primed, as advertised, to produce rice, then the primary staple of the colony.[25] The Company of the Indies utilized these slaves and those who followed in different ways. Most ended up in the hands of company investors who, remaining in France, had bought up vast swaths of cheap land outside New Orleans in hopes of producing rice and sugar for the Atlantic market. But slaves were not as cheap as the sodden ground on which they worked. The average male worker from the Upper Guinea Coast cost a thousand livres, nearly four times the average annual income of a small-scale farmer in rural France at the time. Female slaves of prime childbearing age went for significantly more, occasionally reaching sixteen hundred livres by the mid-1720s.[26] As a result, Governor Bienville and the company directors had to figure out a way to maintain a solid slave force in the colony without spending the money and effort required to find local buyers and subsidize their human purchases. They also needed to attract more people to New Orleans and the surrounding areas, as by the mid-1720s many of the original deportees and volunteers had fallen victim to the rigors of frontier life.[27]

Providing concessions of land and slaves along the fertile, uninhabited Mississippi riverfront, company investors sought to attract a new, more respectable group of settlers and to dispel the rumors painted by travelers and traders of the "Louisiana Penal Colony."[28] These new settlers often arrived as families, seeking reprieve from a banal existence as small rural farmers in the French countryside. Experienced and hardy, they represented something more than peasantry but less than gentry. In Louisiana, they were landed, which meant something in a colony that by 1723 claimed just 373 people, nearly half of whom were slaves and indentured servants.[29] Simply put, by the time the Company of the Indies had attracted enough people to Louisiana to make up for the high mortality of the first generation, granting slaves and land to nearly everyone brave enough to cross the Atlantic, little stood between the social rank and material well-being of the wealthiest settler and the most impoverished. According to Thomas N. Ingersoll, the vast majority—some 80 percent—of settlers arriving in Louisiana from France came from the third "estate" of the French social hierarchy, most notably wage laborers and small landed farmers. Thus, as Ingersoll puts it, "free and independent settlers of relatively low rank who acquired few slaves" formed the "solid core" of Louisiana's free society, especially in New Orleans.[30]

Initially, New Orleans society under the French was not one dominated by Continental notions of class and title. There were simply too few people and too small a gap between wealth and poverty. It was not a microcosm of European society, built on a strict foundation of class, rank, and titular value within a system of "estates." What travelers and early historians such as Henri Gravier and Charles Gayarré called the "gentry" of early New Orleans and the surrounding Louisiana colony was that of Canada, not France. The men and women they described lived lives not of foppish excess but of rugged survival. They were mocked by their French counterparts, who referred to them as *noblesse puanteur* ("stinking nobility") and even *miche quipy* ("fancy loaf"), the Frenchified term for the lowest class among the area's Natchez Indian tribes.[31] To the Continental French, the Louisiana gentry were nothing but frontier imitations of a cultured urban class, more similar in lifestyle to Indians than to urbane French nobility. To the arbiters of metropolitan French society, they appeared to lack intelligence, grace, and hygiene—attributes as important to French social airs as, it turned out, to racial acceptance.

The Louisiana gentry did, however, own land and slaves like their Continental counterparts, and they even attached noble titles to their names, seemingly at random. Christophe Delaune, a native of Québec who migrated to New Orleans in 1729, had somehow entered the ranks of the *noblesse puanteur* by the time he married fellow Acadian Leocade Marguerite Aucoin in January 1753. On their marriage certificate, the groom signed his name "Christophe Delaune, Sieur de Louisiane," yet there is no indication in any record of how he came about that title.[32] According to the first Spanish census of 1769, an aging Delaune and his wife owned three slaves and lived on a small plantation in Assumption Parish, hardly a genteel lot.[33] Although a *sieur*, Delaune lived a standard life. Nearly everyone in the colony who maintained a free status could claim at least one slave and a few squared arpents of land, including the Ursuline nuns, who arrived in 1727. They owned nineteen slaves, all of whom lived on the large Ursuline Plantation just upriver from the city.[34]

In many cases, indentured servants ended up owning slaves and land. Indeed, the Company of the Indies, as well as the men and women who owned the indentures, often wrote into the contracts promises of land and slaves upon the successful completion (or survival) of the given term of service. As shown in the story of Christophe Delaune, as well as the practice of indentured servitude, class, in one form or another, existed in French New Orleans. But it was a rough-hewn, largely meaningless approximation of that found in the metropole. Men who would have been ridiculed in Paris or Lyons as paupers and debtors became members of a landed "gentry" in Louisiana that, in material and social terms, differed little from the state of the menial small farmer or merchant in the colony.[35] Given the abundance of land and slaves, one could, in less than a lifetime, rise from the depths of indentured servitude to inclusion in this *noblesse puanteur*. There was, in essence, no set calculus for what made a man or woman upper-, middle-, or lower-class beyond material substance. And that could change without warning.[36]

Race, or perceived ancestry based on pigmentation, was not as fluid as material condition or even status. According to the science of the time, one's skin color, and the perceived anatomical functions thus attached, defined an individual's status, especially within the colonial setting. According to French society as well as French law, only those people from Africa with black skin could be enslaved for life without "earning" that position through violence, treason, and sometimes debt.[37] As early as 1665, European scientists had been convinced of the biological difference between the *nègre* and the *blanc*. In that year, Italian anatomist Marcello Malpighi "discovered" the *reticulum mucosum*—the layer of skin he claimed caused the *nègre*'s blackness. From that moment onward, race, previously a notion of aesthetic difference, became a measurable, identifiable feature of human anatomy.[38] By the early 1740s, Malpighi's studies had become the centerpiece of European racial science. But French philosophes took Malpighi's skin-deep analyses to deeper anatomical levels, arguing that the blackness of one's skin corresponded to the color and formation of the internal organs, including the brain. In 1741, French naturalist Pierre Barrère wrote that the *nègre*'s "blood and bile" were likewise "stained" black, a result of the hot, humid African climate.[39] Some ten years later, German anatomist Johann Meckel concluded that "the color of the medullar substance of the [*nègre*] brain ... was bluish," which caused a certain delay in the thought processes and mental abilities of the African. Building on Barrère's single-origin climate theory, Meckel further suggested that Africans had somehow developed their internal coloration over many generations; they had "degenerated" from the standard white prototype.[40] In short, the dark pigmentation of African skin served as an external indicator of internal simplicity and corruption. Africans were biologically inferior, or so believed the vast majority of European thinkers, as whiteness, both internal and external, stood as the human standard—the original model from which Africans had diverged.[41]

Indentured servants, though engaged in a form of forced labor for a set term, were guaranteed freedom in the end, assuming they survived the term, obeyed their contractor, and followed the regulations set forth in the indenture. Most importantly, they also had the same internal and external cleanliness, or whiteness, as their contract holders. Between 1718 and 1731, when, in the face of increased slave importation, the number of indentured servants had decreased to less than a hundred in the entire colony, a single nonwhite person appeared in the register of indentures for the colony of Louisiana.[42] This indenture was unique for a number of reasons. Raphael, a *nègre libre*, entered into the contract in France in 1719. The contract required that Raphael travel to New Orleans and work under the "tutelage" of Jean-Baptiste Faucon Dumanoir for a term of three years, after which he would receive his freedom along with two hundred francs and some clothing. But Raphael was not a freeborn man. Before embarking for New Orleans, he belonged to Sieur Paulin Cadot, a Frenchman who promised to free his slave on the condition that he enter into a "contract" to "learn a skill along with the manners of a Frenchman" in the Louisiana colony.[43] Raphael was also never technically an indentured servant, although his contract was recorded in the register of indentures. The word *engagé*—the term given indentured servants under French law and in all other indentures under study—never appeared in Raphael's contract. Instead, Cadot and Dumanoir, as well as a colonial judge in 1724, designated Raphael an *apprenti* (apprentice), a term used to describe both freeborn whites and enslaved Africans sent away to learn skills as young men.[44]

This is important because French colonial administrators never recorded apprenticeship contracts in Louisiana. In fact, apprenticeships were usually verbal agreements made between a father and a tutor, rarely codified in written language.[45] Raphael's "apprenticeship" had all the restrictions and stipulations of an indenture, and it was also recorded in official ledgers. He received transportation to Louisiana from France in return for labor. During a three-year period, he was bound by law to Dumanoir, a business partner of Cadot, his former owner. The only thing separating him from all other *engagés* was the color of his skin and the then-assumed physiological degeneration he suffered from his African ancestry. A *nègre libre*, then, could not be an *engagé*. Colonial officials reserved that word, and status, for whites.

The term itself implied a voluntary condition. The servants were "engaged" in the labor, not forced, placed, or born into it. The condition was secondary, and the *engagé* derived some benefit from it, whether it was a simple skill, a set of clothing, or, in Raphael's case, "the manners of a Frenchman." Most important, colonial administrators assumed the innate freedom of the *engagé*. If a contract holder reneged on the promise of freedom or payment, the servant could sue not only for the stipulated amount but also for damages and additional "sufferings."[46] In 1725, for example, a group of *engagés* complained to the Superior Council of their "slavish conditions" (*conditions esclaveuses*) and late payments. The council, deciding that such treatment was "too common for connivance," ordered that each servant receive full payment *and* the immediate termination of his contract.[47] The petitioners assumed that "slavish conditions" did not befit the *engagé* status, and the freedom they received as a result suggests that the Superior Council agreed. In fact, in the official recapitulation of French colonial law published in 1803, the *engagé* appears under the section titled "Des serviteurs libres" (On free servants).[48]

Slavery was different. As the *engagés*' successful petition, as well as French law, indicate, white European-born men, women, and children could never be slaves in colonial Louisiana. The very name for the law on which French colonial slavery was based—the Code Noir, or Black Code—invoked the color of the people it controlled. In Louisiana, physical blackness signified one's innate enslavement. Whiteness, on the other hand, marked one as innately free, regardless of class, status, or temporary condition. In the 1732 Louisiana census, administrators lumped *engagés* together with *forçats* (forced exiles) as "free French subjects." The former also appeared under the "white" column. It is important to note that the census sheets included three columns—"white," "free *nègre*," and "enslaved." There was a space between "white" and "free *nègre*." But there was no space between "free *nègre*" and "enslaved," implying that slaves were of the same racial category as "free *nègres*."[49] According to the 1724 Code Noir, written specifically for Louisiana, there were two races and three types of people in the colony. Along with Europeans, *Sauvages* ("savages," or natives) fell under *Blancs*. Under *Noirs* stood but a single group, generically identified as *Nègres*.[50]

The difference was in the natural color of the skin. The natives, according to French thinkers in both Europe and North America, were originally the same color, both internally and externally, as the French. "The infants of the natives are white when they are born," wrote Antoine-Simon Le Page du Pratz, a colonist in New Orleans during the 1720s, "but they soon turn brown, as they are rubbed with bear's oil ... [and] roll about naked upon all fours, before they are able to walk upright."[51] While traveling through Louisiana in 1721, Pierre-François-Xavier de Charlevoix confirmed du Pratz's observations, writing that the "color of the Indians" did not constitute a "third species between the Blacks and the Whites." They are "very tawny, and of a dirty and dark red," he admitted, but surmised that this color "is not natural to them," as "the frequent rubs that they use, give them this redness."[52]

Because the native's skin, according to these observations, was covered by tawny grease and rubs, the natural white pigmentation never changed; it was simply hidden, or veiled, beneath a seemingly savage lifestyle and external oils. Following contemporary "science," Indian and French internal physiology was therefore the same, as the darkening of Indians' natural skin color was a result of cultural practices rather than biological degeneration. It was not, in other words, inborn.[53] Once assimilated and adorned with the accoutrements of the cultured French, as historian Sophie White has explained, Indians adopted a "second skin," supplanting the nonwhite "reddish veil" of their skin with the whiteness of French material culture. In essence, the Indians' assumed ability to adapt comfortably to the French way of life and become assimilated into European culture allowed them to cleanse their skin of the tawny grease that covered what observers widely identified as its "original color."[54] The Indians' external appearance was thus "manipulable rather than essential."[55]

Les Nègres, it would seem, did not don a "tawny grease." Their skin, scientists affirmed, was naturally dark, indelibly marked long ago in Biblical times by their ethnic father, Ham. Though expanded into pro-slavery rhetoric during the antebellum era, the story of Ham weighed heavily on the minds of numerous French philosophes in the early eighteenth century. According to the book of Genesis, Ham, one of Noah's sons, witnesses his drunken father "uncovered in his tent." When Noah comes to, his other sons, Shem and Japheth, tell him of Ham's indiscretion and "sinful vision." Angry, Noah casts on Ham a curse that subjects his children, and their children after them, to live as the "servants of servants" for all the people of the Earth.[56] St. Augustine later explained in *City of God* (c. 413 CE) that Ham's son, Canaan, fathered a child named Cush, who went on to people the land of Ethiopia with men and women literally darkened by the sinful acts of their forefather.[57]

Thirteen hundred years after the publication of *City of God*, French philosophes still took Noah's curse of Ham as a valid explanation of dark skin color.[58] But they took the implications of the curse a step further than simple dark skin pigmentation. According to Abbé Jean-Baptiste Dubos, an early anatomist of the 1710s, the curse of Ham, when combined with the arid, sun-soaked climate of Africa, set in motion a physiological transformation within the African body. If Noah's curse made Ethiopians dark, the air and sun of Africa forced that darkness into their blood, affecting both the "physical structure of their organs" and their mental and physical "temperaments." In 1719, Dubos wrote that "two men who have blood that is so different as to make them dissimilar on the exterior, will be even more dissimilar in their minds."[59]

Other philosophes agreed with Dubos's theory of internal difference but thought the change more fundamental and biological. Accepting pigmentary darkness as a given, or as an external stain resulting from the sins of Ham, some philosophes believed that the African body—the "black" skin, "wool" hair, and "primitive" cranial structure—resulted from a degenerative process brought on by the heat and sun of Africa. The darker the skin became, the more irreparably stained and damaged the humors of the body became. And as these humors—the four vital internal fluids: blood, phlegm, yellow bile, and black bile—"degenerated" into blackened varieties of the original, the more simple and "lowly" the African became.[60] This process, wrote one anonymous thinker, "can explain the languidness of the mind and the phlegmatic passions of [African] peoples."[61] Their blackened humors and internal physiology made them, by birth, uncivilized, stupid, and impressionable. It was thus not darkness per se that made Africans imbecilic and brutish. It was the blackness, specifically caused by generations under the heat of the African sun, that created a separate variety of humankind with languid humoral passions and permanent black skin.[62] The Code Noir expressed this modern "science" by placing Indians and Africans in separate categories. For one, color was temporary, secondary, external, and cultural. For the other, it was internal, natural, historical, and hereditary.[63]

The thinkers of the early Enlightenment did not believe that the innate blackness and languid passions of Africans made them a separate species of humanity, as Charlevoix affirmed in 1721. The majority of anatomists, led by Pierre Barrère in his *Dissertation sur la cause physique de la couleur des nègres*, believed that the ability of Europeans and Africans to produce fertile offspring proved the universality of the human species. What contradicts the notion that the African is a separate species, Barrère wrote, "is that, if this were the case, the mulatto, and similar mixed issue, should be sterile, and completely unable to produce offspring, just like male and female mules." But, he contested, this is "not consistent with what we see on a daily basis" in the colonies.[64] Innumerable reports from North America and the Caribbean mentioned a growing mixed-race population of lighter and lighter skin tones, indicating not only that mulattoes could produce offspring with each other but also that they could reproduce with Europeans.

Perhaps most important to this growing awareness and recognition of race in the early eighteenth-century Atlantic world was the acknowledgment that skin color and internal physiology changed with each generation of mixture. "The children that will be born of these people [interracial couples], or at least their grandchildren," wrote a concerned "Author #4" for the Académie Royale des Sciences de Bordeaux, "will have the reticular membranes a few shades lighter than those of the people from whom they came."[65] Administrators and lawmakers on both sides of the Atlantic realized that this caused a problem in the colonies, where it was assumed that natural color determined one's status or one's right to freedom. In Saint Domingue, the active recognition of a mixed-race population and the perceived consequences of racial mixture on skin color and status caused quite a stir in the early eighteenth century. Using only the terms *personnes libres* and *esclaves*, the 1685 Code Noir, written specifically for Saint Domingue by Parisian lawmakers, assumed that status was the determining factor for the granting of rights in colonial society.[66] It did not acknowledge the existence of a free colored population, whether "pure Negro" or mulatto, and "was not concerned about preventing the fusion of the races, either physically or legally."[67]

As early as 1697, however, administrators in Saint Domingue began to notice a number of slaves with skin so light "that you must have very expert eyes to distinguish them from Whites."[68] This created a quandary. If slaves could be as light-skinned as a white man, what, then, separated white from black, or slave from free? Admitting that the 1685 Code Noir "was formulated without having examined this question in depth," colonial minister Adolphe-Joseph Ducasse agreed to propose a law "declaring all *mulâtres* free as soon as they reach the age of twenty-one years."[69] A decade and a half later, administrators decided to restrict the emancipation of slaves "to protect the free population" from black incursions. But the colonial governor's instructions to the Superior Council stressed that "you should not follow this policy with the *mulâtres*. I know they are the declared enemies of the *nègres*."[70]

It seems clear that colonial lawmakers, especially in Saint Domingue, sought to use mulattoes (and other undesignated racial mixtures) as an intermediate racial group between free whites and enslaved blacks, or *nègres*. Around midcentury, Emilien Petit, a Saint Domingue jurist, even dreamed of creating a legally acknowledged system of concubinage between white men and *mulâtresses* to "form a class of freedmen who are always distinguished from the other classes of the free colored people and slaves, with whom they have few ties, and whom they despise."[71] By creating this insular, hate-filled racial intermediary, an earlier jurist proffered, colonists could "overwhelm the black race with so much disdain that whoever descends from it until the sixth generation shall be covered by an indelible stain."[72]

By establishing a color line after the sixth generation of interracial mixture, French colonial lawmakers and thinkers took the first steps toward a movement to "lighten" the free population and "eradicate" the encroachment of "black blood" into the European ancestral pool. This idea, which would be integrated into Louisiana's 1724 Code Noir, was structured around the increasingly influential notion of "racial bleaching"—a theory championed by such early Enlightenment thinkers as Johann Friedrich Meckel, Claude-Nicolas Le Cat, and Cornelius de Pauw. Le Cat, building on Meckel's earlier work, believed that skin color was transmitted through the "spermatic fluids" of an individual's parents. Thus, Le Cat explained, if an African mated with a European, the amount of *animal oethiops*—the fluid that made African sperm "dark"—would decrease by half, creating a "hybrid animal."[73] Picking up on Le Cat's dilution effect, Cornelius de Pauw, a Dutch geographer, constructed a social plan in his essay "*Recherches philosophiques sur les Americains*," which would find a wide readership in Europe and colonial North America, especially among the French. Finding inspiration in Le Cat, de Pauw believed "blackness" was a "tenacious and aggressive" trait. It would not simply disappear from humanity if moved to a colder, wetter climate, as earlier climatists, as well as the more contemporary Buffon, had argued. It was more ingrained than that. To his mind, society would have to combine, through sex, African and European "spermatic fluids" over at least four generations to purge the African "*matière colorante* [dye, or stain]" and the other "coarse and vulgar" effects of blackness from the human genetic pool. Once this happened, he claimed, the blood became "immutable" and pure.[74]

Perhaps most interesting about the theory of racial bleaching, especially as espoused by de Pauw, was that most of its proponents were thinking of North America and the Caribbean when developing the idea. De Pauw's "*Recherches philosophiques*" focused specifically on the history of the human species *in the Americas* and had a deep influence in Paris, especially in the halls of Versailles.[75] This clearly resulted from the concern expressed by colonial magistrates and lawmakers over the growing number of free people of color in Saint Domingue, Martinique, and Louisiana during the early eighteenth century, and from the racial "science" it helped inform. The Louisiana Code Noir of 1724, written in response to this anxiety over race and status, can thus serve as a window into how French colonial lawmakers looked to merge the realities of colonial life with the most influential "scientific" theories and ideas coming out of the early Enlightenment.

Interracial sex, the cause of much of this anxiety in the colonies, held a predominant position in the Code Noir. Article 6 stated that "white subjects, of either sex," were forbidden from "contracting marriage with Blacks," regardless of status, under penalty of heavy fines, imprisonment, or re-enslavement. "All curés, priests, or secular or regular missionaries," as well as ship captains, were also prohibited from marrying an interracial couple, as such a marriage was in "defiance of ecclesiastic and moral law." The Code further outlawed any form of concubinage or domestic relationship between "free people" and "slaves." It was silent, however, on the issues of marriage between free and enslaved blacks and concubinage between two free partners of different races.[76]

Article 6 says a lot. Given that many of the original prostitutes and "irreligious" women who had made the voyage to Louisiana in the 1710s had died off by the late 1720s and 1730s, the French Crown was looking to shore up marriage as a white-white or black-black practice. But interracial sex eluded the Code's reach. While the law forbade concubinage and domestic relationships between whites and slaves, it did not forbid the same between whites and free blacks (called, at the time, *affranchis*, or "free").[77] In fact, the Code Noir specifically forbade "white subjects, along with our free-born blacks, from living in concubinage with slaves."[78]

That the Code Noir allowed interracial sex but denied inter-conditional sex—that is, between a free person and a slave—as well as interracial marriage suggests that French authorities in Louisiana recognized the existence of European blood in the veins of a growing free mixed-race community, as had occurred in Saint Domingue as early as the 1690s. In producing the law they did, the French lawmakers sought to keep the black enslaved (by allowing black-black inter-conditional marriage) and the free as white as possible (by allowing interracial sex among free people but not interracial marriage of any kind). Concubinage and interracial sex between free partners, then, did not, in the eyes of French lawmakers and thinkers, challenge European definitions of freedom and enslavement. The theory of racial bleaching and the creation of an intermediary mixed-race caste allowed for, and even required, such practices. But slavery was different. Allowing sexual relationships to develop between Europeans and enslaved Negroes challenged the theories of degeneration and physiological inferiority so often used to justify whites' enslavement of blacks. Society, to ministers and philosophes alike, could not handle or explain a population of mixed-race slaves. It would raise too many unanswerable questions about the nature of slavery and human development, masculinity, and the obligations of kinship. But if a free black population already existed, a large portion of which was mixed-race, as was the case in Louisiana and Saint Domingue, the latest "science" assured lawmakers that interracial sex would serve only to lighten that population, theoretically erasing the aberrant "free Negro" with patience and time.[79]

The point of Article 6 was thus to protect the connection established in French colonial law and society between freedom and whiteness. As long as freedom remained both legally and socially rooted in the scientific language of whiteness rather than blackness, French colonial authorities and the white-dominated societies they governed could control its meaning and membership on their own terms. European blood could become the defining characteristic for inclusion among the free, while the presumed inferiority of Negro blood could remain at the center of the slave system. Indeed, if any portion of the free population became too physically dark, authorities would have difficulty justifying racial slavery as congruous with the natural biological order of human "varieties." Sex between mixed-race *affranchis* and enslaved blacks, it was feared, would either lighten the enslaved population or darken the free population, depending on the sex of the free partner. But marriage bound the couple and their children together beneath the stigma, if not the status, of enslavement. Of course, the free partner remained free, but the children became legally attached to both parents and were thus forced, at least in theory, to remain in the black, enslaved community for life.[80] This perhaps explains why interracial sex between free partners remained outside the reach of law. And it was this exception to the rule that allowed for the creation of a large, prosperous, mixed-race community in New Orleans.[81]

The Rise and Recognition of a Mixed-Race New Orleans

Around the time the Code Noir took effect in Louisiana, settlers across North America started to take note of race. Between 1700 and 1730, race, with the help of the growing literature on human difference coming out of Europe, suddenly became a central topic in North American social and legal discourse. By the 1730s, as the population of coastal North America increased and slave labor took root as the centerpiece of many colonial economies, authorities began to notice differences in social status and physical appearance emerging within the "free Negro" population. At first, the term *nègre* served as the generic designation for anyone with noticeable or known African ancestry. Nearly every French dictionary published between 1671 and 1730 defined *nègres* in ways that implied natural, or at least assumed, enslavement, painting an image of a distinct people in whom Europeans traded.[82] But the term in colonial vernacular was not as specific. Often, as in the 1719 "indenture" contract of Raphael discussed above, lawmakers and notaries appended the status designation *libre* to the term. Certainly, the notary did not use the established dictionary definition in describing Raphael as a *nègre libre*—which would have translated to "free black slave." He was describing both Raphael's generic African ancestry (*nègre*) and his free status (*libre*).[83] This was also the case with Scipion and his brother, Simon, who entered into a contract with a New Orleans distiller in 1731 to sell rum upriver in the Illinois country. In the contract, the notary referred to both Scipion and Simon as *nègres libres* multiple times, and both men appeared in the census as free landowners of the Chapitoulas district the following year.[84]

But changes in the Atlantic racial lexicon took some time to arrive in New Orleans. As early as 1622, French and Portuguese travelers distinguished between "black" Africans and their "tawny" children of mixed Portuguese blood on the Upper Guinea Coast using the terms *mulâtra* or *mulâtre*—taken from the Spanish *mulo*, meaning "mule," and the Latin suffix *-attus*, meaning "youth."[85] As discussed earlier, by the 1690s administrators and colonists in Saint Domingue used *mulâtre* to describe the real and planned caste of racial intermediaries placed between whites and free and enslaved "blacks" in the colony.[86] Elsewhere in North America, the anglicized term "mulatto" came to define something between white, "black," "Negro," and "slave." In 1691, Elizabeth City, Virginia, declared that if "any English woman being free shall have a mulatto bastard child borne of her body, she shall pay fifteen pounds sterling or be sold for five years ... as [a servant]."[87] Some fifteen years later, Massachusetts outlawed sex between any "negro or mulatto" and "her majesty's English or Scottish subjects" "for the better preventing of a spurious [i.e., bastard] and mixt issue."[88] Following the lead of its northern neighbors, the South Carolina assembly enacted a law in 1717 providing that "any white woman, whether free or a servant, that shall suffer herself to be got with child by a negro or other slave or free negro, ... shall become a servant for and during the term of seven years."[89] Even in Saint Domingue, where custom and code sanctioned racial mixture "for the protection of the free population," the Superior Council passed laws specifically prohibiting marriage and legitimate procreation between "*hommes blancs*" and "*mulâtresses*" in 1731. Their reason, echoing the logic of Article 6 of the 1724 Code Noir, was that "it was a stain upon the whites, and could attach [any children] to the interests of their partners."[90] As in Louisiana, if produced out of wedlock, the stain only lightened and the interests of the parents rested beyond the child's reach. Once made official through marriage, however, the "protection" became a threat.

By 1724, leaders in New Orleans had not codified any form of racialized segregation into law. Beyond the restrictions of the Code Noir, there were no firm legal connections between freedom and color. Yet Louisiana law still created a binary. One could be either black or white but nothing in between. It had no definition for *mulâtre* and made no direct distinction between a *mulâtre* and a *nègre*.[91] Blacks were black—*noir, nègre*—to the French in Louisiana. It was not until the 1730s that *mulâtre* began to appear in colonial or sacramental records with any regularity. On July 13, 1732, in one of the earliest instances on record, Father Raphaël of St. Louis Church recorded the burial of eight-day-old *mulâtre* Catherine, a freeborn infant.[92] That same year, the second French census of New Orleans for the first time listed six *mulâtres*. Of the six, five were not identified by name and lived in households headed by white men, a clear indication of enslavement. Xavier, the sixth, was listed as a *mulâtre libre* and the head of his household. The *mulâtres* did not have their own column on the census sheet. Instead, they were listed in the space between the columns for "whites" and "free *nègres*," symbolically bridging the intended gap between the two.[93] The census record tells us at least one thing: assuming the five unnamed *mulâtres* were slaves, the inchoate racial vocabulary in New Orleans did not, at that point, tend to attach a given status to any of the nonwhite labels. It also tells us something else of great import—namely, that New Orleans officials recognized different levels of racial mixture, regardless of status, and found them important enough to list in the census. The terms were, however, loose, poorly defined, and used only in isolated records.[94]

People with African blood could thus be free. As long as white blood remained in their veins, colonists thought, their existence did not challenge the fundamental notion of white freedom in a slave society. As Thomas Jefferson would write a few decades later, supporting the early Enlightenment ideas of Le Cat and, later, de Pauw, among others, they could even serve as the catalyst for "cleaning the issue of Negro blood" from the free population.[95] But because they lacked a "pure" white line, they could not be as free as "true" white men. There had to be some legal difference, some privilege granted one and not the other.[96] The 1724 Code Noir offered the first explanation of this difference. According to Article 34 of the Code, all free people, whether white or colored, maintained the "right" to their freedom. But this right only protected *affranchis*, or freedmen, from "unwarranted sale and re-enslavement." If caught harboring a runaway slave, an *affranchit* was to pay a fine of thirty francs for each runaway found. If the offender could not pay the fine upon request, he or she was to be "reduced to the condition of slaves and sold." If a white man committed the same crime, he paid a ten-franc fine per harbored runaway and the threat of debtors' prison.[97]

The Code Noir also distinguished between freeborn people of African descent and *affranchis*, who were assumed freed. Although it was illegal for any *nègre libre* to "insult a white person," the Code specifically required all *affranchis* "to convey a singular respect to their former master, their widows, and children." If found guilty of betraying this respect, they would be "punished more seriously" than if convicted of a "standard insult."[98] By definition, a freeborn person of African descent did not have a former master and thus lived outside the reach of this law. In many ways, then, such laws served to strengthen the threat of a growing free colored population, legally setting it apart from the racially similar enslaved community. This further indicates that a perceived difference was developing between the free and enslaved people of African descent, and that the racial vocabulary in use in Louisiana, though underdeveloped, required new terms more focused on degrees of color and perceived ancestry than monolithic definitions of status.

It was not the simple knowledge of this growth or the laws designed to quell it that forced the free colored population into the New Orleans racial lexicon. It was the way in which it grew, and the time during which this growth occurred, that made the difference. According to both manumission records and early census data, the free colored population of New Or-leans more than quadrupled between 1730 and 1769, when France ceded authority of Louisiana to the Spanish, in spite of the prohibitions enacted by the Code Noir.[99] But as anthropologist Shannon Dawdy explains, "although sanctioned manumissions did occur in the French period . . ., they are not numerous enough to account for all the city's free people of color" by the end of the 1760s.[100] There is also no official evidence of any marriages between free women and enslaved men during the French period. This strongly suggests that very few, if any, colored children with an enslaved parent received freedom through matrilineal descent. Two forces can thus explain the growth of the free colored population—intraracial and interracial sex among the free. Even in the case of manumissions, interracial sex more often than not served as the catalyst for granting freedom.

In a number of cases, white slaveholders freed their enslaved mixed-race children. According to the Code Noir, only those manumissions accepted by the Superior Council as "legitimate" could come to fruition. But because the same Code outlawed inter-conditional sex, very few of the manumission petitions cited love or parentage as the reason for emancipation. In most cases, masters granted freedom as a reward for "loyalty" and "good services." It is clear, however, that loyalty and good services often implied something else, something more carnal and personal. For example, when the white French-born settler Lucas Villanausa freed his six-month-old *métisse* slave girl in July 1765, it was hardly for loyalty or good services.[101] Villanausa had maintained a lengthy relationship with the young girl's mother, the *négresse* slave Louisan, and he was the child's father.[102] Even when a master mentioned a slave's parentage in a manumission petition, the reference remained ambiguous, rarely drawing a direct connection to the manumitter. In 1745, Vincent Le Porche affirmed that the *mulâtresse* Marie Louise, his slave, "should enjoy full and complete liberty," for she was "the daughter of a Frenchman."[103]

Le Porche owned more than three hundred slaves during his lifetime, many of whom were mixed race. Manumitting just ten of them over a fifty-year span, he clearly did not believe that freedom should belong to all daughters and sons of Frenchmen. But this situation was different. In this case, he was the "Frenchman."[104]

In the realm of the free, interracial sex was part of everyday life. The offspring of these relations—some long-term, others more fleeting—contributed more toward the growth of the free colored population than any other group in French Louisiana. The 1763 French colonial census provides only the given names of nineteen *affranchis*. Most historians have taken this number as at least a legitimate approximation of the number of free people of color in New Orleans at the time.[105] But historian Cécile Vidal recently uncovered an "Oath of Fidelity" written in 1769 by thirty-four "leaders" of the "*Compagnie des mulâtres et des nègres libres de cette colonie de la Louisiane*," formed in New Orleans by the French during the Seven Years' War with Britain. The militiamen were assuring newly appointed Spanish governor Alexander O'Reilly of their fealty, given that they had once taken up arms in a common cause.[106] Importantly, Vidal's discovery shows that by the end of the French period, colonial officials differentiated between mulattoes and negroes, at least rhetorically, as other North American and Caribbean colonies did in the mid-eighteenth century. It also provides evidence for the existence of a distinct freeborn community of colored men who the French viewed as trustworthy enough to bear arms, but dark enough to term "*de couleur*."[107]

This is important because the vast majority of historians studying the New Orleans free people of color either ignore the French period as immaterial, or state simply that the French did not recognize race as a legitimate social force in the free community, focusing on status alone. The truth is that a free community of African-descended people emerged during the middle to late French period and began to mix with the white population on a regular basis by the 1740s through 1760s. This free population was also not uniformly "black," either by color or designation. According to statistics gathered by anthropologist Virginia Domínguez, 68.7 percent of all free colored people in New Orleans in 1769 were registered as *mulâtres*.[108] This, coupled with the fact that the French, through the restrictions of the Code Noir, attempted to "lighten" the free population and "darken" the enslaved, suggests that the French in Louisiana were, in fact, acutely aware of race as a complex designation and social factor by the final decade of their rule in the colony. They did not simply assign the statuses of *libre* and *esclave* irrespective of skin color, skin tone, and the assumed ancestries thus attached.

The French did not hold on to Louisiana long enough to see the lightening of the free population, however. The largest influx of African slaves arrived in Louisiana in the mid-1730s, just before and immediately following the collapse of the Company of the Indies in 1731. Slave importations dropped sharply thereafter, grinding to a halt by the mid-1740s. This final generation of slaves imported directly from Africa's western coast, or through Martinique, Saint Domingue, or Guadeloupe in the Caribbean, created Louisiana's first black majority.[109] But manumissions did not occur in any meaningful number until the middle to late 1740s, and the free colored population amounted to no more than a hundred across the entire south Louisiana area to that point.[110] Thus, between the mid-1740s and the end of French dominion in 1769, the free colored population had but a single generation left to grow under the French. This may explain, then, why the official racial designation "*mulâtre*" appeared in specific contrast to "*nègre*" for the first time in the early 1760s, when the French formed the Compagnie des Mulâtres et des Nègres Libres toward the end of the Seven Years' War.[111] Before then, *les Mulâtres* did not form a significant enough proportion of the adult free colored population to garner a distinct designation.

It is for this reason, among others, that many modern scholars rightly link the beginning of the Spanish period with the emergence of a recognizable free colored community in New Orleans.[112] But free people of color did not suddenly appear under the Spanish. They emerged out of a social purgatory and an inchoate racial vocabulary. With each successive generation, the free population of "*nègres*" and "*mulâtres*," formed from manumissions, militia service, and interracial relations under the French, took on specific "colors" under the Spanish. Given racial designations by the Spanish government in New Orleans based on specific skin tones and perceived ancestries, the free colored population gradually split into distinct, insular communities codified, in large part, by those designations. As the free population grew on both sides of the racial divide, ancestry, and the correlating surnames and skin tones, came to matter on a more conscious level than during the French period.

The Spanish colonial government aided this separation. As the next chapter shows, corporate entities such as the colored militia officially segregated light-skinned men (*pardos*) from dark-skinned men (*morenos*). Although this legal separation did not produce as strict a phenotypic separation within colored society as some scholars have claimed, it did provide a legal and perhaps psychological foundation on which a consciously mixed-race "Creole" identity could form in the following decades.[113] But the bulk of the colored Creole community emerged from the loins of women like Geneviève Dolliole, who opened this chapter. It is around these shrewd and socially aware women that Chapter 2 takes form, recalling throughout that it all started under the French.

CHAPTER 2

The Vitriolic Blood of a Negro
THE SPANISH

On May 1, 1801, Jean Louis Dolliole gathered with 103 fellow militiamen in front of the seven-year-old facade of St. Louis Cathedral. Part of the official muster of all the militia units active in the Louisiana colony, Dolliole stood beside the twenty-one men of the Third District (*Barrio*) Corps of the Pardo Militia—a group reserved for colored men of at least half-European ancestry and light skin. Just nineteen years old, Jean Louis was a member of the rank and file, given no specific rank on the muster roll and placed in the middle of the group. Beside him stood men who for decades to come would call themselves friends, business partners, and even fictive kin of the Dolliole family. Celestin Populus, a carpenter and already the captain of the Third District Corps in his mid-twenties, Joseph St. Cyr, the thirty-three-year-old lieutenant, and Raimond Gaillard, a thirty-four-year-old carpenter from Saint Domingue, would all emerge from the Spanish period (1769–1803) as members of a colored Creole "elite," a group of which Jean Louis Dolliole was an integral part.[1]

The Third District Corps of the Second Pardo Militia Company of Spanish New Orleans, as it officially appeared on the roll, was part of the Milicias de Pardos de la Nueva Orleans. Although Spanish law declared militia service "compulsory for all able-bodied men" between the ages of fifteen and sixty-five, the Milicias de Pardos numbered just 362 out of a possible 624 men meeting the minimum requirements for membership in 1801.[2] Most scholars agree that the Spanish colored militia rolls served as a who's who of the New Orleans colored elite.[3] Appointments in the militia did not come easily, and they often reflected one's position in society more than willingness to obey colonial law. According to one historian, the free colored militia served as "the key institution in the development of a distinct free colored identity and the collective spokesperson for New Orleans's free community of color."[4] Leaders in the militia petitioned the governor and the Cabildo (which replaced the French Superior Council) for extra pay, awards for bravery in battle, and, most importantly, certain rights that would separate them from slaves and even other free men of color who did not serve. They wore their uniforms with pride during parades, festivals, dances, weddings, and baptisms.[5] In the 1795 census of Louisiana, the commanding officer of the Milicias de Pardos, François Dorville, a quadroon, recorded his primary occupation as "*captaine des mulâtres et quartérons libres*" even though he owned and operated a tavern and served as a wholesale trader six days a week.[6] Clearly, many of the *pardo* militiamen took great pride in their service.

It is easy to overemphasize the role the militia played in the formation of the colored Creole elite and the racial and cultural identity that came to define the community in the first half of the nineteenth century. The social and cultural practices that developed within the colored militia during the Spanish period explain the origins of only half the colored Creole population. In fact, many of the social rituals that recent scholars have attributed specifically to the colored militia—most notably the choice of intraracial marriage over interracial sex—were endemic in the New Orleans colored community by the turn of the century, especially within the group of men and women who did not, for one reason or another, serve in the militia.

Jean Louis Dolliole stood between these two worlds. The eldest child of *mulâtresse* Geneviève Dolliole and Louis Dolliole, a white man, Jean Louis spent his entire life working alongside his brother, Joseph, a builder and architect.[7] They shared many of the same friends, business partners, and contacts in the white and colored communities. They accumulated sizable fortunes, both together and separately, and lived on the same block until Jean Louis's death in 1861.[8] They stood as witnesses at a number of friends' weddings, which group of friends also served as godfathers for each other's children.[9] Their respective successions, recorded seven years apart, contain lists of similar debts and provide nearly identical rosters of friends, relatives, and trusted executors, all possessing equal or greater wealth and social prominence.[10] By all accounts, the two brothers were contemporary members of an organized group of self-aware Creole elites by the end of their lives.

Unlike Jean Louis, however, Joseph Dolliole never served in the colonial militia. Though old enough by two years in 1801, his name never appeared on any muster roll and his succession mentioned nothing of armed service. In fact, of all the members in the extended Dolliole family, including in-laws, uncles, cousins, and sons, Jean Louis stood alone as having served the Spanish Crown.[11] Service in the *pardo* militia certainly helped Jean Louis Dolliole forge social connections with other, similarly complected free colored men. But it did not define his ability to attain social status, earn an income, or gain respect in the colored community. The success his brother and others found in both the colored and white communities without having donned a military uniform suggests that other currents were at play in the development of the colored Creole community in the last quarter of the eighteenth century.

As this chapter shows, the introduction of concepts of whiteness, purity of blood, and legitimacy of kin under the Spanish caused a transformation within the New Orleans colored community. As generations of mixed-race men and women emerged from interracial families established during the late French period, Spanish social and legal practices permeated the New Orleans cultural landscape. Suddenly, new ideas of racial science, mixture, and definition appeared in law, gradually affecting social intercourse. The ambiguous awareness of *mulâtres* and *nègres* under the French gave way to a regimented taxonomy of "races" and "hybrids" developed over more than a century in Latin America and the Caribbean.[12]

This taxonomy, and the laws supporting it, never took firm hold in New Orleans or Louisiana, however. But it did affect the social formation and racial identity of the nascent colored community, especially at the upper reaches of the social structure. As Spanish laws gradually displaced French legal traditions, racial identities and designations became important concerns for colored men and women looking to marry, join the militia, baptize children, and serve as godparents—all functional claims to legitimacy and social belonging in Spanish America. Unlike the French, who haphazardly applied *mulâtre*, *nègre*, or *esclave* in censuses, marriage registers, and baptismal books, the Spanish separated the colored militia into *pardo* (light-skinned) and *moreno* (dark-skinned) units, created two separate baptismal and marriage registers for whites and nonwhites, and even corrected individual phenotypes in sacramental and legal records according to genealogical evidence.[13]

This increased awareness of phenotype, ancestry, and bloodlines ran parallel with a sharp spike in slave importation. In 1782, the Spanish colonial government, looking to bring more profit into New Orleans and the rest of the colony, lifted its previous ban on the international slave trade in Louisiana. Presented with a hungry new market, French Caribbean traders from Martinique and Guadeloupe, who were experiencing massive overflows of slaves from the Congo River area, introduced thousands of African-born bondmen into the largely creolized Louisiana slave population.[14] In the twenty-three years between 1777 and 1800, Louisiana's slave population increased from 9,201 to 24,262, a growth of more than 160 percent.[15] Thus, by the late 1790s and early 1800s, Spanish Louisiana had become "re-Africanized" at the lowest levels of society. African language, religion, and cultural traditions flourished in the newly imported slave population, reinforcing the Enlightenment-inspired connection between enslavement, "corrupted" African skin, and cultural degeneration.[16]

The widespread manumission of enslaved mixed-race children and Negro sexual partners followed. Louisiana slaveowners could finally afford to emancipate their enslaved concubines and children and find seasoned African-born replacements at drastically reduced prices. The introduction of *coartación*—a law granting slaves the right to purchase their own freedom at an officially appraised value—added to the flood. All told, some 1,921 slaves were emancipated in New Orleans under the Spanish, nearly 60 percent of them dark-skinned *morenos*.[17] These *morenos*, as designated by the Spanish, did not fit in with the rest of the free population. Essentially exiled from the slave ranks by cheaper Africans, these semiskilled, relatively young freedmen stood as a cultural and social threat to the light-skinned, freeborn ranks of the Dolliole clan and *pardo* militia.

Such freeborn men and women had never been slaves, and neither had their parents. To associate socially, culturally, or even racially with freedmen and -women would be to accept a social, cultural, and racial position below that which they felt their bloodlines and genealogies deserved. So they shut themselves off. They married, did business, and engaged in social relationships with each other, looking only upward into white society for cultural and social influence and aid. They did not become white. They became "Creole," neither black nor white, Spanish nor French. This chapter traces the development of this Creole cultural and racial identity from its ideological origin in sixteenth-century New Spain to its institutional manifestation in the segregated colored militia.

Racial Revolution in Spanish America

Race and ancestry mattered to the Spanish. For more than two hundred years before acquiring Louisiana, the Spanish had studied, classified, and organized the manifold "races" and "hybrids" found in Latin America into ever-changing categories and groups. Long before Pierre Barrère, Georges-Louis Leclerc, and Johann Meckel investigated the causes of pigmentary darkness and mental degeneration, Spanish officials and proto-anthropologists in Central and South America sought to explain the effects of human "crossbreeding" in the colonial and indigenous populations.[18] As early as 1533, a debate arose in Madrid over whether or not children of Spanish men and Indian women should be recognized by the Crown and educated as vassals of the empire. At the time, King Charles I decided that any child with Spanish blood "to the half" belonged to the empire, and must receive "education and some training."[19]

There was no term for mixed-race individuals in the Spanish lexicon in the mid-sixteenth century. Because the king had decreed that all people with at least half Spanish blood belonged to the Crown, and those with less "belonged to the land," colonial officials referred to mixed-bloods as "American Spaniards" (*Espagnoles Americanos*).[20] Placed well within the circle of citizenship by both social practice and colonial law, American Spaniards associated themselves with the small group of Iberian officials, laborers, and soldiers in the colonial landscape, largely rejecting their Indian families and assimilating into settler society.[21] But as the American Spaniard population grew and the Spanish empire spread across Central and South America during the seventeenth century, the widely assimilated mixed-race community became a problem. Organized into a class of self-described "gentlemen," the American Spaniards threatened the social and racial position of common Iberian settlers. According to one scholar, by the end of the sixteenth century, American Spaniards viewed any nonelite *peninsular* as foreign to the colony. To them, such lowly sorts belonged in the urban capital of Madrid, where colonial resources and morals were not wasted on their upkeep.[22]

Concentrated in New Spain (Mexico), the American Spaniards struck a nerve with the Spanish Crown and colonial administration. By the mid-seventeenth century, the term "American Spaniards" no longer appeared in legal texts or even standard colonial language. Instead, officials recorded these mixed-race "elites" and their children as simply *Americanos*, stripping them of the Spanish blood that made them citizens and members of colonial society.[23] Over time, the term took on a racio-social value in colonial Mexico, in which ideas of race directly informed ideas of social standing. No longer legally Spanish, *Americanos* likewise did not fall as low as the descendants of the indigenous Mayans and Northern Inca in the unwritten social hierarchy. They remained the "elite of their people." But "their people" were no longer Spanish; they were American.[24]

The Spanish obsession with racial mixture and the organization of humanity emerged out of this *Americano* Revolt.[25] The standard seventeenth-century Continental racial system of Europeans and non-Europeans—Spaniards and non-Spaniards, French and non-French, and so on—could not account for the ambiguous position the *Americanos* filled in the established social and racial orders. Educated, wealthy, and socially elite but racially impure, the *Americanos* forced colonial officials and thinkers to expand the dimensions of what separated mankind into different orders, classes, statuses, and colors. In pre-Columbian Spain, human difference was defined by religion, which was thought to be inborn and hereditary. Spanish thinkers, artists, and anatomists saw Jews and Moors as separate versions of humankind. The seemingly bizarre pagan practices of their religions foretold internal corruptions of the body, passed from one generation to the next through the shared experience of pregnancy and the consumption of mother's milk after birth.[26]

The "discovery" of the Americas and the advent of the African slave trade introduced new "forms" of people unnoted in the European racial, social, or linguistic lexicons. Without widespread settlement, and with hardly any intermixture of blood, the pre-Columbian racial system adapted easily to the new environment. The settlers were, of course, Spanish, and the natives, called *Indios*, were not.[27] But with the expansion of colonial settlement came admixtures of blood unseen in Europe. The resulting *Americano* Revolt thus created the need for a new, more diverse, integrated sociracial order, in which social concepts directly informed images and ideas attached to race. More than a century later, this system would serve as the Spanish colonial empire's primary contribution to the development of the colored Creole elite in New Orleans.

Officially termed the Sistema de Castas, the Casta System originated in medieval Spain as a way to organize the world's natural life (excluding humans, which were not thought to be animals).[28] Following the *Americano* Revolt, Spanish officials created new categories within the system for each recognizable human "variety" found in the colonial empire. Through this new system, colonial administrators sought to make sense of a previously indistinguishable colonial mass. One could not simply legislate rights and privileges based on assumptions of sanguinary purity (*limpieza de sangre*). Other factors had to play a role. It is in this way that the Casta System revolutionized the American social and racial landscapes. For the first time in colonial American history, ancestry *and* social standing combined to determine one's *calidad* (quality).[29]

The Casta System, which differed slightly from colony to colony, separated the inhabitants into two primary groups: *Espagñols*, or pure Spaniards, and *castas*, meaning anyone with less-than-pure European blood.[30] Because *Espagñols* included almost all individuals of pure European blood (except, of course, Turks, Moors, and Jews), the group stood alone at the top of the racio-social system. Gauls, Saxons, Germans, and others were all lumped in with the *Espagñols*. The *castas* group broke into between fifteen and twenty *calidad*s progressively based on the percentage of European blood in a given category's ancestry.[31] But as a number of scholars have noted, each *calidad* did not correspond strictly to "quality" of blood. Rather, as one historian has put it, *calidad* "included references to skin color but also often encompassed, more importantly, occupation, wealth, purity of blood, honor, integrity, and place of origin."[32]

Within the Mexican Casta System, the *Americano* stood atop the hierarchy of *calidads*. As educated, indefinably mixed-race, elite *castas*, the *Americanos* had the highest quality of all the racially mixed groups in the Spanish American empire. Although similarly mixed and most likely similarly complected, *mestizos* fell below the *Americanos*. As a group, they had no traceable connection to Spanish high society beyond a claim to at least half Spanish blood. Usually the illegitimate children of *Espagñols* and *Indias*, *mestizos* lacked the cultural accoutrements required for respectability and acceptance into colonial society as subaltern elites.[33] But occasionally lines blurred. A *mestizo* of legitimate birth (meaning his or her parents were married) with education and money could easily pass as *Americano*, so long as the rest of society recognized him as such. These types of performed transformations were possible because Spanish colonial society recognized the unspoken existence of a dual reality. One could perform the social expectations of a certain *calidad* in public, and live as another in the home.[34]

In a sense, the public did not want to know whether or not a given person technically belonged to the *calidad* ascribed to them by society. In court cases filed by those wishing to change their *calidad* from *mestizo* to *Americano*, or even *Americano* to *Espagñol*, judges did not, at first, rely on genealogical investigations. Rather, they would question witnesses—neighbors, friends, slaves, priests—about the petitioner's reputation in society. In one famous case from early eighteenth-century Mexico, Fr. Mariano Aponte testified that Doña Margarita Castañeda was of "pure Spanish blood" because "she demonstrates it in her person and circumstances." While her physical "person," or appearance, evinced Spanish purity, so, too, did her "circumstances," an a posteriori notion requiring at least some personal agency and public acceptance. Another witness further invoked social opinion when he declared that Doña Margarita was "considered and reputed publicly to be a Spaniard," again with her "circumstances and judgment manifesting her good birth."[35] So it seems that "circumstances," which were earned and displayed for the public to analyze and discuss, served as an important tool in the diagnosis of one's *calidad*.

Beyond court cases and public reputation, the caste of *Espagñols* was open to certain people with Indian blood. If an *Americano*, for example, married and had children with an *Espagñol*, the progeny would enter the ranks of the latter. The former, who colonial officials already saw as the closest of all the *castas* to pure Spanish, needed only one more degree of separation to wash clean the stain of Indian blood.[36] *Mestizos*, on the other hand, had a more difficult time cleansing their veins. Taken from the Latin *mixticius*, meaning "mingled together," the term *mestizo* generally referred to a person with any degree of mixed Indian and Spanish blood and unmarried parents.[37] Within the system of *calidads*, if a *mestizo* married and reproduced with an *Espagñol*, the child would be born a *castizo*. The etymology of this tells us a lot. While *mestizo*, the inferior *calidad*, came from the Latin term for "mingled," *castizo* derived its meaning from the Latin *castus*, meaning "unpolluted" or "pure." In the Spanish language, the suffix *-izo* (*-iza*) modifies a term to denote a readiness for, or likeness to, the root word. So the *castizo calidad* contained those who were one step removed from clean blood, or were literally "ready for purity." One more generation of marriage and reproduction with an *Espagñol*, and a *castizo* family joined the pure of blood.[38]

This is important because it explains a demographic shift in late seventeenth-century Central America that directly affected the implementation of the Casta System in Spanish Louisiana some seventy years later. By the 1690s and early 1700s, *castas*—the general term used by officials for anyone of mixed-race—had developed ways to manipulate the fluidity of the Casta System. Because one's *calidad* derived most of its meaning from public acknowledgment and reputation, *castas* of inferior *calidads* would frequently attempt to bring up their children (usually daughters) in a way that would not betray their true origins. Convincing the young girls that their births were legitimate, purchasing them fine clothing on credit, and apprenticing them out to learn the skills of literacy and housewifery, *mestizos* would raise children whose personal and public identities were those of *castizos*. When a girl reached marriageable age, she would travel to the capital, find a Spanish husband, and produce "pure" *Espagñol* children.[39] If she succeeded in constructing "circumstances and judgment manifesting her good birth," no one would ever think to investigate her "mingled" lineage.[40]

Though far from common, these types of marriages were part of a larger increase in racially exogamous unions during the last two decades of the seventeenth century. According to the most reliable statistics available, just four percent of all marriages in Mexico City in 1665 involved a Spaniard and a *casta*. By 1700, racially exogamous marriages accounted for more than 28 percent of all unions. Two decades later, more than one-third of all marriages crossed the *casta* divide.[41] The introduction of Indian blood, however diluted, into the ranks of the racially pure complicated the very notion of *limpieza de sangre*—the centerpiece of the Casta System. As the seventeenth century moved into the eighteenth, the percentage of *castas* marrying, and thus disappearing, into the population of Spaniards likewise increased. By 1720, more than 84 percent of all marriages involving a *casta* also involved an *Espagñol*.[42] In essence, between 1665 and 1720, the *castas* erased themselves from the Casta System, and muddled the fundamental difference between "pure" and "impure."[43]

Alongside the systemic collapse of the impure *calidads* at the turn of the seventeenth century came a lull in the international slave trade to Spanish America.[44] After seeing tens of thousands of African slaves from the Upper Guinea Coast arrive in Spanish American ports between 1543 and 1630, the market fizzled after 1640, when the French Caribbean and British North American colonies stabilized and offered better prices and higher demand.[45] No longer supported by newly imported groups of African-born slaves, the enslaved population in Central and South America grew mainly through natural increase—both intra- and interracially—over the subsequent decades. At the time, no laws forbade interracial sex of any kind. An *Espagñol* could legally impregnate one of his slaves, claim the children as his own, free them, and leave his entire estate to them.[46] The racial order, in the middle to late seventeenth century, only corresponded to levels of Indian blood. African blood, long seen as well contained in the slave population, did not pose an immediate threat to either Spanish purity or Indian impurity. It simply existed outside the colonial purview.[47]

The collapse of the slave trade and the racial corruption of the *Espagñol* caste during the last half of the seventeenth century thus paralleled the emergence of a large free population of African descent throughout the entire Spanish American empire. Largely mixed race, and occasionally of legitimate birth, these *gente de color*, as they came to be known, quickly became the targets of a new Sistema de Castas, one built on the remnants of the old system but expanded to define not only quality (*calidad*) and class but also color and a new concept called *raza*, or race.[48]

Reforming the Sistema

The word "*mulato*" first appeared in Spanish America as a racial designation in a 1614 census of the Peruvian capital, Líma. In that year, "744 Mulattoes" (people with Spanish and Negro parents) resided in the city.[49] In 1648, the term appeared in a Mexican census to describe people "of a mixed nature, of Spaniards and blackamoors."[50] In both of these censuses, as well as a number of others from Guatemala and Argentina, the data for *mulatos* was physically separated from that for Spaniards, *castizos*, *mestizos*, and *Indios*. While the latter groups made up different parts of a single colonial population, the former appeared at the bottom of each page, with no names given, as though included as an afterthought.[51] These tallies did not affect the overall population statistics, either. In all of the censuses under study, officials did not add the number of *mulatos* to the total number of *colonos* (colonists). Instead, they provided two numbers: one for *colonos* and, beneath it, another for *mulatos*. This suggests that colonial administrators were not exactly sure where people of mixed Spanish and African blood fell in the colonial system. In their veins ran the blood of the fundamentally free *and* the blood of the fundamentally unfree. They were, in the eyes of colonial officials and *castas*, a truly exotic "breed," maintaining no connection to the land, and an "impure," illegitimate connection to Spanish society.[52] They were secondary, unnatural, and misplaced.

Another, perhaps more important problem was that of skin color. In 1677, English traveler Thomas Gage provided one of the first physical descriptions of both *Indios* and *mulatos* in Central America. What he observed helps explain the concerns colonial administrators had about the growing number of *gente de color* and the culture they were crafting by the late seventeenth century. "The attire [i.e., appearance] of the baser sort of people of mulattoes," Gage noted, "is so light, and their carriage so enticing, that many Spaniards even of the better sort disdain their wives for them." They wore petticoats and chains of gold, silver, and pearls, Gage explained. They would "swagger" on high-soled, "profane" shoes, and "hang rich silks" from their shoulders and necks.⁵³ Clearly disgusted by the "haughty" culture of the *gente de color*, Gage seemed even more confused by the physical similarities of Indians and *mulatos*. Both "tawny breasted" and "stout," with similar facial features, Gage noticed that Spanish officials and priests "discerned the difference" between the two more by "the wool upon [their] heads" than the color of their skins. Although the Indians often "paint[ed] themselves all over with red or white," their natural color was identical to that of the *mulatos*.⁵⁴

The growth of the *mulato* population in Central America forced Spanish officials to take note of skin color for the first time. Although skin tone never defined one's *calidad*, the Spanish did see skin color as an external indicator of internal corruption, much like the French in the eighteenth century.⁵⁵ To Spanish eyes, *Indios*, *mestizos*, and *castizos* were darker than *Espagñols*; officials just never defined exactly how much darker each one was than the next. But *mulatos* were different. Spanish colonial governors, thinkers, and even the Spanish Crown did not know what to do with this growing population of *Indio*-colored, half-Spanish, half-African freedmen. In 1639, Manuel de Faria y Sousa, a Spanish cleric and legislator in Madrid, wrote that the "blood" of the *mulato* "represents the meeting of opposing objects—freedom and enslavement." "The very name '*mulato*,'" he continued, "likewise comes from 'mule,' an animal derived from two others of different species . . . born to work and never create itself."⁵⁶

The Spanish did not think Africans or *mulatos* were different species of mankind, as a number of pseudoscientists in the antebellum American South would come to reason in the 1830s and 1840s. They simply viewed *mulatos* as the closest human example of a mule-like hybrid. The word did, in fact, combine the Spanish root *mulo*, meaning "mule," with the suffix *-ito*, meaning "derived from," or "youth of."⁵⁷ African blood, to early Spanish "scientists" like Benito Feijoo, was "vitriolic," as historian Magali Carrera has explained. It "corrupted," "destroyed," and "overcame" whatever "bile and matter" it contacted. Echoing the early climatists coming out of the European Enlightenment in the early 1700s, Feijoo asserted that the "brutal air and soil" of Africa caused the acidity of the blood to increase, damaging the internal organs and "burning" the skin black.⁵⁸

It is on this foundation that the Spanish Crown and colonial legislators built the new Sistema de Castas. Using early Enlightenment philosophy and science, as well as observations from travelers and anatomists like Gage and Feijoo, King Philip V, the first French-born Bourbon king of the Spanish Empire, implemented the *Sistema de las Castas* among his other famous "Bourbon Reforms" between 1702 and 1723.⁵⁹ This new system established a separate branch of *calidads* for people of African descent, one significantly more complex than the largely ignored, out-of-date, Indian-based structure. This time, one's *calidad* referred mainly to his or her skin tone and blood composition, although economic and cultural factors, as well as reputation, did retain some influence.[60]

To people of African descent, the new Casta System was cyclical. Because the system was based on the internal and external features of blood and skin color, officials were able to include the entire African-descended population, whatever their specific colors or ancestries. The logic behind the endless hierarchy came from new "scientific discoveries" in Spain. According to Pedro Alonso O'Crouley, an Irish-born Spanish physician, "the *mulato* can never leave his condition of mixed blood" because "it is the Spanish element that is lost and absorbed into the condition of the Negro." Using Feijoo's original wording, O'Crouley explained that the "vitriolic" blood of the Negro "corrupts the unexposed blood of the pure Spaniard," maintaining within the *mulato* child "all internal characteristics" of the African, save the weakest part, "the skin," which "faintly lightened."[61] The system was, in essence, the first legally codified hypo-descendant racial order in American history. No matter what the level of admixture, African blood trumped all.[62]

Introduced first in Mexico in 1702, and then throughout the entire Spanish American empire a decade later, the new Casta System looked to lump people of African descent together at the bottom of the social and racial orders. The aim of this universal subjugation was the creation of a subaltern identity among the *gente de color*, an "intracolonial colonialism," to use Jo-Anna Poblete's term.[63] Spanish officials, especially those in Mexico, recognized that certain actions taken by *castas* over the preceding half century had led to the collapse of the first Casta System. Simple mimicry and constructed ambiguity—the "invention" of a socially superior public identity—exploited the fluid boundaries between *calidads* and eventually rendered the system moot.

Taking away references to land and purity (e.g., *Americano* and *castizo*), the new system categorized the *gente de color* first according to color and then according to levels of African blood.[64] If the law only recognized African blood and the pigmentation it caused, the *gente de color* could not claim relation to, affiliation with, or legal representation as Spaniards or even colonists. They were tied to their African lineage. The terms *pardo* ("brown") and *moreno* ("dark") designated the two color categories within the system. The *morenos*, the darker of the two, included anyone with more than half African blood, or who appeared "darker than the average *Indio*."[65] The lowest of the new *castas*, *grifos* (three-quarters African, or half Indian, half African) and *negros* (full African) received the *moreno* designation. Assumed to be fully African (or nearly so), former slaves, and universally illegitimate, they did not threaten the social order as much as the *pardos*.

The *pardo* designation served as the standard term for anyone of noticeable mixed African ancestry.[66] Literally translated as "brown," the term subjected the group to an assumption of color, regardless of whether or not an actual *pardo* appeared any more or less "brown" than a *mestizo, castizo*, or *Espagñol*. The key is that the color never legally left the skin, whether in theory or reality. Once designated a *pardo* or any of the *calidads* within it, an individual and his or her descendants would always carry the scar of the African sun. *Mulatos* (half African), *cuarteróns* (one-fourth African), and *octavóns* (one-eighth African) all fell under the *pardo* designation.[67]

After *octavón*, however, the system became intentionally vague. In 1749, King Ferdinand IV, clearly inspired by Enlightenment theories of Negro "degeneration" and the white human prototype, added the category of *albino* as the last and catchall *calidad* of the new system.[68] Based on the brand new, progressive theories of the French Enlightenment, the albino (often referred to as *blafard*, meaning "pigmentless human") stood as essential proof that human beings were originally white and that blackness came from secondary, earned, or assumed "corruptions" and "degenerations" within the body. Originally called *nègres blancs*, albinos were thought to be the product of an aberration in the reproductive system in which "vestigial whiteness tends to reappear" in the offspring of two Africans or African-descended people.[69] Anatomically and physiologically, the *nègre blanc* was still a *nègre*; his internal organs, blood, and bile all maintained the corruption his parents passed down to him. His skin simply reverted back to the white human default—the "pigmentless" European prototype.[70]

The use of the *albino* in the new Sistema de Castas allowed for the existence and categorization of "white" *pardos*. Up to that point, each designation represented both a measurement of African blood and its corresponding skin tone. *Cuarteróns* were assumed to be lighter in color than *mulatos*, just as *octavóns* were lighter than *cuarteróns*. Color had to be the initial basis of judgment for the system to stand. The terms *mulato, cuarterón*, and *octavón* implied a direct mixture of African blood and something else. It was that something else—Spanish blood—that caused the collapse of the original Casta System. But the inclusion of *albinos* at the top of the *pardo* racial order allowed for a certain elasticity when color faded but blood remained.

Purity and Color in Spanish New Orleans

When the Casta System arrived in New Orleans with the Spanish, it met a society unused to a structured racial order. Although the terms *nègre*, *mulâtre*, and even *quartéron* existed in the Franco-Louisianan lexicon, they hardly retained definitive meanings.[71] The term *mulâtre*, generally speaking, served a similar purpose to the Spanish term *pardo*. Both described ambiguously mixed-race people, almost universally free, and lighter in color than *nègres* and *morenos*, who were themselves assumed to be darkest and unmixed. The haphazard racial structure in French Louisiana contained no standard *calidads* beneath *mulâtres* and *nègres*. Instead, as explained in the previous chapter, officials simply attached the designation *libre* to separate the free from the enslaved.[72] Society itself did believe most *mulâtres* free, and most *nègres* enslaved, but there was no official status attached to either designation.[73] French priests maintained two separate books for colored and white baptisms and marriages, but both colored and white records appear in the white book. Only a handful of marriages ever wound up in the colored register.[74] By the end of French rule in New Orleans, then, officials, priests, and society as a whole were just becoming aware of the notion of race and racial mixture as definable traits. Thus, with the arrival of the Spanish came an entirely new concept of racial definition, and race suddenly became an important, definable characteristic in the social order.

New Orleans was the first newly acquired Spanish colony to experience the Casta System. Introduced to the Spanish American empire in 1712, the system became law only in colonies that had fallen under the authority of the first Sistema de Castas and maintained majority *Indio* and *casta* populations.[75] None of these colonies had belonged to another European power for any meaningful period of time. But New Orleans was different. Its people spoke French and many of them saw the French metropole as their original or ancestral home. French law and culture still pervaded and French-based Atlantic notions of race defined the order of society (see chapter 1). It was not until 1763 that *mulâtres* numbered more than ten individuals in the census, and that year marked only the second time the term ever appeared in an official enumeration.[76] Introducing a highly structured system of racio-social categorization, then, would not be easy.

The Spanish Crown did not force the new *Sistema Institucionalizado de las Castas* on the francophone people of Louisiana. Instead, it wisely merged the *Sistema* with Louisiana's decades-old Code Noir of 1724. Published on November 5, 1769, by Alexander O'Reilly, an Irish-born Spaniard and the first effective Spanish governor of Louisiana, the "Ordinances and Instructions of Don Alexander O'Reilly" sought to ease Louisiana into the new system. By maintaining many of the major regulations and privileges found in the Code Noir, Spanish officials could justify certain new restrictions and rights to the skeptical new Spanish subjects. They also needed to close the holes in the Code Noir that allowed racial bleaching and the so-called "whitening" of free society. While the French in Saint Domingue, and later New Orleans, saw the "indelible stain" of Africa lasting "until the sixth generation," the Spanish had worked for nearly a century to establish the "vitriolic" and "corruptive" nature of African blood.[77] It never went away, they theorized, no matter how "white" the person.

The key to this plan was the expansion of rights for freemen and the creation of avenues to freedom for the enslaved. Considering what happened in Mexico and Central America a century before, Spanish officials wanted to establish at least three separate legal corporate entities, between which there were no questions of status or race.[78] Once they established this three-tiered order, they could move on to implementing the new Casta System, with all its *calidads* and divisions of pigmentation. At the top, like most of Central and South America, stood the Euro-Louisianans (often called *blancos*), or people of pure European descent. Because Louisiana contained so many Frenchmen and -women and so few Spaniards, the term *Españols* simply did not fit. Between the Euro-Louisianans and the third group, slaves, stood the *libres*, or the general mass of free people of color.[79]

O'Reilly's Code, as the November 1769 laws came to be known, shifted the weight of the system more toward race and color than status and freedom. Although the three-tiered structure resembled the system forming in New Orleans at the end of the French period, the new code strengthened the difference between whiteness and blackness and largely ignored the difference between freedom and slavery. Under O'Reilly's Code, freedom cast a wide net. It was not restricted to the light of skin or pure of blood. Slaves could receive freedom for any number of services, actions, or claims. If a slave "aided the state through good actions," prevented the "rape of a virgin," or "avenged the death of his master," he or she would receive "the happy fruits of liberty."[80] If a master forced his or her slave into a life of prostitution, the slave could sue for freedom. In like manner, courts often granted freedom to slaves who had suffered "great personal injury" at the hands of their owners.[81] As late as March 1801, *negro* slave Jean Léon Olivier sued his Spanish master, Benito Pardo, for "right injuries and abuses." The Cabildo

(Spanish city council) freed Olivier "with immediacy" after hearing the testimony of a single witness.[82]

Perhaps the greatest avenue to freedom opened by O'Reilly's Code was the privilege of *coartación*. First introduced in Cuba by then-commandant Alexander O'Reilly around 1748, *coartación* granted slaves the ability to purchase their own freedom without a master's approval.[83] This represented a marked shift from French policy, which revoked a slave's right (or privilege) to own, inherit, or purchase property of any kind. Although French New Orleans society did not strictly adhere to this rule, as the slave markets of Congo Square evince, a slave could not sue or represent anyone in court if a master refused an act of self-purchase.[84] With *coartación*, the Cabildo guaranteed a slave's freedom if he or she provided the appropriate funds based on two or three official appraisals. On March 30, 1771, the aging *negro* Bautista provided the small sum of thirty pesos and received his freedom from Joseph Meunier, his owner. Later that year, the *mulata* Juana Catalina invoked the "favor that the laws concede to her" when she presented her master, Jean-Baptiste Destrehan, with her appraised value of three hundred pesos.[85] Neither Meunier nor Destrehan solicited these sales. In both cases the slaves acted on the "favor" granted them by law to purchase their own freedom. If an owner refused, the petition would go before the Cabildo, which almost universally sided with the slave.[86] In all, less than 15 percent of self-purchases under *coartación* went to court. Most owners recognized the profit *coartación* could bring them, especially with the reopening of the slave trade in New Orleans in 1782.[87]

O'Reilly's Code also loosened restrictions on manumission. French law placed an age requirement of twenty years on each master looking to manumit a slave, and the Superior Council had to approve each act. Under the new Spanish code, an emancipator had to be at least fourteen years of age and in "good standing" with society. However, if the owner was related to the slave within "three degrees"—ranging from great-grandparents to first cousins—the age requirement did not apply. Each act of emancipation also required five free witnesses over the age of twenty years.[88] Beyond these simple requirements, slaves could receive freedom from anyone at any time as long as the owner obtained a "reasonable price."[89] And the government claimed the right to set that price.

Spanish officials were not necessarily planning to expand the free colored population for its own sake. Rather, they saw slavery as "the basest and most despicable thing on earth, (except sin,)" and viewed freedom as "the most dear and precious."[90] They did not wish to abolish slavery, however. They simply wanted to offer freedom as a just reward for those who earned it, refreshing the system with new, African-born slaves. Regardless of whether slavery was "despicable" and "base," it was still, according to many Spanish and French thinkers, the natural state of dark-skinned Africans. And that could not change with a simple shift in morals.[91]

Expanding the free population also made it easier for Spanish administrators to order society based on race rather than status. In 1769, when Governor O'Reilly instituted his "Ordinances and Instructions," a new racial language took root in Louisiana. Suddenly, phenotype and perceived ancestry became fundamental to an individual's social and corporate identities. This new lexicon came directly from King Philip V's *Sistema de las Castas* of 1712, but it was not as complex and structured as its Central American predecessor. Initially, O'Reilly required notaries, priests, and judges to record each individual's phenotype in contracts, sacramental registers, and official court documents. And they had to be specific. Beginning around 1771, *cuarteróns*, *mulatos*, *grifos*, and even a *tierceron* started to appear in baptismal and marriage registers as well as all forms of official documentation.[92] Where *mulâtres* once stood as the socially and racially ambiguous buffers between white freedom and black enslavement, a varied group of former slaves and freeborn Frenchmen now spanned the racial spectrum. A true "colored" population was forming.

Five years later, the process resumed. In 1776, King Charles III, a devout Catholic, issued the *Real Pragmática*, an edict designed for the "preservation of the social and political order through marriage."[93] The "royal sanction" required priests in all "urban colonies" to record the marriages and baptisms of whites and coloreds in separate registers. In New Orleans, these books took the form of *libros de blancos* and *libros de gente de color*.[94] Blood purity was clearly not the issue. With a book for whites and a book for people of color, phenotype, or one's degree of color, was the obvious centerpiece in the new colony.

One of the most important aspects of the *Real Pragmática*, especially in the formation of a self-conscious, mixed-race Creole population, was its regulation of "unequal" marriage. Clad in the language of patriarchy, the *Pragmática* decreed that all men and women under the age of twenty-five years must receive their fathers' "blessings" in marriage. The father of the groom had primary authority, and it was his duty to determine whether "substantial social inequality" existed between the two partners. If he decided, for whatever reason, that the match was unequal, he had the right to "stop all ceremonies and plans." If the bride's father challenged the blessing of the groom, the decision went to the Cabildo, which took testimony from friends and neighbors of each partner.⁹⁵ The blessing served as an expression and test of legitimacy, an important social and moral trait in Catholic society. The presence of a father in a groom's life indicated legitimate birth. A father's blessing indicated that society also viewed and understood the bride to be legitimate and from a respectable family.⁹⁶

But there was a racial element to the *Pragmática* as well. The "equal station" restriction and the requirement of parental blessing did not apply to "mulattoes, Negroes, Coyotes, and individuals of the castas and similar races."⁹⁷ The assumption was that mixed-race individuals came from illegitimate relationships between colored women and white men that did not last beyond the birth of the child. By exempting all people of African descent and lumping all phenotypes and variations into a generic group of "castas and similar races," the Crown reinforced the social and racial border between blackness and whiteness. Regardless of whether or not a *cuarterón* was the legitimate issue of two similar parents, he or she was assumed illegitimate and exempt from seeking public recognition of legitimacy and equality. The Crown did "remind" mixed-race individuals of their "natural obligation to honor and veneer [*sic*; read, "venerate"] their Fathers and superiors," encouraging them to seek the approval of their parents.⁹⁸ But this approval, if it was ever granted, never made it into the official record. Colored legitimacy did not matter to the law.

The importance here lies in the context of O'Reilly's Code and the *Real Pragmática*. Just eight years into Spanish rule, the racial landscape of New Orleans had changed. The legal language of race, previously an inchoate combination of status and color, became a complex system of shades and fractions within which status had little or no meaning; freedom became something nearly anyone could purchase or earn for the right price, act, or claim; and color became something both complex and simple—one was either purely white or some variation of black. On a legal level, the Spanish had succeeded in implementing the same reforms that revolutionized Mexico's racial system decades before, just in a more subversive way. By the early 1780s, a hypo-descendant racial order had taken shape in Louisiana and New Orleans. White was not black, and black could never be white. In the standard style of the Casta System, *pardos*—the general term for anyone of light skin with African ancestry—capped the mixed-race hierarchy. Although *albino* never appeared in Spanish Louisiana, *pardo* served the same purpose. It drew the racial line, protected the white community from anyone trying to "pass" as something their ancestry proved they were not, and created the impetus for the development of a self-conscious colored Creole community in New Orleans.

The Emergence of a Colored Creole Community under the Spanish

All was not lost for the colored population under O'Reilly's Code and the *Real Pragmática*, especially for the likes of Jean Louis Dolliole and his brother, sister, and friends. Born in the 1770s to mixed-race mothers and white French fathers, the Dollioles and the members of their social group were the first freeborn francophone generation to come of age under the Spanish. Like most of the free colored population at the time, these light-skinned *pardos* were almost universally illegitimate. Just nineteen free colored marriages occurred in Louisiana under the French.[99] At the time, there was no pressing reason for a colored woman to marry within her racial group. Legitimacy, though important at the highest levels of French society, did not matter on the colonial frontier. Colored women also vastly outnumbered colored men. In 1777, there were just forty-seven colored men for every hundred colored women in New Orleans.[100] There were simply not enough men to marry every woman.

The women, as well as their mixed-race progeny, could also benefit more from illegitimate relationships with white men than legitimate marriage with colored men. Even before the *Real Pragmática* affirmed the universal illegitimacy of people of African descent, there was no precedent for free colored marriage. Under the French, a population of *gens de couleur libre* existed, but it did not yet function as a self-conscious corporate entity. Each family, usually headed by a single mother, was a separate social unit. The bonds of fictive kinship and social networking did not unite the community under a common cause. Brothers and sisters, rather than friends and neighbors, stood as godparents for each other.[101] If a son did not go into business with his father, he often settled into unskilled or semiskilled labor or agrarian work, hardly establishing the business contacts that defined social preeminence. Rarely did one's social group extend beyond the filial clan. As a result, many colored women looked outward rather than inward during the late French period. By establishing relationships across the color line, they saw a way to give their children and possibly their children's children a step out of the insular familial unit. By attaching their kin to white society, however loosely or unrecognized, they introduced a new subliminal unifying concept to the New Orleans colored community—social "legitimacy" through whiteness.

Born between 1760 and 1780, the first generation of freeborn Spanish Orleanians came of age at a pivotal moment in the racial history of the city. As O'Reilly's Code and the *Real Pragmática* essentially finalized the implementation of the new Casta System in New Orleans, the colored community began to divide along demographic lines. It is here that the new racial language introduced by O'Reilly provides an insight into the social workings of the colored community. By looking at the specific phenotypes attributed to slaves freed during the Spanish period in combination with marriage records and baptisms, one can start to see a color line (or lines) develop *within* the free colored population, separating the light from the dark, the legitimate from the illegitimate.

Coartación and lax manumission laws muddled the line between freedom and enslavement in the 1770s and 1780s. In all, some 1,921 slaves received "the happy fruits of liberty" during the Spanish era.[102] At no point during that period did the free colored population number more than three thousand. In fact, between 1771 and 1800, the number of freeborn *gente de color* in New Orleans increased by just 1,327.[103] Such a comparatively large increase in freedmen certainly complicated the colored social order. Of the 1,921 former slaves, notaries and judges listed 1,037 (54 percent) as *morenos*, or pure blooded, dark-skinned Africans. Just 112 *cuarteróns* (6 percent) and 710 *pardos* (37 percent) received their freedom papers during the same period.[104] Of the 112 *cuarteróns* who became free under the Spanish, 52 (46 percent) of them did not pay for it. In all 52 cases, former owners freed their sons or daughters *graciosa* out of "love and kindness."[105] In contrast, just 346 of the 1,037 *morenos* (33 percent) received *graciosa* manumissions. In these cases, very few owners used a language of kinship or love. Most cited "good services" and "honesty" as the reasons for granting freedom.[106] On occasion emancipators would include a line of affection, but rarely signs of paternity or partnership. In December 1779, Don Alexander Boré freed his slaves Magdalena and her son Joseph, declaring that his "soul was moved to desire their freedom." That desire came about from a heartfelt plea by Magdalena's recently manumitted *pardo* husband, Joseph Casenave, who asked Boré to free his wife and son for a fee of 111 pesos. Boré accepted the money and freed the two slaves *graciosa*, making only passing reference to the payment.[107] Thus, the vast majority of *morenos* had to purchase their own or a relative's freedom through *coartación*, an act that cost an average of 244 pesos—a steep price that likely drained the majority of their life savings.[108]

During the Spanish period, then, a large, impoverished, dark-skinned contingent of former slaves entered the ranks of the largely skilled, light-skinned freeborn. The latter did not welcome the former into their community. In fact, they moved away from the primarily dark-skinned former slaves and slowly created a community for themselves and those like them. Spanish law and lasting French social practices already created simple divides within the free community based on skin color, ancestry, skill, and status (freeborn or freed). But as the number of manumitted *morenos* and newly imported African slaves increased over the Spanish period, these once fluid, loosely defined social prescriptions became conscious markers of class, culture, and race. The contrast between men like the Dolliole brothers—wealthy, socially active, literate, professional *cuarteróns*—and Silvestre, for example, an illiterate *moreno* carpenter who purchased his freedom through *coartación* in 1784 for 300 pesos, drove an emerging self-conscious elite away from the growing "black" mass.[109]

Over the first two decades of Spanish rule, *pardos* and other light-skinned freemen started to adopt the social characteristics celebrated within white society. Although the law did not recognize colored legitimacy, marriage was all but universal in the upper echelons of the socioracial hierarchy by the time the second generation of freeborn Orleanians came of age at the end of the Spanish period.[110] Debarred by law from the trappings of whiteness, socially prominent free people of color looked to create their own sense of elitism, their own set of social and cultural markers identifying the purported legitimacy of some and illegitimacy of others.

Although many scholars claim that marriage, legitimacy, and social formation first appeared with the expansion of the colored militia during the 1780s and 1790s, other evidence suggests that such practices and concerns were widespread before the militia held much meaning in the free community.[111] By the end of the French period, most free people of color were either one generation removed from slavery or had been born slaves.[112] In most cases, freeborn people of color took the surnames of their mothers, which were in turn the surnames of their mothers' masters. Geneviève Azémare's first child, François, took his mother's surname at his baptism in 1764. Geneviève was the daughter of Louis d'Azémare, a French slave-owner, and one of his *négresse* slaves.[113] At her 1757 baptism, Prudence Cheval received the name of her mother, Maria Theresa Cheval, a recently manumitted slave of Paul Cheval.[114] Prudence's father was Luis Antoine Blanc, a white French-born jeweler. Although he did not recognize Prudence as his daughter at her baptism, he accepted the responsibility of her power of attorney in 1796, admitting in the declaration that she was "my daughter."[115] This suggests not only that Prudence knew who her father was but also that she knew him for quite some time. With two grown children and an older brother, Prudence could easily have granted one of them her power of attorney.[116] Instead, she chose her father, which implies a level of trust forged over years rather than months.

Over the first decade of Spanish rule, naming and sexual practices among freeborn women started to change. During the 1770s and 1780s, white fathers of mixed-race children started acknowledging their paternity more frequently at baptism.[117] Along with this wave of paternal recognition came a new trend in free colored naming and sexual practices. Nearly every mixed-race child born to a *mulâtresse*, *pardo*, or *cuarterón* mother and *blanco* father during those two decades took the surname of the father rather than the mother.[118] In many cases, too, these children resulted from life partnerships between mixed-race women and white men, an uncommon practice under the French. All nine *cuarterón* daughters of Luison Cheval, a free *mulâtresse* from St. Charles Parish, took the names of their white fathers. After having a child each with Léonard Mazange, a prominent notary in New Orleans, and Juan Prieto, a Cuban-born Spanish planter, Luison settled into a thirty-year-long relationship with Charles Vivant, a French-born trader, that produced seven more children.[119]

Geneviève Dolliole, who opened chapter 1, maintained a relationship with Louis Dolliole, a builder and native of southern France, for nearly forty-five years. All four of their children took the Dolliole surname and were raised by both parents in the same house.[120] Although born with the surname Azémare, Geneviève's first son, François, adopted the surname of his common-law stepfather as he grew into adulthood. The five children he had with his wife, Julia Camps, a free woman of color, likewise took the adopted Dolliole name at birth.[121] Marguerite Pantalon also gave birth to children who did not share her last name. Between 1773 and 1780, she had four daughters by Martin Barthelemy Toutant Beauregard, a French-born merchant and great-uncle of famed Confederate general P. G. T. Beauregard. All four daughters received the Toutant surname at baptism, yet Martin Barthelemy never signed his name in the register. Only in his will did he acknowledge his relationship with Marguerite and his paternity of their four daughters.[122] After Martin's death in 1792, Marguerite publicly adopted the Toutant name as well, connecting herself socially to the man with whom she spent nearly twenty years of her life.[123]

Elsewhere in colonial America, the free colored populations had already moved on to more insular sexual practices. In French Saint Domingue, the massive, well-to-do free population of color saw marriage as the provenance of virtue, or of a bourgeois morality.[124] As early as the 1710s and 1720s, free people of color consistently married within their own phenotypes. Most notably in the Aquin region of Saint Domingue, *mulâtres* married other *mulâtres* with near universality. In like manner, *nègres* either married other *nègres* or took slaves as mates.[125] In 1720, fewer than 20 percent of all mixed-race baptisms in Saint Domingue involved an interracial couple or "unknown" father—a tell-tale sign of interracial parentage. By the time free coloreds in Spanish New Orleans were coming around to interracial life partnerships, their counterparts in Saint Domingue were pushing marriage onto their slaves, further isolating their own family lines from those of their enslaved brethren.[126]

A veritable obsession with marriage came upon the New Orleans free colored community around the time the second generation of freeborn Orleanians attained the age of majority in the last decade of the eighteenth century. A concern for "legitimacy," both legal and social, had grown in the free community ever since the introduction of the *Real Pragmática* in 1776. But the impetus for a growing insularity within the colored community did not rest entirely on legal sanctions and the Crown's rejection of mixed-race legitimacy. The external threats and forced ambiguity of O'Reilly's Code and the *Real Pragmática* merged with a community's inherent need for definition and a conceptual identity in a new social system.

Though numerically few and socially disconnected for most of the French period, the mixed-race families that emerged from interracial partnerships during the 1770s and 1780s shared certain traits that naturally brought them together. Francophone and Catholic, debarred from the "professional" realm, illegitimate by birth and law, these young freeborn Orleanians with white surnames and brown skin found themselves growing, both physically and culturally, alongside each other. A cultural endogamy thus developed around the social and racial ambiguity that had kept their parents separate and culturally undefined. In the face of an expanding population of darker-skinned freedmen and -women, they found definition and structure in their light color, free birth, mixed ancestry, and white surnames. They created an identity with the tools given them by their parents and the Casta System.[127]

Just as their mothers planned, their white blood became a point of pride. On a number of occasions, colored men and women asked parish priests or colonial officials to change or correct the phenotypes given them in sacramental records. At baptism, priests usually recorded racial designations based on observation alone, especially when the father was "unknown" and genealogical evidence unavailable. These records thus stood as representations of how individuals appeared to an informed third party, rather than reflections of their actual racial backgrounds. Under Spanish law in New Orleans, baptismal records specifically served as official colonial records. Men and women of color legally took the designation given them in the sacramental registers, regardless of their reputations in society.[128]

As a result, the baptismal registers for the Spanish period are dotted with alterations and changes to individual's phenotypes. On July 20, 1777, Marie Adelaïde Cheval was baptized as a *mulâtresse* in St. Louis Church. At some point over the next twenty-six years, a priest went back to the entry, scratched out "*mulâtresse*," and wrote "*cuarterón*" above it.[129] The alteration almost certainly occurred sometime after the original baptism. It is unlikely that the same priest would have made the first recording in French and then corrected it in Spanish. In all likelihood, a second priest changed the record years later, probably at the behest of Marie herself, who was in fact the quadroon daughter of a free *mulâtresse* and a white man.[130] The baptismal records of Adelaïde and Isabelle Cazelar, two sisters, reveal a similar process. Baptized later in life, at the ages of ten and twelve, respectively, the two sisters originally appeared in the register as *mulatos*, the Spanish variation of the term. At some point, probably around the time of their brother's baptism thirteen years later, a priest or official scratched out "*mulato*" and wrote the French term "*quartéronne*" below it in a clearly different hand.[131] Their brother's record, written entirely in French, lists him as a *mulâtre*, indicating that some external force, rather than simple correction, led to the changes in the sisters' entries.[132]

Although Spanish law maintained no legal difference between a *mulato* and a *cuarterón*, it clearly meant something to the increasingly insular freeborn population. By correcting specific phenotypes in sacramental registers, these socially and racially ambiguous people created official records of each family's racial history. They provided proof of one's bloodline and pedigree, serving as another indicator of elite status and upbringing, regardless of wealth, education, and other European standards of class and refinement. That most of the changes appeared on the records of women, and all of them provided a step up in the racial hierarchy, suggests that these alterations were intended for some internal process of racial and familial development.

Perhaps more importantly, these freeborn Orleanians started marrying each other. Unlike the *Americanos* of seventeenth-century Mexico, who sought "purity" through marriage with *Espagñols*, freeborn Orleanians looked to take control of the family names they received from their white fathers. Because the Spanish Crown did not recognize colored legitimacy, endogamous marriage not only challenged the racial logic of the *Real Pragmática*, it also provided a claim to legitimacy and ownership of family lines. Marriage legitimized the illegitimate. Once married, a colored couple became a church-sanctioned family unit with the moral obligation to expand as far as possible.[133] In essence, it gave the children of illicit interracial couples the ability to purify their impure bloodlines. It was a restart on the genealogical map. Each child born to one of these couples shared the same surname, skin color, and claim to legitimacy. It gave the colored Creole community a starting point, the ability to produce a single string from many threads. It allowed free people of color with light skin and white blood to claim the same familial and moral ties that defined European society.

In forging this new web of legitimacy and marriage, Creoles of color kept a keen eye on skin color. Not once, in all the marriages that occurred within the freeborn colored community, did phenotypes differ between partners by more than one generation of African blood.[134] Although these freeborn people of color clearly understood the fractions and meanings behind each designation, they did not always follow strict patterns of racial hierarchy in choosing their marriage partners. Somewhat surprisingly, men did not universally marry women of equal or inferior phenotype. For example, on November 16, 1801, Pierre Aubri, a *mulato* officer in the *pardo* militia, married Marie Françoise Aurélie, a *cuarterón* who had changed her original baptismal record from *mulâtresse*.[135] Three years earlier, Firmin Perrault, a *mulato* bricklayer, likewise married Hortense Toutant, a freeborn *cuarterón*.[136]

More often than not, however, freeborn Orleanians married people of their own phenotype, attaching specific racial designations to the families they were creating. Between 1777 and 1803, ninety-three free colored couples entered into the bonds of marriage. In seventy-one unions (76 percent), both partners shared the exact same phenotype as recorded on the marriage certificate (and baptismal records when available). Both partners were freeborn in sixty-one of these couples (85 percent). On only nine occasions were brides lighter than grooms.[137] Simply put, these new Creoles of color actively sought out those who looked like them and came from the same general background. *Cuarteróns* married other *cuarteróns*, and *mulatos* married other *mulatos*. On the rare occasions that both partners did not share a single phenotype, the difference did not cross the *pardo/moreno* divide. In all twenty-two cases, including the two mentioned earlier, a *cuarterón* married a *mulato*.[138] Not once between 1777 and 1803 did a *grifo* marry up in the racial order, or a *mulato* marry down.

The colored militia followed this same pattern. Resurrected by Alexander O'Reilly in the late 1770s when Spain joined France in support of the American colonists against the British, the colored militia split into two regiments based entirely on skin color—one for *pardos* (light skinned) and one for *morenos* (dark skinned).[139] But many scholars claim that militia-led social practices, like marriage, did not reflect this pigmentary line. As one scholar recently argued, colored militia members led the campaign in support of "European family formation for purposes of advancement and community building," ignoring the color line drawn by the Casta System.[140] Men like Noël Carrière, the captain of the *moreno* regiment, for example, stood as witnesses to thirty wedding ceremonies, twelve of which involved members of the *pardo* regiment.[141]

This suggests that the *moreno* and *pardo* regiments shared the same social space and cast their lots in the same camp. It also suggests, as has been argued, that the colored militia served as "the collective spokesperson for New Orleans's free community of color," leading the rest of the community by example.[142] But the intraracial color line that had developed in colored Creole marriage practices as a whole did not go away when one of the partners donned the uniform of the Milicias de la Nueva Orleans. In all, about half of the free colored marriages that took place between 1777 and 1803 involved a militia member. In every case, regardless of who stood as a witness, the militiaman married a woman of the same *calidad*. Even in the twelve *pardo* weddings that Noël Carrière, a *moreno*, witnessed, the *pardo* serviceman married a *pardo* bride.[143] In nine of those same weddings, the captain of the *pardo* regiment, François Dorville, also stood as a witness. In fact, Dorville witnessed fourteen other weddings, all of which united two *pardos*.[144] The *pardos*, then, were clearly more interested in defining themselves than in challenging the color line drawn by the Casta System.

Unlike his *moreno* counterpart, François Dorville recognized the importance of marriage in both the militia and civilian circles. All but one of the thirty ceremonies Noël Carrière witnessed involved a militiaman—the one exception being that of his father, Joseph Leveillé, and mother, Marie Thérèze Carrière, both African-born *negros*, in 1786.[145] Of the twenty-three witnessed by Dorville, eight involved friends or family members who did not serve in the militia. In 1801, he stood witness as his only daughter, Julia, a quadroon and "natural daughter of François Orville [*sic*], captain of the *pardo* companies of this place, and of Isabel Boisdoré," married Philippe Azur, a quadroon native of New Orleans.[146] Like so many other freeborn *pardos*, including Isabel's three brothers, Philippe Azur never served in the militia.[147] Yet somehow he managed to marry the only daughter of the highest-ranking *pardo* officer in that body, and receive his blessing. As for Isabel's brothers, François witnessed two of their marriages and lived down the street from them for nearly three decades.[148]

François Dorville cared greatly for the militia. He considered his position as captain of the *pardos* his profession, while he simply worked as a dry goods merchant and tavern keeper. But even in his dedication to the militia, Dorville exposed his true allegiance. In the 1795 Census of New Orleans, François Dorville was the only member of the militia to mention his service. In the space provided for "*profesión*," he wrote: "*captaine des mulâtres et quartérons libres*."[149] Instead of using the official, accepted term for his regiment (Milicias de Pardos), he used the French versions of the two specific phenotypes classified as *pardo* in the Casta System. He never actually mentioned the militia at all. By choosing French over Spanish and dropping the generic term "*pardo*," Dorville made clear the emergence of an as-yet-unnamed Creole identity. He referred back to the racial ambiguity and status identification of the late French period, but showed how the inklings of a cultural and racial identity back then had found definition and classification under the Spanish. He could have phrased his six-word history of his people differently, but the words he chose painted an honest picture. They were not simply *pardos*, and neither were they all militiamen. They were francophone Creoles of Spanish Louisiana, privileged by the white blood that ran in their veins.

A Creole community was thus forming, but not along lines dictated by Noël Carrière and his *moreno* militia. If anything, the *morenos'* actions were reflections of where François Dorville, Jean Louis Dolliole, and the other "*mulâtres et quartérons libres*" were headed. Beginning in the late French period, it was the mixed-race women who, for reasons largely beyond their control, decided to imbue within their children a pride of place and clan. Through patriarchal naming practices and lifelong interracial partnerships, these women, the mothers and grandmothers of the first true Creoles of color, promoted "European family formation" long before militiamen witnessed a single marriage. The Casta System that arrived with the Spanish gave their children and grandchildren a language of race and degree, a social order all their own. By ascribing meaning to each level of the system, free-born Orleanians were able to forge a social hierarchy independent of status, yet perfectly in line with the expectations of the white community.

They never claimed a position in the white system. They simply used the tools given them by the Casta System to differentiate themselves from the lower orders of colored people—the *morenos* and freedmen. And by marrying each other, they created physical and nominal legacies for themselves and their kin. They preserved the social order in blood, making sure that certain families remained light skinned, French, and eventually Creole. This could not have occurred without the Casta System and Spain's experiences in Central and South America centuries earlier. But it also took form in the hands of a self-conscious community in need of cultural and racial definition. Under the Spanish they rebuilt one and found the other. But a new sun was rising in the east, and in 1803, they had more work to do.

CHAPTER 3

A Sensible Equivalent to the Original Blood

THE AMERICANS

François Boisdoré and Manuel Moreau had no idea that the man they heard on September 21, 1814, would become president of the United States. That day, the two childhood friends stood as part of a multinational, multilingual force that mustered to protect the United States from invasion by the British. The War of 1812 had been raging for more than two years in the Northeast. Just a month earlier, British forces under Major General Robert Ross burned the United States Capitol along with much of the city of Washington. American pride was damaged. The British, American military officials concluded, had only one place left to raze—the newest American state capital at New Orleans.[1]

There are few indications that François Boisdoré and Manuel Moreau worried about American defeats in the North. The only local newspaper, the Orleans *Gazette*, barely covered the actual fighting of the war. It focused on what really concerned the heavily commercial and trade-oriented people of New Orleans: the threat of a British blockade and the illicit trade in human cargo and Cuban rum out of Barataria Bay, the sanctuary of the Lafitte brothers some forty-five miles south of the city.[2] Boisdoré and Moreau both understood English, but they spoke and read French. Born to unmarried, interracial, francophone parents, Boisdoré and Moreau grew up at the heart of the colored Gallic community in New Orleans. They cared little about the white anglophone North.[3]

Men like Boisdoré and Moreau defined themselves in both racial and cultural terms. As members of a colored Gallic community, they solidified their sense of belonging by maintaining social and familial bonds with those of similar mixed-heritage backgrounds. By the time of the Louisiana Purchase in 1803, Boisdoré, then twenty-five years old, was an established cabinetmaker. He owned a shop on St. Philip Street in the middle of the Vieux Carré, a business he owned and maintained until his death in 1859. He never married. But he did have two children by Isabelle Gaitan, a freeborn, French-speaking *mulâtresse* with whom he spent nearly thirty years.[4] Shortly after Louisiana became an American territory, Boisdoré went into business with the upstart undertaker and Saint Domingue refugee Pierre Casenave, the mixed-race father of one of New Orleans's most prominent colored Creole families.[5] For the next four decades, Boisdoré constructed the caskets and Casenave handled the bodies and funeral arrangements for nearly every elite colored francophone family in New Orleans.[6]

During that time Boisdoré built a considerable social network stretching across the color line. With a surname rooted in the French colonial period and more European than African blood in his veins, François Boisdoré had a claim to membership in the New Orleans cultural and social elite. He owned property, a business, and slaves. He followed local and national politics, was a member of the highly exclusive Société d'Economie, and stood at the vanguard of his society.[7] Although of partial African descent, he muted his "tainted" blood by celebrating his Gallic lifestyle. As this chapter shows, along with many other colored Creoles he clearly recognized that racial ambiguity did not translate into whiteness, equality, or full citizenship within American society. Yet he also knew that other aspects of social life could reduce the importance of racial differences. Property and cultural status could forge less rigid racial categories within America's language of citizenship.

This process of social manipulation was seamless for Boisdoré and others. Among a select few light-skinned Creoles of means, Boisdoré never appeared in a city directory with the letters "f.m.c."—"free man of color"—behind his name. In court papers, the white clerks, judges, and notaries likewise left off the required racial indicator.[8] To New Orleans white society, Boisdoré and his social and racial equals were not colored, black, or negro. They were something else altogether, members of a self-conscious socioracial caste established nearly half a century earlier. In fact, the only practical thing separating this localized group from full citizenship in the American nation was the franchise; and that privilege hardly fell to the majority of Americans at the time.[9]

The man speaking to Boisdoré, his colleague Moreau, and the 350 other free colored men that day in 1814 expanded the idea of citizenship further than any public figure had before. He opened the address to his "fellow brave citizens" with an apology. "Through a mistaken policy," he admitted, "you have heretofore been deprived of a participation in the Glorious struggle for National rights, in which this Country is engaged." The time was at last at hand for these "Free Coloured Inhabitants of Louisiana" to take up their new national banner and, as "sons of freedom," defend that "most estimable blessing" of American "confidence." As "adopted Children" of the United States, he called for them "to rally around the standard of the Eagle," an instinct that any intelligent and honorable American would have, especially in the face of "false representations" of freedom offered by the British invader.[10]

Major General Andrew Jackson, this future president and the commanding general in charge of Louisiana's defense, knew his audience well. "Your country," he assured them, "does not wish you to engage in her cause, without amply remunicating [*sic*; read, 'remunerating'] you, for the services rendered." He offered them a very reasonable $124 in cash, along with 160 acres of land, following the ultimate defeat of the advancing British force. He promised that these rates were in line with those "furnished to every American Soldier"; and as members of their own battalion, these colored "Americans," all "brave citizens" of the nation, would not "be exposed to improper comparisons or unjust sarcasm."[11] Indeed, by granting 160 acres to each individual, Jackson established these colored Louisianans as freeholders, the very definition of voting citizens in states like Virginia, Maryland, and North Carolina.[12]

But there was a catch. Echoing the uncertainty of nearly every American politician, military leader, and white citizen at the time, Jackson refused to allow these colored "citizens," the nation's "adopted Children," to serve as officers. Although participating in the "Glorious" defense of a shared country, men of color could not be trusted with direct representation in the military order. They could exist and function as nominal citizens when needed, but their voice in the hierarchy, their representatives in the national body—realized at this moment in the defense force itself—were to be chosen from among their "White fellow Citizens."[13] People of color could only participate as loyal subjects, not full citizens in the American nation. They could take up arms in its defense and carry the banner of their new nation and state against a universal foe, but they could not take on leadership roles. They could not stand in proxy for their social and racial superiors—white Americans—in battle or in the political sphere. That was too much to ask, and well beyond long-established natural and political hierarchies. But they could consider themselves "American."[14] That much Jackson promised.

This concession of "citizenship," similar in effect to the nominal privileges granted François Boisdoré and Manuel Moreau over the next forty years, came more than a decade after New Orleans became American, and two years after it became the capital of a new state. Yet Andrew Jackson's address was the first public decree of its kind. Before 1814, before the United States needed manpower to defend its newest port against the British, the New Orleans Creoles of color endured an uncomfortable and unique silence. Nonwhites, as a whole, had no place in the expanding American empire of liberty, an empire forged in the crucible of an enlightened republican revolution.[15]

Republican virtue, the altruistic force that bound Americans together, existed, it was held by many, in the hearts and minds of white men only. All others, though loyal members or denizens of the Republic, were incapable of embodying the true meaning and value of the Revolutionary cause. It was a movement dominated and defined by a select, white, male aristocracy. Patriotic virtue demanded the liberty that came from property ownership and manly honor, which excluded dark-skinned Africans and tawny-skinned Indians.[16] Except in rare cases, the concepts of "citizen" and "American," at least on paper, did not reach much further than white, landowning men.

But after the Louisiana Purchase of 1803, things were different. The very treaty through which the purchase was effected made it that way. Signed on April 30, but dated April 28, 1803, the Louisiana Purchase Treaty granted the United States, "for-ever and in full Sovereignty," more than 828,000 square miles of land west of the Mississippi River, including the so-called Isle of Orleans, located on the east bank between the river and Lake Pontchartrain.[17] Along with the territory came several million people—Spaniards, Frenchmen, a few frontier yeomen, free people of color, slaves, Indians, and every admixture of the different classes. Expressing American leaders' ambivalence about defining and regulating citizenship, or membership in the American nation, the treaty decreed that the "inhabitants" of Louisiana would be "incorporated" into the American union "as soon as possible" with the full "enjoyment of all rights, advantages and immunities of citizens of the United States." Until then, the new American government would protect each individual's right to "liberty, property, and religion."[18]

There was no mention of race, color, language, or culture. That much was assumed. Because free people of African descent (and Native Americans) had no defined or conceived place in the American national body, the authors of the treaty, as well as top officials in the Jefferson administration, did not consider them in the language of the agreement. The inhabitants referred to in the Purchase Treaty were the French émigrés, white Creoles, and leftover Spaniards who, according to one American merchant, exhibited manners and habits "totally foreign to those of the citizens of the U[nited] States."[19] These were the people the Jefferson administration needed to woo over to their side and "incorporate" into the expanding body politic.[20]

Men like François Boisdoré, Manuel Moreau, and their mutual friend Jean Louis Dolliole, as well as other Creoles of color who came of age at the end of the Spanish period, never expected citizenship or representation in the virtuous American Republic. The very concept of a republic—virtuous representation—was alien to their subaltern, colonial experiences and expectations. The United States was not their heroic savior. It did not liberate them from political tyranny and cultural darkness as it made its "providential journey" westward.[21] But it also was not the debilitating oppressor that many historians have made it out to be.[22] More than anything else, it invited a more fluid and less settled process. As this chapter shows, following a period of surprising ignorance, American officials in both New Orleans and Washington came to appreciate where the colored Creoles stood under the Spanish. They understood that these light-skinned, francophone, literate, and prosperous free people of color had fashioned their own self-image. They had established a sense of racial and social pride, unlike what white officials expected from the aggregate free "negroes" of Virginia, Maryland, and New York. They had to tread carefully when working with civic customs that already existed in Louisiana.

In large part, Jefferson, Madison, and the new American governor of Louisiana, William C. C. Claiborne, let the Creoles maintain that conscious racial and social identity. But they also wanted to codify it into law and define it in no uncertain terms. They were curious about these people; and these people, in turn, were curious about them. But as will become clear, the idea of citizenship, of full and ordinary membership in the American political framework, never crossed either of their minds—at least not until Jackson came to town to face a dangerous British foe. Only then did the Creoles realize that actual citizenship demanded more than the protection of "liberty, property, and religion."

Before Jackson and the Battle of New Orleans, however, the Creoles of color worked to define their own place in the new American community, one that challenged the legislative standard of the "free Negro" and the "black slave." The established community of free people of color in New Orleans, in ways similar to like populations as far north as Richmond, Virginia, used socially reinforced notions of complexion, culture, and local belonging to carve a social space beyond the constructed bounds of law.[23] Although dismissed or ignored by state and federal legislators, elite free "Negroes" in both the Upper and Lower South, not just New Orleans, used social strategies as a way to reject universal "Negrohood" and create something altogether different.[24] By law they were Negroes and free men of color, fundamentally debarred from full citizenship. But through social definitions of class and complexion, they forced the nation's hand, remaking themselves into denizens, subjects, and, at times, even "brave Citizens."

Citizenship and Local Belonging in the Early Republic

Of course, before General Jackson, no one had ever told them they would be citizens of anything, much less a new nation. To the Creoles of color, the emerging elite of the growing New Orleans colored population, membership in society meant the maintenance of freedom and land, not much more. Under the French, their forebears fought for simple recognition in a colony of the French Crown. Citizenship itself did not entirely exist. Instead, vassalage defined belonging and political place on the colonial frontier. By the 1760s, they had succeeded in becoming, if nothing else, recognized as a mixed breed, somewhat distinct from blacks and entirely distinct from whites. But still, citizenship never entered their minds.[25]

The Spanish were equally silent on the matter. Citizenship, if it ever existed in New Spain or *Luisiana*, required the *limpieza de sangre* ("purity of blood") inherently denied people of African descent. The Casta System, as explained in chapter 2, organized nonwhites into *calidads* representative of their fundamental impurity. For people of African descent, the system never changed. The "vitriolic" blood of their progenitors locked them forever in place as stained or tainted, regardless of color or ancestral distance.[26] Given a social and racial place in the community, however, their relative ambiguity and mixed-race backgrounds became the Creoles' equivalent to citizenship under the Spanish. In fact, the concept of Creolehood emerged in New Orleans under the Spanish and within their detailed racial hierarchy.[27] But privileges did not amount to rights, and acceptance as a social and racial other, or *casta*, did not make them citizens of anything, much less the metropole across the Atlantic.[28]

The Louisiana Purchase introduced the notions of citizenship and national belonging to Louisianans for the first time. Unlike the new Americans, Louisianans, both white and colored, had not fought their own virtuous revolution. They had not challenged the yoke of colonialism and the ills of taxation without representation. They had never fought and died for the "inalienable rights" and "natural rights of man" invoked by Jefferson and many other English-minded thinkers. They had fought with those who did, but for different reasons and with different expectations.[29] So when the United States literally purchased them out of colonial denizenship, everything was new. The average Louisianan, especially of African descent, had neither read about nor understood the principles of American nationhood and republicanism. The ideas might have floated around the highest circles, but the newspapers neither printed the Constitution nor provided any serious detail about what to expect from the Americans and their government.[30] In less than three years, between 1800 and 1803, Louisianans had shifted between three separate colonial ventures, each with a different language, culture, and code. By April 30, 1803, the people of Louisiana were, if nothing else, confused.

The Americans were no more prepared following the Louisiana Purchase than their new subjects. Louisiana stood as the first major expansion of American principles to a previously foreign colonial population. No one knew exactly what to do with the thousands of new potential citizens living along the Mississippi River. Precedent had established few rules for such a massive expansion of the American state. Until relatively recently, some twenty-seven years prior to the Purchase, American colonists had prided themselves on their status as British subjects, their inclusion in the body politic of a distant but protective monarchy.[31] Indeed, it was the betrayal of that very protection and membership that ultimately justified the Americans' break from their "*mother* country."[32] The matter of citizenship as an official position in society was thus relatively new. American independence had arisen from a breach of the natural order defined by sovereign protection and representation in parliament—the two fundamental English liberties. As a result, American leaders defined membership, or citizenship, in the new nation as an expression of an honest and voluntary *allegiance* to both an individual state and the federal government.[33]

The problem was that no state had the same definition of membership, or even the same word for it. As early as 1783, before the United States Constitution bound together the separate, sovereign states, the Supreme Judicial Court of Massachusetts decided that a new idea "favorable to the natural rights of mankind" and "innate Liberty" demanded that "all men are born free and equal" and "entitled to liberty, ... as well as life and property" without regard to "color, complexion, or shape of noses, [and] features."[34] The court referred to this entitlement as "subjectship," the same term used by British courts and parliament to describe the "natural" allegiance and protection exchanged between the people and their monarch.[35]

Elsewhere it was more complicated. In most southern states, the basis of political membership came down to allegiance and how one proved his ability to maintain that allegiance to the given state. Nearly every state granted citizenship—or whichever word it used—to any white male born in the state after independence. Founded on the seventeenth-century British notion of *jus soli* subjectship, "natural-born citizenship" assumed that each individual born in a state would be raised under both the influence and protection of the given state's government. These citizens' allegiance to the state, therefore, went unquestioned, as it became a part of their lives from the beginning. The very act of being born wedded the individual to the state—an idea the British called "birth within the allegiance."[36] In 1790, a North Carolina court declared that "all free persons born within the State are born citizens of the State."[37] A Tennessee court in 1799 established that all "good and white men born within our state" were immediately "adopted into the body politic a new member."[38] Both Virginia and Pennsylvania decided that all "freeborn men of good character" entered "into political partnership" with the state due to their "natural and free birth" within its territory.[39]

Natural-born citizenship—or partnership, or membership—was easy. The state could trust a child to grow into a virtuous citizen simply by growing up under the protection of the government. He had theoretically inherited his membership in the community by the right of descent. The consensual allegiance of his forefathers granted him that status.[40] But aliens—those born outside the borders of the nation, state, or political community as a whole—posed a more difficult problem. Because these men maintained prior allegiances to other political entities, or did not fall under the basic descriptions of citizens established by law, they could not necessarily be trusted without somehow proving their at least tacit consent to be governed.[41] It is within this process of naturalization—proving the consent and allegiance of aliens—that one first sees the question of colored citizenship arise. And in Louisiana after the Purchase, the question became one of the central issues delaying the "incorporation," or adoption, of the territory into the American union.

The most important aspect of the naturalization process was, according to the state of Virginia, the "assurance of fidelity" through "oath ... and residence."⁴² If an alien could live alongside natural-born citizens within the bounds of the law and the territory for a certain number of years, he could show that his allegiance to the new state was not fleeting or corrupt. Nearly every state in the union included a residency requirement for naturalization in its original constitution. Vermont set a one-year term of residency, while New York required three years and an oath forcing each applicant "to abjure and renounce all allegiance and subjection to all and every foreign king, prince, potentate and state, in all matters ecclesiastical as well as civil."⁴³ Both Virginia and Maryland demanded two years "beyond initial settlement" along with a standard "oath of allegiance" and the purchase of property. Maryland also required "belief in the christian [*sic*] religion" to achieve the status of citizen.⁴⁴

The purpose of residency requirements was simple. They "evinced a permanent attachment to the state" and demonstrated that the applicants had "exerted themselves in behalf of the freedom and Independence of the United States of America."⁴⁵ According to Jeffersonian notions of expansion and conquest, the dominance of the land through ownership, tillage, and production thereon created a natural, individual claim to that land. Because the land was part of a growing nation-state, the owner, tiller, or producer of the land, when doing so of his own volition, was entitled to membership in the community built upon it. The key was work and service. If a man labored for and by way of the land of the nation, serving both his family and the state as a whole, he proved his allegiance to both.⁴⁶ This work, and the land it involved, bred good character and honesty—two basic requirements for legal citizenship. Newspapers, politicians, and travelers extolled the "happy, neighborly cultivator" of the American countryside.⁴⁷ Alexander Hamilton, as early as 1775, celebrated the "industry of our country men," claiming that it produced "jealousies" across the Atlantic and gave birth to a "dawning splendour" of "affection" and "independence."⁴⁸

The grounds for citizenship were not as simple as birthright, property ownership, and volitional allegiance, however. Although the law set these claims as the basis for national and state membership, society worked on a different level, one that complicated the very notion of what it meant to be American in the early Republic. Of the states that defined citizenship in their original constitutions, only Virginia, South Carolina, and Tennessee provided that "all free *white* persons born within the territory of this commonwealth" (emphasis added), or "residing therein" for two years, "shall be deemed 'citizens' of the state."⁴⁹ The rest seem to have forgotten about or never considered the issue of race and color. The number of free people of color in the United States remained small for most of the eighteenth century. It was not until the mid-1790s that manumissions picked up in a wave of Revolutionary fervor, creating the "free Negro" populations that would cause social and legislative unrest decades later.[50] Before that, the free colored populations of most states lived on the periphery, recognized by society but not necessarily by law.

Left out of most initial attempts to define local and national citizenship, free people of color were never accepted as members of the local political community either. Only in North Carolina, where "all freemen" were given a political voice, could a man of color vote in an election.[51] But this was not entirely based on racial difference. The science of the time, especially that coming out of Europe, focused on the perceived "natural" differences between the African and the European. Men like Johann Friedrich Blumenbach of Göttingen led the way in declaring the two "races" fundamentally separate in development rather than origin. The African had developed dark skin and corrupted internal organs not from a distinct creation, they claimed, but from the climate in which Africans had developed as a people. As a result, these climatists insisted, Africans represented an essential subspecies of the human race. They had started at the same level as Europeans but never reached the same levels of development in the hot, moist African air.[52]

Society did not adopt such high-minded views. In the same way that American revolutionaries decried "natural hierarchies" yet oversaw a society constructed upon them, face-to-face interactions between workingmen on the streets of America's growing cities functioned more on the basis of reputation and character than scientific declarations of racial superiority.[53] And this translated into the legal system. Citizenship in states like Maryland, New York, Pennsylvania, and Virginia required "good character" and "respectability" along with residency because, on the ground level, reputation and service did more for one's status than more quantifiable aspects of allegiance. As chapter 2 made clear, reputation, character, and "circumstances" in New Spain could not only decide where a person stood socially but also where they stood racially.[54] These same aspects of personal identity also helped define early American notions of virtue and belonging. "[A man] equally removed from the temptations of poverty and the allurements of opulence," wrote one Virginian, "is uniformly the most virtuous."[55]

This idea, broadly considered, transcended race in cities like Petersburg, Richmond, and especially New Orleans after the Purchase. The historical record is full of examples of courts and people throughout the South placing reputation, good character, and, in the case of New Orleans, military service before or alongside skin color and race as markers of social and personal virtue. When Robert Battles, a free mulatto from Albemarle County, Virginia, for example, attacked Patrick Johnson, a free Negro, in Richmond in 1804, the Albemarle County Court found in favor of the defendant. The court cited the "freeman" Battles's reputation as "the best known, most respectable, most independent, best connected member of the Battles family" as partial justification for his acquittal. It also did not hurt that his father, Robert Sr., was a known Revolutionary War veteran. And while the plaintiff appeared in the record as a "free Negro," the court never referred to Battles as anything but a "freeman."[56] Four years later, a white transient merchant accused free mulatto Charles Forgason of stealing seven dollars' worth of merchandise outside of Richmond, near Farmville, Virginia. The character of the two men came up in the court proceedings some eight months later. The many wealthy and middling white witnesses who came to Forgason's aid—a testament in itself—assured the court of his "solid appearance," "honest and upright manner," and "industrious and economical" lifestyle. The plaintiff, Richard Foster, did not fare so well, as witnesses claimed that his "sister & mother are whores" and that he was a "known and common drunk in Petersburg." Without any further testimony, the court acquitted Forgason and ordered Foster to pay court costs.[57]

In both cases, the courts accepted reputation and social status as reasons for acquittal. In the eyes of the court as well as the white witnesses who, in the words of more than one historian, "rescued" their colored neighbors, Battles and Forgason passed the test of allegiance and belonging through their social actions. They had lived in town, owned or worked the land, and maintained "good character" and "upright manners," all attributes required for membership in Virginia's political community. As a result, local society granted them the basic rights and privileges of acceptance and belonging in that community. There is a chance that their mixed-race backgrounds played a part, especially in the case of Robert Battles. But their upright reputations clearly played more of a role in their acceptance and acquittal than race. According to legislation passed in Virginia in 1785 and again in 1806, free people of color were not supposed to remain in the state for more than six months after the acts were passed without legislative permission, much less defend themselves in court against white plaintiffs—against whom they could not legally testify in any capacity.[58] But both Battles and Forgason, and countless others, remained, went to court, and lived their lives as accepted members of Richmond's free society in spite of the law.

Full membership in the political systems of both the state and nation, however, eluded them. Historian Laura Edwards has noted that, as the United States took social and legal form in the decades after the Revolution, "state law developed alongside the localized system, but never completely displaced it." Indeed, in places like Virginia and the Carolinas, the states' legal institutions and the laws they crafted and passed "did not provide the only, or even the primary, legal site or conceptual framework for addressing public matters," including how best to assign value and standing in the local community.[59] To the planters in the state legislature as well as many whites throughout the country, free people of color, even those best known and most respected in their local areas, fit neatly into an "aggregate free black category" with no name, face, or reputation.[60] For example, the act passed in 1785 looked to quell what one legislator called the "great and alarming mischiefs of freedom amongst slaves." Another Virginian referred to free people of color as "persons obnoxious ... or dangerous to the peace of society." As a whole, the Virginia legislature was convinced that "free Negros [sic]" were "attendants of unpleasant incidents" as well as "notorious thieves" and "suspects of rebellion within the freest republic on earth."[61]

This faceless aggregate category, legislated in nearly every state in the union, specifically relegated people of color, both enslaved and free, to the status of "Other." In effect, they were informal pieces—objectified and with no formalized status within the body politic—of the social landscape, lacking a political voice or legal recognition. According to Senator William Smith of South Carolina, "the act of manumission," whether by "birth or personal act," did not "constitute [Negroes] citizens." At best, he concluded, they stood among "quasi-citizens, aliens, or denizens," incapable of claiming *all* the "rights and privileges of true citizenship."[62] But as the cases of Robert Battles and Charles Forgason in Virginia suggest—along with many others throughout the country—reputation and culture held serious weight in the local, face-to-face negotiation of who belonged and who remained alien or Other. Indeed, on a larger, more political scale, it was the lack of face-to-face knowledge, this lack of personal attachment—and a recognized local practice to govern it, suffered by both territorial and federal American leadership—that made Louisiana a difficult child to adopt smoothly into the American national family.

Simply put, white anglophone Americans did not know Louisiana or its strange, foreign, capital city. Both were purchased, brought in, and their denizens were not members of the original Revolutionary clan. The localized systems their people had negotiated and built before becoming legally American, even where similar to those found in older, original areas of the country, had taken form under foreign allegiances—at best confusing and external, at worst extralegal and unwanted in the new united system of states.[63] On the ground, the work had been done—in reputation, land ownership, and militia service. Geneviève Dolliole, her sons, the Boisdorés, and the established community of Creoles of which they were a part had made sure of it. But at the highest, most disconnected levels of governance, it was all brand new: the proverbial chain of recognition forged under the French and Spanish had broken with the Purchase of 1803. Beyond the standard notions of naturalization and volitional allegiance retained from an ancient, white, and British system, American citizenship had no explanation or place for the free, light-skinned, reputable, francophone people of color it encountered in south Louisiana.

Color, Class, and Culture in Louisiana and the Nation

Somewhat surprisingly, given his penchant for measurement and planning, Thomas Jefferson knew very little about the people and the land he purchased on April 30, 1803. Almost immediately, letters started flooding out of New Orleans asking questions and providing important information about the newest American territory. The people "are all anxious to know what kind of government will be first given to us," wrote Benjamin Morgan, a merchant from Philadelphia who had lived in New Orleans for three years by August 1803. Whatever the type, Morgan informed his friend Chandler Price, the transition would be difficult. "Our population consists," he cautioned, "of people of allmost [sic] all nations accustomed to arbitrary prompt decisions." They were ignorant of the freedoms of American rule, yet also "free from the distresses occasioned by" their previous despotic conditions. Only "the talents of virtuous good men" could "make the laws of freemen palatable to them."[64] The next month, John Pintard, a businessman from New York and a close friend of Thomas Jefferson, wrote a letter to Albert Gallatin describing a similar scene. "The manners & habits of [the] people," he warned the secretary of the treasury, are "totally foreign to those of the citizens of the U[nited] States." The implementation of an American-style ethos in the region, he admitted, "may require a system modified to their prejudices."[65]

The people of New Orleans were aliens to the American system. Although many worked, owned their own property, and maintained the "upright manners" befitting an American citizen, they did not, according to American migrants like Morgan and Pintard, have even a basic understanding of American principles of government and life. They were used to the "arbitrary prompt decisions" of a colonial oligarchy. They lived for themselves rather than for society as a whole. Most importantly, as Morgan pointed out, they seemed unbothered by the disadvantages brought about by tyrannical oversight. They lacked virtue and thus could not stand under American law as it was then written. It would take time to test and treat their allegiances.[66]

But the letters from Morgan and Pintard offer an interesting perspective, one that highlights the disconnect between local practice and national image. Both men had lived in New Orleans for extended periods by the summer of 1803—Morgan for just over three years, and Pintard for just under four.[67] Although relative newcomers, both men served in the vanguard of the American presence in New Orleans. They did business throughout the city, owning a number of properties and running a series of trading houses along Levee Street, the central business district of the entire region.[68] They certainly had interactions with the local white Creole population. In 1804, both Morgan and Pintard worked with Michel Fortier, a wealthy Creole, along with John McDonogh of Maryland and Edward Livingston of New York, to create the first Bank of Louisiana, an institution that served the entire white population of the city.[69] Morgan even described Fortier, along with fellow Creole Antoine Cavalier, as "good acquaintances" and "honest men."[70] In 1802, Morgan went so far as to praise Barthélémy Lafon, the white father of the wealthy Creole of color Thomy Lafon, as "the true picture of virtue."[71]

These men did not represent the wider New Orleans public in the eyes of Pintard and Morgan. Like Robert Battles and Charles Forgason as well as countless Others and aliens across the country, their reputations for honesty and virtue set them apart from the aggregate whole. Yet both Morgan and Pintard still wrote of the foreign manners and habits of the people of New Orleans. Although Fortier, Cavalier, and Lafon were unique in their combined wealth, their shared French culture and language, nativity in the early Spanish period, and general lack of republican knowledge fell in line with the rest of the population of their city.[72]

This was the primary conundrum Jefferson and his administration encountered in Louisiana. Adoption of an entire target population—in this case white Creoles and leftover Spanish merchants—could not work without a standard practice. As required by democratic ideology, all prospective citizens had to be treated equally. Accepting men like Fortier and Lafon into the political union based on personal knowledge created a legally proscribed hierarchy antithetical to nearly every principle of republicanism. "They [individual Louisianans] must be treated as one element," argued Republican congressman John Smilie of Pennsylvania. "Neither the conquest nor the purchase [of the territory] can incorporate them into the Union."[73] Equality of treatment was the key, declared Samuel Latham Mitchill, a Republican from New York. "All inhabitants of Louisiana willing to stay," Mitchill explained, "are to be trained in the knowledge of our own laws and institutions." They will "serve an apprenticeship to liberty; ... be taught the lessons of freedom; and by degrees ... raised to the enjoyment and practice of independence." All of this "to make them safe in the rights of conscience."[74]

It was their choice to stay in the new American land and become "apprentices to liberty." Their allegiance, then, was volitional, as required by American principles of national and state belonging. Although Lafon, Fortier, and Cavalier had friends in the federal system and could have passed easily into the American fold, they had to complete the required three-year residency and "conform" to the "quiet possession" and "actual cultivation" of land and "good manners" just like the rest of their fellow creoles.[75] In effect, native Louisianans, or at least those noncitizens resident in the area before the Purchase, were legal aliens of the federal system, children groomed for adoption into a new national family.

This idea originated in Britain following the unification of the English and Scottish crowns in 1603. According to Chief Justice of Common Pleas Lord Coke, nativity defined one's status within the empire. Although local "legiance" was, he admitted, quite "real and basic," the concept of *ligeantia naturalis* (natural allegiance) held sway over all other lines of judgment. Thus, according to Coke's 1609 decision in the famed Calvin's Case, Scotsmen who were born before the unification of the crowns—*antenati*—were aliens fit only for naturalization once their allegiance was established by the court, akin to "adopted sons of the Crown."[76]

Louisianans were, in essence, equivalent to *antenati* Scotsmen. They had lived as subjects of a foreign sovereign and were brought into a new system by the replacement of authority. As John Smilie stated above, "neither the conquest nor the purchase [of the territory] can incorporate them into the Union" without a test of allegiance. And that test, according to both the Purchase Treaty and Congress, applied to "all the inhabitants of the ceded territory," without any exception or restriction noted.[77] If the Jefferson administration treated everyone the same, granting no localized exceptions to the incorporation and naturalization process, the system, in theory, would fall into place. But such a broad view of a local community betrayed one simple, blatant fact—everyone was not the same, especially in the eyes of the nation at large.

In his letter to Chandler Price, Benjamin Morgan first noted the problem. "Upon what footing will the free quadroon mulatto & black people stand?" he inquired. "Will they be entitled to the rights of citizens or not[?]" In most other circumstances, the question would serve very little purpose. A number of states directly excluded people of color from citizenship or membership in the local community. Others strongly implied their prohibition and often passed retroactive laws eliminating any ambiguity in the state constitution.[78] But there was a reason for Morgan's question. "Many," he continued, seemed "very respectable," and might even "be good citizens" if given the chance. But Morgan quickly backtracked. Everything depended on the treatment they received from the United States government, he warned. If flatly rejected, they could just as easily prove "formidable abettors of the black people say slaves if they should ever be troublesome." To Morgan, a white man from the North, they presented the perfect dichotomy—helpful, respectable citizens, and agents of racial apocalypse.[79] Local practice told him one thing, and national image told him another.

His letter, then, tells us a lot. From his perspective, the "numerous class" of "very respectable" free people of color could not possibly be as trustworthy and enlightened as they seemed. After all, they represented two opposing factions in American society—white citizens and black slaves. They held themselves aloof from the dregs of society and, aside from a darker exterior, displayed characteristics in line with the standards of white citizenship. But in the end, Morgan could not escape the national fear of racial brotherhood among people of African blood. Their respectability, though notable, did not make them the "true picture of virtue," as it did Barthélémy Lafon, who fathered at least one of these "quadroons." It allowed only for the "consideration" that they may, in time and under the right conditions, "be good citizens." It could never suppress the passions rooted in African blood. The slightest misgiving, he feared, whether from above or below, would awaken their natural, sanguinary allegiance to "the black people."[80] The bonds of race, it seemed, transcended the bonds of society.

In this way, Benjamin Morgan was no different than most other white Americans at the time. In December 1803, General James Wilkinson, a Revolutionary War veteran and personal agent of President Jefferson at the exchange ceremony in New Orleans following the Purchase, wrote Secretary of War Henry Dearborn in a near panic concerning this odd and conflicting population. "I apprehend difficulties from various causes," he wrote. "The formidable aspect of armed Blacks & Malattoes [sic], officered and organized, is painful & perplexing, and the People have no Idea but of Iron domination at this moment." He went on to request a "Garrison of 500 regulars" for the "continuation of tranquility" in the city.[81] Evidently, the presence of armed colored men, even "officered and organized," constituted an innate threat to the public peace. Three months earlier, the new governor of the Territory of Orleans, the young William C. C. Claiborne, wrote to President Jefferson with similar concerns. It would be "advisable," he explained, for the president to release some "*four to five thousand* stand of Arms, and a suitable proportion of ammunition" to New Orleans in the coming weeks. "The negroes," he declared, "are very numerous, and the number of free mulattoes is also considerable." Without the extra arms, "these people may be disposed to be riotous." Complete reformation, he reminded Jefferson, "is best calculated for enlightened minds."[82] For all others, arms would do.

Again, it was not New Orleans itself or the reputable "free quadroon mulatto & black people" that caused this reaction among American administrators and correspondents. In places farther north and more "American," such as Richmond, Virginia, whites lived two separate lives—one as citizens of the state and its nation, and the other as members of the local community. State law and local practice throughout the South did not coincide, especially concerning the social and racial status of free people of color. In October 1785, the Virginia legislature declared that "every person of whose grandfathers or grandmothers any one is, or shall have been a negro, . . . shall be deemed a mulatto."[83] There was not much of a legal difference between a Negro and mulatto at the time, and the legal titular distinction likely came as a result of local knowledge. In the minds of the legislators, mulattoes and Negroes were not the same. In the same way that Morgan was unsure of the political status of the "respectable" mixed-race caste, the 1785 Virginia statute implies a similar confusion, a similar ambiguity of status as between local knowledge and national stereotype.

Throughout Virginia, free people of color, especially those of mixed race with filial connections to white society, stood at the center of these two divergent visions of society. Although Virginia law forbade any "free negro or mulatto" from returning to the state after he or she had left, local practice hardly recognized the law's existence.[84] Throughout the first three decades of the nineteenth century, men like William N. Colson, a quadroon merchant from Petersburg, traveled back and forth across state lines with no trouble. In fact, Colson himself traveled to New York, a state with a known and growing antislavery voice despite the rather benign gradual emancipation legislation it passed first in 1799, and more than a dozen times between 1810 and 1833.[85] Not once did he petition the local or state authorities for permission. He simply booked his passage, did his business, and returned home without incident.[86] At the port of Richmond, along the James River, hundreds of free colored sailors embarked and disembarked on ships destined for ports of call along the entire Atlantic coast. Joseph Anderson, a mulatto coal trader in Richmond, personally ran shipments to Maryland and North Carolina without incident for more than three decades.[87] James Roberts, the father of future Liberian president Joseph Jenkins Roberts and a resident of Norfolk, likewise made his living transporting tobacco and other staples along the James River to Maryland, Delaware, and New Jersey. A "bright mulatto" of "intelligence and poise," no one ever questioned his perceived right to free travel.[88]

It is interesting to note that none of these men ever registered as a free Negro or mulatto with the county court. After the Virginia legislature in 1793 required each "free Negro and Mulatto" living in a "town or city" to be "registered and numbered in a book to be kept ... by the clerk of court," hundreds of free people of color recorded their names, ages, heights, colors, and birth statuses in the county registers.[89] But as historian Kirt Von Daacke recently pointed out, "In actuality, the 1793 registration law did little to alter Virginia's social landscape."[90] Very few free people of color, especially those of noted mixed ancestry and "good characters," ever bothered to report at all. And if they did, it was either on their deathbeds or after many, many years of unregistered living.[91] Indeed, of the 318 free people of color who registered in Petersburg between 1800 and 1808, 53 percent (168 individuals) were from out of state. Of the remaining 150 Virginians, 111 registered as "Negro" or "black" (74 percent). Nearly that many (72 percent) of the out-of-state registrants appeared as "mulatto," "yellow," or "light brown."[92]

Reputation, mixed bloodlines, and local nativity seem to have skewed the numbers in an interesting way. According to many loose estimates, unlike in the Lower South, the majority of free people of color in the Upper South were of unmixed African ancestry. The consensus among early scholars is that some 60 percent of the free people of color in the Upper South were "black" or "Negro," while the remaining 40 percent were "mulatto."[93] The native Virginians who registered in Petersburg between 1800 and 1808 betray a similar trend—74 percent "black" and 26 percent "mulatto," "yellow," or "light brown." But the overall picture tells a different story. Out-of-state residents, it seems, though primarily mixed race and occasionally quite wealthy, existed outside of accepted Petersburg society. Many were born free to mixed-race, or interracial, parents. Most had full-time employment and some even owned property in town. At the other end, the native registrants were mainly poor unskilled laborers. Most of them had been born slaves, although a few were a generation removed. Very few owned any land or appeared in property-tax lists. A vast majority were dark-skinned "Negroes" of no perceptible white blood. Of the few native "mulattoes" who registered, just six appear to have owned any taxable property.[94]

Men like William Colson, James Roberts, and his four sons, Joseph, James Jr., John, and Henry, did not fit any of these rough molds, and, with one exception, they also never registered.[95] James Roberts, a native of Norfolk, owned two houses in Petersburg by 1807 and ran a successful boating company off Sycamore Street, in the heart of downtown. Six years later, he owned one slave and seven boats in addition to the two houses.[96] Perhaps most importantly, on his death in 1827, a number of his white business colleagues wrote his wife, Amelia Jenkins, offering their condolences. In one letter, Samuel Pennington described Roberts as a "decent, honest man, not just in busniss [sic] but in all conveyance." "He shall be placed in the hands of god," he promised, "and recalled warmly by us left here."[97]

William Colson, along with James Roberts's sons, carved out a similar social niche for themselves and each other. Much like the colored Creoles in New Orleans, Colson and his friend Joseph Roberts used their education and familial connections to break into lucrative fields. Before joining Joseph's trading firm in the late 1810s, Colson was a successful barber, just like his father, James Colson. He owned one slave and employed three "negro" teenagers at his shop. Described as "Good-looking, ... smart and quick," Colson had a reputation in Petersburg that made him, in the words of one white colleague, "known and established" in town.[98]

To the white men with whom Roberts and Colson and those like them did business, these "colored" entrepreneurs blended into the fold. They held them above the poor, unskilled "Negroes" forced to register with the county clerk. Although recognized as something other than white, Colson, Roberts, and countless others ignored the registration law and the restriction on out-of-state travel because the local community, the social and racial circle in which they actually lived, allowed them to do so. In the eyes of the nation, they were noncitizens, aliens at best, freed slaves at worst. But on the ground, in the eyes of the people with whom they shared lived experiences, they were "known and established." They did not need to register with the county clerk; to do so would relegate them to the level of poor blacks and unknown, out-of-state mulattoes with no fictive or filial roots in the local community—the aliens and aggregate free Negroes targeted by the registration laws. They stood apart, just as the respectable "free quadroon mulatto & black people" of New Orleans did to Benjamin Morgan, Chandler Price, and the president to whom they and others reported—as outsiders—from the ground. They were mulattoes, distinct and separate from Negroes according to law, but skin color and ancestry combined with local knowledge and reputation to place this group, along with that in New Orleans, outside the contemporary language of race and citizenship in the young nation.

"We the Subscribers, Free Citizens of Louisiana"

It is clear, of course, that President Thomas Jefferson never set foot in Louisiana and relied on friends, administrators, and traveling businessmen for details of the sounds, shapes, and skin tones found in the newest American territory. But the question of what to do with the "free quadroon mulatto & black people" of the territory confounded him more than perhaps anyone else. Again, as Laura Edwards has explained, and as the preceding section likewise showed, the dynamics of change were obscure, "composed of inconsistent local rulings" that muddled and even countered the attempt at universal measurement and definition Jefferson and state and federal legislators sought in everything they governed. Indeed, as Edwards puts it, "there was no uniform 'law' to appeal to" for leaders and thinkers like Jefferson when faced with a community endowed with no legal "rights," so to speak, but a recognizable, established, and even respected place in the local community.[99] It is unclear whether or not Jefferson knew about men like Charles Forgason, Joseph Roberts, and William Colson in his own backyard, and it is even more uncertain whether or not he knew of any of the fifteen hundred free people of color who inhabited New Orleans alone in 1803.[100] The questions he asked those who did visit the area read like honest inquiries about a land and people he largely did not understand. He asked Governor Claiborne about the borders of the territory—a topic on which Claiborne "ha[d] not been able to obtain any satisfactory Information." He asked which crops would best grow in the climate and which side of the Mississippi River was best suited for farming. He asked about "whites" and "blacks"—but he never mentioned freedom or status. He let the recipients determine that.[101]

In most of his public writing, Jefferson ignored free people of color. In *Notes on the State of Virginia*, he only hinted that those Negroes already free should be "removed beyond the reach of mixture," and emancipated slaves were his main concern in that regard.[102] In his political schemes, his plans for the "dreamed-of future," free people of color seemed aberrant, and thus outside of serious consideration. As two recent scholars put it, "Jefferson saw nationhood in racially untainted hues."[103] But he saw humanity as a spectrum of measurable racial varieties, each of which exhibited distinct physical and mental characteristics. As early as 1705, the Virginia legal code defined a "mulatto" as "the child of an Indian, and the child, grandchild, or great grandchild of a Negro." In essence, the "stain" of blackness washed out after the fourth degree of separation—when, in New Spain, an individual would fall under the *octavón* or albino designations.[104] In 1785, the Virginia state legislature reworked its definition of the term, referring to all people of at least "one-fourth part or more of negro blood" as "mulattoes."[105]

Jefferson agreed with the law but saw much more detail in the explanation. When asked his opinion about the state's definition of a "mulatto," Jefferson replied with startling detail, suggesting that he had put enormous thought into the query. He fell in line with the "true canon, which is that one-fourth of negro blood, mixed with any portion of white, constitutes a mulatto." But blackness was not simply a matter of conjecture with Jefferson. He saw it as a "mathematical problem," something that could and should be made scientific. It was, to him, "of the same class with those on the mixtures of different liquors or different metals."[106] Blood was the "biological instrument of production," it contained "the life of the body."[107] African blood and European blood, then, to Jefferson's Enlightenment, scientific mind, were different varieties of the same substance. They contained different codes, and even different physical colors, that manifested in the pigmentation of the skin. Like any measurable substance, its mixture with something else would produce consistent outcomes. As Emily Clark recently described it, "Jefferson's calculus of race was meant to be precise, immutable, reliable, knowable."[108] It had the support of science behind it.

Following a racial arithmetic measuring the remnants of African blood through a series of cross-mixtures, Jefferson arrived at the result of what he called "the 2.d crossing"—that between h (half-blood; or $a/2 + A/2$) and B (pure white). According to his measurement, the result of this (written "$h/2 + B/2$") would be "$a/4 + A/4 + B/2$, call it q (quarteroon) being ¼ negro blood." Although placed under the blanket term "mulatto," the progeny of a "half-blood" and a "pure white" did not simply receive that general designation of mixture from Jefferson. It received its own specific taxonomic code—quarteroon—due to the measurable amount of "negro" blood within its veins. Further into the arithmetic, Jefferson found the line at which blood became clean and purified. "Let *q* [quarteroon] and *e* [eighth] cohabit," he wrote pragmatically. The result would be "3/16 of *a* [pure negro]," which, according to Virginia's 1785 law, "is no longer mulatto." But it was not simply Virginia law that dictated the result. "It is understood in natural history," Jefferson explained, "that a 4th cross of one race of animals with another gives an issue equivalent for all sensible purposes to the original blood." Thus, a "quarteroon" and any other person with a lesser degree of "negro" blood (one-eighth or lower) would produce a child of pure white blood.[109]

But freedom did not automatically arise from this sanguinary purity. "Sensible" equivalence to the "original blood" did not trump natural-born condition. "Observe," Jefferson wrote, "that this does not re-establish freedom, which depends on the condition of the mother." Although "pure" of blood, the offspring did not stand above the level of enslavement. His or her mother could still be a colored woman, and thus pass on her condition to all of her progeny, regardless of actual or fictive color. Whiteness, then, had to be granted through emancipation. If this occurred, Jefferson concluded, "he [the 3/16 offspring] becomes a free *white* man, and a citizen of the United States to all intents and purposes."[110]

Jefferson sustained the widely held notion that whites could not, under any circumstance, be enslaved. The condition of slavery somehow darkened the offspring beyond any possible measurement. It in essence disqualified him or her from measurement compared to whites. This, then, may explain why Jefferson specifically asked about the "white" and "black" populations of Louisiana, yet never used the word "black" in either his arithmetic or any previous discussion of free people of color. *Slavery* made people "black." It did not matter how closely they approximated whites, either externally or internally. Whites could not be slaves, so slaves were, by definition, nonwhite. If free, however, they could take on any number of mixtures. It is clear that Jefferson did not view the "negro" in the same light as the "quarteroon," either. They had different sanguinary formulas. The "negro" was an element. The "quarteroon" was a compound. Four years earlier, Thomas Jefferson's close friend and advisor, Dr. Benjamin Rush, wrote of the varying intellects among mixed-race people. "It is possible," he said in a lecture at the University of Pennsylvania, "the strength of intellects may be improved in their original conformations ... by certain mixtures of persons." Indeed, he continued, "the mulatto has been remarked, in all countries, to exceed, in sagacity, his white and black parents."[111] There is every reason to believe that Thomas Jefferson agreed, at least in part, with this conclusion. The "mulatto," whatever the variety (quarteroon, eighth, etc.), was not a "negro" and could not be lumped together with one under a single designation. It would defy natural science to do so.

But the question of citizenship remained. Did whiteness and freedom make a man a citizen? Or was it something else altogether? Before his letter to Francis Gray in March 1815, Jefferson remained eerily silent on the matter, especially when the issue became central to the incorporation of the new Territory of Orleans, and its "numerous" "very respectable" quadroons and mulattoes.[112] Article 3 of the Louisiana Purchase Treaty dictated that "the inhabitants of the ceded territory shall be incorporated in the union of the United States, as soon as possible, . . . to the enjoyment of all the rights, advantages and immunities of citizens of the United States." The implication of the article was that "the inhabitants" were not *yet* incorporated into the union, and thus not *yet* privy to the rights of citizenship. It would take time for the many American appointees and transplanted merchants moving daily to the region to "convert" the Catholic, French-speaking former subjects of European crowns into honest, trustworthy Americans. Until they earned the rights of citizenship, the basic principles of the Bill of Rights would do. "In the mean time," Article 3 provided, "they shall be maintained and protected in the free enjoyment of their liberty, property, and the religion which they profess."[113]

The treaty provided no definition for the ideal candidate for incorporation, and eventual citizenship. As evinced in his repeated ignorance of free people of color, Jefferson's main concern was the initiation of "so many foreigners" into the American nation, not the delineation of a racial citizenship.[114] Jefferson, along with Secretary of State James Madison and treaty negotiators James Monroe and Robert Livingston, assumed that nationhood and citizenship excluded colored people, both free and enslaved. Again, before the United States actually took possession of the land, the Jefferson administration knew very little about the demographics of Louisiana. The concept of free colored citizens never existed.[115] If the United States was a nation of empathy, sensibility, and virtue, Africans and their descendants could never be part of its citizenry.[116] Jefferson, along with a number of other Enlightenment thinkers, had already set forth in no uncertain terms that Africans lacked the ability to balance reason and sensation, making them fundamentally incapable of understanding the rigors of virtuous citizenship.[117]

The largely Jeffersonian Legislative Council of the Territory of Orleans, appointed by the governor and designed specifically to keep policy decisions out of the hands of locals, agreed. Between 1804 and 1808, the council passed a series of laws specifically highlighting the subordinate social position of free people of color. An 1805 statute required free coloreds who claimed nativity in the city to produce proof of their freedom and to register with the mayor for a residency permit.[118] The next year, the territorial legislature declared that "no free man of color shall be admitted into this territory" without giving "security, to the satisfaction of the mayor," for his departure "within three months." Failure to do so warranted a hefty fine of twenty dollars a week and possible imprisonment.[119] In 1808, the legislature further separated the free colored population from slaves and whites by ordering all "notaries, or other public officers," to insert following the surname of each person of color "these words—*free man or free woman of color.*"[120]

These laws assumed an inherent duplicity within Louisiana's free colored population. They forced the Creoles of color to prove that they were not like some of their enslaved neighbors and were simply pretending to be free. They tried to isolate the Creoles from corruptive forces in the outside world, especially the "devious," "rebellious" American freedmen, as well as those of the francophone islands of the Caribbean, then in the midst of a violent civil war in Haiti. They also attempted to brand the mixed-race, light-skinned Creoles as "colored" on all public documents, theoretically eliminating any questions of identity based on appearance or legal ambiguity. But still citizenship never came up. The laws, though specifically designed to undermine the social (or, better, racial) standing of free people of color, never granted or took away any specific rights of citizenship. They could not vote, along with women, children, and many propertyless white men. But Creoles of color, and other African-descended people, could still own property, carry guns with relative freedom, and represent themselves in court. Indeed, many of these and other laws, although passed by a local body, went ignored on the streets.

As elsewhere, reputation, bloodlines, and culture remained highly influential in New Orleans society. As mentioned at the beginning of this chapter, men like François Boisdoré, Manuel Moreau, Jean Louis Dolliole, and others of their ilk, never appeared in city directories or court proceedings as "free men of color," as required by the 1808 law. In the succession of François Lacroix, one of the wealthiest colored men in the United States during the antebellum era, the words "man of color" appear only three times in nearly fifteen thousand pages of testimony, court records, receipts, and business transactions covering a span of nearly seventy years. Taking testimony about Lacroix's physical appearance, a judge asked Barthélémy Lafon's son, Thomy, "Did Mr. Lacroix pass in this community as a white man or a man of color?"

Lafon's answer spoke volumes. "François Lacroix," he replied, "was known in this community & in society as a colored man. [But] he would pass for a white man in a community where he would not be known as a colored man."[121]

Society knew Lacroix as a "colored man," yet never referred to him as such in any formal documentation. Indeed, the very fact that the judge had to ask Thomy Lafon, himself of "nearly white" complexion, whether or not his lifelong friend was in fact colored speaks to the longevity of the colored Creoles' ambiguous status in the city. Lacroix was born in Cuba, the son of a free *mulâtresse* and a white trader in exile from Saint Domingue. He and his widowed mother emigrated to New Orleans in 1806, a full year after the passage of an anti-immigration law.[122] In fact, nearly five thousand colored refugees arrived in New Orleans from Cuba and Haiti between 1803 and 1814 (see chapter 4), very few of whom were imprisoned, fined, or enslaved after the three-month grace period elapsed.[123] Pierre Casenave, François Boisdoré's future business partner, arrived in this flood and stayed until his death fifty years later, never appearing as an "f.m.c."[124]

These men also stuck together, and called on their white neighbors and partners when needed. In 1809, a white merchant accused Joseph Fouché, a quadroon coastal trader, of stealing a shipment he had left on the dock overnight. In spite of laws forbidding colored testimony against whites beyond cases of self-defense, young Murville Cheval, a quadroon with French colonial roots, defended Fouché as "the finest gentleman of *our class*" and "a humble servant of the court." Likewise, A. J. Gomila, a wealthy white sugar factor and later a business partner of François Lacroix, described Fouché as "a man of diverse and trusting character agreeable to all who know him." He went on to say that he would never expect Fouché to "take possession [of anything] without payment," as "it is not his nature." After one meeting, the court adjourned, with the plaintiff ordered to pay all costs and warned "to make no light of this court" in the future.[125]

The dedication to a Gallic culture bound these men together, and their white blood and "good characters" gave them social pedigree. But militia service also served as a social tool for a number of colored Creoles, especially those of noted mixed ancestries and colonial bloodlines. In January 1804, a full year before the first of the repressive regulations, fifty-two members of the former *pardo* militia and one *moreno* sent Governor Claiborne a letter.[126] "We the Subscribers, free Citizens of Louisiana," they wrote, "beg leave to approach your Excellency with Sentiments of respect & Esteem and sincere attachment to the Governance of the United States." They set themselves apart from the American nation while declaring their allegiance to the new regime. "We are Natives of this Province," they assured the governor, "and our dearest Interests are connected with its welfare." They expressed "a lively joy" that the "Sovereignty of the Country" was "united" with the "American Republic." Again, they did not include themselves in this "Republic." They clearly recognized that they had recently come under the domain of the United States but were not yet members of its national community. They did not look for citizenship as the Americans defined it. They looked for assurance and protection of property and condition. "We are sensible that our personal and political freedom is thereby assured to us forever," they declared. "And we are also impressed with the fullest confidence in the Justice and Liberality of the Government towards every Class of Citizens which they have here taken under their Protection."[127] They were not "Americans." They were Louisianan. And they did not expect to be made citizens of the American nation, at least not immediately or necessarily on equal footing with whites.

To the Creoles who signed the letter, the term "citizen" meant "resident." Less than a year after the American acquisition of Louisiana, the inhabitants of the former French and Spanish colony would not have fully understood the notion of republican national belonging or the concept of a single, equal class of citizenship. They had been vassals their entire lives. The ideas of representation within the government or of inalienable rights did not exist to them. The colored Creoles who had served in the Spanish militia and fought in the American Revolution wanted to maintain the same status and privilege given them by the Spanish and New Orleans society as a whole. But this privilege and status did not, in their view, come freely from the distant, unfamiliar Constitution of their new "nation." Under the Spanish, they declared, "our Conduct in [the military] Service has ever been distinguished by a ready attention to the duties required." They had earned their position in society not only from their shared French roots and mixed ancestries but also through honest and zealous service in the colonial militia. "We therefore respectfully offer our Services to the [United States] Government as a Corps of Volunteers," concluded the men, "agreeable to any arrangement which may be thought expedient."[128]

They expected nothing. As a separate "Class of Citizens," they had earned their stripes under the Spanish by serving in the militia. Under the Americans, they saw no reason for that to change but realized that they had to play a role in its maintenance. Had they expected more, they would have sent Claiborne a letter similar to that signed by some three dozen local white

"Citizens who know their Rights and disdain to flatter the man [Claiborne] who has betrayed them," following something as simple as a hike in docking fees.[129] But instead, they offered services, not demands, allegiance and zeal "agreeable to any arrangement," not threats of reprisal if betrayed. They offered flattery to "your Excellency" and the "Governance of the United States," for the "personal and political freedoms" invoked in the letter were not, according to the signers, necessarily rights protected by a promise of citizenship and equality. There was no threat of betrayal if the freedoms and privileges were not seen as guaranteed in the first place.

Apparently the plan worked, at least in part. It was not until Andrew Jackson recalled the colored militia in September 1814 that the Creoles of color again took up arms in defense of their homeland. In the meantime, Claiborne remained silent on the issue as the territorial legislature left the colored militia out of the Militia Act of 1806, and then again in 1807 and 1809.[130] But more immediately, Claiborne had faith in these mixed-race elites. After having met with "8 or 10 of the influential characters among the free people of colour," Claiborne assured James Madison that "the Mulattoes" expressed a "friendly pacific disposition, and devoted attachment to the present Government."[131] Some months earlier, James Wilkinson admitted that the "free people of colour ... have universally mounted the Eagle in their Hats & avow their attachment to the United States." On the other hand, Wilkinson complained that the white inhabitants of the city "still demonstrate their love for the Mother Country" (i.e., France) and hope that "War, may return them to Her Bosom."[132] The colored Creoles had clearly made their case for allegiance and trust within the new American regime. But still, no one, the Creoles included, put citizenship and "colored" together.

It makes sense, then, that when Andrew Jackson addressed his "fellow brave citizens," the "adopted children" of the American nation, the tone and meaning had changed. The Creoles of color—Jean Louis Dolliole and François Boisdoré, both signers of the Claiborne letter, among them—had dressed for battle for the first time since the very war that created their adoptive mother country. The term and notion of citizenship had remained for more than a decade part of a "dreamed-of future" for Louisiana, a possible, but hardly guaranteed, result of incorporation "as soon as possible."[133] Left out of the militia and isolated by oppressive legislation, the colored Creoles, by September 1814, existed in a political and social void. "Colored" by law, relatively wealthy, literate, freeborn, and socially respectable, they amounted to the ultimate paradox in American racial thought. But the letter to Claiborne in 1804 proved, if nothing else, that the Creoles had a voice. Their reputations on the ground, their lived experiences in face-to-face interactions with white Americans and locals, showed that life existed outside the categories of black slavery and white freedom. Like their contemporaries in Richmond and Petersburg, they lived as accepted members of the local society and community. But citizenship never really came up. Generations of mixture and character building had lifted the perceived veil of black from their skin, but the stain of Negro blood remained. Ever short of "pure white," they could never, it seems, take that last remaining step further into full citizenship. But that did not stop society from treating them as equals, at times even looking past race for the "diverse and trusting character" that made them more acceptable than others not quite of "their class." Of course, Jefferson and his representatives in Louisiana could never admit that they saw it. To recognize an intermediate caste, a people in nearly every way "equivalent ... to the original blood" of the American Republic yet debarred by natural science from equal standing in that republic, would produce too many questions and challenge the very foundation of the Jeffersonian ideal.[134]

The Battle of New Orleans changed a lot for the Creoles of color, as well as reputable free people of color throughout the South. It coincided with a massive influx of Saint Domingue refugees, many of mixed race. Jackson's declaration regarding citizenship, however fleeting and nominal, confirmed to the Creoles that their place in New Orleans, if not the nation, was secure, that their offer of military service had perhaps had its effect. Following the battle, they could lay claim to the same sacrifice made, the same full measure given to a shared nation that sparked the "patriotic fire" of the 1810s and 1820s.[135] As the next chapter shows, that fire burned brightly within free colored communities throughout the South, especially those of Charleston, Richmond, and New Orleans. But to the Creoles of color it was not necessarily a fire of national pride and belonging. It was a fire of cultural and racial identity, stoked by the arrival and eventual integration of mixed-race émigrés from Saint Domingue, and the pride of place that Jackson gave Creoles of color on January 8, 1815, at the Battle of New Orleans. Race and nation were there, but it had become much more complicated than that.

CHAPTER 4

A Fire of Color and Class
THE SOUTH

According to the New Orleans *Daily Picayune*, on June 13, 1861, François Lacroix went insane. In the first of two similar incidents in ten years, Lacroix was arrested by the Municipal Guard for "failing to abandon delinquent property" on which he owed "substantial back-taxes and damages."[1] In a fit of anger no doubt brought on by "advanced age," the paper claimed, Lacroix locked himself in a second-floor bedroom of a property on Dauphine Street in the heart of the Vieux Carré. Showing signs of an "infirm & afflicted mentality," the colored tailor attacked the approaching guards with "riotous insults & invective, spits & bottles still half-full." It was "madness," the *Picayune* declared, "unfit of M. Lacroix's known character in this city."[2]

François Lacroix was neither charged with a crime nor as infirm as the newspaper claimed. Following the arrest, the Municipal Guard released Lacroix without recording the incident in the arrest log.[3] To pay off the delinquent taxes, the city seized the Dauphine Street property and sold it at auction on July 10 to Julien Lacroix, François's brother and a wealthy grocer, who held the property until his death seven years later, bequeathing it back to his brother.[4] At fifty-six years old, François Lacroix was in good health and of sound mind, if slightly too old to join some of his colleagues and their sons in the Louisiana Native Guards—a Confederate regiment formed by New Orleans Creoles of color in 1861.[5] His friends and business partners called him "eccentric" and "colorful" his entire adult life. After his death in

1876, his daughter-in-law, Sarah Brown, a white woman, described him as an "interesting, odd man, but an affectionate husband and father."[6] A tailor by trade, he wore fine silks and linens during the spring and summer, imported cashmere overcoats, suede trousers, and cravats in the fall and winter.[7] He often wore facial hair, combed smooth, in a goatee or mustache. He was tall and slim and rarely took a dray or carriage, preferring to walk whenever possible.[8]

If the *Daily Picayune* got anything right, it was Lacroix's "known character" in the city. By 1861, François Lacroix had stood at the center of a growing, increasingly self-conscious colored community in New Orleans for nearly forty years. The son of Jean Lacroix, a relatively wealthy Frenchman, and his mixed-race, Saint-Dominguan wife, Anne Batecave, François was educated, light skinned, francophone, and had an eye for profit.[9] By the late 1820s, he had opened a tailoring shop with his friend Etienne Cordeviolle, a francophone of Italian and African descent. Lacroix & Cordeviolle, as the shop came to be known, served "the finest clientele one could boast" and sold "the best and most extensive assortment of clothing of every description, made in Paris."[10] Their clientele ran the gamut of Creole elites, both white and of color. The famous white real estate mogul and land developer Bernard Marigny purchased nearly $1,500 worth of clothing from the store, as did Félix Grima, a powerful notary and public figure. On the other side of the color line, Albin, Norbert, and Lucien Soulié, wealthy Creole financiers and real estate speculators, as well as the celebrated philanthropist Thomy Lafon, all did business with Lacroix & Cordeviolle for nearly twenty years.[11]

His success as a tailor translated into success in other ventures. By the 1830s, Lacroix owned more than two dozen properties throughout the city, most located in the desirable faubourgs of Vieux Carré and Marigny. In 1838, he rented to no fewer than thirty-four white and colored tenants on twenty-six separate properties. Known as a "fair and honest" landlord, he collected rent and checked on properties personally, earning the good graces of those with whom he did business.[12] Over the next decade, Lacroix amassed a real estate portfolio valued at more than $250,000—the largest of any free person of color in the state. In 1848, the New York credit firm of R. G. Dun and Company reported that Lacroix was "a Creole, long in business, rich, and among the most fashionable businessmen in the city."[13]

But François Lacroix was not a "Creole," at least not in the most technical sense of the term. As discussed earlier, the term "Creole" most often described those born within a given colony, whether slaves, free coloreds, or whites. Lacroix, unlike his close friends Jean Louis Dolliole, Thomy Lafon, and François Boisdoré, was born in Cuba, not New Orleans. Indeed, he was not even a native of French land. His parents, in exile from the revolution in Saint Domingue, had taken refuge on the Spanish island along with nearly thirty thousand other refugees of all colors and statuses at the turn of the century. In 1809, when François was just three years old, the Spanish government, threatened by the increasingly violent civil war in Haiti and repeated confrontations with the French along the Pyrenees, expelled all French citizens and subjects from Spanish lands.[14] The Lacroix, along with some ten thousand others, ended up in New Orleans, where François and his brother, Julien, were raised by their mother after their father's early death.[15]

The Lacroix family arrived in New Orleans at the perfect time for a mixed-race, francophone family in need of acceptance and peace. Far too young to defend their new home under General Jackson at the Battle of New Orleans, François and Julien came of age in the midst of the cultural and racial identity formation that followed, a time when the very notion of national and cultural belonging came under renewed scrutiny throughout the United States. With victory declared (perhaps unjustly) in the War of 1812, the concept of nativity—and its New Orleans counterpart, "Creolehood"—took on a new meaning.

The United States had proven itself before the entire world, fending off Great Britain for the second time in a generation. The questions surrounding the Louisiana Purchase had in large part been settled. Expansion finally had precedent on which to move forward. A rebuilt federal city stood as the symbol of a unified nation. It was a time for Americans of all colors and pedigrees to redefine themselves as a people and as a nation.[16]

This "patriotic fire" inaugurated a revolution in the way New Orleanians defined themselves as members of the American national community. Victory at the Battle of New Orleans had carved out a space for the white, francophone Catholics who American officials had deemed "too foreign" for equal standing in 1803. Now a state, Louisiana and its capital, New Orleans, were home to a group of rag-tag, frontier Americans who had proven themselves on the field of battle. At last, Louisiana had its Revolutionary Generation, its American founding on the fields of Chalmette. As the *Louisiana Gazette* declared following the victory, "the State of Louisiana now has her voice."[17]

When it came to the colored community, the sense of pride and place was not so clear. Although rightly proud of the part they had played in the defense of New Orleans, colored Creoles never received the effective citizenship General Jackson had promised them before the war. With the arrival of thousands of Saint Domingue refugees between 1809 and 1815, increased sensitivity to the expansion of French culture and ideology in the South, and new developments in American racial "science" over the next two decades, the place of free people of color throughout the United States became increasingly complicated. In cities across the South—Charleston, Richmond, and especially New Orleans—free colored communities were forced by both law and society to create mechanisms, organizations, and practices through which they could reinforce their own corporate identities, while also improving their social and cultural stock in the ever-expanding, ever-changing American nation.

In New Orleans, these mechanisms led to an expansion of Creole identity, shifting away from specifics of ancestry and toward the acceptance of a cultural definition based on the French language, the Catholic religion, and the unifying effort to protect them. In some ways, this involved people like Jean Louis Dolliole, François Lacroix, and others, who looked to the white Creole community—the "foreign French" now accepted into the American body politic—for a model of success in a relatively new and culturally foreign nation. In other ways, it required cultural and racial insularity. Although nonwhite, these mixed-race Creoles of color, especially those with some wealth, skill, and social standing, needed to prove to both the white Creoles and the advancing Americans that they did not fall within broad "scientific" parameters of the "Negro"—a group continually defined and redefined between 1820 and 1860, and beyond.[18]

Free people of color in Charleston, Richmond, and New Orleans reacted in similar ways to this growing nationalism. They did not take to the streets in protest against laws targeting an aggregated image of the "Negro" held in the minds of state legislators. And neither did they reject the model of white society in order to form their own, strictly insular community. Likewise, they did not entirely dismiss those people of color with less hope, less wealth, and darker skin. They chose to sit in the middle, that same position defined by their pedigrees. Neither black nor white, colored Creoles in New Orleans, the "Brown Elites" of Charleston's Brown Fellowship Society, and free people of color in Richmond accepted that they were different from the American standard on both sides of the color line. And they used it to their advantage.

Between the end of the War of 1812 and the beginning of the Civil War, wealthy, skilled, primarily mixed-race people of color—those whom Joseph Willson of Philadelphia termed the "higher class of colored society" in 1841—founded benevolent and burial societies, literary and spiritual groups, anything that could prove, beyond the new racial "science" and oppressive legislation, that they stood more alongside than below the white community.[19] Some of these organizations vowed to help others, especially the indigent, the orphaned, and the poor. Others sought to escape direct connection with those same members of a lower class, charging high initiation fees and embracing language, occupation, and skin-color requirements. Most acted on a sense of morality and duty to one's fellow man, whether through direct aid, education, uplift, or communal support. They collected fees for libraries, held debates and discussions, public lectures, and parades. In effect, they mirrored the social role of the colored militia immediately following the American Revolution.[20] Membership in or association with these societies served as a badge of belonging, proof of a fruitful, moral, socially progressive lifestyle. It attached each member or associate to a tradition and obligation higher than themselves. It gave them social and moral value within and outside their own communities. And in many ways, perhaps only personal, it made them more "American" than ever before.[21]

But it also had a wider effect, one more national in scope. As this chapter shows, these colored benevolent societies, organizations, and intellectual clubs fell in line with a growing middle-class value system spreading throughout white American society. The values of industry, thrift, sobriety, and self-discipline, among others, came to define an entire national community between the 1820s and 1860s in both the North and South.[22] White merchants, doctors, lawyers, clerks, and other professionals likewise created benevolent, debating, and moralist societies to help define their positions in the cultural landscape of America. Through these societies as well as shifts in cultural mores, this new middle class developed new styles of fashion, religion, social intercourse, and even family formation. They intermarried with each other, established social value through surname, comportment, wealth, pedigree, and associational membership—both religious and social. They viewed themselves and their values as fundamentally different from those of planters and unskilled laborers, dockworkers, simple artisans, and paupers.[23] They were something new, and needed a voice.

The free community of color throughout the South was not immune to this phenomenon, as early scholars of the "free Negro" suggested they were.[24] Though the "elite of their people," as Julie Winch rightfully termed them, these colored elites embodied the cultural and social workings of the white southern middle class, fashioning themselves, at times literally, into a legitimate social movement. This chapter traces the development of this colored middle class and the evolution of their shared values in Charleston,

Richmond, and New Orleans. In each city, the wealth projected by members of this colored elite/middle class varied greatly. Indeed, very few free people of color in the United States, much less the slave South, came close to maintaining anything like the $329,000 estate that François Lacroix claimed in 1861.[25] But wealth became relative, just as nativity and Creolehood did, in the formation of this group. Foreign nativity—Saint Domingue, Cuba, another state or city—gave way to shared cultural values, ancestry, skin color, and associational memberships. François Lacroix, then, although born free in Cuba, found acceptance in the New Orleans colored Creole community in the same way that Anthony Weston, born a slave in Statesburg, South Carolina, found acceptance in Charleston's Brown Elite. Each used the fluid nature of the time to earn and build the same values, practices, and organizational memberships as those born free and locally. And although these values and practices differed in root and origin from place to place, they all came together in similar communities to produce a self-conscious, proud, and socially influential middle class of colored people, a group largely ignored by current scholarship.[26]

"Birds of Passage": The Rise of a Southern Middle Class

The years immediately following the War of 1812 in the United States were a time of flux for the entire Atlantic community. To the south, on the island of Haiti, the world's first black republic inched past independence beneath the weight of a violent civil war.[27] There was unrest in the British colonies of Barbados and Jamaica, as well as in Cuba and Santo Domingo under the Spanish.[28] Across the Atlantic, France, having lost its largest and most productive colony just ten years earlier, now set about rebuilding a republic from the imperial rubble of Napoleon's second coming. In Britain, a tired and unstable King George III had to answer for his second costly war with the Americans while scrounging to pay debts incurred from ten years of conflict with France.[29] Although threats to American sovereignty remained in Europe and its collective colonial grasp, the United States was no longer the youngest and most vulnerable of the world's nations.

Many Americans remembered this time with fondness, and those who lived through it recognized the change. The United States had survived fifty years of independence and war. In July 1817, as the newly inaugurated president James Monroe entered Boston on his Presidential Jubilee tour, Benjamin Russell celebrated the start of an "era of Good Feelings" in the United States, a time of "festive boards, in pleasant converse," a time of peace and unity in a previously divided nation.³⁰ John Milton Niles of the Hartford *Times* likewise celebrated a "New Era" of American political "character." He announced the end of "political dominion, founded on mystery and delusion," a system which "galvanized political fraud, encouraged dissimulation ... [and] fanaticism," and "enveloped itself in darkness." The "authority of reason and common sense," he declared, had come to light, and the "abusive, fraudulent" system of the past "FELL, NEVER TO RISE AGAIN."³¹

Men like Russell and Niles had reason to look up. The last of the Virginia Dynasty begotten by the Revolution, James Monroe, in his ankle-length trousers, laced shoes, and naturally grey head, embodied the direction of the nation from revolutionary youth to victorious adolescence. A close friend of Madison and Jefferson, Monroe set aside his personal and political qualms about John Adams and the remaining Federalists to inaugurate an era notably lacking a definitive political agenda. He stood as representative of both progress and memory—a child of the Revolution, apprentice to the Jeffersonian cause, yet a man of the new America, aware of the mistakes of his predecessors and witness to the ills of the institutionalized "revolution" of the past decade.³²

This meeting of generations and cultures found expression in every corner of the nation. Cities, once seen as the headquarters of a political elite and urban aristocracy devoid of virtue, became the target of thousands of small farmers in search of profits opened by safer seas, postwar rebuilding efforts, and a newfound dedication to domestic production.³³ An American editor in New Orleans wrote that the "relentless pioneer push" from the east brought "countless seekers-after-power" to the "once frontier town, now a city." New Orleans, he claimed, was "on the make," and this "promise of a golden avalanche" bred ambition and guile "resistant to considerations of justice and mercy." But from each "mercantile killing," he admitted, came a new man to try again, a cycle that gave "hope, expectation, and continual rebirth" based upon the belief that "tomorrow would be his day."³⁴

In Richmond, the lure of profit brought droves of speculators and dreamers to the small capital of Virginia. Like New Orleans, the town quickly converted to a city. Samuel Mordecai, a prominent Jewish merchant, recalled how "corn-fields, Slashes and Piney thickets were laid out into streets and squares," dirt roads were paved, and outlying towns soon became suburbs, then neighborhoods, as the city expanded.³⁵ Suddenly, there were coffeehouses and tearooms, taverns frequented by "men of airs" rather than dockworkers, and restaurants serving oysters, steak, and fine wines. Along the James River, "dry goods palaces," such as Kent, Paine, & Co., "rose on the spot" of old warehouses and taverns. The city had become "an attraction,... handsomely situated and respectably inhabited."[36]

Charleston made similar leaps. With more than $10.8 million in exports reported in 1816, Charleston went from a midrange, rice-based coastal port in the early 1800s to the second-largest exportation port in the nation in less than a decade.[37] As with towns around Richmond, the surrounding villages of Radcliffe and Mazyck quickly became Radcliffeborough and Mazyckborough. The Second Bank of the United States built one of its main offices on a newly paved King Street, surrounded by townhouses, trading offices, and parks funded by docking fees and private citizens.[38] The "Old Families," the city-dwelling planters who had dominated Charleston's coastal trade for generations, derided the new merchants as "mere *birds of passage*" dedicated only to "their fortunes" rather than "its source."[39] But the townhouses and trading offices along King Street and the shares in the Bank of the United States all belonged to these "birds," who by 1819 owned more than half the property in the city.[40]

It was this transience that gave birth to a new middle class in the South. In some ways, Charleston's Old Families were right. As historian Jennifer Goloboy has explained, "merchants rarely stayed in Charleston for very long." They knew how to play the system—set up an office in a growing town and then move on down the coast, leaving agents and clerks to manage the profits. Some bought houses and lots, but most never made a home, instead collecting rents under a hired landlord. They operated under the principle of *caveat emptor*, focusing on profit over quality, salesmanship over service. And when a town ran dry, they sold their wares, fired their employees, and left.[41]

But it was not this class of "noblemen" and "birds of passage" that formed the middle class in the antebellum South. Indeed, it was the clerks and agents who ran their offices, the skilled artisans who produced their wares, and the friends and families with whom this more local collective did business and spent time that produced a class of Americans literally stuck between the landed gentry in the upcountry and the tavern-goers on the docks. Forming first and most strongly in the port towns, these young professionals and skilled artisans arrived from all over the Atlantic world. Between 1809 and 1815, more than thirty thousand white and colored refugees from Saint Domingue turned up at American ports, many settling permanently where they landed—Philadelphia, Charleston, and New Orleans.[42] The Irish, ever on the move, came in droves following the "year without a summer," placing nearly twenty thousand individuals each year along the Atlantic and Gulf coasts between 1816 and 1840.⁴³ Germans, too, spread throughout the South following the end of the Napoleonic Wars in 1815. Between that year and the start of the Civil War, an estimated 1.7 million Germans settled permanently in the South.⁴⁴

Although most of these immigrants made their livings as unskilled laborers, a large number of the agents, artisans, clerks, and factors for urban merchants were foreign born.⁴⁵ Many immigrants with education, wealth, and skill had a choice in their final destinations. Saint Domingue refugees, as a whole, tended to choose New Orleans and Charleston, two cities with historic and cultural connections to France, while hundreds of skilled and educated Irishmen and Germans looked to Richmond, Norfolk, and New Bern, North Carolina, where similar communities already existed and the markets were open and growing.⁴⁶ In each of these towns, well-placed immigrants settled alongside local men "on the up." Traders and factors from Dublin, Berlin, Paris, and Cap-Français used the only skills they knew to carve out both a living and a social space in their new homes. As the "birds of passage" set up their offices and shops by the dozens, outsiders and ambitious locals found steady employment in nonlabor trades, the likes of which had never existed in such numbers.⁴⁷

Over time, as trade expanded during the long Atlantic peace of the antebellum decades, the group of professionals who entered at the start became the ancestors of a hereditary, self-conscious class of middling capitalists. Indeed, by the 1830s, the term "middle class" had entered the American lexicon as a definitive social position between the planter elite and the working poor. But the term did not simply define one's imagined place in the social hierarchy. It defined a way of life, an image consciously performed in society, a culture actively maintained and vigorously defended from outsiders and fakes.⁴⁸ Men who worked together, and even competed against each other, recognized the need for an identity early on. Catholic francophone refugees from Saint Domingue who landed in Charleston in the late 1810s learned English and became Episcopalian and Methodist in order to assimilate and find a space within which to grow. The opposite occurred in New Orleans, but for the same reasons. The nearly ten thousand "Foreign French" who landed in what had until very recently still been officially named Nouvelle-Orléans never needed to drop their native tongue and faith. They attracted the interest and empathy of the francophone Creoles, who were in the midst of their own struggle to protect French cultural practices from the advancing "Anglos" from the east. Germans gave up their language, at least publicly, and the Irish, too, became Protestant, or allied with the French to maintain a subdued Catholicism, as they did in New Orleans.[49] This explains in part why the city of Charleston, home to more than two thousand Saint Domingue refugees and their children and in 1850 to more than ten thousand Irish, had but a single Catholic church, run by a small Irish benevolent society called the Hibernians.[50]

Perhaps most important to the development of a southern middle class was the notion of consciousness and community. In dropping, or subduing, the cultural features that made them different in a Protestant, anglophone nation, the educated and skilled immigrants placed themselves on the same level as locals with the same goals and skills. Just as the Creoles in New Orleans adopted many Saint Domingue refugees into their protective community, the skilled carpenters, masons, and teachers of Charleston and Richmond saw potential and protection in the new arrivals. Living in the same neighborhoods and working in the same shops, young professionals, both local and immigrant, came to see their shared education, skill, and experience as virtues that needed protection and development. They believed themselves to be distinct from planters, yeomen, and laborers, and their interests differed drastically from those of the ruling elite and the urban poor.[51]

In Charleston, New Orleans, Norfolk, and Richmond, young professionals opened schools, founded benevolent societies, and developed a material culture unseen elsewhere in the nation. Intellect and intellectual culture flourished within the ranks of this young community. Literacy, book ownership, and intellectual engagement came to define the "middle-class" lifestyle first coined in the 1830s and celebrated in the 1840s and 1850s. As with the passing on of skills, schooling remained strictly within the community of like-minded families and friends. Public and common schools, though virtuous and beneficial to society as a whole, served a "lesser" type than the children of middle-class clerks, artisans, and merchants.[52] While the children of these "paupers" learned to read and write in public schools, middle-class children were trained in bookkeeping, literary and oratorical display, and philosophical debate—tenets invaluable to moral purity and civic responsibility—in private, independently funded classrooms.[53]

Benevolent associations and moralist unions provided a base for this system of internal education, acceptance, and training. Founded in 1831 by men of property and some wealth between the ages of twenty-one and fifty-six, the Norfolk Humane Association dedicated itself publicly to the "relief and improvement of the poor" throughout the Virginia port.[54] Over the course of three decades, the Humane Associations funded "pauper schools" and "common schools" for the "indigent and illiterate." Such virtuous acts, the public acknowledgment of which fueled the growing moralistic tenor of the southern middle class, appeared in Norfolk and Richmond newspapers several times a year.[55] But association members sent their children not to the schools they publicly funded, but to the small private school run by the Dorcas Society—an educational and benevolent organization managed by educated and wealthy women, many of whom married members of the Humane Association.[56]

The Charleston Library Society, founded in 1749, had grown to more than three hundred voting members when it reconstituted itself in 1826. The purpose of the society, as stated in its published constitution, was the study and sanction of "personal and private morality; . . . the mutual duties of husband and wife, of parent and child, perhaps also of master and servant," and the promotion of the "duties which man owes to his Creator." The natural state of humanity, the society claimed, was one of curiosity and learning. The ancient Greeks and Romans established "doctrines and systems of ethics" now lost "among the wanderers of the desert or congregated multitudes of the populous cities." In holding and maintaining a library for its membership "and their trusted friends and families," the Library Society promised to replace "the rude and simple arts of past ages" with the "literature, arts, and science of an enlightened age."[57]

Although dedicated to the education of its membership, the society also served to construct a reputation of high-mindedness and intellectual verve in the public eye. In publishing its catalogue of nearly twelve thousand titles along with a detailed constitution and history of officers for public consumption in 1826, the society made clear the distinction between the interests of its members and those of the rest of society. Attributing the "rude and simple arts of past ages" to the "congregated multitudes of the populous cities," they explicitly separated the educated, "enlightened," philosophically pure members of the society from the illiterate, laboring majority of Charlestonians. Their goals likewise differed from those of the planter elite, the "wanderers of the desert" dedicated to exploitation and deaf to the call of progress and enlightenment. Theirs was a vision of mobility and cultural growth. Others were too far below, or too safely above, to share in their recognition.[58]

These and other societies across the South gave meaning and protection to the developing middle-class identity. Maintaining a calm, sober, learned demeanor in public demonstrated a masculine self-mastery, a confidence bred by education, morality, and personal ambition. These men, and the organizations to which they belonged, protected their skills, education, and wealth, however modest, by distinguishing themselves from these "congregated multitudes" and "wanderers of the desert."[59] Conscious of their status and in many ways the creators of it, they produced a stereotype of themselves in the public mind predicated on values they considered to be distinct from the values of those around them—the education, charity, and professional skills that had brought them together in the first place. Public displays of benevolence and charity thus veiled insular modes of personal refinement, apprenticeship, and commerce taking shape behind closed doors. By the start of the Civil War, this class of people, not the politically dominant planter elite, controlled the urban centers of the South, including, of course, New Orleans. But, as will become clear, counterparts across the color line sprouted from both seeds, one sown in the elite planters' rural domain and the other firmly set in the emerging middle class of Louisiana's urban center. Importantly, however, they remained separate, existing within similar liminal social, racial, and legal settings yet rarely, if ever, overlapping on the larger social and cultural maps of their shared time and space. They seemed to move away from each other in every measurable way, the one joining (and in many ways challenging, at least in terms of how race interacted with popular definitions of class) the ranks of the American planter elite and the other cementing its identity as established, middle-class, urban Creoles of color.

A Decent, Orderly Behavior:
Colored Benevolence and Middle-Class Character

By the middle of the antebellum era, rural Louisiana had become increasingly "American," as white anglophone migrants from the eastern states found their way to the cheap, fertile land of the Mississippi Valley and Delta.[60] In many places throughout the state, the symbolic walls that had separated the foreign from the local—in any direction—had largely crumbled into impediments rather than ramparts. Although exceedingly small, a collective of demonstrably "elite," consciously upper-class people of color had formed in the rural parishes that surrounded New Orleans and its river. In Plaquemines Parish, southeast of New Orleans, one of these elites, Andrew Durnford, lived on his plantation, St. Rosalie. Born in 1800 to a British officer stationed in West Florida and a free *mulâtresse* from New Orleans, Durnford quickly scaled the ranks of colored men in New Orleans, inheriting an estate of nearly $40,000 from his father in 1826, and subsequently purchasing vast tracts of land in the rural parishes outside the city.[61]

Through his father, later a merchant specializing in sugar cane, Durnford became a close friend and business partner of John McDonogh, the famed philanthropist, sugar planter, and shipping mogul of the Crescent City. Indeed, he purchased his St. Rosalie plantation from McDonogh in 1831 for $22,500, a price indicating the potential of the land.[62] Over the next three decades, Durnford, with McDonogh as his agent, created one of the largest sugar cane plantations in the state, complete with seventy-seven slaves, 2,660 acres of land, and three houses.[63]

Durnford did not simply look the part. He acted and thought like a true elite, a model planter of the sugar parishes. In 1835, he traveled to Richmond, Virginia, to purchase slaves directly from dealers, rather than at auction in New Orleans. Once there, he wrote McDonogh complaining of the high prices in the Virginia capital. "I went to see a family of four children, mother & father for 1800$ of *yellow complexion*," he told his friend. "I expect to have a better bargain."[64] He eventually got one. After nearly a month of shopping around, he ended up with twenty-five individuals "of all descriptions" and a bill for $6,876. He got as good a deal as he could find. "I could have bought some cheaper," he informed McDonogh back home. "But, they are what I call rotten people, . . . and are getting higher every day."[65] As a man of color, albeit extremely light skinned, Durnford spoke with surprising pragmatism concerning "the Blacks," as he repeatedly called the slaves. To Durnford, as well as to Thomas Jefferson and countless other slaveholders across the South, "blacks" were not free Negroes or people of color. They were, in the language and thought of the day, products, property, items for sale, "black" because they were slaves, not because it most closely approximated the pigmentation of their skin.[66]

Durnford, of course, did not belong to this group, either socially or racially. Himself of "yellow complexion," Durnford placed no premium on similarly complected slaves. Indeed, he felt $1,800 for a "yellow" family of six too dear for his liking. And although he purchased twenty-five men and women "of all descriptions," they remained "Blacks" in his eyes. He clearly had an understanding of where he stood in the social and financial hierarchy of the nation. Race aside, Durnford seemed no different than any other planter on the lookout for a good deal in the world of the slave trade. He bartered, struck deals, refused sales, and traveled at will across a nation dedicated to retaining people like him—those written out of the standards of white American citizenship—in perpetual bondage. He even complained to McDonogh that the captain of the ship *Harriet*, recently returned from

Liberia and en route to New Orleans, "would not agree to take Blacks," although Durnford was welcomed.[67] It was not the segregation that bothered him. It was the cost of finding other arrangements to transport his new property.

The way Durnford lived his life, and the people with whom he interacted, did business, and befriended, shaped the way he viewed himself and the society in which he lived. He placed himself in a broad group of producers and employers, men who created jobs and unpaid labor for others by purchasing wares, making orders, and maintaining a farm worked by slaves and hired hands—the quintessential planters of the rural South. "I think society is made up of two distinct parts," Durnford wrote McDonogh in 1844, "on the one hand, wolves and foxes and, on the other hand, lambs and chickens to provide food for the former."[68] He was one of these wolves—a producer of fortune, a man imbued with a natural ability to create what others valued and needed. The rest of society, whether slave, consumer, debtor, or merchant, existed because of him, and for his benefit.

But Andrew Durnford did not represent the class of colored people taking form in southern cities following the War of 1812. Nearly all of his interactions, throughout his entire life, were with other planters, all of whom were white. At his death in 1859, his chief creditors were white plantation owners, as were most of those owing him debts. In his lengthy succession document, beyond his children and wife (who all appear as "colored" in at least one official document), no free people of color show up. It seems as though Andrew Durnford, a free man of color living outside while doing business within a city with a free colored population of more than eleven thousand in 1860, had no colored friends, partners, or acquaintances. Even those giving testimony to his character, marital status, death, and business relationships came from the white caste.[69] Indeed, his only recorded interaction with a well-to-do Creole of color in New Orleans was in 1834, when Norbert Rillieux, a French-trained engineer and chemist, offered Durnford $50,000 to rent his entire plantation in order to test his new "multi-effect vacuum pan," designed to refine cane sugar. Durnford flatly rejected the offer, claiming that he did not want to "give up control of [my] people."[70] He would not release his slaves into the hands of another colored gentleman. Either he did not know Rillieux, or he did not trust him. Either way, throughout the 1830s and 1840s, Durnford did loan some two dozen of his "people" to John McDonogh and William Erskine, two white men, for nominal fees.[71] Rillieux's offer simply did not matter.

Men like Norbert Rillieux and his close friends François Lacroix, Bernard Soulié, and Pierre Casenave did not cross paths with Andrew Durnford: they lived in different social, cultural, and even racial spheres. Just like in the white community, colored merchants, skilled artisans, and professionals in the cities saw themselves as fully separate from both the planter elite and the working poor. They used men like Durnford and his white colleagues as counterpoints to their own social image and identity. And they did this through the same measures as middle-class whites across the urban South.

The lives of prominent colored people in the urban South constantly overlapped. Social networks—friends, business partners, lovers, kin—expanded each year and gradually came to define the concepts of belonging and acceptance in the community. In New Orleans, wealthy and known Creoles of color appeared as witnesses for each other's wills, baptisms, marriages, and funerals. In 1857, François Boisdoré named Joseph Dolliole as first executor of his estate, a trusted position of enormous responsibility. Joseph's brother, Jean Louis, served as the godfather of Boisdoré's second son, Jean Baptiste, twenty years earlier. The godmother was Cécile Édouary, the wife of François Lacroix.[72] Many of those giving testimony on Boisdoré's life and relations appear in dozens of other successions, all claiming to have been "very intimate" (or saying the same thing in other words) with the deceased, often "since childhood."[73] They loaned money to one another, sold each other land and slaves, and visited each other's homes and businesses for dinners, shopping, and mourning.[74]

They lived their lives together, defining the parameters of their community—of their class—in a complex social dialogue stretching over several decades. But this dialogue was not necessarily public, nor was it necessarily written or even spoken, except, perhaps, in the language they used among themselves to indicate such a thing. More than anything, it was *performed* in the public sphere through the actions of everyday life—through one's occupation, fashion, language, and comportment. This dialogue extended beyond the reputations and "good character" that gave individuals faces and names in the larger, white-dominated society. It turned inward, defining what degree of pigmentation, skill, or style warranted the protection and acceptance of this distinct community at large.[75] The conscious identity that developed out of this dialogue was middle-class rather than elite, urban rather than rural, mercantile and skilled rather than yeomanly or aristocratic. And it developed within the same nationalistic fervor as that of the white community, both in New Orleans and in other urban spaces across the South.

As early as the 1790s, free communities of color across the South recognized a need to unite. Following the American Revolution, a war in which hundreds of colored men fought, militia rosters often served as indicators of social memberships. In places like Virginia and Louisiana, where dozens of free men of color took up arms for the American cause, veteran status created both camaraderie within the colored community and a place of respect and character within the local community as a whole.[76] In South Carolina, however, free people of color did not serve in the local militia, and very few, if any, qualified for pensions as veterans. This explains, at least in part, why Charleston saw the first and perhaps most exclusive of all the colored social clubs and benevolent societies in the South, while those in other important southern cities developed decades later.[77]

On November 1, 1790, five men met at the home of James Mitchell, located next to Vanderhorst's Wharf at the end of Tradd Street in downtown Charleston.[78] All five men lived in the area, known for its merchant houses and trading offices. They all worked in skilled or professional trades. George Bampfield and William Cattle, for example, were partners in the coastal rice trade. George Bedon was a carpenter specializing in cypress, a popular and useful wood that required exceptional skill to craft. Mitchell, who owned the home at Vanderhorst's Wharf, owned and operated a cooperage, complete with sixteen slaves, a furnace, and three rooms of storage.[79] Little is known about the last of the men, Samuel Saltus. Together, they were the founders of the Brown Fellowship Society, the first colored benevolent society in the South to survive well into the antebellum era.

At Mitchell's house they wrote a constitution explaining the reasoning for forming the society and delineating exactly who could become part of its membership. Race took center stage from the beginning, but it was not the tension between black and white that one would expect from the early slave South. "We, free brown men, natives of the city of Charleston," they began, recognize "the unhappy situation of our fellow creatures, and the distresses of our widows and orphans" on the occasions of "sickness and death." Their "fellow creatures" were not the negro masses on the docks and in the cities, or the black slaves in Mitchell's cooperage, or in the fields of St. Rosalie. This "fellowship" included only "free brown men" and their families. Indeed, "observing the method of many other well disposed persons of this State, by entering into particular societies," they continued, "we comply with this great duty ... to contribute all we can towards relieving the wants and miseries" of all members and their families.[80] Not only were they "free brown men," they were also "well disposed," just like the many other men and women founding similar organizations in the white community. Immediately, then, it becomes clear that these five "originators," and the dozens of members initiated in the decades that followed, recognized themselves as separate and distinct from both "black" people and the poor. There was no innate allegiance, no fundamental caste identity that attracted these men to others who did not share their complexion and lifestyle.

All members of the Brown Fellowship Society had to fit the same mold. Only fifty men could hold a place in the fellowship at any time. One became a member by writing a letter to the Society stating his interest in joining. After three separate readings, a simple majority in either direction decided the applicant's fate. According to the constitution, as well as the membership certificate, a member had to be a "free brown man." Upholding the "well disposed" character of the roster, the initiation fee stood at $50, the highest of any known benevolent society of the era.[81] Monthly dues followed at $1.00 per month, and punishments for various infractions—including skipping a meeting, showing up late, or drinking in public—ran between 25¢ and $5.00.[82]

These fees helped fund the primary purpose of the Fellowship. As the constitution declared, the Fellowship formed to relieve the "distresses of sickness and death" among members and their families. It also promised to lend a helping hand to any member in need. When the Fellowship reconstituted itself in 1844, it included a new rule allowing members to borrow money from the Society at extremely low interest. It also provided $60 per annum for any widow or orphan of a member. Beyond that, each child, whether orphaned or not, was to receive schooling "until arrived at the age of fourteen years," the standard age at which a youth entered into a professional apprenticeship at the time.[83] The Fellowship required that members visit the sick and dying among them (who received $1.50 per week during their illness). Upon a member's death, all other Brown Fellows attended the funeral "in full dress" with "a black crape around the left arm," to signify solidarity and mourning. Failure to perform either duty resulted in a 25¢ fine at the next meeting.[84] Not once, in nearly fifteen years of extant records, did such a fine occur.[85]

The Brown Fellowship Society clearly existed to support a specific group of people, protecting them from the pitfalls of life and death. It created a community of its own, one highly selective in its membership and candid concerning its insularity. Beyond publishing its *Rules and Regulations* in 1844 as a celebration of its official jubilee, members had to maintain a certain public appearance, a certain comportment that fell in line with the standard of respectable society. "[A] decent, peaceable, orderly behaviour [must] be observed by all members" in public and at meetings, the 1844 regulations declared. They were not to utter "God's name in vain" at any time, or, as mentioned earlier, become intoxicated in public.[86]

"Decorum" evincing the good character and manners of a well-disposed gentleman was fundamental not only to the Brown Fellowship but to the southern middle-class identity as a whole. It also makes sense that the Brown Fellowship would add many of these rules and regulations in 1844. By that time, a middle-class identity was entrenched in urban communities across the South. In 1790, the Fellowship formed to distinguish its membership from the growing population of freedmen manumitted in the humanitarian rush following the American Revolution.[87] Unskilled, impoverished, and largely dark skinned, these freedmen often moved to the cities to find work and to escape the fields in which they had come of age. State legislatures in Virginia, South Carolina, and eventually Louisiana passed laws intended to quell the growth of this feared population. It follows that the free colored population, with its skills, property, and slaves, would take the same action—establishing both physical and ideological separation from this new, impoverished, but racially similar group.

By the time of the Brown Fellowship's jubilee, a number of similar organizations had formed in other cities. Each one, fueled this time by the nationalistic fervor of the 1810s and 1820s, as well as the influx of foreign immigrants to the cities, maintained the same standards of membership, decorum, and internal aid as the Charleston original. New Orleans was host to a number of such organizations, all nearly identical in purpose but targeting different segments of the population. In January 1836, the Société d'Economie et d'Assistance Mutuelle formed in the faubourg Tremé, just outside of the famed Vieux Carré. Like the Brown Fellowship, the Société d'Economie developed out of the consideration of "all the advantages and the benefits that are repaid to a group of men joined together in Society." But membership in the Société was not universal. "We have committed ourselves to perseverance," the founders declared, "and to put all our efforts into instituting a society ... composed of men distinguished by their private lives, noble sentiments and virtues." They called themselves "*les anciennes*," a term referring to their familial roots in the "original" French settlement of Louisiana.[88] They were natives of distinction, literate, property-owning men of high character and virtue. The average "Negro," immigrant, or freedman simply had no place beside them.

They mentioned nothing of race, however, and only loosely referred to any form of benevolence for the rest of mankind. To the members of the Société, race was only an issue insofar as society was concerned. Their primary consideration was social and cultural belonging, constructing a public identity that defied racial prejudice. Indeed, the "perseverance" noted in the Société's constitution referred more directly to the challenge of proving separation from the Negro masses than allying themselves with their oppressed brethren. They played on class more than anything else. As *les anciennes*, they had as much claim to the land and culture of New Orleans as anyone, especially white Creoles like Barthélémy Lafon and Michel Fortier, discussed in the last chapter. Likewise, such rooted pedigree all but guaranteed that European blood flowed in their veins. This group of distinguished, sentimental, and virtuous mixed-race men played to the expectations of class identity rather than racial identity.

Just like the Brown Fellowship, which did have an explicit racial, or, rather, pigmentary mandate, the Société d'Economie looked to maintain and inspire a certain quality of citizenship, one dedicated to personal and communal uplift, as well as public exhibition. The Société intended "to help one another, teach one another while holding out a protective hand to suffering humanity." Internal aid and education came first, and "suffering humanity" took what remained.[89] But even charitable aid did not extend to all people.

Although a separate organization with slightly different membership, many of the known members of the Société d'Economie served on the board of the Institution Catholique des Orphelins Indigents (Catholic Institution for Indigent Orphans). Listed in the Prospectus and Constitution of the Institution, published in 1847, seven of the ten *directeurs* are known to have belonged to the Société d'Economie at the same time.[90] No school for colored children had existed in New Orleans since 1813, and the public and common school legislation of the preceding decades had ignored free people of color altogether. Although the *directeurs* of the Institution recognized that "the needs of society have, for a long time, called for a solid and durable institution like this one," they did not offer their services to those who did not fit a certain mold, or who did not have the financial wherewithal to cover tuition.

The Institution offered classes only in French, with basic English grammar and writing taught in the third grade (*troisième division*). Similar to the private schools attended by white middle-class children, the Institution Catholique focused on professional training and intellectual pursuits rather than basic literacy and arithmetic. By the sixth grade, which carried a

$6.00 monthly tuition cost, students took classes on logical analysis, literary composition, elements of physiology, rhetoric, and musical composition.[91] This was hardly the level of learning offered to or directed at the children of dockworkers, freed slaves, or even native English speakers. The *directeurs* looked to develop young intellectuals with the knowledge to seek out profit and conduct business with their minds rather than their hands, capable of analyzing society and politics, exhibiting a cultured refinement in both language and comportment, and demonstrating high moral character—those virtues that defined the growing middle-class identity of the antebellum United States.

Supported only loosely by the Catholic Church, the Institution Catholique served as the "charity" work of middle-class Creoles of color. François Lacroix served as one of the *directeurs*, as did his business partner and friend Etienne Cordeviolle. François Escoffié, Barthélémy Rey, and Nelson Fouché, men who appeared in each other's wills, business papers, and testimonies, also took turns serving on the board.[92] But few actual orphans attended the so-called École des Orphelins. Indeed, beyond the published Prospectus and Constitution, the Institution Catholique served as a school for the children of the *directeurs*, members of the Société d'Economie, and their friends and partners. If the Catholic Church or a kind donor could provide the tuition required for an orphan's education, he or she could have a place in the school. Of course, all children attending class also had to understand French in order to learn. But that was no matter to the Creoles who founded it.

The connection to the Catholic Church and the nominal dedication to "indigent orphans" allowed the Institution to skirt an 1847 law declaring any private educational facility for colored people, free or enslaved, illegal. The state considered religious institutions and those affiliated with them "neither public nor private in matter," and thus outside the new law.[93] If anything, the École des Orphelins allowed well-to-do Creoles of color to educate their children with a curriculum, and at a cost, that insulated them from their intellectual and social subordinates while reinforcing the standards of the wider middle-class identity among the youth. Additionally, those orphans who did find a way into the classroom came out of it trained in those same standards, culturally, ideologically, and socially detached from lower-class "black" life.[94]

The movement toward a middle-class identity among professional people of color was not limited to the Lower South. In nearly every developing city across Virginia, colored benevolent societies sprung up in the decades following the War of 1812. Each of them shared the same insular tilt as the Brown Fellowship and the Société d'Economie. In 1824, for example, the Mutual Relief and Friendly Society formed in Alexandria, Virginia. Membership required nomination from a current member and a two-thirds majority vote. Monthly dues stood at $3.00, the highest of any organization under study. It required no initiation fee (50¢ if "probationary"), but "in case any member should unfortunately get into difficulties," the constitution required each member to raise "an appropriate individual sum" for the "distressed brother." If a member refused or could not provide the given sum, he was fined "double the monthly fee."[95]

They took care of their own, and when a member died, each of his brethren wore "a black crape sash around his hat" for six months. At the funeral, surviving members marched before the casket in their "finest cloth." Any member notably absent paid "a fine of twelve and a half dollars," a forceful penalty. Public appearance and reputation clearly meant a lot to these self-described "free men of color." In addition to public acts of mourning, members upheld a strict code of respectability, both in public and within the Society. Expulsion attended conviction of "any crime, felonious or otherwise," and any member "or his wife and family" could receive the benefits of the Society as long as they conducted themselves "with prudence in public affairs." A two-thirds vote of the membership could deny benefits to any spouse or relative of a member if found "imprudent and no longer deserving the protection of the Society."[96] They did not associate with cuckolds, swindlers, and criminals—the same character types associated with the aggregate "free Negro" community in legislation and popular imagination. They, like their brethren in Charleston and New Orleans, had an identity to form, a reputation to uphold, and a society to convince.[97]

"The Good Fight of Usefulness": Intelligence and Artisanship in the Colored Middle Class

Internal aid among the colored middle class stretched well beyond basic charity, benevolence, and mutual assistance, however. Although the majority of colored organizations with urban memberships focused, at least publicly, on the "betterment of mankind," or "our fellow members," or "brethren," or "creatures," they often stood alongside—and even shared membership with—other, more culturally centered groups. Education of children in the tenets of middle-class life, financial support for a friend or widow, and the maintenance of an outward image of affluence, decorum, and class could only go so far in establishing a true identity for the entire community. Colored professionals wishing to create a place in society, a known identity in a white-dominated world, needed more than just images. They needed substance. They needed education for themselves—the grandfathers and fathers of the newest generation. They needed confidence in themselves and their community. And they needed a way to embody the growth of America's cities, the urban lifestyle, and the money that accompanied success within it.[98]

Alongside the Brown Fellowship in Charleston, the Société d'Economie in New Orleans, and the Friendly Society in Alexandria came organizations intent on expanding the cultural fluency of the professional and artisanal colored class. The largest and most organized of these groups formed in Charleston in 1847. Called the Clionian Debating Society, its membership included the wealthiest, most prominent colored men in Charleston, well over half of whom also belonged to the Brown Fellowship.[99] Joseph Dereef, a land speculator, wood factor, and member of the Brown Fellowship, owned more than $40,000 in property in 1850 and served as a leader in the colored community as a whole. His reputation in the city as a man of "great business habits, . . . respect and influence" blurred the lines of caste and race in the urban South.[100]

Following a series of 1823 laws requiring all free people of color in the state to acquire "white Guardians" as representatives in court, contracts, and other official capacities, Joseph Dereef and his brother Richard stood as the "white Guardians" of at least three other free people of color. Although recognized in tax books and some court documents as colored, no one ever questioned the Dereefs' eligibility.[101] Moreover, just six of the forty-one members of the Clionian Debating Society, along with three of the fifty Brown Fellows, ever addressed the law and appointed guardians. And nearly every member of both organizations successfully brought suit as individuals against at least one white person between 1820 and 1860, a legal privilege specifically reserved for white people. Some, like Joseph Dereef, Richard Holloway, and Anthony Weston, by far the most prominent of the lot, appear consistently in dozens of cases, suing and being sued by white men of similar standing.[102]

The Clionian Debating Society created a culture of learning and discourse for these men. It allowed them to realize the same principles of enlightenment, intellectual growth, and moralism taking form in the salons of Paris, the Free Library Society in New Orleans, and even the Literary and Philosophical Society in London.[103] They dedicated themselves to the "vehement preservance [sic], order and fortitude necessary for the promotion, conviction and improvement of intellect." This, they declared at their first meeting, was "our first celebration . . . to see our star of improvement in the ascendant." They likewise believed "education to be one of the most important duties devolved upon man," as it offered "resolution among our fellow members" to keep up "the good fight of usefulness to ourselves and society."[104] In December 1848, the Committee of General Interests gathered $2.00 from each member to create a library for the Society. Every attending Clionian gave willingly, and within two months, the Society had acquired a library of more than six hundred titles, an accomplishment President Enoch G. Beaird called "a liberal collection which gives us great encouragement to continue on."[105]

The main purpose of the Clionian Society, however, was not the establishment of a library or school for its members and their families. That much was assumed. Members had to be literate, a skill tested by each initiate signing the Society's roster "in his own hand" and producing a handwritten letter requesting a "reading before the Society." These requirements accompanied two letters of recommendation confirming the applicant's "character for honesty and intellect." Tellingly, there was no initiation cost or monthly dues. Clionians only paid when requested by the administration for maintenance of the library or furnishings for the meeting hall or a public debate.[106]

Again, this was not a benevolent society. The Clionians, almost all of whom belonged to a benevolent society or two, focused instead on the production and development of an intellectual identity for themselves and their fellow members, a collective air of intellectual prowess and enlightenment. "With vigor and heat," often over multiple weekly meetings, they debated questions on the past and present. They showed surprising knowledge of current events, especially in Europe. In late 1849, they discussed whether or not "the late Revolutions of Europe [have] benefited the condition of the people of that continent" for nearly three weeks, concluding "with unanimity" in the affirmative. Any revolution, they decided, "whether of violence or peace, justifies a Republic."[107] Such a conclusion should come as no surprise. The revolutions across Europe in 1848 resulted in the mobilization and expansion of an urban middle class akin to that which populated American cities after the War of 1812—a *petite bourgeoisie* of employees rather than employers, skilled producers and clerks rather than investors.[108]

Race, slavery, and citizenship never came up for debate. Even privately, the Clionians never seemed to question their own standing as colored men in American society or the injustice of racial slavery—a practice in which a majority of them partook.[109] The closest they came to discussing slavery was on August 1, 1849, when they decided that "the treatment of the English to the Irish" was indeed "tyrannical." But then again, they also determined that Oliver Cromwell was a "usurper" with "no right to the reins" of English government, and that George Washington was "the greatest and most virtuous general of all history."[110] They clearly held an anti-British tilt.

Perhaps most importantly, though, the Clionians analyzed their own lifestyles, goals, and notions of self, as though justifying the lives they had chosen for themselves, their families, and their community. On multiple occasions, the virtues of wealth and education became the focus of debate. In a "heated discussion" approaching "insensibility," Henry Cardozo, a college-educated Jewish mulatto of extensive wealth, and Jacob Legare, an artisan painter with more modest property, debated whether or not there were "any benefits derived from riches." It was not a question of whether benefits existed. Rather, it was a question of how much good could arise from the benefits attached to wealth—a question built upon virtue and morality. Of course, they decided, there were "benefits to riches." But were those benefits personal or communal? Did they aid in uplifting an individual and those around him, or did they corrupt him? In the end, the Clionians settled on the affirmative, but noted that "opulence injures the Soul and Mind." Riches only benefited those who "work for one and all," and "endeavour to build culture and intellect" among their peers.[111]

Repeatedly, over nearly five years of debates, the topics and subsequent decisions emphasized the middling, self-conscious position these men held in society. One could be wealthy, as nearly all of them were, but he could not allow that wealth to harm his moral judgment, his virtue as a "citizen" of his community. If he did not give to the Society, join a benevolent organization, or pursue an honest career and business practices, he defied the image and identity upheld and promoted by his colleagues and friends. Indeed, the Clionians decided in 1848 that "dishonesty," rather than "intemperance," "tends most to the ruin of the human race." To them, the intellectual was innately moral, as "intellectual excellence" constituted "moral excellence" and was "the greatest beneficial influence upon Society" as a whole. It was "ambition alone" that led Napoleon to defeat at Waterloo, they likewise decided, as "the promotion of self corrupts the moral and intelligent mind." This virtuous balance, this moralistic control over ambition, wealth, and greed, came only with "education, reason, and affiliation with others."[112] The Clionian Debating Society, along with the Brown Fellowship and its sister organizations, provided this affiliation, this protection of the definitive moral trait of the class, this middling notion of balance between emotional extremes.

Under these conditions, the various identities of colored professionals and skilled artisans living in a growing southern port crystallized into that of a single middle-class community of colored men and their families.

This trend flourished across the entire South and took a remarkably similar form in New Orleans. In the shadow of the prestigious Société d'Economie—which, as the name indicates, catered to an almost universally professional membership—came a partner organization with a vastly different approach to community and cultural development. The founding of what came to be called the Société des Artisans remains unclear. However, multiple sources suggest that by 1847 it had existed for at least a decade. In fact, the "orphan" school at the Institution Catholique stood as a joint effort between the moneyed Société d'Economie and the more intellectual Société des Artisans. The chief *professeur* at the school was the poet Armand Lanusse, who served as president of the Société des Artisans for many years.[113]

The "artisans" of this Society did not fit the common mold of woodworkers, blacksmiths, and wheelwrights. They practiced fine arts and literary pursuits. Indeed, the Société des Artisans existed for the promotion and development of fine arts within a classically trained, often internally educated community. The members of the Society made their money painting portraits rather than homes, sculpting marble busts and ornamental tombs rather than laying sidewalks and runners for streetcars. They wrote poems and plays and taught others to do the same, finding ways to supplement their incomes with real estate and even the sale of slaves.[114] They met to hear, view, and critique each other's work. And before the creation of the Institution Catholique alongside the Société d'Economie, they educated their own children in the rules and ways of the arts.[115]

Louis Séjour, for example, a prominent and active member of the Society, introduced his young son, Victor, to the Artisans in the late 1830s. Louis, born in Saint-Mârc, Haiti, immigrated to New Orleans in 1809, part of the same wave that brought François Lacroix and Pierre Casenave to the city.[116] He had a fascination with the theater, allegedly working as a young hand at an opera house in Saint-Mârc before his exile. As a man of the arts, with money and slaves from his white father, Louis entered New Orleans society as an alien. But he fit the cultural mold of many Creoles of color, especially those who twenty years later would go on to form the Société des Artisans. By the time of his son's birth in 1817, Louis had opened a dry goods store at the corner of St. Philip and Bourbon. He owned six slaves, all born in Haiti, and held nearly $8,000 in property.[117] If his modest success did not earn him the respect of his peers, his service at the Battle of New Orleans did, where he was quartermaster of Major Louis D'Aquin's famed 2nd Battalion of Free Men of Color. He fought beside Bazile Thierry, the Haitian-born father of the Creole poet Camille Thierry, both future Artisans, as well as Louis Daunoy, François Boisdoré, and Jean Louis Dolliole, all lifelong friends of François Lacroix and members of the Société d'Economie.[118]

On the fields of Chalmette, more than anywhere else, Louis Séjour became a Creole. He had fought for the land and its people, mixing the land with his blood. But it was among the members of the Société des Artisans that he found acceptance and merit as a cultural equal. Tellingly, Louis never joined the Société d'Economie, although he fought alongside and often did business with a number of its members. The Artisans, then, were no less middle class and culturally "Creole" than the members of the Société d'Economie. Both groups celebrated the local past, maintained rosters of propertied, francophone, mixed-race men, and accepted a number of veterans of the Battle of New Orleans into their ranks.[119] The two groups simply represented different paths to the same end. Instead of sustaining a community of honest, financially endowed professionals, the Société des Artisans looked to develop the minds and talents of respectable, highly skilled artists, writers, and performers.

Joseph Colastin Rousseau, the son of Haitian-born Battle of New Orleans veteran Jean Rousseau, had the rare honor of belonging to both societies. Through the Société d'Economie he donated money to the Institution Catholique, and he ran his contracting business with the help of fellow members Pierre Soulié and Henry Louis Rey.[120] But with the Artisans, he could ignore the troubles and stresses of the financial world and focus on his love of poetry and literature. On three different occasions, he read works before the Société des Artisans that later appeared in French-language journals across the region. One of those works, his tribute to the colored soldiers at the Battle of New Orleans titled "*Les contemporains*" (The witnesses, 1846), appeared in *La réforme*, a highly respected, white-run literary journal known for publishing poems and stories by the likes of William Cullen Bryant and Victor Hugo.[121]

Rousseau's concurrent success in the artistic and professional realms suggests, at the very least, that affiliation with one did not preclude affiliation with the other. As with Louis Séjour, many Artisans owned businesses and property to fund their artistic pursuits. And almost universally, they exchanged money, slaves, and merchandise with members of the Société d'Economie.[122] But men like Louis Séjour did not raise their sons to be traders, merchants, and speculators (though out of necessity they often made money as such). They introduced them early to the world of art. As mentioned earlier, Louis's son, Victor Séjour, made his literary debut at the age of twenty before the members of the Société des Artisans. There he read a scene from his unfinished play, *Les volontaires de 1814*, in which he likened the free men of color at Chalmette to the "honest republicans" of the French Revolution and celebrated both events as "formative for our people."[123]

Victor Séjour's "people" were not necessarily native New Orleanians, though. His father, who introduced him to the Société des Artisans, was born in Haiti. His friend Julien Lacroix, brother of François, came from Cuba by way of Saint Domingue. Fellow Artisan and poet Camille Thierry was born in Bordeaux, France, to a Haitian father and mother.[124] To be part of "our people" meant more than local nativity. Proper knowledge of the French language, education, public decorum, and a professional skill, though not explicitly required for acceptance in the Society, came to bear as universals in its membership. The pride of place that defined the colored Creole identity in the territorial period translated into a pride of culture following the Battle of New Orleans. The public appearance of education, fashion, and French roots, whether colonial or continental, came to define belonging in the New Orleans colored middle class.

The members of the Société des Artisans embodied this identity in ways that only public exhibition could justify. In 1843, Armand Lanusse, the president of the Artisans, along with members Joanni Questy, Camille Thierry, and Michel Saint-Pierre, founded a literary journal of their own called *L'album littéraire: Journal des jeunes gens, amateurs de littérature* (The literary album: A journal of young men, lovers of literature). In *L'album*, members of the Société des Artisans could distribute their works beyond the confines of the meeting hall. During its short run of just over a year, *L'album*, which Lanusse edited, published dozens of poems and short stories written exclusively by young colored artists from New Orleans.[125] It was a public exhibition of artistic talent, a signature on a public work, an expression of pride and proof of ability. It served the same purpose as Florville Foy, a talented colored marble cutter and headstone scribe, signing the front of every headstone he made, regardless of complexity. He had something to prove to those interested. He had to claim his work and talent to let others know he was there.[126]

The pages of *L'album* were a testament to where this young colored Creole class found its cultural origins outside the bounds of nativity. Written primarily in the French Romantic style, the poems and stories published in the journal celebrated the French past, the rise of Napoleon, and the dream that all men are "capable of creating, believing, and living in liberty."[127] Like the founders of the Clionian Debating Society, the Artisans in *L'album* attached liberty, progress, and even the destiny of humanity to education and the realization of intellect. In an essay titled "Philosophy of History," Armand Lanusse described artistic expression as "this liberating action" that eases the human predilection for "brute force and accident." "Organic society," he explained, "emerges only when intelligent people come together." Without this "divinely inspired" order, he concluded, "history would only be a mysterious and endless labyrinth."[128]

Lanusse clearly believed that education and art, whatever the medium, held the key to cultural and social advancement. But like his counterparts in Charleston, Lanusse's actions fell short of his universalist rhetoric of widespread "liberation." The truth is that Armand Lanusse, along with nearly every contributor to *L'album*, owned slaves, and often sold them for profit.[129] He also publicly differentiated between the "moving words" of "gentlemanly French" and the "verbiage and commonplaces" of the "barbaric French" spoken by "Negro vagrants and beggars."[130] He was of an enlightened class, mixed race, propertied, and highly educated. He spoke perfect French, wrote poetry and verse, owned slaves, and taught a select group of mixed-race children the pleasures of intellectual fulfillment. In 1845, he edited and published *Les cenelles* (The hawthorns), the first collection of African American poetry in the United States. In his introduction to the volume, he described education as a "shield" against "indifference and maliciousness." Again, he stopped short of universal protection. "It is with great pride," he wrote, "that with each day we see the number increase of those among us who now resolutely undertake the difficult pursuit of the arts and sciences." But "against the spiteful and calumnious arrows shot at us" by stereotype and law, the "only ones to have earned our sympathy are the young men whose imagination has been forcefully captured by everything that is great and beautiful."[131]

Those forcefully captured by slavecatchers, traders, and social oppression stood outside the Artisans' shield. Lanusse and his colleagues in the Société des Artisans, as well as nearly every other literary, debating, and benevolent society in the South, sympathized with those they considered worthy of protection. They did not publish *Les cenelles* and *L'album* to publicize the plight of the impoverished freedman or the lifelong slave. They published these books and journals, formed debating societies, and collected money for libraries to perform an educated, professional, middle-class identity. They created the means by which their culture could continue and grow with each generation, separate from those outside the accepted circles. Education, learning, and an expansive intellect "liberated" them from the lumpen masses. It made clear their cultural, social, and intellectual distinction from Negroes and slaves in the same ways as professionalism, ancestry, and wealth. They were all paths to the same end—publicly acknowledged separation from social, and in some cases racial, inferiors.

So François Lacroix did not necessarily lose his mind that day in 1861. He rather stepped outside of the expected standards of a man of his class. A member of neither the Société d'Economie nor the Société des Artisans, Lacroix nonetheless stood as a talisman of both schools. A talented and wealthy tailor of progressive French fashion, he was a practitioner of sartorial artistry, the products of which he sold at great profit to men of similar ilk. He owned massive amounts of property, collected thousands of dollars in rent, and sat on the boards of at least two charitable institutions and one insurance company, all as a colored man.[132] When the Municipal Guard arrested him, the *Daily Picayune* could think of no other reason than old age or insanity for a man of such standing to act that way. He was not a mad colored man to them or to the police. He was a respectable, professional, wealthy, middle-class man who was acting unnaturally.[133]

This was the image middle-class men of color across the South sought to create. Through the establishment of benevolent and literary societies, professional, educated, self-conscious men of color could control the public perception of their actions. They could make a high-minded attitude, well-mannered decorum, and professional and intellectual lifestyle seem natural and suitable to their class of people. In the eyes of broader American society, especially among whites, they could separate themselves fundamentally from the actions, appearance, language, and culture of Negro freedmen and slaves. To be arrested, for example, would be seen as unnatural, and thus excused as an aberration or mistake, hardly an expression of the innate character of an aggregated "free Negro" population. These men had money, property, fashion, literature, and advanced educations. They were clearly more "American," more self-made than a slave or an impoverished, poorly spoken, illiterate freedman. They were not "Negroes" because they did not act, look, or think like "Negroes."

The colored middle class likewise did not simply mirror that of white society. They embodied the same notions of self, personal and communal advancement, and social protection as their white contemporaries. And they came of age as a class at the same time. The social and cultural standards and protective tendencies seen in the Brown Fellowship Society are the same as those seen in the Norfolk Humane Association, both groups reconstituted within years of each other. The need for protection in a changing world drove all men of professional and intellectual merit to the same actions and conclusions. Following the War of 1812, the United States was no longer a nation of planters and paupers, "Americans" and foreigners, "blacks" and "whites." It was a nation of fluidity and insularity; a nation of class construction and caste disintegration; a nation where two mixed-race, extremely wealthy men doing business in the same area of the same city could go an entire lifetime without meeting, because their cultural and social values did not align.

Benevolent and literary societies took form on both sides of the color line to harness this fluidity and protect the insularity that followed. The Clionians discussed the questions they did because they needed reassurance from themselves and each other that their experiment was working. They felt obligated to read, research, and debate the human experience simply because they could. That was the point—the perception and reality of ability. This was not an elite of colored men. To apply that term implies that the target population functioned outside of the standard social hierarchy of the time. Just because François Lacroix, Henry Cardozo, Joseph Dereef, and Armand Lanusse, to name a few, were men of color does not separate them from the society in which they lived. Indeed, with the development of a middle-class identity across American society, these men became more aware of themselves and their surroundings, perhaps even more "local" than ever before. Simply put, they started to belong, if not consciously within the archival borders of national "whiteness," then at least in their own communities, their own minds, and everyday life—each one a product of the local present. But they were certainly not planters like Andrew Durnford, nor were they detached merchant-traders with hundreds of employees and clean hands. They worked, made money, and lived self-conscious lives as middle-class Americans of the same "race" with different backgrounds, origins, and even, as the final chapter suggests, future visions of "home." Race, then, was not the only thing that made them distinct. And neither was language, religion, nor, it turns out, location. Class, as much or more than all others, also played a central role, and so, too, did their understandings, at once both collective and divergent, of what a future in the United States would hold for them and their people.

CHAPTER 5

"A Call Back to the Original"
THE ATLANTIC

The idea of colonization never seemed to die in the nineteenth century. The question of what to do with the free colored population of the nation, especially those born enslaved, caused endless debate, confusion, and fear in nearly every state legislature from the founding of the Republic to the end of the Civil War and beyond.[1] During that time, as well as several decades before, legislation and ideology coalesced in the creation of a theoretically aggregated community described variously as "free Negroes," "the Negroes," "freedmen," and "recently manumitted slaves."[2] This population, in the minds of legislators and politically active citizens alike, represented "great and alarming mischiefs" in society, a threat to the slave system, and an example of the possible disintegration of Western society through either slave rebellion or cultural and moral degeneration.[3] Their presence, many feared, corrupted slaves with an image of freedom; they made up an anomalous class in a seemingly regimented society, neither citizens nor enslaved others; and, as chapter 3 made clear in the case of territorial New Orleans, they implicitly questioned the character and meaning of America's God-given, Anglo-Saxon republican identity. They were different and foreign, all, even the native born—valuable "creoles" if enslaved products, strange and dangerous "Creoles" and "free Negroes" if left to their own devices.

The so-called great men of the eighteenth and nineteenth centuries, from Thomas Jefferson to Abraham Lincoln, commented on this "troublesome group" and what it would take for the United States to advance socially and culturally without it. As early as 1785, Jefferson presaged the common argument for colonization when he wrote that, without question, the African population of North America should be free. However, he continued, following a prolonged process of emancipation, "they should be colonized to such place as the circumstances of the time should render most proper." To Jefferson and to many who followed him, Europeans and Africans could not and should not live in the same society. "Deep rooted prejudices entertained by the whites," as well as "the real distinctions which nature has made," dictated it so. The two groups were, to his mind, politically and socially at war with each other, so naturally different that continued coexistence would "produce convulsions which will probably never end but in the extermination of the one or the other race."[4]

It was on this logic that the American Colonization Society (ACS)—the independent philanthropic organization entrusted with the task of relocation—formed in late December 1816. Led by the likes of Supreme Court Justice Bushrod Washington, House Speaker Henry Clay, and Congressmen John Randolph and Charles Fenton Mercer of Virginia, the ACS was an organization attempting to answer to the interests of both the emerging antislavery fringe of the North as well as the embedded proslavery gentry of the South. It passed itself off as a benevolent society, resolute in both the maintenance of the American cultural and social lifestyle and identity, and the protection and relocation of the "masses of free people of colour of the United States" to a place "more suitable to their capabilities, needs and wants."[5]

At once, it admitted the need to find a safe haven for this "peculiarly situated class" and rid the United States of a "useless and pernicious portion of its population," which, for reasons outside the control of any individual, could never enjoy "equal rights and privileges with those around them." It never chose one side of the "free Negro" question, only claiming to work on behalf of "all those thus engaged in our enterprise," whether they be "anomalous" free people of color in Virginia or Louisiana, or slaveholding planters in South Carolina and Georgia.[6] The ACS struck the perfect chord of neutrality amid an increasingly divided American public, and it held their attention for more than five decades.[7]

In recent years, scholars have depicted the ACS, and colonization ideology more generally, as an abject failure. They have pointed to the lack of support in the African American community, both North and South, the inability of the organization to woo any consensus or lasting support from either side of the slavery debate, especially abolitionists in the Northeast, and its lack of sustained federal funding following the Slave Trade Act of 1819, which granted the Society $100,000 to establish an "anti–slave trading colony" on the west coast of Africa.[8] The ACS has, more simply, become the historical standard-bearer of colonizationist thought in the antebellum era and has come to represent, beyond slavery itself, the most public example of whites imposing their collective will on a helpless, oppressed Black community in the United States.[9]

Indeed, it is through this veil that many recent scholars have discussed the ACS and the idea of "black removal." In some ways they are correct, as long as the perspective is restricted to that of the white leaders and organizers of the movement who believed that "the African is a degraded member of the human family" who must "live and thrive elsewhere," or of leading African American abolitionists who publicly denounced the movement as a "scheme [by whites] to drive us from our country and homes."[10] To be sure, many people thought this way, as the vast majority of free people of color in the United States never thought of going to Liberia—the colony the ACS founded on the west coast of Africa in 1822—or anywhere else, except when caught in the momentary depths of hopelessness. And a great many white men, especially those in power, likewise viewed the "free Negro" as a degenerate mass unsuited for membership in the American body politic.

But the idea of removal, of leaving the United States for another land believed better than the last, meant more than just falling under the spell of the ACS Board of Managers and traveling blindly to the distant "land of your ancestors."[11] To some free people of color, especially those of education, mixed ancestry, some wealth, and middle-class sentiments in the South, the idea of changing location came with a sense of empowerment and hope, of mobility and protection. In cities as geographically and culturally distant as Richmond, Petersburg, and New Orleans, middle-class colored families saw colonization and emigration not as a white scheme for displacement and exile, but rather as a chance to make more of themselves, their cultures, and their communities, to maintain the insularity, both social and racial, they had protected and built over the preceding century or more.

They differed in important ways, though, ways that evince the separate paths each community took to achieve the same end, the same sense of belonging in and fulfilment of a conscious national and social self. Whereas in New Orleans middle-class Creoles of color moved rather haphazardly, many looking elsewhere at the height of emigrationist fervor but most ultimately remaining in place or quickly returning to the perceived comforts of home, similar communities in Richmond and Petersburg left in force, consciously and collectively constructing a new "home" in what some have called "another America" across the sea.[12] Such different paths, highlighted in this chapter, tell similar stories but in different words. Like other important aspects in the development of New Orleans's culture, society, and people under the gaze of an encroaching, external "American" identity, the convergence across the antebellum United States of questions concerning nationhood, citizenship, and the place free people of color held or could hold within that nexus took on unique forms in New Orleans and its environs. Because of their distant, external, French origins, their Catholic faith, their conscious, mixed-race, middle-class identities, and their late, purchased admittance to the Union, New Orleans's colored Creole community was never fertile ground for a version of emigration or colonization hawking a new America in black Africa, a place to live within the same liberal model built by the American Revolution and enshrined in its Declaration of Independence. General Andrew Jackson, decades earlier, had already promised them such a place right where they were, before their national baptism at Chalmette in 1815, and the places they had carved out for themselves in the local *terroir* over the course of nearly a dozen decades still betrayed a hope of its realization.

But the same expectations of liberty and membership in the American national image, the social body politic of the land, that led certain free mixed-race, middle-class people of color in the Border South to embrace the ACS and its new, more liberal, multicolored transatlantic America also drove Creoles of color in New Orleans and southeast Louisiana to imagine new possibilities. Their destinations simply differed, in the same way the directions from which they had arrived had differed. To the former, the search for liberty and belonging lay outside the United States, outside their collective origins. Born subaltern, they would remain subaltern until they found liberty elsewhere. To the latter, a similar search had brought them into the United States, its promise sealed with blood spilled and virtuous sacrifice recognized. Born externally, foreign, brought in rather than pushed out, they already had their home when they arrived, and they received the promise of belonging in a nation that itself, to them, was external and new.[13]

Although separate in orientation, perspective, and origins, the identities and purposes that drove both groups were more similar than different. As this chapter shows, in the face of a legislative and social movement across the South to universalize the "free Negro" and erase any distinction, legal or otherwise, between mulattoes, Negroes, and slaves in the 1850s, men like François Lacroix, Armand Lanusse, Joseph Jenkins Roberts, and Louis Nelson Fouché, among countless others, discussed the idea of moving away from their lives in the United States. But the reasons for these discussions, and indeed, for some, the act of removal itself, did not align with how previous scholarship has depicted the colonization movement as a whole, whether through the ACS or individual will. These mixed-race, middle-class men and their families used the idea and possibility of removal as ways of fulfilling personal and communal legitimacy, expanding business opportunities, and taking a step up into an aristocratic, politically active class.

They were not part of the huddled masses of freedmen leaving for Liberia, Haiti, Mexico, and Canada at the behest of their former masters and white "philanthropists" in Philadelphia and Washington, D.C., highlighted in other studies of the colonization movement and the social upheaval of the antebellum decades. Rather, they were self-promoting entrepreneurs, savvy businessmen, and ambitious, talented craftsmen in search of expanded wealth, cultural protection, and a definitive sense of belonging in the political and social realms. They did not simply want freedom. They already had that. What they wanted was legitimacy—a recognized position in a society that honored ancestry, business acumen, and traditional cultural institutions, whatever forms they took locally. If they could not be citizens in the United States, they would make themselves citizens elsewhere. A feeling more than an action, a possibility more than a plan, the idea nevertheless was present in every corner of the South, and some groups took it more literally than others. The same story of political and social uplift and cultural empowerment that drove the ACS's success with free people of color in Virginia failed miserably among the Creoles in Louisiana. But the possibilities of what that story promised, the sense of legitimacy and recognition to which that story appealed, had a place in many Creoles' visions of an American future. Only, to them, the story remained to be written in place, on their own local, once-distant shores.

"The Popular Will of Our Bleeding Nation": The "Free Negro" and the Last Decades before War

The 1850s were not kind to free people of color, no matter where they lived. As though planned throughout the nation, state legislatures across the North and the South began passing, and repassing, restrictive legislation almost as soon as the clock struck midnight on December 31, 1849, inaugurating the new decade. The reasons for this legislation remained consistent throughout the decade and even after the Civil War broke out. White legislators worried about the growing population described almost universally in law as the "free Negroes of this state." Those with the motivation to publish their thoughts explained, for example, that "a natural distrust affects itself between our society and that of the Negro. Indeed a more ridiculous or dangerous falacy [sic] could hardly be designed by men than the idea of rearing up three classes of people in a Republic like ours."[14] The division between white and nonwhite, colored and "clean," had to be rigid and defined. It was only natural, they claimed. "The will of God has declared the separation of the negro and the white man," declared Virginia governor William Smith in 1846, "and our laws and feelings approve it." In fact, the governor continued, "if freed from negro association," the average white man "would not feel so hopelessly his moral degradation" and would benefit from "increasing self-respect, and reviving hope," reinforcing the "productive industry" of the white community.[15]

To many legislators, politicians, and leaders of all classes, the "free Negro" threatened white autonomy, freedom, morality, and the very existence of republican government. Not only was the reality of their freedom anomalous and confusing to many southerners, their supposedly universal traits of moral decrepitude, hypervirility, alcoholism, and pride struck terror in the hearts and minds of "reasonable, moral, hard-working" whites everywhere.[16] Even the most debased of whites fell above the "free Negro" in the social and moral hierarchy of the antebellum South. As early as 1822, the superintendent of the new Virginia State Penitentiary, Edmund Pendleton, explained that "although the free white persons usually confined in this institution, are, for the most part, of the lowest order of society; the free Negro prisoners are certainly a grade or so below them, and should not be associated with them."[17]

Anti–free colored legislation and ideology were nothing new to the South. Nearly every southern state maintained laws requiring the registration of "all free Negroes and Mulattoes" within the state as early as the 1790s.[18] Likewise, free people of color, no matter how reputable, wealthy, light skinned, or trusted, could not vote in any southern state (except for a handful of years in North Carolina and Tennessee). Neither could they, by law, own a tavern, serve alcohol to slaves, or congregate in large numbers from the earliest years of the nineteenth century.[19] But as the century progressed and the American public, white and colored, became more urban and culturally and socially diverse, many of these laws fell to the wayside, as face-to-face interaction and local reputation and character held sway over the enforcement of laws designed to universalize treatment of certain social, racial, and cultural groups.

This changed in the 1850s, at least from the perspective of enforcement. Suddenly, decades-old laws all but forgotten by the public began to pass through state legislatures with massive majorities as "reinstatements" and "reissues" of the originals. For example, in Louisiana, although the law had been on the books for nearly four decades, in 1852 the General Assembly reissued a bill declaring it "against *understood* and *engrained* law for any free Negro to sell, dispose of, or make available to slaves any form of spirituous liquor, or to maintain a house in which spirituous liquors are sold or consumed."[20] John King, the author of the law, used the terms "understood" and "engrained" to emphasize the fact that the law was not original to his mind or time, and that the enforcement of the law was now his and the legislature's main concern.

And enforce it they did. Between 1852 and 1856, the City Guard arrested more than three dozen free people of color on such charges.[21] One of these men, the wealthy, mixed-race, well-connected Creole of color François Escoffié, petitioned the legislature, claiming false accusations and "basic insults" to his character. "It is well known to all the inhabitants of this town," he explained, "that since eight years your petitioner live[d] in the same place, he has never met a complaint similar to that of which he recently became a victim." Indeed, he insisted, "this is the first complaint of that kind or any other whatsoever ... since 8 years he has kept a grog shop."[22] Not only was this the first time he had ever been arrested, he had also been living in contravention of the law for eight years, and "all the inhabitants of [the] town" had known about it and never said a word. There is no wonder that he was embarrassed, surprised, and insulted by the arrest. In the end, Escoffié paid an $80 fine, but retained his license and establishment for at least ten more years, a testament to his "well known" respectable status in the community.[23]

Throughout the decade, and across the South, stories like this arose. On August 7, 1860, seventy "Negroes," both enslaved and free, were arrested in Charleston, South Carolina, for "working without the proper badges required by law."[24] The law requiring "all slave mechanics, draymen, and day labourers hired by their owners" to wear an "impressed badge designating [their] status" had been in place since 1806, and was most recently revised in 1843.[25] But in 1854, the South Carolina legislature "reissued" the law, citing a "determined lack of deposits [for the badges] to this point accounted by the Treasurer."[26]

Although the *Charleston Courier* and the city police admitted that "most of those arrested" were in fact free, and thus did not fall under the law, the *Courier* expressed what many whites in the South were starting to believe, and what many free people of color—especially men like Joseph Dereef, one of those arrested, as well as a high-ranking member of the Brown Fellowship Society and himself a slaveowner—feared would become a reality.[27] Refusing to admit fault on the part of the police arresting dozens of innocent freemen, some even freeborn and "nearly white," the *Courier* explained that the arrests were justified because those claiming freedom "were under a mistaken notion that they were free and did not require [a badge]." In the end, according to the paper, "they remain Negroes in practice and in law, and they should require the same badges as their companions."[28] At least from the perspective of the paper and the police, "Negroes" were, or should be, slaves. Freedom no longer automatically extended to the ranks of even the lightest-skinned, freeborn, respected, and skilled free people of color. They were, to the most public voices in southern society, as well as the minds of legislators everywhere, simply "Negroes," and the slaves were their "companions."

The active creation of an aggregated "free Negro" class and the legal and social consolidation of people of color, both enslaved and free, into a single racial category in the two decades before the Civil War developed from a number of major shifts in the American political and intellectual landscape. The growth of Know-Nothingism (also known as "Americanism" and "Nativism"), especially in the Border States as well as Louisiana and Georgia in the Deep South, brought temperance, zealous Christian moralism, and "American" cultural nationalism to the public mind in the late 1840s and 1850s.[29] Fearing and moving against anything outside of evangelical Protestantism, the English language as understood in the United States, and the Anglo-Saxon racial "variety," Know-Nothings across the South gave legs to notions of American exceptionalism and cultural superiority begotten by the Second Great Awakening and disseminated through the egalitarian rhetoric of the once-popular Whig Party. Those deemed outside the "accepted American standard"—a motley group including African Americans, the Irish, Germans, the French, and Catholics as a whole—became targets of pointed legislation, vitriolic rhetoric, and even physical violence.[30] It was, Know-Nothings claimed, the "popular will of our bleeding nation ... to carry out her proper spirit."[31]

Increased immigration, especially by the Irish following Ireland's Great Famine of 1845–47, as well as Italians, Poles, Frenchmen, and Germans fleeing the revolutions that swept Europe in 1848, fed the flames of nativism and tested the abilities of many American cities, as well as their inhabitants, to feed, house, and find jobs for waves of desperate families.[32] Free people of color, then, especially among the lower, unskilled classes, were perfectly suited to join these huddled masses as scapegoats for nativist fears and rhetoric about increased competition for work, overcrowding, and cultural degeneration. Indeed, the Know-Nothings, whose numbers swelled within the unskilled white population in many southern towns, saw the increased immigration from Europe as a threat to slavery more than anything else—a menace often attached to free people of color as well. That most "American of institutions," according to New Orleans Know-Nothing Charles Gayarré, required "a shield against the Northern abolitionist horde made manifest in those now challenging at our docks our most precious cultural institutions."[33] Given the perceived threat to white American values, jobs, and institutions now "manifested" in the immigrants themselves, a number of state legislatures with large Know-Nothing contingents—Louisiana and Virginia most notably—saw an opportunity to rid themselves not only of the immigrant threat but also of that posed by the "free Negroes of this state."[34]

This, however, was not simply an example of white politicians finally stumbling on an opportunity to paint people of color as un-American in the eyes of an increasingly discontented southern populace. Society as well as law, in both the North and the South, had never fully recognized people of African descent as members of the American body politic, or even as active members in American society as a whole. Men like François Boisdoré, Jean Louis Dolliole, Charles Forgason, and Richard Holloway were exceptions in their collective abilities to craft public reputations of honesty, respectability, and "good character" through social interaction, celebration of mixed ancestry, and a dedication to a middle-class lifestyle—those attributes that separated them and those like them from archival images of salacious, dishonest, and intemperate Negro masses developing in the minds of those empowered with defining citizenship and belonging in the antebellum South.[35] Dark skin, poverty, emancipation papers, and/or a lack of local roots condemned the rest of the free colored population to being a mass of "Negro denizens" at best, or simply unwanted public burdens at worst.[36]

By the 1850s, this was all but written in stone. And it was supported by a new, popularized racial science. Over the last two decades of the antebellum era, new ideas in American racial science gave substance to the growing anti–free Negro agenda and served to justify the wider consolidation of the so-called "free Negro caste" into one amorphous legal and social population. Most importantly, this new science—or pseudoscience—focused, for the first time since Jefferson's racial arithmetic of 1815, on the place of mulattoes, and other people of mixed racial backgrounds, in the taxonomy of the human race. In doing so, ethnographers, as this new group of racial scientists called themselves, succeeded in doing what American society had tried desperately to do for nearly seven decades—define the place, meaning, and condition of the "mulatto" in a slave society.[37]

"Lymphatic & Scrofulous": The "Mulatto" as "Negro" and Leader

What separated this new wave of ethnography from the wide-ranging studies of the Enlightenment a century earlier was its widespread popularity among the laity. Indeed, as far as theory goes, very little of what American ethnographers had to say was original, or even scientifically accurate. But they wrote their ideas for a popular audience, made stump speeches, traveled across the South speaking at colleges, town halls, benevolent and intellectual societies, and any other venue that would have them. Perhaps more importantly, the ideas came from known and respected members of the American medical community, men who had already established their reputations in other fields and saw a profitable opportunity when, in the mid-1830s, abolitionists, especially those from the more radical branches of the movement, set out to bring racial slavery into public discourse across the country.[38]

For the first time since the middle of the eighteenth century, the question of whether or not the different races of mankind represented different species, complete with different creation stories and anatomical structures, came up for debate. Before the 1850s, the Atlantic world, religiously and socially, had all but concluded that, although vastly different in ability and "born-nature," the races of mankind were simply "varieties" of the same European default corrupted over time by climate, geography, and mating practices.[39] But this consensus, ethnographers claimed, dealt only with the "collective wholes of each variety" and failed to see "the challenge where two wholes meet."[40]

The problem of "amalgamation" was key to men like Josiah Nott, George Gliddon, Samuel Morton, and Louis Agassiz—all advocates of the so-called American School of Ethnography.[41] The "moral repugnance" of racial mixing—called "miscegenation," "amalgamation," and even "cross breeding" at various times—was well known and widespread long before Nott and Agassiz ever published a word. Even the likes of Walt Whitman, the famed American Romantic poet and author of *Leaves of Grass* (1855), conflated intemperance with the "moral debauchery" of interracial sex in his only novel, *Franklin Evans*, in 1842, as did many temperance authors of the early antebellum era.[42] John Bachman, a well-known medical doctor and early ethnographer, likewise found that "mulatto progeny," and the process by which it was created, "insults our American feelings and morals." But he did not go so far as to declare it wholly unnatural or degenerative.[43] That was the job of the new wave of ethnographers coming into prominence in the 1850s.

The very existence of free people of color, or free labor in general, unnerved the American School of ethnography. Because, they claimed, Africans and people of "pure" African descent could not control their "lust for Anglo-Saxon blood," slavery suited them well. It tamed them, gave them the control and structure in life that would not, indeed could not, exist if left to their own devices. Moreover, the "organic structure of the African," from the brain to the heart to the skin, was "primitive in comparison to that of the Anglo-Saxon of Europe," Josiah Nott declared in an 1849 speech. And there existed "not a particle of proof," he claimed, that this "primitive structure resulted from some form of degenerative external cause," or that "the different races of mankind ever have shared a family tree." The "disharmonies" he had found between Africans and Europeans were "too various and too fundamental to offer an honest comparison."[44] There was but one conclusion that Nott and his fellow ethnographers could promote: the African and the European (or "Anglo-Saxon") were two separate species of mankind, created at different times and under different conditions.

The importance of this movement is reflected in the expansion of anti–free Negro legislation, especially its ability, or at least its intent, to consolidate all free people of color into one highly structured, controlled caste. People of mixed race—those often left outside of racialized legislation, whether intentionally or through local social preference, in the past—stood at the heart of the ethnographic revival. Indeed, according to both Nott and Agassiz, "the mulatto" served as the proof behind their multispecies, polygenist conclusions.[45] "Nobody can deny," wrote Agassiz, an extremely charismatic and popular Swiss-born natural historian and Harvard professor, "that the offspring of different races is always a half-breed, as between animals of different species, and not a child like either its mother or its father." This distinction—called "hybridity"—went deeper than "the mere differences of skin color" seen between Europeans, mulattoes, and Africans. It defined the "variation" between "the *natural* abilities and propensities" of each.[46]

Because "mulattoes" were "half-breeds" of two separate human species, their kind could not functionally exist as members of the human community. "Among the characteristic[s] of the halfbreeds," Agassiz wrote after a meeting with Nott, "one of the most important is their sterility or at least their reduced fecundity."⁴⁷ Mulattoes, the theory of "hybridity" claimed, could produce young "on the rarest of occasions"; and that progeny, "if surviving an awkward and uncaring childhood," was "on all known occasions completely sterile and effeminate," incapable of sustaining a life of its own.⁴⁸ According to Nott, "mulattoes are [also] the shortest-lived of any class of the human race," being "particularly delicate, and subject to a variety of chronic diseases." As youths, they were "lymphatic & scrofulous," blistering in the sun and weakened by hard labor. It is important to remember that, according to this new ethnography, mulattoes were "a mixed form of both parent stocks," and thus maintained "the weaknesses of one as tempered by the strengths of the other." But unlike the mule, for example, "which is derived of [two] working stocks," its human namesake, the mulatto, "derived of but one"—the "black."⁴⁹

It was on this notion that the mulatto became important to both legislators and advocates of colonization and removal as a whole. Although it was thought they were destined to fade away over time due to their supposed "lack of fecundity," mulattoes served two opposing purposes in—or indeed, to some, were threats to—society. On the one hand, the danger of amalgamation remained if "a mulatto intermarries with a member of the parent stock," especially a female. While two mulattoes could rarely produce young, a mulatto man and white woman "have been known to reverse the condition," as "in Mobile, New Orleans, and Pensacola, [Nott] had witnessed many examples of great longevity . . . and manifest prolifacy [sic]" between mulattoes and "Caucasians."⁵⁰ To make things worse, as both Samuel Morton and Louis Agassiz noted, certain cases had arisen of "young Southern gentlemen" becoming "confused" and "ever in search of spicy partners" after sexual contact with a "negress or mulattress," which threatened the very existence of American society.⁵¹ "Viewed from a high moral point of view," Agassiz argued, "this characteristic production of halfbreeds is as much a sin against nature, as incest in a civilized community is a sin against purity of character."⁵² If left unchecked by law and society, mulattoes ran the risk of becoming "absorbed, diluted & finally effaced" by the white blood they both possessed and "unconscionably attracted." The best approach, he warned, was to "allow them to move among us as negroes," and force them into the "opposite dilution."⁵³

This is exactly what many state legislatures did. By "reissuing" and "reinstating" long-since-ignored laws using generalized target terms such as "free Negroes," "Negroes," and even "free people of color," legislators used the weight of "science," and the renewed fear of "amalgamation" and "effacement," to force men like François Escoffié and Joseph Dereef into the same caste as lower-class, illiterate, largely dark-skinned freedmen with whom they did not relate or identify, either racially or socially. Nott's and Agassiz's theories drove this crusade. Their works ended up in the libraries of nearly every major literary society in the South, as well as on the desks of many prominent lawmakers. Indeed, Josiah Nott himself became a veritable celebrity across the South, with his and George Gliddon's *Types of Mankind* (1854) selling more than fifty thousand copies by 1856, and his personally commissioned translation of Arthur de Gobineau's *Essai sur l'inégalité des races humaines* (1855) selling more than twenty thousand copies in its first three printings.[54] "For the present," wrote one reviewer of *Types of Mankind*, "we can only say that we of the South should now consider them, more even than [Samuel] Morton, as our benefactors, for aiding most materially in giving to the negro his true position as an inferior race."[55] These ideas were not simply science at this point. They had become popular culture.

But there was still another side to the mulatto, a side that even Nott admitted "opened up a place for them amongst the blacks."[56] As renewed legal pressure mounted against the southern free colored community, the idea of colonization and the "voluntary removal of free people of colour" out of the United States grew in popularity. In 1822, the American Colonization Society had founded the colony of Liberia on the west coast of Africa. In 1847, that colony, by then a "commonwealth," declared its independence from the ACS as the Republic of Liberia—the first of its kind on the African continent.[57] Naturally, the apparent success of Liberia flew in the face of the new ethnographic "truths" championed by Nott, Morton, Gliddon, and Agassiz, who collectively and continually argued that "Negroes, or more simply blacks, are perfectly incapable of self-government."[58]

Nott, the most public of the American School, recognized the problem, and addressed it at the 1850 meeting of the American Association for the Advancement of Science in Charleston, several years before the appearance of *Types of Mankind*. In his well-attended address, Nott explained that the reason for Liberia's success reduced entirely to "the support which [the colony] receives from the whites without, and by the white blood coursing through the veins of their leaders at home."[59] As "halfbreeds," Nott later wrote in *Types of Mankind*, and had argued as early as 1843, "mulattoes are intermediate in intelligence between the blacks and the whites." As a result, they "can, and do in some capacities, serve as leaders of the Negroes," at least as far as intellect, state building, and social discourse were concerned.[60] Of course, as largely sterile, sickly "amalgamations," they could not lead forever, and would soon "leave the equation." But their white blood, according to Nott and his colleagues, gave them the "quality of mind" to "sustain the Liberian experiment." Indeed, Nott concluded in 1850, "President [Joseph Jenkins] Roberts is three-fourths white blood, with florid skin, red hair, etc., and with one or two exceptions, all those who have figured in Liberia are Mulattoes."[61]

Advocates of colonization and removal agreed. From the very beginning of the colonization and removal movements, reformers and supporters specifically recruited freeborn people of color, or at least those free people of color who had been free for many years, for the first wave of settlement abroad. Some even went so far as to restrict their focus to "mulattoes and men of mixed race only." "The mulatto," wrote Thomas Hodgkin, a well-known doctor and member of the ACS, "may inherit so much of the constitution of the father," who he assumed would be white, that "although unavailing of climatic endurance, he may express a positive intellectual influence on the making of the colony."[62] Nearly twenty years later, in 1853, the ACS continued to emphasize the importance of people of mixed race in the feasibility of Liberia's future. "The plan of organizing the free people of color into a political body," wrote Rev. Charles H. Read of the ACS, "is absurd and impossible without a mixed race leadership, must they think and lead with their minds." If they do, he declared, these men "will stand far above all" as the "bold and successful pioneers of their race."[63]

People of mixed race, then, were the ideal settlers. They were smart, capable leaders, able and willing to represent the virtues of American culture abroad while also protecting the colony itself from the "uncivilized and far less capable nature" of the "Negro of pure blood."[64] If given leadership positions in Liberia and elsewhere, they could also serve as examples of the superiority of white blood and European ancestry as a whole, if successful, or examples of the vitriolic nature of "Negro blood," if unsuccessful. But most importantly, they stood as convincing leaders of a questionable movement. If placed outside the reach of "amalgamation" and the resultant "effacement" and racial "absorption," people of mixed race in the 1850s maintained the same unique role in the American racial structure that they had forged over the past century. But this time their role came with both "scientific" support and a ticket out. At last they could be leaders, aristocrats, elites, and presidents, but they had to do so outside the United States. Indeed, as science, law, and society would have it, they could only do so outside the United States.

"Vastly Superior to His Sable Successor":
Colonization, Removal, and the Place of Those Who Left

Joseph Jenkins Roberts, the man Josiah Nott described as "three-fourths white blood, with florid skin, [and] red hair," epitomized the image and temperament of the "mulatto leader of pure Negroes." Light skinned, pious, well-spoken, and wealthy, he lived lives of respect, freedom, and relative comfort in two drastically different lands. Freeborn in Norfolk, Virginia, Roberts came of age in Petersburg, was educated at the reputable, all-white Union Street Methodist Church as a youth, and employed as a clerk in a trading firm on Sycamore Street for several years thereafter.[65] In 1826, he started a trading firm of his own with boyhood friend William Nelson Colson, a freeborn "mulatto" barber and part-time river trader in Petersburg.[66] Just one year later, Roberts, Colson, & Co. was thriving, trading with at least twenty-six different firms along and across the Mason-Dixon line, all run by white men. That same year, they employed seven "Negro youths" as well as three of Colson's slaves, and brought in more than $9,800 in profit after expenses.[67]

They were both men of taste, trading in perfume, tobacco, leather knickers, and silken vests, stockings, and cravats. They advertised "fine imported silks" and the "latest designs of Europe" in local newspapers and directories appearing as far away as Charleston, South Carolina, and Providence, Rhode Island.[68] Roberts alone owned three houses in Petersburg by the end of the 1820s, and Colson, successful before establishing the firm, owned at least seven properties throughout town as well as the firm's downtown office.[69] As far as records show, both men ran with similar social groups, naming among their friends men who likewise owned property, came from mixed-race families, and whose names consistently appear in the rosters of benevolent and literary societies, property-tax lists, and city directories as skilled artisans and merchants.[70]

But life in the United States, even as a respected, middle-class trader and merchant, was too much for Joseph Roberts. Unlike many of his acquaintances in Virginia, Roberts left his native land for the seven-year-old ACS colony of Liberia on February 9, 1829, on board the *Harriet*. He brought along his mother Amelia, brothers John and William, and sister Elizabeth.[71] But his older brother, Henry, and business partner William Colson stayed behind, instructed to "see to the business of the firm until our arrival" in Liberia, something they did for nearly twenty years.[72]

This offers the first and earliest hint as to why men like Joseph Roberts and other like-minded, mixed-race Americans would look to remove themselves from the United States for socially, culturally, and geographically distant shores. If anything, Roberts saw opportunity in Liberia. His mother, still relatively young at the age of sixty-three, had lived in the same house as her son for more than seven years by 1829, an arrangement that implies some form of reliance on or support from him, given that he had owned three separate houses since 1823.[73] Roberts easily could have left his mother with his brother (and her first-born son), Henry, and William Colson had he considered the trip to Liberia one of exploration, potential freedom, and an isolated, frontier lifestyle. Certainly his mother and younger sister, then just eighteen years old, would not take kindly to or even survive such an uncertain, perilous future, however free from legal, social, and cultural oppression it seemed.[74]

His family served a purpose in Liberia, one that essentially guaranteed their comfort and survival. Immediately on arrival, Roberts introduced his sister, Elizabeth, to Beverly Page Yates, a freeborn native of Richmond and a skilled tailor and merchant. The coupled married in 1831, combining what would eventually become two of the largest, most powerful families in Liberian history.[75] With the two brothers who joined him in Liberia, Roberts set up a branch of Roberts, Colson, & Co. in Monrovia, the colony's capital, partnering with his brother-in-law's newly formed trading company, Payne & Yates, to purchase three coastal cruisers and schedule regular packet lines between Monrovia and the more established British settlement of Freetown, Sierra Leone, some 225 miles north.[76] He continually wrote to his partner Colson, still in Petersburg, asking him about the viability of new African products like camwood and palm oil in the American market. Indeed, over the next fifteen years, even after achieving a great deal of wealth, notoriety, and political power in Liberia, Roberts traveled to New York, Philadelphia, Richmond, and Petersburg at least three separate times, not as a representative of his new home or of the ACS, but as a representative of his firm.[77]

This is not to say that men like Joseph Roberts, Beverly Yates, and James Payne rejected Liberia as a land of hope for people of color, or the ACS as a legitimate vessel of that hope. Roberts, and others like him, represented and supported the ACS and the idea of removal in a number of important ways. Within ten years of their arrival, Roberts, Yates, members of the Payne family, and dozens of others of similar ilk rose through the ranks of the ACS's colonial bureaucracy, taking on appointed positions that ranged from

Head Jailer in charge of law enforcement to seats on the white-run Colonial Council—the chief lawmaking body in the colony. After making his way through several smaller appointments, including brief tenures on the Colonial Council and as lieutenant governor of the colony, Joseph Roberts became the first colored governor of the Liberian colony on January 20, 1842, paving the way for his eventual election as the first president of the Republic of Liberia in 1847.[78]

In his inaugural address, given on January 3, 1848, President Roberts repeated the message of racial and national rebirth hawked endlessly by the ACS for nearly three decades. Gone was any rhetoric of personal profit, intermarriage, or American markets. He said all the right things to win over both the skeptics across the sea and the thousands of new citizens he now represented to the world, without exposing his own personal ambition. "I feel, fellow citizens, that the present is a momentous period in the history of Liberia," he declared. Through the grace of an "all wise Providence," Liberians everywhere had "taken upon their shoulders the legacy of *a mere handful of isolated pilgrims*, in pursuit of civil and religious liberty." "Free people of color of the United States," the new president continued, had grown "tired of the oppressions which weighed them down" in their native land, where "society had withheld ... those civilities and that comity which marks the friendly intercourse between civilized and independent communities." But with the help of the "Divine Disposer" and the "wealth, vigor, virtue, and consequent happiness of our national past," he announced, "we have fashioned a land of liberty from a wilderness of difficulties."[79]

But Joseph Roberts was no "isolated pilgrim." He was a smart, savvy, ambitious businessman dedicated to achieving power and influence he could not claim in the United States. He did not look to free himself from an oppressive American past, as the ACS-created motto of his new republic pronounced—"The Love of Liberty Brought Us Here."[80] In fact, it was quite the opposite. He sought to root his new nation's history in that of the United States—"isolated pilgrims" carving out a "land of liberty" from a "wilderness of difficulties" using the "wealth, vigor, [and] virtue" given them by their native connection to the United States. The Liberian "national past" was, indeed, the American national past. Only this time, men like Roberts, Yates, and Payne, along with many others, could design and dictate the construction, implementation, and eventual expansion of a new national, and in this case racial, identity. They were the "pilgrims" on whose legacy the story of Liberia would be written. And with the help of the ACS, they designed it that way.[81]

By the time of Liberia's independence, President Roberts and his colleagues—Yates served as chief justice of the Liberian Supreme Court and James Payne served as the third president of Liberia—fit the mold of the ideal "mulatto." They used public, universalist rhetoric of national and racial growth to attract the "degraded and troublesome population" of freedmen from the United States while more privately creating an American commercial and cultural outpost on the west coast of Africa, upholding the middle-class values and entrepreneurial spirit simultaneously on the rise in America's cities.[82] But their reputations as leaders in Liberia, the Canaan of colonization and removal at the time, rested equally upon their demonstrated business acumen and their physical complexions as "mulatto hybrids."

In 1859, William Proby Young Jr., a Virginia doctor hired by the ACS to treat "returned Africans" in Liberia, met and recorded his impressions of several Liberian leaders in his diary.[83] After dining with then-President Stephen Allen Benson, a freeborn "very dark mulatto" from Maryland, Young minced no words.[84] "He's a great *loaf* of a nigger," the doctor wrote, "terribly inflated by the dignity the office [of the president] is supposed to confer, and scarcely able to *descend* to the level of those around him." A day later, Dr. Young, clearly disgusted by the character and appearance of President Benson, "had the pleasure to be introduced to Ex-President Roberts," whom he described as "a sensible and intelligent yellow man; vastly superior in every respect to his sable successor."[85]

Although Stephen Benson was just as accomplished as Joseph Roberts, having built and operated the only lumber mill in Monrovia and likewise made his way through appointive positions in the ACS bureaucracy, his color and perceived "pure" African ancestry fueled the prejudicial flames of Young's Virginian worldview. He could not possibly accept the existence of a dark-skinned president, however valid and deserving he was of the office. Benson, to Young, represented everything about which science had warned the ACS—the inability of the Negro to rule over and support a civilized society, their penchant for laziness without the organization and structure of slavery.

But Joseph Roberts, though still "yellow," and thus not "white" by American standards, stood as the validation of both the Liberian experiment and the ethnographic theories spreading across the South at the time, at least in the minds of the young doctor from Virginia and the ACS Board of Managers. Benson's attempt at respectability and power made him a "terribly inflated ... *loaf* of a nigger"; Roberts's made him "sensible and intelligent," deserving of the "dignity" attached to leadership on the world stage. Science had already presaged Young's perspective. Roberts was indeed "superior" in nearly "every respect to his sable successor," for he clearly had "the white blood coursing through [his] veins" that Josiah Nott had by then long claimed would protect Liberia from "utter and speedy failure."[86] Benson, it seemed, did not.

The respect and "dignity" garnered by Joseph Roberts, Beverly Yates, and other leading mixed-race Liberians made sense to men like Young, Nott, and the ACS leadership because it was earned *outside* the United States. The voyage across the Atlantic distanced Liberia's "mulatto" leadership from the aggregated Negro whole taking form across the South in the 1840s and 1850s. They could be "sensible and intelligent," "vastly superior" to their "sable" countrymen and counterparts, because they no longer posed a threat to the American racial ideal. Indeed, they fortified it; they lived it. Their individual success seemingly proved, to those interested, the positive effects of white blood in the weakened, sterile bodies of mulattoes, while their public leadership provided marketable language and symbols of hope, success, and racial rebirth in a newly independent nation far from American shores.

But Roberts's actions and rhetoric, however oddly contradictory they seemed, were not unique to Liberia, the ACS, or even those who ended up leaving the United States for Africa. Although many historians have painted those who stayed put as fervent anticolonizationists, proud abolitionists, and even proto-racial nationalists, the rhetoric and actions of many who stayed fell in line with those of Roberts, Yates, Payne, and other so-called Americo-Liberians.[87] And simply because they stayed in an increasingly strict, racialized United States did not mean their minds never wandered to other shores. It simply meant that those shores did not necessarily seem any more golden than the ones they called home.

"Where We Better Fit":
The Dream of Leaving and the Reality of Staying Put

In the pages of *L'union*, an increasingly radical French-language newspaper in New Orleans, Armand Lanusse penned a series of articles. A freeborn native of the town, Lanusse had gained local renown for publishing *Les cenelles*, a collection of romantic poetry, the first of its kind by an African American, in 1845, and serving as the principal and primary instructor at L'Institution Catholique des Orphelins Indigents since 1847.[88] Of mixed race and proud of it, Lanusse walked at the highest levels of New Orleans colored society—educated in Paris, president of the posh and selective Société des Artisans, editor of the literary journal *L'album littéraire*, and a friend of the Dolliole brothers, the Boisdoré family, François Lacroix, and even the one-time criminal François Escoffié.[89]

His public articles, crafted between 1857 and 1862 as responses to the French-born mulatto Édouard Tinchant, an outspoken supporter of the new Republican Party, echo those same sentiments of civil and racial oppression invoked by Joseph Roberts in his inaugural address more than ten years earlier and several thousand miles away.[90] In a complicated time of legal prohibition and increasing isolation, Lanusse sounded more like an activist than a comfortable, middle-class educator. "The title of 'fellow citizen' with which the gentleman [Tinchant] honors me," he wrote, "unfortunately belongs neither to him nor to me," for in Louisiana, "the land for which I have shouldered my rifle and marched," the "man of color cannot be a citizen."[91]

This had always been the case, Lanusse insisted. Even after "all our boys and men had gathered under the call of Jackson" and "shared blood" against a common foe in 1815, "the inhabitants [of the United States] professed only the greatest indifference or the deepest contempt" for "the race of men born on this ground."[92] He could find only one solution. "When oppression makes a revolution necessary," he wrote, citing the Marquis de Lafayette rather than the better-known American Declaration of Independence, "insurrection is the most sacred of duties." But that insurrection, whether social or political, he admitted, "cannot happen here."[93]

Much like the Liberian "pilgrims" mentioned in President Roberts's speech, Lanusse sought citizenship of some sort, legitimacy and freedom from a legally enforced second-class life. And he was not alone. Between the founding of the ACS and the outbreak of the Civil War, a number of New Orleans colored Creoles considered voluntary exile. Even François Lacroix, the extremely wealthy, cosmopolitan tailor, flirted with the idea in the 1840s. In a letter to his close friend and business partner, Etienne Cordeviolle, Lacroix admitted that "I have often thought to leave here." Although he owned nearly $180,000 in landed property at the time, held six slaves, and operated two tailoring shops for primarily white clients, he apparently felt "stuck to my reputation" in New Orleans, "not able to stand between the two sections" of the city—the French First Municipality where he lived, and the "American" Second Municipality where one of his shops was located. "I think I may join you where we better fit," he mused to his friend.[94]

Despite their universalist language and use of the French pronoun "nous," meaning "we" or "us," neither Lacroix nor Lanusse had their eyes set on Liberia or on finding freedom, or a "fit," for all people of color. Indeed, when asked by the City Court of New Orleans in 1847 whether his partner, Cordeviolle, had left for Liberia, Lacroix responded sharply: "M. Cordeviolle did not remove to the negro Country. He found his place in Paris, in France."[95] Over the next decade and a half, nearly two dozen wealthy, mixed-race, francophone New Orleanians would also leave for Paris. In court cases and successions, endless references to friends and business partners "recently removed" to the French capital appear. Joseph Dumas, a close friend of Lacroix as well as one of the wealthiest colored men in the South, packed up his tailoring business in 1849 and moved his family to Paris, where he died in 1880.[96] Erasme Legoaster, Bernard Soulié, and Julien Colvis, all wealthy, educated, respected businessmen, withdrew to France together in 1853, where they set up a lending and brokerage firm, as they had in New Orleans for nearly twenty years.[97]

Once in Paris, many of these men disappeared into the metropole, reappearing in the records only when they returned to New Orleans on business or to visit friends and family.[98] For many, if not most, the trip to France served as the end of their American lives, as visits were infrequent and very few maintained active business relationships with anyone in the United States—Etienne Cordeviolle standing as the primary exception.[99] They clearly left because they could not see a future in the United States as mixed-race, francophone Catholics with wealth, education, and acknowledged ambition. France was not a "negro Country," as François Lacroix described Liberia, or a nation in which, according to Lanusse, the "man of color cannot be a citizen." It was a nation of *égalité* and citizenship for all, having recently overthrown its own monarchy in favor of a Second Republic predicated on the notion of universal personhood. They worshipped men like Victor Hugo and Alphonse de Lamartine, quoting them often and even hanging their pictures on the walls of their homes. It only made sense for them to seek citizenship and political legitimacy in a land that celebrated the same culture they had worked more than a century to sustain in the United States.[100]

The tenets of American culture and memory espoused in Liberia's public image, colonization rhetoric, and the recent wave of cultural nationalism stretching across the South did not appeal to François Lacroix or Armand Lanusse either. But neither of them ever followed their own advice and set out for a "better fit," even after a number of their friends had left, never to return. Lacroix simply, and quietly, stayed. He continued to expand his empire in New Orleans, write to his friend Etienne in Paris, and raise a close-knit, well-connected family in his adopted home.[101] He never made much of the Civil War when it finally came, and, in spite of his social prominence and wealth, he never showed any interest in running for office or serving as a leader of the colored population after the war ended. It was said that he lived a happy life after dreaming of Paris, visiting his grandchildren daily and hosting dinner parties attended by "every respectable character in colored society." According to his son, François Edgar, he "passed in society & in the community for a colored man," and "visited and frequented the society of colored men," although "his complexion [sic] was white." He was a loving father and grandfather, and "made clothes his entire life."[102] He was happy where he was and felt no need to explore other venues. In his last recorded letter to Cordevielle, dated February 12, 1862, just two months before New Orleans fell to the Union, he expressed this feeling. "We are fine here. I am fine.... Business has slowed, but I will stay as long as it takes.... We are all fine. We are all happy."[103]

Armand Lanusse did not remain so quiet. And he continued to dream of other places. In 1857, when his close friend, Louis Nelson Fouché, a wealthy, freeborn quadroon with French colonial roots, led a group of locals to eastern Mexico in hopes of starting a "Colony for Foreign Nationals Known as Eureka," located between the towns of Tampico and Veracruz, Lanusse applauded the effort but declined to join.[104] In an article in *L'union*, he praised the emigrants as "pioneers of their class" whose "patriotism cannot be questioned."[105] But their patriotism was not necessarily wrapped in the historical memory of America's founding, as it was in ACS rhetoric and the speeches of Liberia's national leaders. Indeed, what drove Fouché and his fellow emigrants to Mexico was not really patriotism at all. It was the same sense of economic opportunity, social mobility, and elitist ambition that drove similar men and women—the likes of Roberts, Yates, and Payne—to Liberia.

From the very beginning of the enterprise, Fouché and his partner Lucien Donato, a freeborn mulatto originally from St. Landry Parish, planned to bring "a considerable fortune and technical equipment which promises to make our experiment a success."[106] Even the local Mexican newspapers reported on their financial and technical well-being. In July 1857, the Mexico City newspaper *El siglo XIX*, which published simultaneously in English and Spanish, described "more than forty families with a significant amount of capital, knowledge in different areas of agricultural cultivation and trade practices, strong moral character, customs, courteousness, [and] good dispositions with wishes and hopes for the progress of industry." The paper went on to explain that "their principle work consists of the cultivation and processing of sugar cane, which they plan to sell in the American markets."[107] By late fall, *El siglo* reported that "the mulattoes have acquired machinery, vessels, formed factories and plantations, and are not waiting for their relatives and friends to arrive."[108]

This was, in Lanusse's words, "a call back to the original," a step away from an increasingly uncomfortable life in New Orleans, into a place where Catholicism and African blood, however faint, did not amount to stains on one's position in society and sense of cultural belonging.[109] To Fouché and his clan, it was a "movement to recognize all the rights of ambition and destiny, and to evade superficial barriers, in lieu of other colonization projects" like Liberia or even Haiti, which, despite its prominent place in the lives and legacies of people like Fouché, Lacroix, and Lanusse, could not offer the ambitious, liberal future Fouché and others had in mind.[110] They called each other *les associés* (associates) and set as their primary goal (*l'article premier*) "the establishment of a plantation built by us and worked by the people of the area" to produce goods for "the global trade."[111] They were ambitious traders with dreams of plantation life, not racial nationalists seeking to found a safe haven for the colored population of America—a nation of which they always considered themselves "Nationals," even in Mexico.[112] They were mixed-race men and women of middle-class standing looking for that same social step up denied Liberia's Virginia-born leaders.

And the ACS saw them as such. Indeed, men like Lanusse, Lacroix, Fouché, and Donato, all of whom owned property, businesses, and wealth in New Orleans, likewise fit the mold of the ideal "mulatto." The concept did not simply vanish from the minds of white leaders because these men lived in a place considered somewhat exotic, French, and foreign in its racial structure. The ACS wanted Louisiana as a market, especially New Orleans. As early as 1836, it formed an auxiliary branch in the city, which quickly grew to become the Louisiana Colonization Society (LCS) in 1840.[113] Between that year and the end of the 1850s, the ACS and LCS placed no fewer than 417 advertisements in New Orleans newspapers alone.[114] In studying the New Orleans free colored population for possible removal, the ACS found that among "the mulattoes of New Orleans many are sober and industrious mechanics, quiet and useful citizens, who are susceptible of noble sentiments and virtues." As a result, they concluded, "throughout the Union there is no field of better promise to the cause; none from which emigrants in larger numbers, *or more suitable*, are to be expected" than the "Auxiliary Society of Louisiana."[115]

But the emigrants never came. Between the founding of the auxiliary in

1836 and the fall of New Orleans to the Union army in April 1862, just sixteen individual freeborn Louisianans left for Liberia. Of those sixteen, eight were from New Orleans, none of whom spoke French, were Catholic, or held any meaningful property in the city. They were all "mulattoes," but few knew who they were, and even fewer lamented their loss once they left.[116] The "mulattoes" the ACS hoped to woo over to their cause had their eyes fixed either on Mexico or on the land they had made their collective home for decades. Men like Lanusse never even mentioned the ACS or Liberia, while Lacroix, far quieter than his friends, simply referred to it as "the negro Country" and moved on.[117]

The Mexican experiment excited many wealthy, mixed-race New Orleanians, young and old. In English composition class at L'Institution Catholique, the selective school for colored Creoles run by Armand Lanusse and the Société d'Economie, Lanusse had his seventh-year students (aged fifteen to eighteen) practice the art of letter writing. In hundreds of letters written between November 1856 and September 1863, Lanusse's students, nearly all of whom were francophone and from wealthy Creole families, wrote to friends in places like Cincinnati, New York, Natchez (Mississippi), Paris, and Marseilles. They wrote business correspondence, discussing shipments of "fine silks, cravats, hats, handkerchiefs, Claret wine, and lace," sometimes with a value of $6,000 or more. They asked for advice from friends, mentioning inheritances (often $10,000–$15,000) and prospects of starting up a trading firm or grocery store with their "newly acquired" wealth.[118]

Although the content of these letters says a lot about who these young men were, what their families were like, and what they expected from life, they also provide a unique look into what the common discussions were in their social circles, what they found interesting, or, if nothing else, what their *professeur*, Armand Lanusse, wanted them to learn. It should come as no surprise, then, that between letters of advice and business matters, nearly every other letter written between the summer of 1857 and 1859 dealt directly with the experience, successes, failures, and prospects of the Mexican experiment.[119]

The students imagined themselves as settlers, occasionally writing to friends "back home" in New Orleans. And in each letter, the same dream appeared—that of plantation life, leisurely trade on the backs of the locals, and immediate, unrestrained success. "You will be very well here," wrote Armand Grégoire, the "mulatto" nephew of famed Creole poet Pierre Valcour, to his friend Joni Beltier in New Orleans. "I will give you an apartment in my own house, [and] you will be able to do whatever you please."[120] In another letter, Armand Nicolas, a cousin of the Dolliole family and future member of the First Louisiana Native Guards under the Confederate state militia, lamented the difficulties of controlling his "servants" in Mexico. "Last week I took 2 servants," he wrote, "who stole me fifty dollars, and ran away in the night.... I assure you that I am very plagued, and cannot leave my plantation. I had twenty five men on it, but only fifteen now remain."[121] Henry Vasserot, who was listed as "white" in the 1850 census, and who would later serve in the First Louisiana Native Guards, seemed to have more luck in his imaginary life. "You can get some Mexicans to work for you for five dollars a month and some others for four," he told his friend Lucien Picou. "The inhabitants of this country are simple and good natured fellows. I am rich and a king here!"[122]

Others reported to friends what they had heard from those who had left, spreading gossip and stories of easy success. Ernest Brunet wrote to M. Lombard in St. Martinville, Louisiana, that his father, who had traveled to Mexico with his friend Louis Duhart, "had bought two plantations and says if I come, I shall have one for sixty dollars." His father's production, too, was nothing short of extraordinary. "He has just bought some boys about fourteen years old, who make one or two thousand bricks a day; They are constructing many buildings on his plantation; He has three thousand lemon trees, and a very fine house."[123]

Whether detailing their own imaginary exploits or spreading the news of others' successes, an image of the great southern plantation appeared. When Etienne Pérault wrote that he "would like better to be a farmer than carry on any other profession," he was not referring to the hardy yeoman of Jefferson's idyll. Rather, he wanted to "make money by it in the markets," for he had heard that "Vera Cruz is a good country for commerce" and that the "local people make a suitable peasant class."[124] He was not interested in moving to Mexico to till his own fields and plant his own seed. The "peasants" from the surrounding villages would do that while he, the planter, sorted out his business affairs down the coast in Veracruz. Indeed, fieldwork was the domain of the masses, not the educated, wealthy aristocracy. "If you become a man lazy in your habits," warned Armand Nicolas, "you will be forced to work in the fields to get your living," and lead an "idle, failed life."[125]

It was the same in New Orleans, just without the plantation and the possibility of fieldwork. Commerce drove the minds of the students' parents, as well as of their teacher, Armand Lanusse, and his social circle. When Nelson Fouché designed the plan for Eureka, he did not look to separate himself and his people from life in New Orleans. Far from it. He sought to expand the commerce they had already established in the city and open up new frontiers, new possibilities, new products, services, trade routes, and ideas. That is precisely why he referred to his fellow emigrants as "associates" rather than colonists, "foreign nationals" rather than Mexicans, Eurekans, or any other demonym establishing a new identity and a new home. The plan was not to colonize or even permanently move, but to grow, hand-in-hand, with those they had left "back home" in New Orleans. They wanted to become that same aristocracy monopolized by the white gentry (with very few exceptions) of the rural parishes and counties, and redirect trade southward. They would become the producers, the planters, the sources of trade, all the while protecting both themselves and their families from schemes and laws seeking to lump them together with a population more foreign to them than anything they would encounter on the banks of the Papaloapan River. There they could be Creoles, Catholics, Frenchmen, mulattoes, quadroons, and gentlemen again, and still make that step into the planter class, into the aristocracy.

In the end, few followed the likes of Joseph Roberts, Beverly Yates, and the more than ten thousand others who left the United States for Liberia before the Civil War.[126] In fact, the vast majority of New Orleans Creoles of color, especially those who had lived and succeeded in New Orleans for the past half century, stayed put. Very few of the men encountered here ever left New Orleans, and neither did their children. François Boisdoré, for example, died in 1858, a veteran of the Battle of New Orleans and a patriarch of his class.[127] His friend Jean Louis Dolliole died in 1861, beloved and wealthy, leaving two sons, two daughters, and a wife, none of whom ever considered leaving for Mexico, Paris, or Monrovia. Instead, they stuck together, continued their father's business, and married into respectable Creole families.[128]

As for Nelson Fouché and Lucien Donato, the leaders of the Mexican experiment, they both returned to the United States in 1860, just in time for war. After three years in Eureka, none of the dreams Lanusse's students described had come true. A mere one hundred colored New Orleanians made the trip, and those who did not die of "the fever" stayed no longer than six months at the longest. In fact, neither Fouché nor Donato ever set up a plantation or even a permanent home in Eureka, as they continuously traveled back and forth in search of "associates," funding, and provisions.[129] After 1860, they simply faded into their old communities, returning to the property they never sold and the skills they never abandoned, working and living alongside those same people with whom they had once sought change.[130]

But the dream was there. And for a brief moment, between fits of racially reductionist legislation and science, cultural nationalism, and lost hope, it took hold of the imaginations of far more people than passenger lists, death tolls, and newspaper reports could possibly express. For that moment, the free colored population of New Orleans merged with the larger colored population of the United States in its interest and curiosity about life outside of home. For more than a century, francophone, Catholic, mixed-race men and women in New Orleans had worked to create a space of belonging and legitimacy, whether social or racial or both, in a city far different from, but quickly assimilating into, the American political and cultural body. And when threatened, those same visions of commercial expansion, political power, and social legitimacy that drove Joseph Roberts and the Americo-Liberians to the West African coast likewise drove Lacroix, Lanusse, Fouché, Donato, and many of their friends to dream of similar success.

The key is that they were all "mulattoes" in the eyes of powerful white men. Although the ACS did not succeed in attracting most New Orleanians into the fold, they rested easy knowing that they, too, wanted out. In either case, the plan was set, the end was achieved—the intelligent yet weak and sterile "mulattoes" were leading the "debauched" and "insubordinate" Negroes out of the country, perhaps saving them, perhaps condemning them; it mattered little. As Charles Gayarré, a well-known white Creole and colonizationist, put it to the ACS board, "Your committee cannot conceive the expectation that a colored man, born in Louisiana, will break so many ties, which need not be enumerated, to cross the ocean and settle among men whose origin, whose language, and whose manners are so different from his own.... A colored man, of French origin, born in Louisiana, would not voluntarily go to Liberia." And he was correct. None of them went to Liberia; but Liberia was not the only choice. Beyond even Paris, Eureka, Veracruz, and Tampico, they could be "mulattoes," *Créoles de couleur, gens de couleur libre*, simply by acting the same, encouraging the face-to-face interaction that made them who they were, and continuing on with life as socially and racially ambiguous denizens of the state. But for those with further ambition, or at least the will or desire to see that ambition through, removal was always an option—an option some took while most rejected, but all for the same reasons.

In 1861, civil war came, cutting off most emigration movements and dreams, at least for several years. But still the Creoles of color in New Orleans, the mixed-race, francophone Catholics who form the chorus of this work, never left. They stayed, raised a militia, and took up arms for both sides—the same way their forefathers had when French became Spanish and Spanish became American. The will to fight, to protect their homes, and to legitimate themselves through the same means provided whites of the same ilk never ceased. They were Confederates and Unionists, blacks, whites, mulattoes, and Negroes. But most importantly, more than anything else, they were natives; they were home; they were American. It just took them a while to admit it.

NOTES

INTRODUCTION

1. Jean Blandin to Henry Vasserot, Natchez, Miss., May 29, 1861, L'Institution Catholique Copy-Book, Archives of the Archdiocese of New Orleans, New Orleans, La. Also cited, in slightly different form, in Mitchell, *Raising Freedom's Child*, 42–43.

2. On this insularity, see O'Brien, *Conjectures of Order*, 1:285–87; Thompson, *Exiles at Home*, 138–44; Charles E. O'Neill, "Foreword," in Desdunes, *Our People and Our History*, ix–xix.

3. See Olwell, *Masters, Slaves, and Subjects*, 44–47; Burton, *Afro-Creole*, 22–30; and Kenneth Morgan, *Slavery and the British Empire*, 84–90.

4. See Domínguez, *White by Definition*, chap. 1; Burnard, *Creole Gentlemen*, chap. 7; and Nicole King, *C. L. R. James and Creolization*, 10–21.

5. See Cole, *Krio of West Africa*, chaps. 1, 3, and 4; Fanon, *Wretched of the Earth*, 138–42; Wyse, *Krio of Sierra Leone*, 23–36; Usner, "Facility Offered by the Country,'" 38–45; and Wegmann, "'Upon This Rock,'" 63–68.

6. The historiography of Enlightenment racial science is vast, but very few studies either look at the New World as a testing ground for scientific theories or consider the place of people of mixed race in the creation and development of those theories. For the best, most objective, historical treatment of American adaptations of Enlightenment racial science, see Stanton, *Leopard's Spots*. Other, more subjective treatments include Stephens, *Science, Race, and Religion*; Dain, *Hideous Monster of the Mind*; Horsman, *Race and Manifest Destiny*; Fabian, *Skull Collectors*; Irmscher, *Louis Agassiz*; and Dugatkin, *Mr. Jefferson*. The best study of the racial theories of the Enlightenment, especially as they related to slavery and the Atlantic world, is Curran, *Anatomy of Blackness*.

7. The books that cite Berlin's *Slaves without Masters*, or use it with abandon, are far too numerous to list. The most notable are Koger, *Black Slaveowners*; Curry, *Free Black in Urban America*; Horton and Horton, *In Hope of Liberty*; Schweninger, *Black Property Owners*; Johnson and Roark, *Black Masters*; Myers, *Forging Freedom*; Bristol, *Knights of the Razor*; Ford, *Deliver Us from Evil*, chaps. 1 and 3; and Gudmestad, *Troublesome Commerce*.

8. See Berlin, *Slaves without Masters*, chap. 4.

9. For New Orleans as an isolated, unique, largely "un-American" city and culture, see ibid.; Myers, *Forging Freedom*, especially introduction and chap. 2; Schweninger, *Black*

Property Owners, chap. 4; Hirsch and Logsdon, *Creole New Orleans*; Toledano et al., *New Orleans Architecture*, vol. 4; Kein, *Creole*; Powell, *Accidental City*; Bell, *Revolution, Romanticism*; Brasseaux, Fontenot, and Oubre, *Creoles of Color*; Dormon, *Creoles of Color*; and Everett, "Free Persons of Color."

10. For excellent, but purely regional studies of race in New Orleans, Louisiana, and the Gulf Coast, see Hanger, *Bounded Lives, Bounded Places*; Ingersoll, *Mammon and Manon*; Gary B. Mills, *Forgotten People*; and Usner, *Indians, Settlers, and Slaves*. For the few studies that expand the standard area of investigation, see, most notably, Spear, *Race, Sex, and Social Order*; Emily Clark, *Strange History*; Gwendolyn Midlo Hall, *Africans in Colonial Louisiana*; and Vidal, *Louisiana*.

11. Most notable among recent studies focused in large part on the territorial period in Louisiana and New Orleans is Eberhard L. Faber, *Building the Land of Dreams*. For an analysis of the transition from French and Spanish to American legal systems, see Fernandez, *From Chaos to Continuity*.

12. See Kastor, *Nation's Crucible*, chap. 4; Spear, *Race, Sex, and Social Order*, chap. 7; Logsdon and Bell, "Americanization of Black New Orleans"; Blassingame, *Black New Orleans*, chap. 1; Sterkx, *Free Negro in Ante-bellum Louisiana*; Sharfstein, *Invisible Line*, primarily chaps. 6 and 8; and Hobbs, *Chosen Exile*.

13. See Arnold R. Hirsch and Joseph Logsdon, "Introduction" to part 2, in Hirsch and Logsdon, *Creole New Orleans*, 91; Tregle, "Creoles and Americans," 132; and, more generally, Tregle, "Early New Orleans Society," 30–35.

14. Vidal, *Caribbean New Orleans*, 23–34. Vidal challenges the assumption that "the existence of differences between North American and Caribbean slave systems" evinces the existence of "two antithetical models" (23–24). The discussion of the evolution of racial systems and their "contingent and pliable" natures appears on p. 34.

15. On the increasing "Americanization" of New Orleans and the resultant fading of "Creole" culture, see Bell, *Revolution, Romanticism*; Hirsch and Logsdon, *Creole New Orleans*, chaps. 4 and 5; Kastor, *Nation's Crucible*; Thompson, *Exiles at Home*; and Aslakson, *Making Race in the Courtroom*.

16. On racial science, the mulatto, and concepts of racial mixture, see note 6 of this chapter, in addition to Curran, *Anatomy of Blackness*, chap. 4; Williamson, *New People*; Wolf, *Race and Liberty*, esp. chap. 4; Wolf, *Almost Free*; Stewart R. King, *Blue Coat or Powdered Wig*, chaps. 3, 4, and 6; Lemire, *"Miscegenation,"* chaps. 1 and 2; Buscaglia-Salgado, *Undoing Empire*; Gossett, *Race*; Sweet, *Bodies Politic*, chap. 4 and part 3; von Daacke, *Freedom Has a Face*, esp. chaps. 5 and 6; Greg Carter, *United States*, introduction and chap. 1; Shuffelton, *Mixed Race*, chaps. 12 and 13; and Sussman, *Myth of Race*, chaps. 1 and 2.

CHAPTER 1. *Genèse Française*

1. Succession of Jean Louis Dolliole (f.m.c.), March 4, 1861, #17,714, Second District Court of New Orleans, New Orleans Public Library Special Collections (hereafter NOPL); Toledano, *National Trust Guide*, 19.

2. Deed of Inheritance of Real Estate, June 1, 1845, Succession of Jean Louis Dolliole (f.m.c.), #17,714, Second Dist. Court, NOPL; also Succession of Louis Dolliole, 1822, Court of Probates, NOPL.

3. Gwendolyn Midlo Hall, *Databases for the Study*.

4. Will of Louis Dolliole, 1815, book 3, 242, NOPL. There are no birth certificates for any of the children, but in his will, Louis acknowledged his paternity of all four. He described them as his "natural children" (as opposed to "legitimate"), meaning that their parents never married. Also see Toledano et. al., *New Orleans Architecture*, 4:91.

5. The two sons and Marie Françoise survived into the antebellum era. In the 1850 census, Jean Louis and Joseph appear as "mulatto." The officers of the Louisiana militia in 1815 likewise list Jean Louis and Joseph as "free mulatto." See *1850 Manuscript Census Rolls*, Orleans Parish, NOPL, and "Muster Roll of First Colored Battalion (Fortier's), Louisiana Militia," in Pierson, *Louisiana Soldiers in the War*, n.p.

6. "Petition of Heirs," Succession of Geneviève Dolliole, f.w.c., 1838, Court of Probates, NOPL.

7. Petition to the Honorable Charles Maurin, Parish Court of Orleans, August 24, 1834, NOPL; also *1850 Manuscript Census*, Orleans Parish, Municipality 1, Ward 4, NOPL.

8. 1843 City Directory of New Orleans, NOPL.

9. The *1840 Manuscript Census* lists Pierre Deverges as living with four others, all white. The *1850 Manuscript Census* has Pierre Deverges residing with his widowed mother, wife Coralee, and three white children—Marie Louise (12), Louise (10), and Eugénie (8). The three children attended school, and their father, a gardener by trade, maintained a personal wealth $115,000. See *1850 Manuscript Census*, Orleans Parish, Municipality 1, Ward 4, NOPL.

10. Both brothers are listed as "carpenters" in the *1850 Manuscript Census* for Orleans Parish. Jean Louis also did work on the Soulié brothers' (Albin and Norbert) property on Rampart Street in 1844. See Soulié Family Ledgers, June 18, 1844, Historic New Orleans Collection, New Orleans, La. (hereafter HNOC).

11. See Soulié Family Ledgers, October 30, 1844, December 21, 1844, September 20, 1845, HNOC. Also, Octave de Armas, Notary, 1853, book 61, #161, New Orleans Notarial Archives (hereafter NONA).

12. Succession of Jean Louis Dolliole, March 4, 1861, #17,714, Second Dist. Court, NOPL; Succession of Joseph Dolliole, *fils*, March 31, 1868, #32,582, Second Dist. Court, NOPL; "Muster Roll of First Colored Battalion (Fortier's), Louisiana Militia," in Pierson, *Louisiana Soldiers in the War*, n.p.; and Achille Chiapella, Notary, 1854, vol. 36, #1253 and #1755, NONA.

13. See Succession of Jean Louis Dolliole, March 4, 1861, #17,714, Second Dist. Court, NOPL; Succession of Joseph Dolliole, *fils*, March 31, 1868, #32,582, Second Dist. Court, NOPL; Succession of Joseph Valcour Dolliole, August 30, 1854, #8,126, Second Dist. Court, NOPL; and *1850 Manuscript Census*, Orleans Parish, NOPL.

14. Death Certificate of Geneviève Hermina Dolliole, January 7, 1852, NOPL; and *1850 Manuscript Census*, Orleans Parish, NOPL.

15. See Will of Louis Dolliole, 1822, book 3, 242, NOPL; and Succession of Louis Dolliole, 1822, Court of Probates, NOPL.

16. Will of Louis Dolliole, 1822, book 3, 242.

17. Spear, *Race, Sex, and Social Order*, 8.

18. This concept of metropolitan/colonial interaction and distance comes from a number of sources. It is principally, but not entirely, founded upon the concepts of the "image archive" and the "iron cage." The former term, coined by Sue Peabody in 2004, describes the process by which metropolitan governments came upon their "knowledge" of colonial society through a series of descriptions and tales given by travelers rather than their own eyewitness experience. These "images," implanted in the minds of metropolitan legislators by third-party witnesses or writers, created an "archive" from which these lawmakers constructed legally bound notions of what they *thought* they knew about Africans, Indians, and the needs of the colonists. On the image archive, see Peabody, "'Nation Born to Slavery,'" 113; and Spear, *Race, Sex, and Social Order*, 2–5. A Weberian term, the concept of the "iron cage," first invoked in a historical context by Ronald Takaki in 1979, refers to the process by which members of a dominant social or racial group become bound or "chained" to legal notions of value and meaning within the realm of "corporate discourse"—macro notions of social dominance and subordination, the principles of virtue, political rights, etc. Yet in social intercourse, these same people are free to function outside of the iron cage, inventing their own, very personal concepts of dominance and virtue that often stand in stark contrast to the self-renunciation and alienation practiced within the corporate iron cage. See Takaki, *Iron Cages*, viii–x, 3–16, 254–60. For the perspective of the subordinate, or "subaltern," group, see Fanon, *Black Skin, White Masks*, 25–40, 64–73.

19. For descriptions of the earliest settlers of New Orleans, as well as a few demographic figures, see Powell, *Accidental City*, 54–55; Gwendolyn Midlo Hall, *Africans in Colonial Louisiana*, 5–6; and Ingersoll, *Mammon and Manon*, 11.

20. On the border conflict and exploratory rivalry between the French and Spanish in the early eighteenth century, see Weddle, *French Thorn*, chap. 11.

21. Gwendolyn Midlo Hall, *Africans in Colonial Louisiana*, 6. Also see Ingersoll, *Mammon and Manon*, 10–11.

22. Dawdy, *Building the Devil's Empire*, 10–11.

23. Lachance, "Growth of the Free," 206–7; Ingersoll, *Mammon and Manon*, 11; Gwendolyn Midlo Hall, *Africans in Colonial Louisiana*, 7; and Giraud, *History of French Louisiana*, 182–83.

24. Ingersoll, *Mammon and Manon*, 11; and Gwendolyn Midlo Hall, *Africans in Colonial Louisiana*, 7–10.

25. Gwendolyn Midlo Hall, *Databases for the Study*.

26. See Spear, *Sex, Race, and Social Order*, 57–58; and Morrisson and Snyder, "Income Inequality of France," 66.

27. For mortality rates in early Louisiana, see Pritchard, "Population in French America," 207.

28. A number of historians, especially those focusing on the development of the North American colonial landscape as a whole, incorrectly argue that, beyond the first

generation, France and Spain used Louisiana primarily as a penal colony. For this understanding of events, see, most notably, Taylor, *American Colonies*, 384–87; and Sublette, *World That Made New Orleans*, 52–53.

29. Lachance, "Growth of the Free," 206, 213; Ingersoll, *Mammon and Manon*, 11; and Paul Lachance, "Louisiana Census Data Set," in Gwendolyn Midlo Hall, *Databases for the Study*.

30. Ingersoll, *Mammon and Manon*, 10–11; and Gravier, *La colonisation de la Louisiane*, 73–76.

31. Gravier, *La colonisation de la Louisiane*, 74; and Gayarré, *Louisiana*, 318.

32. Rieder and Rieder, *Crew and Passenger Registration Lists*, 81; and Marriage of Christophe Delaune, Sieur de Louisiane, and Leocade Marguerite Aucoin, "Registre des Mariages pour la Colonie de la Louisiane, 1718–1763," January 1753, book 5, NOPL.

33. Gwendolyn Midlo Hall, *Databases for the Study*; Lachance, "Louisiana Census Data Set."

34. On the Ursulines, see Emily Clark, *Voices*, introduction; and Emily Clark, *Masterless Mistresses*, esp. 41–83, 169–70, 206. By 1770, the Ursulines owned sixty-one bondpeople who lived at the plantation. By 1795, they had twenty-four living in New Orleans at the Ursuline convent in the Vieux Carré. Clark contextualizes these numbers: "The number of bondpeople they claimed in 1731 put them among the top 30 percent of slaveowners among those with plantations on the Lower Mississippi River. In 1770, they were among the top 6 percent of slaveholders in this category" (*Masterless Mistresses*, 169).

35. See Ingersoll, *Mammon and Manon*, 9–12; Dawdy, *Buildings the Devil's Empire*, 29–30; and Berlin, *Many Thousands Gone*, 205–8.

36. Some recent scholarship makes the argument for a class-based society in French New Orleans. See Dawdy, *Building the Devil's Empire*, 142–43. Dawdy claims that New Orleans maintained "a hierarchy based on legal status, particularly sensitive to degrees of servitude." She also notes, however, that "considerable fluidity remained among the other social classes," and that "racial features were probably noted as an approximation of legal status and clan pedigree." Thomas N. Ingersoll argues that although "class" differentiation existed in white society, the lowest stratum of white society—a tie between indentured servants and soldiers—still stood above any and all black "classes," making the social structure in French New Orleans inherently racial, or biracial. See Ingersoll, *Mammon and Manon*, 12–17.

37. On the French rejection of Native Americans as slaves in the *pays d'en haut*, see Richard White, *Middle Ground*.

38. Curran, *Anatomy of Blackness*, 120–21.

39. Barrère, *Dissertation sur la cause physique*; and Klaus, "History of the Science of Pigmentation," 7–8.

40. Meckel, "Recherches anatomiques," 99; and Curran, *Anatomy of Blackness*, 124.

41. The notion of racial degeneration was also made popular by Georges-Louis Leclerc, Comte de Buffon, in his important decades-long (1749–88) study, *Histoire naturelle, générale et particulière*. Hereafter, most references to this work come from Leclerc, "Natural History, General and Particular"; or Curran, *Anatomy of Blackness*.

42. A total of 2,653 indentured laborers arrived in Louisiana between 1718 and 1731. See Ingersoll, *Mammon and Manon*, tables 1 and 4; and Usner, *Indians, Settlers, and Slaves*, 46–49.

43. Raphael Bernard, n.l. v. Cadot, May 9–10, 1724, Records of the Superior Council (hereafter RSC), in *Louisiana Historical Quarterly* 1, no. 3 (1917): 238–42; and Raphael Bernard, n.l. v. Dumanoir, July 26, 1724, September 20, 1724, RSC, ibid., 242.

44. Langlois, *Des villes pour la Louisiane française*, 340–41.

45. Usner, "From African Captivity," 34–35; Sophie White, *Wild Frenchmen*, 47–48, 245n66; and Gayarré, *Louisiana*, 513–14.

46. Spear, *Race, Sex, and Social Order*, 54.

47. See "Petition for Fair Treatment," September 1, 1725, RSC, *Louisiana Historical Quarterly* 2, no. 1 (January 1919): 468; "Petition for Fair Treatment," October 22, 1725, RSC, *Louisiana Historical Quarterly* 2, no. 1 (January 1919): 479; and Spear, *Race, Sex, and Social Order*, 54.

48. See Spear, *Race, Sex, and Social Order*, 310. For an explanation of who and what an *engagé* was, see "Des serviteurs libres," chap. 2 of title 6, *Du maitre et du serviteur*, in *A Digest of the Civil Laws Now in Force in the Territory of Orleans* (New Orleans: Bradford & Anderson, 1803), 37.

49. Dawdy, *Building the Devil's Empire*, 156–57; and Charles R. Maduell Jr., comp. and trans., *The Census Tables for the French Colony of Louisiana from 1699 through 1732* (Baltimore: Genealogical Publishing Company, 1972), vi–xix, 41–72. The term *mulâtre* also first appears in this census, but as a seeming afterthought listed between columns at the end of each section, and tallied only in the total population. As we will see below, the census takers did not seem to know where to place this newly recognized population.

50. Dawdy, *Building the Devil's Empire*, 155; and Sala-Molins, *Le code noir*, 219, 243. All further quotations and citations of the Code Noir are from this source and edition.

51. Le Page du Pratz, *History of Louisiana*, 308.

52. Charlevoix, *Journal d'un voyage*, 6:15; also see Sophie White, *Wild Frenchmen*, 203–4. All translations, unless otherwise noted, are by the author.

53. Curran, *Anatomy of Blackness*, 82–85.

54. For a detailed and profoundly nuanced analysis of the meaning of Native American skin tone and foreign ideas about its natural appearance, see Sophie White, *Wild Frenchmen*, 120–25, 192–95, and 203–7; and Havard, *Empire et métissages*, 570–78.

55. There are two important things to note here. First, the belief that indigenous people had a "second skin" that could be shed, allowing them to accept, understand, and enact the cultural and social features of French whiteness, did not protect them from the act and status of enslavement. The "manipulability" of Indians' external appearance only related to the possibility of assimilation and at least qualified acceptance. It did not, however, suggest an assumption of assimilation and acceptance or any legal or practical right to it. Second, native people in early French Louisiana, and especially French New Orleans, were not met with a strict ultimatum of assimilation or abject cultural annihilation. Although colonial in nature, the relationship between native peoples and French authorities in the young colony was extremely complex and fluid. Like many claims based more on maps than people, the French hold on New Orleans and its envi-

rons did not erase what came before it. Indeed, a number of remarkable studies over the past thirty years have shown conclusively that New Orleans and Louisiana under the French was as much a native space as a French colonial space. The relationship, both on the ground and in the minds of French colonial administrators and thinkers, between people of African descent and native people along the French colonial frontier has not received as much scholarly focus, and although it is beyond the practicable scope of this book, it is a topic ripe for future study. On Native American enslavement and racial identity, adopted and given, see Englebert, "Making Indians"; Havard, "'Protection' and 'Unequal Alliance'"; Brasseaux, *French, Cajun, Creole, Houma*, chaps. 1 and 4; Havard, *L'Amérique fantôme*, chap. 1; and Vidal, *Caribbean New Orleans*, chap. 2. On the creation and maintenance of native spaces in colonial North America, and particularly French Louisiana, see Usner, *Indians, Settlers, and Slaves*, chaps. 1 and 3; Carson, "Sacred Circles and Dangerous People"; Usner, *American Indians*, chaps. 1 and 2; William Brown, "Mask of the Colonizer"; Elizabeth Ellis, "Petite Nation with Powerful Networks"; and Holly, "From Itsa'ti to Charlestown." For the quote in the text, see Sophie White, *Wild Frenchmen*, 204 and Kupperman, "Presentment of Civility," 194.

56. Gen. 9:21–25 (King James Version).

57. Augustine, *City of God*, 104–6; and Curran, *Anatomy of Blackness*, 78.

58. By the 1720s and 1730s, the concept of polygenesis, or multiple human origins, a largely heretical belief, had started to fade as the leading theory of human difference. Most philosophes and thinkers in Europe had switched to a monogenist system in which biblical lore served as the basis for human development, and any difference in appearance (especially that of skin color) developed over time rather than as result of separate origins. In other words, humanity was but a single species with multiple variations of color and physiological features. See Curran, *Anatomy of Blackness*, chap. 2.

59. Dubos, *Réflexions critiques*, 2:14–15, 251–52, HNOC; Curran, *Anatomy of Blackness*, 79–80.

60. On varieties of humankind, see Barrère, *Dissertation sur la cause physique*, 11–15; Leclerc, "Natural History, General and Particular," 17–20; Terrell, *Man Who Flattened the Earth*, 122–26; and Curran, *Anatomy of Blackness*, 84–86, 91–98. On humoral theory, see Vardi, *Physiocrats and the World*, 61–66; and Wheeler, *Complexion of Race*, 27–29.

61. Author #2, papers submitted to the Académie Royale des Sciences de Bordeaux, 1741, in Curran, *Anatomy of Blackness*, 85. Curran provides the first academic investigation of a series of papers submitted by the top anatomists and thinkers in Europe to the Académie Royale des Sciences de Bordeaux on the topic "What is the physical cause of blackness and African hair?" These sixteen papers, Curran claims, provide the clearest picture of how the highest thinkers in Europe understood and interpreted the pigmentary differences between Europeans and Africans, and their causes.

62. Barrère, *Dissertation sur la cause physique*, 9–13; Fontenelle, "Observations de physique générale," 15–17; Terrell, *Man Who Flattened the Earth*, 124–26; and Leclerc, "Natural History, General and Particular," 17–20.

63. Cohen, *French Encounter with Africans*, 9–11; also see Sophie White, *Wild Frenchmen*, 169.

64. Barrère, *Dissertation sur la cause physique*, 11.

65. Author #4, Papers Submitted to the Académie Royale des Sciences de Bordeaux, 1741, in Curran, *Anatomy of Blackness*, 85.
66. Spear, *Race, Sex, and Social Order*, 64.
67. Gwendolyn Midlo Hall, "Saint Domingue," 184–86, where she refers to Peytraud, *L'esclavage aux Antilles françaises*, 156.
68. Moreau de Saint-Méry, *Loix et constitutions*, 2:185.
69. "Extrait de la lettre du ministre à M. Dacasse," February 5, 1698, in Moreau de Saint-Méry, *Loix et constitutions*, 1:579.
70. "Extrait de la lettre à le marquis de Fayet," March 29, 1735, in Moreau de Saint-Méry, *Loix et constitutions*, 3:420. Also see Gwendolyn Midlo Hall, "Saint Domingue," 184–86.
71. Petit, *Traité sur le gouvernement*, 2:72–75.
72. d'Auberteuil, *Considérations sur l'état present*, 2:73; and Gwendolyn Midlo Hall, "Saint Domingue," 184.
73. Le Cat, *Traité de la couleur*, 58–59, Troy H. Middleton Library, Louisiana State University. Some translation and discussion of Le Cat can be found in Curran, *Anatomy of Blackness*, 125.
74. Curran discusses this at length in *Anatomy of Blackness*, 127–129. For the original, see De Pauw, "Recherches philosophiques," 1:97–100 and 175–83.
75. Sens, "Dutch Debates on Overseas Man," 82–83; and Wokler, "Ideology and the Origins," 698–99.
76. Sala-Molins, *Le code noir*, art. 6. Also see Spear, *Race, Sex, and Social Order*, 62–63.
77. The word *affranchi[t/s]* translates to "freed," but in the 1720s and 1730s the term loosely meant "free," regardless of birth.
78. Sala-Molins, *Le code noir*, art. 6. The original text of the Code Noir reads, "Défendons aussi à nos dits sujets blancs, même aux Noirs affranchis ou nés libres, de vivre en concubinage avec des esclaves."
79. Recall the theories espoused by de Pauw and Le Cat and discussed by Curran above. See Curran, *Anatomy of Blackness*, 124–29; Le Cat, *Traité de la couleur*, 58–59; and de Pauw, "Recherches *philosophiques*," 1:175–83. Even the likes of Thomas Jefferson saw lightening, or, as he called it, "cleaning," as having the potential to rid the free population of African blood. As Andrew Burstein writes, Jefferson "was clear in his mind that 'cleaning the issue of Negro blood,' as he put it, occurred when a quadroon (one-fourth black, like Sally [his mistress and slave]) bore a white man's child." On top of this, Jefferson believed the remaining free nonwhite population would have to be "deported" from the United States. See Burstein, *Jefferson's Secrets*, 145–47.
80. It is important to note that Article 6 of the 1724 Code Noir largely ignores gender as a legal variable. Although Brett Rushforth and Jennifer Palmer have individually shown that custom almost universally bound children to the condition or status of their mothers, legal codes varied drastically. Indeed, although certainly customary throughout French colonial North America, the condition of children does not come up in Article 6. Implicitly, of course, children of two slaves were born enslaved. But the only clear reference to gender or sex of any kind in Article 6—the only section of the law di-

rectly governing sexual relationships between different races and conditions—forbids "white subjects, *of either sex*," from "contracting marriage with Blacks" (Sala-Molins, *Le code noir*, 76; emphasis added). In all other cases, the code uses gender-neutral language—"free people," "slaves," "Blacks," "Negroes," "French," etc. Although it is difficult to say with certainty, given that French is a heavily gendered language and plural nouns referring to persons generally take the masculine form unless only referring to female subjects, it is possible to see such widespread use of gender-neutral language in Article 6 as a conscious choice by its authors to avoid turning custom into law. For more detailed discussions of the dynamics of gender, status, and family in eighteenth- and nineteenth-century North America, see Rushforth, *Bonds of Alliance*, chap. 2; Palmer, *Intimate Bonds*, chaps. 4 and 6; Moitt, *Women and Slavery*, chap. 5; Daina Ramey Berry, *Price for Their Pound*, chap. 1; and Hunter, *Bound in Wedlock*, chap. 2.

81. A number of scholars have discussed the issue of interracial sex in the Code Noir. The above discussion was based in part on these studies as well as personal interpretation. See Spear, *Race, Sex, and Social Order*, 60–66; Powell, *Accidental City*, 286–87; Gary B. Mills, *Forgotten People*, 21–22; and Sterkx, *Free Negro in Antebellum Louisiana*, 16–18. For a detailed description of the other articles of the Code Noir, especially those related to slaves' "rights," see Spear, *Race, Sex, and Social Order*, 61–64.

82. For a concise discussion of early eighteenth-century definitions of *nègre*, see Peabody, *"There Are No Slaves,"* 59–61.

83. Raphael, n.l. v. Cadot, May 9–10, 1724, SRC, in *Louisiana Historical Quarterly*, vol. 1 (1918): 238–42; and Raphael, n.l. v. Dumanoir, July 26, September 20, 1724, SRC, in *Louisiana Historical Quarterly*, vol. 1 (1918): 242.

84. "Contract of Scipion and Simon, *nègres libres*, and Jean La Croix," July 17, 1731, #1739031003, RSC; and *Census of Inhabitants along the Mississippi River*, 1731, Archives Nationales de France, cited in Spear, *Race, Sex, and Social Order*, 93, and held in NOPL.

85. The earliest example of the word's usage, according to the Oxford English Dictionary, is Alemán, *Rogue*, 2:328. In later years, these mixed-race people of Portuguese ancestry and African culture came be called Luso-Africans. See Mark, *"Portuguese" Style and Luso-African Identity*; and Brooks, *Eurafricans in Western Africa*.

86. See "Extrait de la lettre du ministre à M. Ducasse," February 5, 1698, in Moreau de Saint-Méry, *Loix et constitutions*, 2:209; and "Extrait de la lettre à le marquis de Fayet," March 29, 1735, in Moreau de Saint-Méry, *Loix et constitutions*, 3:47–48. Also see Gwendolyn Midlo Hall, "Saint Domingue," 184–86.

87. See Johnston, *Race Relations in Virginia*, 175–76; and Williamson, *New People*, 8–9.

88. "An Act for the Better Preventing of a Spurious and Mixt Issue, October 24, 1705," *Acts and Resolves, Public and Private, of the Province of the Massachusetts Bay* (Boston: Wright and Potter, 1869), 1:578–79; Spear, *Race, Sex, and Social Order*, 64; and Jordan, "American Chiaroscuro," 184n2.

89. Cooper, *Statutes at Large*, 3:20. Also see Williamson, *New People*, 17.

90. Leroy-Beaulieu, *De la colonisation*, 1:165; also quoted, in slightly different form, in Spear, *Race, Sex, and Social Order*, 64.

91. Spear, *Race, Sex, and Social Order*, 63–65.

92. "Funeral of Catherine," July 13, 1732, Sacramental Records of St. Louis Cathedral, Archives of the Archdiocese of New Orleans, book 1, 76; also see Spear, *Race, Sex, and Social Order*, 96, 263.

93. *Recensement général de la ville de la Nlle. Orléans*, 1732, Bibliothèque et Archives Canada, accessed January 15, 2013, http://collectionscanada.gc.ca/. The original is housed at the Archives des Colonies, Archives Nationales de France, series G1, as cited most clearly in Spear, *Race, Sex, and Social Order*, 261–64. Also see Maduell, *Census Tables for the French Colony*, 133–47.

94. For a detailed account of how racial terminology and taxonomy appeared in early French New Orleans (particularly as it related to the codification of slavery in French colonial society) that challenges previous accounts of a strict racial binary and unflagging two-caste system in the colonial town, see Vidal, *Caribbean New Orleans*, 369–78.

95. Thomas Jefferson to Francis Gray, March 4, 1815, quoted in Burstein, *Jefferson's Secrets*, 146. Likewise, see the theories of racial bleaching discussed in Curran, *Anatomy of Blackness*, 124–29; Le Cat, *Traité de la couleur*, 58–59; and de Pauw, "Recherches philosophiques," 1:179–80.

96. There is very little recent scholarship on this subject not focused on the twentieth century. For somewhat antiquated but still generally useful material, see Zack, *Race and Mixed Race*, 79–80; and Williamson, *New People*, 9–10. For a brief but more recent approach, see Sophie White, *Wild Frenchmen*, 137–38, 149–57.

97. Sala-Molins, *Le code noir*, art. 34. Also see Spear, *Race, Sex, and Social Order*, 66–67.

98. Sala-Molins, *Le code noir*, art. 53.

99. As far as censuses are concerned, the free colored population of New Orleans increased from twelve individuals in 1732 to eighty in 1763. One must take census data with a grain of salt, however. Nearly every scholar to study the topic has asserted that the censuses severely underrepresented free people of color in New Orleans and the surrounding areas. See Dawdy, *Building the Devil's Empire*, 178–79, 292n93; Spear, *Race, Sex, and Social Order*, 94–95; Sophie White, *Wild Frenchmen*, 36; Bell, *Revolution, Romanticism*, 11; and Hanger, *Bounded Lives, Bounded Places*, 22–23, 184n11. Hanger shows that ninety-seven free colored individuals resided in New Orleans in 1771. Just six years later, that number had increased to 312 (*Bounded Lives, Bounded Places*, 22, table 1.3).

100. Dawdy, *Building the Devil's Empire*, 181.

101. The term *métis(se)* referred to anyone of mixed race in general, but usually half white and half black. Strictly translated as "mongrel" (*métis*) or "crossed" (*métissé*), *métis(se)* became the standard term for mixed-race individuals who had adopted the African culture of their *indigène* mothers in the French colonies of West Africa, specifically Senegal, Saint-Louis (later part of Senegal), and Côte d'Ivoire. The term never became part of the vernacular in colonial Louisiana, although it does appear in official documents occasionally. French colonial Louisianians preferred the term *mulâtre(sse)* in describing people of mixed ancestry. See Hilary Jones, *Métis of Senegal*.

102. See Certificate of Manumission, July 20, 1767, RSC; also see Spear, *Race, Sex, and Social Order*, 86–87.

103. *Certificat de liberté pour Marie Louise*, November 14, 1745, RSC; Gwendolyn Midlo Hall, *Africans in Colonial Louisiana*, 260; Spear, *Race, Sex, and Social Order*, 85.

104. Gwendolyn Midlo Hall, *Databases for the Study*. Between 1740 and 1811, Vincent Le Porche bought and sold 306 slaves out of his plantation in Pointe Coupée Parish, northwest of New Orleans. No fewer than fifty of the slaves were of mixed race. He freed just ten of them. To this day, the Le Porche family straddles the color line in Pointe Coupée.

105. See Brasseaux, Fontenot, and Oubre, *Creoles of Color*; Domínguez, *White by Definition*; Ingersoll, *Mammon and Manon*; Din, *Spaniards, Planters, and Slaves*.

106. Cécile Vidal, "The 1769 Oath of Fidelity and Allegiance to the Spanish Crown of the French 'Company of the Free Mulattoes and Negroes of This Colony of Louisiana': Dual Genealogy of a Social Event." Unpublished paper presented at the American Historical Association Conference, New Orleans, Louisiana, January 3, 2013. These findings also appear, expanded and contextualized, in Vidal's groundbreaking book, *Caribbean New Orleans*, 414–33.

107. Most scholars see French New Orleans as a fundamentally status-based society, arguing that it was broken up into two distinct categories—free and slave. To these scholars, race or skin color had no bearing on the social order, and that rights were granted on the basis of status alone. Shannon Dawdy, who fully rejects race as a structural force in the free community, argues that "Creole New Orleans was a hierarchical society in which slavery was a defining fact of life. Disparities in the quality of life between the legally free and unfree could be great. But these were *legal* categories tied to specific personal histories and specific documented transactions" (*Building the Devil's Empire*, 179–80; emphasis in original).

108. Domínguez, *White by Definition*, 24.

109. Powell, *Accidental City*, 228; and Lachance, "Politics of Fear," 240–51.

110. See Gatien de Salmon to the Ministry of the Colonies, October 10, 1739, in Gwendolyn Midlo Hall, *Africans in Colonial Louisiana*, 174. Hall quotes Gatien de Salmon, an administrator in New Orleans, complaining that only "one-fifth of the colony's *nègres*" were eligible for service in the militia. In his report, Salmon states that he has 270 slaves and fifty "*nègres libres*."

111. See Vidal, "1769 Oath of Fidelity."

112. See Berlin, *Slaves without Masters*, 108–9; Powell, *Accidental City*, chaps. 9 and 10; Hanger, *Bounded Lives, Bounded Places*, chap. 1.

113. Kimberly Hanger argues that the *pardo* and *moreno* militias directly created the familial and social links that formed the colored Creole "elite" of the antebellum era. See Hanger, *Bounded Lives, Bounded Places*, 87–91.

CHAPTER 2. The Vitriolic Blood of a Negro

1. 1801 Militia Rosters, May 1, 1801, folio 358, roll 160–A, Papeles Procedentes de la Isla de Cuba, Archivo General de Indias (herafter PC-AGI), Hill Memorial Library, Louisiana State University, Baton Rouge, Louisiana (hereafter LSU-HM).

2. There is much speculation as to the number of light-skinned free coloreds in New Orleans at the turn of the century. Using census data, which admittedly provides only a rough estimate if taken by itself, one can determine that there were 624 free colored men

between the ages of fifteen and sixty-five with at least half European ancestry in 1801. That is out of a total free colored population of 1,566, which included darker-skinned men (*morenos*) as well as women and children. See ibid., folios 347–68; Hanger, *Bounded Lives, Bounded Places*, 113, 115 (table 4.2); and Flannery, *New Orleans in 1805*, 5–8.

3. Perkins, *Who's Who in Colored Louisiana*, 109; Hanger, *Bounded Lives, Bounded Places*, 86–87, 107–12, 136–37; and Aslakson, "Making Race," 162.

4. Aslakson, "Making Race," 157.

5. Hanger, *Bounded Lives, Bounded Places*, 125; Aslakson, "Making Race," 162; and Emily Clark, *Strange History*, 90–100.

6. City Treasury Accounts, 1787, vol. 3, no. 2, Records and Deliberations of the Cabildo, New Orleans Public Library Special Collections (hereafter NOPL); 1795 Census, folio 34, roll 1-B, PC-AGI, LSU-HM; and Hanger, *Bounded Lives, Bounded Places*, 126.

7. See Soulié Family Ledgers, October 30 and December 21, 1844; September 20, 1845, Historic New Orleans Collection, New Orleans, La. Also, Octave de Armas, Notary, book 61, #161, 1853, New Orleans Notarial Archives (hereafter NONA).

8. Joseph died intestate in 1868 with an estate worth an estimated $17,000, including inheritance from his father and mother, nine slaves, and some property brought to the marriage by his wife, Josepha Rodriguez, a quadroon of Spanish descent and native of New Orleans. In 1861, Jean Louis claimed assets valuing $15,959, including two slaves and four lots in the faubourg Marigny. See "Inventory of the Estate of Joseph Dolliole," Succession of Joseph Dolliole, *fils*, March 31, 1868, #32,582, Second District Court, NOPL; "Inventory," September 18, 1849, Succession of Joseph Valcour Dolliole, f.m.c., 1854, #8,126, Second District Court, NOPL; "Inventory of the Estate of Jean Louis Dolliole," Succession of Jean Louis Dolliole, March 4, 1861, #17,714, Second District Court, NOPL; and *1840 Manuscript Census*, NOPL.

9. Emily Clark notes that a "Jean Doliole," who, if one traces the records, is clearly Jean Louis Dolliole, witnessed ten weddings between 1812 and 1818 alone. Some, but not all, of these weddings were of fellow militiamen. Joseph Dolliole witnessed at least four marriages between 1810 and 1830, including both of his brother's weddings. See Marriage of Joseph Beaulieu and Josepha Jalío, April 24, 1811; Marriage of Juan Castelan and Juana Nivet, November 22, 1811; Marriage of François Boisdoré and Marie Joseph Sophie Olivier, June 3, 1828; and Louis Découdreaux and Rose Fillier, April 4, 1830, *Libro Primero de Matrimonios de Negros y Mulatos de la Parroquia de Sn. Luis de la Nueva Orleans, 1777–1830* (hereafter "Libro Primero"), Archives of the Archdiocese of New Orleans (hereafter AANO).

10. Succession of Jean Louis Dolliole, March 4, 1861, #17,714, Second District Court, NOPL; and Succession of Joseph Dolliole, *fils*, March 31, 1868, #32,582, Second District Court, NOPL.

11. 1793 Militia Roster, November 6–7, 1793, folio 286–301, roll 159-B; and 1801 Militia Roster, May 1, 1801, folio 347–63, roll 160-A, PC-AGI, LSU-HM.

12. The best, most concise treatment of Latin American racial taxonomy is Mörner, *Race Mixture in the History*, 57–59.

13. See chap. 1 of this work; Powell, *Accidental City*, chaps. 5 and 7; Mörner, *Race Mix-*

ture in the History, 53–62; Spear, Race, Sex, and Social Order, 129–37; and Aubert, "'Blood of France'."

14. Gwendolyn Midlo Hall, Africans in Colonial Louisiana, 277–86; Ingersoll, "Slave Trade"; Ford, Deliver Us from Evil, 102–5; and Powell, Accidental City, 262–69.

15. Gwendolyn Midlo Hall, Africans in Colonial Louisiana, 279; and Powell, Accidental City, 262–63.

16. For the Enlightenment theories of "corruption" and "degeneration," see Barrère, Dissertation sur la cause physique; Klaus, "History of the Science of Pigmentation," 7–8; Leclerc, "Natural History, General and Particular"; and Curran, Anatomy of Blackness, 120–24.

17. For statistics on manumissions in the late Spanish period, see Hanger, Bounded Lives, Bounded Places, 28–33. According to Hanger (29, fig. 1.3), of the 1,825 emancipated slaves for whom a racial designation was given, 54 percent were morenos (fully African), 37 percent pardos (one-half African, one-half European), 6 percent cuarterón (one-fourth African, three-fourths European), and 3 percent grifo (three-fourths African, one-fourth European).

18. Branche, Colonialism and Race, 90–94; Mörner, Race Mixture in the History, 55–56; and Spear, Race, Sex, and Social Order, 158–59.

19. Konetzke, Colección de Documentos, 1:147; also cited in Mörner, Race Mixture in the History, 55. All Spanish translations done by translator Ian Malcolm Bromham and the author, unless otherwise noted. All French translations done by the author, unless otherwise noted.

20. Konetzke, Colección de documentos, 1:147–48; Mörner, Race Mixture in the History, 56; and Herzog, Defining Nations, 144–45.

21. See Parry, Spanish Seaborne Empire, 334–36.

22. Ibid., 344–45; and Lafaye, Quetzalcóatl and Guadalupe, 147, 196–98.

23. Lafaye, Quetzalcóatl and Guadalupe, 107–8; and Eastman, Preaching Spanish Nationalism, 125–26.

24. Lafaye, Quetzalcóatl and Guadalupe, 107–9; Parry, Spanish Seaborne Empire, 335; and Patch, Maya Revolt and Revolution, 85–87.

25. Also known as the Creole Revolt, the Americano Revolt is largely cited as the catalyst for Mexican national consciousness. Most scholars claim that from the mid-sixteenth century to the mid-seventeen century, the Spanish Crown slowly lost its grip on colonial Mexico, and the ideological nation of Mexico was born. See Parry, Spanish Seaborne Empire, chap. 18; and Brading, First America, 478–80, 535–37.

26. Kuznesof, "Ethnic and Gender Influences," 154–62; Nieto-Phillips, Language of Blood, 18–22; and Fuchs, Passing for Spain, 1–5.

27. Kuznesof, "Ethnic and Gender Influences," 160–61; Fuchs, Passing for Spain, 5–6; and Carrera, Imagining Identity in New Spain, 9–10.

28. For a brief description of the history of castas, see Mörner, Race Mixture in the History, 53; and Carrera, Imagining Identity in New Spain, 35–36.

29. Twinam, Public Lives, Private Secrets, 42–43; and Carrera, Imagining Identity in New Spain, 6–11.

30. Mörner, *Race Mixture in the History*, 54; Spear, *Sex, Race, and Social Order*, 158; and Carrera, *Imagining Identity in New Spain*, 36–38.

31. Ronald J. Morgan, *Spanish American Saints*, 130–32; and McCaa, "*Calidad, Clase*, and Marriage," 477–78.

32. Carrera, *Imagining Identity in New Spain*, 6. Earlier historians of colonial Spanish America focused entirely upon skin color. Magnus Mörner, one of the pioneers of Spanish racial studies, referred to the *Casta* (and *calidad*) System as a "pigmentocracy." Other, more recent scholarship has rightfully complicated the issue, claiming that skin color and pigmentation played a major role, but economic and social factors also served as criteria for categorization. See Mörner, *Race Mixture in the History*, 54; and McCaa, "*Calidad, Clase*, and Marriage," 477.

33. Carrera, *Imagining Identity in New Spain*, 36–37, 66–67; Twinam, *Public Lives, Private Secrets*, 25–27; Vento, *Mestizo*, 51–55; and Jack D. Forbes, *Africans and Native Americans*, 160–63.

34. Twinam, *Public Lives, Private Secrets*, 42.

35. "Petición de aclaración de la partida de bautismo de Margarita Castañeda, colocados en los libros correspondientes de los de color quebrado siendo ella esagñola," in Castro, *Biblioteca de autores españoles*, 293. This case is also cited in Carrera, *Imagining Identity in New Spain*, 3–11; and Bass, *Drama of the Portrait*, 101–5.

36. Magnus Mörner provides two fascinating and detailed maps of racial nomenclature within the Peruvian and Mexican Casta Systems. Only in the Mexican system do *Americanos* (termed "Criollos") appear. See Mörner, *Race Mixture in the History*, 58–60. On the "stain" of Indian blood and the degrees of separation from "absolute impurity," see Twinam, *Public Lives, Private Secrets*, 45–50; Nieto-Phillips, *Language of Blood*, 24–26; and Gutiérrez, "New Mexico, Mestizaje," 271–72.

37. In some regions, *mestizo* referred to those with exactly one-half Spanish and one-half Indian blood. But even in these regions, it was by far the most commonly used designation for mixed-race people as a whole. See the maps in Mörner, *Race Mixture in the History*, 58–60. The issue of legitimacy and purity of lineage will be discussed in much greater detail later in this chapter. The best treatment of the topic in Spanish America is Twinam, *Public Lives, Private Secrets*. Also see Spear, *Race, Sex, and Social Order*, chap. 5, for a more concentrated but highly detailed discussion of family formation in Spanish New Orleans.

38. On the specific *calidads* and required blood mixtures, see Carrera, *Imagining Identity in New Spain*, 66–67; Mörner, *Race Mixture in the History*, 58–60; and McAlister, "Social Structure and Social Change," 356. There are a number of nineteenth century travel texts that lifted the Central American *calidad* map, combined with the well-known racial hierarchy of French Saint Domingue, to describe that of the American South. Most (in)famous is Olmsted, *Cotton Kingdom*, 1:294.

39. See Fuchs, *Passing for Spain*, 3, 15–18, 105–6; Katzew, *Casta Painting*, chap. 2, esp. 56–57; and Knight, *Mexico*, 112–16. For examples of social "passing" in late-colonial Spanish America, see Twinam, *Public Lives, Private Secrets*, chap. 7.

40. See "Petición de aclaración de la partida de bautismo de Margarita Castañeda, colocados en los libros correspondientes de los de color quebrado siendo ella esagñola,"

in Castro, *Biblioteca de autores espagñoles*, 293; Carrera, *Imagining Identity in New Spain*, 3–11; and Bass, *Drama of the Portrait*, 101–5.

41. See Valdés, "Decline of the *Sociedad*," 37–41, tables 1.5, 1.6, 1.8, and 1.10. Also see Carrera, *Imaging Identity in New Spain*, 38–40.

42. See Valdés, "Decline of the *Sociedad*," 37–39, tables 1.5 and 1.8.

43. Ibid., 40–42; Carrera, *Imagining Identity in New Spain*, 40; and Cañizares-Esguerra, *Nature, Empire, and Nation*, 90–93.

44. Rout, *African Experience in Spanish America*, 30–33.

45. Ibid., 59–60, 97–98, 108; Alencastro, "Apprenticeship of Colonization," 163–67; and Eltis, *Rise of African Slavery*, 129–30.

46. See Seed, *American Pentimento*, 148–50; Nash, "Hidden History of Mestizo America," 17–20; and Hood, *Begrimed and Black*, 122–23.

47. See Mörner, *Race Mixture in the History*, 62–65; Rout, *African Experience in Spanish America*, 152, 179–82; and Kinsbruner, *Colonial Spanish-American City*, 86–90.

48. On the emergence of color and *raza* in Brazil and parts of Central America, see Jack D. Forbes, *Africans and Native Americans*, 118–30.

49. "Pedro de León Portocarrero's Description of Lima, Peru," in Mills, Taylor, and Graham, *Colonial Latin America*, 186.

50. The census data no longer survives in manuscript form, but the definitions of each racial category can be found in Englishman Thomas Gage's 1677 travel narrative. See Gage, *New Survey of the West-Indies*, 86–87. Also quoted in Jack D. Forbes, *Africans and Native Americans*, 204.

51. See Mills, Taylor, and Graham, *Colonial Latin America*, 186–89; and Gage, *New Survey of the West-Indies*, 86–87. On Argentina, see Hill, *Hierarchy, Commerce, and Fraud*, 123–25, 210.

52. Jack D. Forbes, *Africans and Native Americans*, 130–32; Carrera, *Imagining Identity in New Spain*, 12–13; and Rosenthal, *Race Mixture*, 93–99.

53. Gage, *New Survey of the West-Indies*, 86–89.

54. Gage, *New Survey of the West-Indies*, 20–23, 203–7, 322.

55. See chap. 1 of this work; Barrère, *Dissertation sur la cause physique*; Leclerc, "Natural History, General and Particular"; and Curran, *Anatomy of Blackness*, 120–22.

56. De Faria y Sousa, *Lusiadas de Luís de Camoens*, 503–4. Also quoted, in shorter form, in Jack D. Forbes, *Africans and Native Americans*, 132.

57. See *Oxford English Dictionary*, s.v. "mulatto"; and Jack D. Forbes, *Africans and Native Americans*, 133–34.

58. See Carrera, *Imagining Identity in New Spain*, 10–12, 37–41; Feijoo y Montenegro, "Color Etiópico," in *Feijoo y Montenegro, Obras Escogidas*, 474–79; Aldridge, "Feijoo and the Problem"; Mörner, *Race Mixture in the History*, 22–27; and Robertson, *Enlightenment*, 294–97.

59. The Bourbon Reforms, as a wider movement, are well studied and well represented in current literature. See Kinsbruner, *Colonial Spanish-American City*, 99–106; Carrera, *Imagining Identity in New Spain*, 10–12, 32–34; Twinam, *Public Lives, Private Secrets*, 17–20; Cope, *Limits of Racial Domination*, 24–25; and Carroll, *Blacks of Colonial Veracruz*, 120–25.

60. Mörner, *Race Mixture in the History*, 54–55; Rout, *African Experience in Spanish America*, xiv–xv, 80–83; and Bennett, *Colonial Blackness*, 185–85, 214–16.

61. O'Crouley, *Description of the Kingdom*, 20–25. Also cited in Carrera, *Imagining Identity in New Spain*, 13–14.

62. The concept of hypo-descent was made famous by the "One-Drop Rule" in the antebellum and Jim Crow–era American South. The notion held that black blood was so strong that a single drop of it in the bloodstream nullified the genetic effects of all other ancestries, save external appearance, which increased in lightness in tandem with the amount of white blood in the body. This is how Jim Crow laws and antebellum restrictions on free people of color justified the enforcement of color-based legislation at the fringes of the color line. See Gotanda, "Critique of 'Our Constitution,'" 258–62; Voss, *Archaeology of Ethnogenesis*, 85–88; and Singh and Iwamasa, "Biracial," 72–76.

63. See Poblete, "Multitasking Mediators," 294–99.

64. See Rout, *African Experience in Spanish America*, 128–29.

65. See ibid., xv; Spear, *Race, Sex, and Social Order*, 311; and Hanger, *Bounded Lives, Bounded Places*, 223.

66. There are many definitions of *pardo* floating around, most of which are similar to that which appears in the text. However, Ann Twinam, in *Public Lives, Private Secrets*, defines the term as the exact opposite of the consensus. In her glossary, Twinam defines a *pardo* as a "dark-skinned person." In turn, she defines *moreno* as the opposite—a "person who is racially mixed; mulatto." Because there are no notes for the section, it is unclear how she came across these definitions.

67. See Mörner, *Race Mixture in the History*, 58–59; Carrera, *Imagining Identity in New Spain*, 65–66; Rout, *African Experience in Spanish America*, 129; and Jack D. Forbes, *Africans and Native Americans*, 122–23.

68. That year, the Crown passed a series of reforms called the *doctrinas de indios*, meant specifically for the American colonies. Among these was a slight reform in the Casta System, to which was added the *albino* category, and which infused many of the new Enlightenment theories into the racial order. On the Enlightenment, see chap. 1 of this work. On the *doctrina de indios*, see Andrien, "Coming of Enlightened Reform," 190–93.

69. See Moreau de Maupertuis, *Venus physique*, 141–42. Also cited in Curran, *Anatomy of Blackness*, 94.

70. See Curran, *Anatomy of Blackness*, 86–95, for a brilliant, detailed discussion of the albino in Enlightenment thought.

71. See chap. 1 of this work; *Recensement général de la ville de la Nlle. Orléans*, 1732, Bibliothèque et Archives Canada, accessed January 15, 2013, http://collectionscanada.gc.ca/; Spear, *Race, Sex, and Social Order*, 261–64; and Charles R. Maduell Jr., comp. and trans., *The Census Tables for the French Colony of Louisiana from 1699 through 1732* (Baltimore: Genealogical Publishing Company, 1972), 133–47.

72. Raphael, n.l. v. Cadot, May 9–10, 1724, SRC, in *Louisiana Historical Quarterly*, vol. 1 (1918): 238–42; and Raphael, n.l. v. Dumanoir, July 26, September 20, 1724, SRC, in *Louisiana Historical Quarterly*, vol. 1 (1918): 242; "Contract of Scipion and Simon, *nègres libres*, and Jean La Croix," July 17, 1731, #1739031003, Records of the Superior Council (hereafter RSC); and Peabody, *"There Are No Slaves,"* 60–61.

73. See Spear, *Race, Sex, and Social Order*, 63–65; and *Recensement général de la ville de la Nlle. Orléans*, 1732, Bibliothèque et Archives Canada.

74. See "Registre des mariages pour la colonie de la Louisiane, 1718–1763," vols. 1–4, NOPL.

75. The one exception to this is Argentina. Still today, Argentina maintains a majority Spanish population, with just three percent of the total population mixed-race, or "nonwhite." See Kingstone, *Political Economy of Latin America*, 9–12.

76. The *mulâtre* population of New Orleans increased from seven individuals in 1732 to sixty-one in 1763. Although these early censuses provide only a rough estimate, nearly every scholar in the field has used them and recognizes them as the best indication we have of the New Orleans population. See Dawdy, *Building the Devil's Empire*, 178–79, 292n93; Spear, *Race, Sex, and Social Order*, 94–95; Sophie White, *Wild Frenchmen*, 36; Bell, *Revolution, Romanticism*, 11; and Hanger, *Bounded Lives, Bounded Places*, 22–23, 184n11.

77. See d'Aubertuil, *Considérations sur l'état present*, 2:73; Carrera, *Imagining Identity in New Spain*, 10–12, 37–41; Feijoo, "Color etiópico," 474–79; and O'Crouley, *Description of the Kingdom*, 20–25.

78. Spear, *Race, Sex, and Social Order*, 100–101.

79. Ibid.; and Domínguez, *White by Definition*, 23–24.

80. Lislet and Carleton, *Laws of Las Siete Partidas*, 1:589–91. Also see Sterkx, *Free Negro in Ante-bellum Louisiana*, 36–37.

81. Lislet and Carleton, *Laws of Las Siete Partidas*, 1:589–90.

82. "Petición de Juan León de Olivera," March 7, 1801, #349, vol. 3, Petitions, Letters, and Decrees of the Cabildo, 1770–1803, NOPL. Also referenced in Din, *Spaniards, Planters, and Slaves*, 234.

83. See "Declaration by fugitive negroes, Manuel and John, belonging to M. de Benac," March 22, 1748, RSC. Also cited in Spear, *Race, Sex, and Social Order*, 270n68.

84. On Congo Square, see Jerah Johnson, *Congo Square in New Orleans*, 10–16. Also see Sala-Molins, *Le code noir*, art. 22.

85. "Manumission of Bautista," March 30, 1771, #112, book 12, Notary Jean-Baptiste Garic, NONA; and "Manumission of Juana Catalina," December 14, 1771, #242, book 44, Notary André Almonaster, NONA. Also see Spear, *Race, Sex, and Social Order*, 116.

86. The only examples of the Cabildo refusing self-purchase are when the appraised value appeared too low to the Cabildo's third appraiser. In these cases, the Cabildo rejected the original price, forcing the slave to continue saving. On most occasions, if a *coartación* petition went to court, the owner had refused the slave's original request. Considering this, the likelihood is slight of any slave successfully saving enough money after his or her petition was denied by both the master and the Cabildo. See Hanger, *Bounded Lives, Bounded Places*, 27–33, 42–44.

87. See Hanger, *Bounded Lives, Bounded Places*, 27, table 1.4; Spear, *Race, Sex, and Social Order*, 117; and Gwendolyn Midlo Hall, *Databases for the Study*.

88. Lislet and Carleton, *Laws of Las Siete Partidas*, 1:587–88; and "Ordinances and Instructions of Don Alexander O'Reilly," in French, *Historical Collections of Louisiana*, 5:285.

89. Lislet and Carleton, *Laws of Las Siete Partidas*, 1:589.

90. Ibid., 1:592.

91. For the French, see the discussion of Barrère, Meckel, and Le Cat in chap. 1 of this work. For the Spanish, see Carrera, *Imagining Identity in New Spain*, 10–17, 30–44; Feijoo, "Color etiópico," 470–83; Mörner, *Race Mixture in the History*, chap. 4; and O'Crouley, *Description of the Kingdom*, 10–38.

92. "Registry for Baptisms of *Negro esclavo* and *mulatos*," 1771–1783, Sacramental Records of St. Louis Cathedral, Archives of the Archdiocese of New Orleans (hereafter SR-SLC); "Marriages of Negros and Mulattos," 1777–1830, SR-SLC. The origin of the term *tierceron* is unclear. Derived from the French *tierce*, meaning "third," and the Latin suffix *-oon*, meaning "small," "diminutive," or "derived from," the term likely refers to a person of approximately one-third African blood. This would require one *cuarterón* parent and one *mulato* parent, resulting in 37.5 percent African blood. The term itself appears just twice in any record. See "Baptism of Marie Françoise and Jean Pierre Cuillon," book 23, #48 and 49, SR-SLC.

93. Emily Clark, *Strange History*, 77–78; and "Pragmática Sanción para evitar el abuso de contraer matrimonios desiguales, El Pardo, March 23, 1776," in Konetzke, *Colección de documentos*, vol. 3, book 1, 406–13.

94. See "Libro de bautizado esclavos y gente de color," 1777–1802, 5 vols., SR-SLC; Spear, *Race, Sex, and Social Order*, 161; Emily Clark, *Strange History*, 77–78, 237–38; and Baade, "Law of Slavery," 44–45.

95. "Pragmática Sanción," in Konetzke, *Colección de documentos*, vol. 3, book 1, 408–9; Emily Clark, *Strange History*, 77; Hanger, *Bounded Lives, Bounded Places*, 92; and Twinam, *Public Lives, Private Secrets*, 44–48.

96. See Emily Clark, *Strange History*, 77–78; and Twinam, *Public Lives, Private Secrets*, 44–46, for brief discussions of the *Real Pragmática*, legitimacy, and marriage.

97. "Pragmática Sanción," in Konetzke, *Colección de documentos*, vol. 3, book 1, 412–13. The term "coyote" was used primarily in northern New Spain, in what is now the American West, to describe people of mixed African, Indian, and European blood.

98. For the final quote, which came from a 1778 amendment to the *Pragmática*, see Saether, "Bourbon Absolutism and Marriage Reform," 490–91; Mörner, *Race Mixture in the History*, 38–39; and Emily Clark, *Strange History*, 78.

99. Din, *Spaniards, Planters, and Slaves*, 288; and Miceli, "Influence of the Roman Catholic Church," 93.

100. For an account of the sex ratios within both the colored and white populations in Spanish New Orleans, see Hanger, *Bounded Lives, Bounded Places*, 22–23, table 1.3. According to Hanger, there were 175 white men for every 100 white women in 1777. By 1805, that ratio had decreased to 115:100.

101. There are dozens of examples of insular godparenthood under the French. See "St. Louis Cathedral Baptisms," 1731–1733, 1744–1753, and 1759–1762, books 1, 3, and 5, SR-SLC.

102. Lislet and Carleton, *Laws of Las Siete Partidas*, 1:591; and Hanger, *Bounded Lives, Bounded Places*, 21, table 1.2.

103. See Kinnaird, *Spain in the Mississippi Valley*, 2:196; Census of New Orleans, November 6, 1791, NOPL; Flannery, *New Orleans in 1805*, 5–8; and Hanger, *Bounded Lives, Bounded Places*, 18, table 1.1.

104. These numbers and percentages come from the data provided in Hanger, *Bounded Lives, Bounded Places*, 27–29, table 1.4 and fig. 1.3.

105. All 52 of the *graciosa* manumissions used the same or similar language. For the given quotes, see "Manumission of Francoise and Baptiste," February 11, 1772, book 3, #35, Notary André Almonaster y Roxa, NONA. For statistics, see Hanger, *Bounded Lives, Bounded Places*, 27, table 1.4.

106. See "Manumission," March 13, 1773, #58, Notary Pierre (Pedro) Pedesclaux, NONA; "Manumission of Adelaïda," September 4, 1777, book 4, #245, Notary Jean Baptise Garic, NONA; and "Manumission of Raymundo," March 29, 1791, book 12, #296, Notary André Almonaster y Roxa, NONA.

107. "Manumission of Magdalena and Joseph," December 9, 1779, book 12, #553, Notary Jean Baptiste Garic, NONA; and "Manumission of Joseph," December 18, 1779, book 12, #591, Notary Jean Baptiste Garic, NONA. For unknown reasons, Garic drew up two manumission papers for Joseph nine days apart. Also see Sterkx, *Free Negro in Ante-bellum Louisiana*, 48–49.

108. See Hanger, *Bounded Lives, Bounded Places*, 31, table 1.6.

109. On Silvestre, see "Inventory of the Estate of Andres Juen," Succession of Andres Juen, September 14, 1784, Spanish Judicial Records (hereafter SJR), in *Louisiana Historical Quarterly*, vol. 24 (1941): 1262; and Valentin v. Succession of Andres Juen, September 23, 1784, SJR, in *Louisiana Historical Quarterly*, vol. 24 (1941): 1279.

110. Most scholars attribute the growth of marriage and legitimacy to the emergence of the colored militia. They claim that the "free black militia . . . adopted the European family formation for purposes of advancement and community building," and that a man named Noël Carrière, the captain of the *Moreno* Militia, "introduced" this "new set of values in the free black community." See Emily Clark, *Strange History*, chap. 3, esp. 72–84 (quote at 72); and Hanger, *Bounded Lives, Bounded Places*, chap. 4.

111. On the militia as the birth of free colored cultural formation, see Emily Clark, *Strange History*, chap. 3; Hanger, *Bounded Lives, Bounded Places*, chap. 4; and Powell, *Accidental City*, chap. 10, which largely repeats Hanger's argument.

112. See chap. 1 of this work. Noting that the slave trade ended in Louisiana in 1743 and the French period technically ended in 1763, the free colored population had just a single generation to grow through natural increase. Thus, if there were freeborn men or women in French Louisiana with freeborn parents and grandparents, they made up an incalculably small percentage of the population. The vast majority of free people of color were either born slaves or had enslaved parents.

113. "Baptism of François Azémare," St. Louis Cathedral Baptisms and Marriages, 1763–1766, September 9, 1764, SR-SLC. François's father was not marked, as was common in colored baptisms. On Geneviève, see "Petition of Heirs," Succession of Geneviève Dolliole, f.w.c., 1838, Court of Probates, NOPL.

114. "Document A," appended to "Death Certificate," Succession of Christoval alias

Léandre Cheval, f.c.m., December 19, 1839, Court of Probates, NOPL; and Gwendolyn Midlo Hall, *Databases for the Study*.

115. "Declaration of Power of Attorney," Prudence Cheval to Louis Antoine Blanc, December 6, 1796, book 10, #592, Notary Carlos Ximenes, NONA.

116. Her two children were Léandre Cheval, born around 1778, and Françoise Sebatier, born around 1780. See "Death Certificate," Succession of Christoval alias Léandre Cheval, f.c.m., December 19, 1839, Court of Probates, NOPL; and Orleans Parish Death Indices, #126, vol. 6, NOPL.

117. A number of studies have looked into father recognition for a variety of reasons. The most recent, looking at the marriage practices of Saint Domingue refugees in New Orleans and the Atlantic world from 1790 to 1812, is Emily Clark, *Strange History*, chap. 4. Also see Rebecca J. Scott, *Degrees of Freedom*, 12–15; and Spear, *Race, Sex, and Social Order*, 142–45, and more generally chap. 5.

118. There are dozens of examples. In general, see "Registry for Baptisms of *Negro esclavo* and *mulatos*," 1771–1783; "St. Louis Cathedral Baptisms," 1772–1776, 1777–1786, and 1786–1796; and "Libro de bautizados de negros y mulatos," 1786–1792, all AANO.

119. Léonard Mazange's paternity is not certain. The baptizing priest did not record a name for Eulalie Mazange in the baptismal register. However, considering that very few other members of the Mazange family lived in New Orleans at the time, and considering Léonard's place in society, it is likely that he and Luison shared at least several sexual encounters in the late 1760s. See Death Certificate of Eulalie Mazange, February 6, 1846, NOPL; Death Certificate of Henriette Prieto, April 25, 1860, NOPL; Long, "Macarty Family of Orleans Parish.". In her article, Long provides a detailed genealogy of Henriette Prieto's children, providing racial designations for both mother and children.

In order of birth, Luison Cheval and Charles Vivant's children were Adelaïde, Constance, Lucile, Louis, Louise, Aimée, and Rosette. See Francisco Broutin, Notary, book 25, #169, June 9, 1793, NONA; and "Petition of Heirs," March 20, 1839, Succession of Louison Cheval, f.w.c., Court of Probates, NOPL; and *Orleans Parish Death Index*, Letter v, Reel 1, NOPL.

120. See Succession of Geneviève Hermina Dolliole, January 7, 1852, NOPL; Succession of Jean Louis Dolliole, March 4, 1861, #17,714, Second Dist. Court, NOPL; Succession of Joseph Dolliole, *fils*, March 31, 1868, #32,582, Second Dist. Court, NOPL; Succession of Joseph Valcour Dolliole, August 30, 1854, #8,126, Second Dist. Court, NOPL; *1850 Manuscript Census*, Orleans Parish, NOPL; Will of Louis Dolliole, 1822, book 3, 242, NOPL; and Succession of Louis Dolliole, 1822, Court of Probates, NOPL.

121. See Succession of Geneviève Hermina Dolliole, January 7, 1852, NOPL; Succession of François Dolliole, 1816, book 2, Court of Probates, NOPL; Succession of Joseph Dolliole, *fils*, March 31, 1868, #32,582, Second Dist. Court, NOPL; and Succession of Joseph Valcour Dolliole, August 30, 1854, #8,126, Second Dist. Court, NOPL.

122. See "Document G," in Succession of Françoise [Toutant] Populus, f.w.c., 1834, Court of Probates, NOPL; Succession of Louise Toutant, f.w.c., 1817, Court of Probates,

NOPL; and Will of Barthelomé Toutant Beauregard, February 27, 1792, book 15, #39, Notary Francois Broutin, NONA.

123. See Succession of Louise Toutant, f.w.c., 1817, Court of Probates, NOPL; and Marriage of Honoré Toutant Beauregard and Maria Jacques Kernion, February 5, 1823, SR-SLC.

124. On "bourgeois morality," see Stewart R. King, *Blue Coat or Powdered Wig*, 181–82.

125. Moreau de Saint-Méry, *Description topographique, physique, civile, politique*, 1279; and Garrigus, *Before Haiti*, 42–43.

126. See Garrigus, *Before Haiti*, 198–200; and Stewart R. King, *Blue Coat or Powdered Wig*, 182–83.

127. On cultural and social endogamy, see Spear, *Race, Sex, and Social Order*, 142–43.

128. See Emily Clark, *Strange History*, 82–83; and Hanger, *Bounded Lives, Bounded Places*, 14–15.

129. "Baptism of Marie Adelaïde Cheval," July 20, 1777, book 13, #21, SR-SLC.

130. Ibid.; and "Petition of Heirs," November 3, 1842, Succession of Marie Thérèze Cheval, f.w.c., 1842, book 6, #450, Court of Probates, NOPL. She was the daughter of Marie Thérèze Cheval, a *mulâtresse*, and Jean Dubois, a white Frenchman.

131. "Baptism of Adelaïde Cazelar," September 15, 1787, book 12, #282, SR-SLC; and "Baptism of Isabelle Pompona Cazelar," May 5, 1791, book 12, #1,223, SR-SLC. Also cited in Emily Clark, *Strange History*, 106–7.

132. "Baptism of Jean Pierre Cazelar," April 18, 1800, book 14, #820, SR-SLC.

133. The Catholic Church viewed all marriages in the same light, regardless of law. See Hanger, *Bounded Lives, Bounded Places*, 92; Bell, *Revolution, Romanticism*, 12–13; and Din, *Spaniards, Planters, and Slaves*, 127–28.

134. See "Marriages of Negros and Mulattos," 1777–1830, SR-SLC; and *Libro Primero de Matrimonios de Negros y Mulatos de la Parroquia de Sn. Luis de la Nueva Orleans, 1777–1830* (hereafter "Libro Primero"), SR-SLC, esp. vols. 1 and 2.

135. "Marriage of Pierre Aubri and Marie Françoise Aurélie," November 16, 1801, *Libro Primero*, vol. 2, SR-SLC.

136. "Marriage of Firmin Perrault and Hortense Toutant," July 14, 1798, *Libro Primero*, vol. 2, SR-SLC.

137. Statistics gathered from *Libro Primero*, vols. 1 and 2, SR-SLC; and Hanger, *Bounded Lives, Bounded Places*, 95. Hanger provides the total number of marriages (93), and the initial number of shared phenotypes (71). Also see "Registry for Baptisms of *Negro esclavo* and *mulatos*," 1771–1783, SR-SLC; and "Libro de bautizado esclavos y gente de color," 1777–1802, 5 vols., SR-SLC.

138. *Libro Primero*, vols. 1 and 2, SR-SLC; and Hanger, *Bounded Lives, Bounded Places*, 95. There are a few examples, most of which occur after 1803, in Emily Clark, *Strange History*, 82–83.

139. McConnell, *Negro Troops of Antebellum Louisiana*, 15.

140. Emily Clark, *Strange History*, 72.

141. Ibid., 79

142. Aslakson, "Making Race," 157.

143. See *Libro Primero*, vols. 1 and 2, SR-SLC.

144. See ibid.

145. See "Marriage of Joseph Leveillé and Marie Thérèze Carrière," May 14, 1786, *Libro Primero*, vol. 1, SR-SLC.

146. Marriage of Philippe Azur and Julia Boisdoré, December 10, 1801, *Libro Primero*, vol. 1, SR-SLC. Julia was the illegitimate daughter of François Dorville and Isabelle Boisdoré. Philippe was twenty years old at the time of his marriage.

147. Philippe Azur, or the Spanish version of the name, "Felipe Asur," does not appear in any of the extant militia rosters. For reference, see 1793 Militia Roster, November 6–7, 1793, folio 286–301, roll 159–B; and 1801 Militia Rosters, May 1, 1801, folio 347–63, roll 160–A, PC-AGI, LSU-HM.

148. See Marriage of Jean Baptiste Boisdoré to Louise Firmin, December 27, 1807, St. Louis Cathedral Marriages, 1806–1821, vol. 1, SR-SLC; Marriage of François Boisdoré to Josephine Sophia Livaudais, May 24, 1807, St. Louis Cathedral Marriages, 1806–1821, vol. 1, SR-SLC; and "Petition of François Boisdoré," January 10, 1843, Succession of François Lemolere Dorville, NOPL.

149. 1795 Census, folio 34, roll 1–B, PC-AGI, LSU-HM; and Hanger, *Bounded Lives, Bounded Places*, 126.

CHAPTER 3. A Sensible Equivalent to the Original Blood

1. The historiography on the War of 1812 is expansive. The most widely cited works are Hickey, *War of 1812*; Latimer, *1812*; and Taylor, *Civil War of 1812*.

2. See Orleans *Gazette*, June 14, 1813; December 20, 1813; May 17, 1814; and August 29, 1814, New Orleans Public Library Special Collections (hereafter NOPL).

3. There is no evidence that either Boisdoré or Moreau spoke or read English. They clearly understood it and probably spoke enough to get by, as they both did direct business with a number of anglophone merchants, tenants, and customers. They also fought in the militia under anglophone officers, which suggests that their orders were given in English. Of course, bilingual friends and colleagues could have easily translated. Given their social status and educated backgrounds, however, both men most probably had a functional understanding of the English language. See Succession of François Boisdoré, December 9, 1859, #16,146, Second District Court, NOPL; and Succession of Manuel Moreau, 1872, #35,212, Second District Court, NOPL.

4. Some court records refer to Isabelle as "Isabelle Gayetano," adopting the Spanish version of the name. As the American period wore on, however, her surname consistently appeared as "Gaitan," the original French spelling. See original manuscripts in A. Boisdoré v. Zabelle Gayetano, f.w.c., wife of B. Populus & als., December 20, 1860, #17,923, Second District Court, NOPL; and "Testimony of Acquaintances," Succession of François Boisdoré, December 9, 1859, #16,146, Second District Court, NOPL.

5. The Casenave family legacy stretched well into the late nineteenth century. Pierre's son, Gadan, continued the family undertaking business beyond the Civil War and Re-

construction, eventually passing it on to his son. By the late antebellum era, the family was among the wealthiest in the city, white or colored. See Testimony of P. Carenov [Casenave], Succession of François Boisdoré, NOPL; and Succession of Pierre Casanave [sic] and Wife Rose Baraquin, December 5, 1865, #28,597 (misplaced at #25,597 in the collection), Second District Court, NOPL.

6. The name Casenave is endemic in colored Creole successions. For some examples, see the successions of François Lacroix, François Boisdoré, Myrtille Courcelle, Joseph Dumas, Jean Louis Dolliole, Joseph Dolliole, *fils*, Rose Gignac, Michel St. Pierre, and Bazile Desmazilière, all located at NOPL.

7. Boisdoré's social relations encompassed nearly every prominent colored Creole of the time. His list of friends, creditors, and debtors crossed the color line and connected him with some of the biggest names in Louisiana, white and colored. In 1859, he owned $6,025 in slaves alone, as well as $40,219 worth of real estate. He also subscribed to both the Louisiana *Gazette* and *L'abeille*, the major English and French newspapers in the city. See "Inventory," February 27, 1860, Succession of François Boisdoré, NOPL. For more on the Société d'Economie, see chap. 5 of this work.

8. In 1808, the Louisiana territorial legislature passed a law requiring all notaries, clerks of court, and judges to include the letters "f.m.c." or "f.w.c." after the names of colored people of any phenotype or claim to European ancestry. There were a number of colored Creoles who received this "exemption." All of them were extremely wealthy, and maintained widespread commercial and social connections. See New Orleans City Directories for 1849, 1850, 1851, 1854, and 1857, all at NOPL; and Succession of François Boisdoré, NOPL. On the 1808 legislation, see Ingersoll, *Mammon and Manon*, 329; Mascou, *New Orleans' Free Men of Color*, 36; and Strekx, *Free Negro in Ante-bellum Louisiana*, 160–61.

9. Many scholars have studied the value of the franchise in forming a national community and sense of citizenship. The best treatment of how nationhood stood at the center of Louisiana's development is Kastor, *Nation's Crucible*, esp. chaps. 5 and 6. On citizenship and the franchise more generally, see Isenberg, *Sex and Citizenship*; Greenberg, *Manifest Manhood*; and Stephen G. Hall, *Faithful Account of the Race*.

10. "To the Free Coloured Inhabitants of Louisiana," in Bassett, *Correspondence of Andrew Jackson*, 2:58.

11. Ibid., 2:59.

12. The freehold, defined as 160 acres of individually owned land, served as the Jeffersonian standard for full American citizenship. In early Virginia, once a man accrued 160 acres of land, he became a veritable yeoman farmer and a freeholder, allowing him to participate in the creation, expansion, and legislation of the new American nation. See Curtis, *Jefferson's Freeholders and the Politics*, 12–13, 97–106; and Burstein and Isenberg, *Madison and Jefferson*, 263–64.

13. "To the Free Coloured Inhabitants of Louisiana," in Bassett, *Correspondence of Andrew Jackson*, 2:59.

14. On the idea of representation, membership, and disfranchised citizenship, see Isenberg, *Sex and Citizenship*, chap. 2; Curtis, *Jefferson's Freeholders and the Politics*, 97–106;

Bradburn, *Citizenship Revolution*, 238–39, 262–66; and Kettner, *Development of American Citizenship*, chaps. 4 and 5.

15. On the idea of an "empire of liberty," the "republican revolution," and how Americans lived and remembered them, see Onuf, *Jefferson's Empire*, chaps. 2 and 3; Wood, *Radicalism of the American Revolution*, chaps. 9, 10, and 11; Royster, *Revolutionary People at War*; and Burstein, *America's Jubilee*.

16. On the republican self-image, see Burstein, *Sentimental Democracy*, chaps. 5 and 7, esp. 158–65, 235–37; Jordan, *White over Black*, 332–35; and Appleby, *Inheriting the Revolution*, 149–60.

17. "Textual Transcription of the Louisiana Purchase," National Archives and Records Administration, http://www.archives.gov/exhibits/american_originals/louistxt.html; and Kastor, *Nation's Crucible*, 38–41.

18. Louisiana Purchase Treaty, art. 3; and Kastor, *Nation's Crucible*, 42–43.

19. John Pintard to the Secretary of the Treasury, September 14, 1803, in Clarence Edward Carter, *Territorial Papers*, 9:51.

20. This idea is derived mainly from Kastor, *Nation's Crucible*, chaps. 2 and 4. Also see Kukla, *Wilderness So Immense*, chap. 14; and Vernet, *Strangers on Their Native Soil*, 17–25.

21. The providential rhetoric of early American expansion into the west is well documented. A series of scholars have recently reconsidered this rhetoric through a number of different cultural lenses, to great effect. See Douglas, *Stand Your Ground*, 93–102; Conroy-Krutz, *Christian Imperialism*, 1–6, 132–45; Park, *American Nationalisms*, chap. 2; Guyatt, *Providence and the Invention*, 150–72; Israel, *Expanding Blaze*, chap. 13; Hopkins, *American Empire*, chap. 4; and, not as recently, Horsman, *Race and Manifest Destiny*, chap. 5.

22. Most scholars who have studied colored Louisianans under the American territorial government have focused on the implementation of a racial binary system opposite that in force under the Spanish, and even the French. A three-caste system, encompassing whites, free blacks, and slaves, these scholars claim, emerged from social and racial protest from the ranks of the free black community. This, however, maintains the racial binary, as it fails to note the complexity of this free "black" caste. See, for example, Aslakson, "Making Race," esp. 10–24; Lachance, "Formation of a Three-Caste Society"; and Laura Foner, "Free People of Color," 406–12. Thomas Ingersoll, in *Mammon and Manon*, argues that New Orleans was always under a racial and social binary system.

23. For more on this idea, called the "image archive," predicated on the social limits of legislative acts, see Peabody, "'Nation Born to Slavery,'" 113; and Spear, *Race, Sex, and Social Order*, 2–5. Also see chap. 1 of this work.

24. The idea of face-to-face interaction, also called "personalism," as a form of social protest and reformation comes primarily from von Daacke, *Freedom Has a Face*, 3–10.

25. See chap. 1 of this work; Dawdy, *Building the Devil's Empire*, 178–79, 292n93; Spear, *Race, Sex, and Social*, 94–95; Sophie White, *Wild Frenchmen*, 36–40; and Bell, *Revolution, Romanticism*, 11–15.

26. See chap. 2 of this work; Mörner, *Race Mixture in the History*, 53; and Carrera, *Imagining Identity in New Spain*, 35–36.

27. See 1795 Census of Louisiana, folio 34, roll 1–B, Papeles Procedentes de la Isla de

Cuba, Archivo General de Indias (herafter PC-AGI), Hill Memorial Library, Louisiana State University, Baton Rouge, Louisiana (hereafter LSU-HM); and Hanger, *Bounded Lives, Bounded Places*, 126–29.

28. See Carrera, *Imagining Identity in New Spain*, 137–40.

29. When Spain allied with the American colonies during the American Revolution, Louisiana mobilized its militia in force. Whites, *pardos*, and *morenos* participated in campaigns against Baton Rouge, Pensacola, and Mobile, fighting and serving with valor on numerous occasions. The Mobile campaign specifically served as the apex of the colored militia's service, as nearly a dozen *pardos* and *morenos* received medals of valor from the Crown. On the military expeditions of the Spanish colored militia during the American Revolution, see McConnell, *Negro Troops of Antebellum Louisiana*, 10–15; Hanger, *Bounded Lives, Bounded Places*, 133–34; Bell, *Revolution, Romanticism*, 24–25; and Landers, *Atlantic Creoles in the Age*, 50–52.

30. There was no primary newspaper in New Orleans under the Spanish. The smattering of short-lived or irregular publications found at Tulane University's Historical Louisiana Newspapers Collection produced nothing on the principles of American government. See Historical Louisiana Newspapers Collection, series 1, box 1–2, Howard-Tilton Library, Tulane University.

31. On the American colonists' Britishness, see Anderson, *Crucible of War*, xvii–xxv; Bradburn, *Citizenship Revolution*, 4–10; and Kettner, *Development of American Citizenship*, 87–89, 180–83.

32. See Bradburn, *Citizenship Revolution*, 7–8. Quote from *Boston Evening Post*, October 8, 1759 (emphasis added).

33. The historiography on American citizenship is surprisingly limited. On the development of the notion of citizenship and its connection to allegiance, see Kettner, *Development of American Citizenship*, chaps. 3, 7, and 8; Bradburn, *Citizenship Revolution*, chap. 1; and Isenberg, *Sex and Citizenship*, chaps. 2 and 7.

34. Commonwealth v. Jennison (Massachusetts, 1783) in *Proceedings of the Massachusetts Historical Society: 1873–1875* (Boston: Massachusetts Historical Society, 1875), 293. Also see Kettner, *Development of American Citizenship*, 315.

35. On subjectship as a concept, see Kettner, *Development of American Citizenship*, chap. 1; and Smith, *Civic Ideals*, 54–60.

36. The concept of *jus soli* subjectship/citizenship originated in the famous 1609 British suit at law focusing on naturalization known as Calvin's Case. Addressing the question of whether or not parliament should consider Scots born under the combined English and Scottish crown subjects of both England and Scotland, the Court of King's Bench decided that nativity under "a crown" subjected a given person to that crown and all it represented at the time. In other words, Scots born under the combined English-Scottish crown became subjects of both, because the crown itself represented both. Their parents, on the other hand, were consider "aliens" because, at the time of their birth, the Scottish and English Crowns had separate monarchs, and represented different national communities. On Calvin's Case, see Kettner, *Development of American Citizenship*, chaps. 1 and 2; and James Wilson, *Considerations on the Nature*, 2–24.

37. This quote comes from a similar 1838 decision in which Judge William Gaston re-

fers to an unnamed 1790 decision. See State v. Manuel (North Carolina, 1838) in William Gaston Papers, folder 78, Southern Historical Collection, Louis Round Wilson Special Collections, University of North Carolina–Chapel Hill, http://www2.lib.unc.edu/mss/inv/g/Gaston,William.html#folder_78#1. Also quoted, in slightly different form, in Kettner, *Development of American Citizenship*, 317.

38. See Vaughn v. Phebe (Tennessee, 1827) in Freeman, *American Decisions*, 17:772–73.

39. See Foreman v. Tamm (Pennsylvania, 1853) in Grant, *Reports of Cases Argued*, 1:23–24. For the Virginia case using similar language, see Benjamin F. Hall, *Official Opinions*, 1:506–9; also cited in Bradburn, *Citizenship Revolution*, 236–37.

40. On the concept of descent and citizenship or subjectship, see Isenberg, *Sex and Citizenship*, 21–28; Kettner, *Development of American Citizenship*, 24–26, 55–58, 80–86; and Sollors, *Beyond Ethnicity*, 5–7, 150–54.

41. Of course, women were not considered members of the political community, and thus not citizens of the nation or state. This would change in the late 1840s and 1850s. But in the early Republic, women, and children generally, stood outside the bounds of citizenship, membership, or partnership. See Isenberg, *Sex and Citizenship*, chap. 2; Bradburn, *Citizenship Revolution*, 51–54; Kettner, *Development of American Citizenship*, 7–10, 32–41, and chap. 7; and Brewer, *By Birth or Consent*, 6–16.

42. Hening, *Statutes at Large*, 10:129.

43. See Kettner, *Development of American Citizenship*, 214–15. Quote from Constitution of the State of New York (April 20, 1777), art. 42, in Thorpe, *Federal and State Constitutions*, 5:2637–38.

44. See Hening, *Statutes at Large*, 11:263; and Maxcy, *Laws of Maryland*, 1:364. The latter also cited, in slightly different form, in Kettner, *Development of American Citizenship*, 215.

45. See Hening, *Statutes at Large*, 11:264; and "Act for Preventing Improper or Disafected [sic] Persons Emigrating from Other Places, and Becoming Citizens of this State," August 5, 1782, in Chandler, *Colonial Records of the State*, 19:164.

46. On the yeoman ideal and citizenship through labor and production, see Burstein and Isenberg, *Madison and Jefferson*, 52–58, 106–8; Eric Foner, *Free Soil, Free Labor*, xii–xvi; Applebaum, *American Work Ethic*, chap. 8, esp. 73–80; and Hofstadter, *Age of Reform*, chap. 1, esp. 23–31.

47. See Burstein and Isenberg, *Madison and Jefferson*, 106–8.

48. Alexander Hamilton, "The Farmer Refuted, &c.," February 23, 1775, in Syrett, *Papers of Alexander Hamilton*, 1:93–94. This quote is also cited in different form, ibid., 108.

49. See Kettner, *Development of American Citizenship*, 215; and Wolf, *Race and Liberty*, 5–6. Quotes from Hening, *Statutes at Large*, 10:129–30; and "Constitution of 1778," in Cooper, *Statutes at Large*, 1:140–41.

50. The free colored population in the United States increased from an estimated 59,466 in 1790 to an estimated 108,395 in 1800. See Berlin, *Slaves without Masters*, 46, table 2. There is an active scholarly debate surrounding the causes behind the expansion of the free colored population following the American Revolution. Ira Berlin and many others have argued that the Revolutionary mindset of equality and liberty drove many

slaveowners to manumit at least a portion of their slaves. In some cases, this resulted in the freedom of slaves on entire plantations. In others, it resulted in the freeing of favored house servants or mixed-race children of the master. For this argument, see Berlin, *Slaves without Masters*, 15–51. Others have more recently argued that the Revolutionary fervor existed, but was not long-lived or widespread enough to cause such a drastic increase in the free colored population. Eva Sheppard Wolf, most notably, argues that the rise in manumissions in the Upper South, especially Virginia, resulted from masters holding out freedom as an incentive to produce better work in the declining economy following the Revolutionary War. See Wolf, *Race and Liberty*, ix–xvi, 3–15.

51. Franklin, *Free Negro in North Carolina*, 110–16; Bishir, *Crafting Lives*, 47–52; and, on the disfranchisement of free people of color in North Carolina in 1835, Ford, *Deliver Us from Evil*, chap. 14.

52. On Blumenbach and others of the monogenist, climatist school, see Wheeler, *Complexion of Race*, 181–87; Dain, *Hideous Monster of the Mind*, 57–60; and Blumenbach, "Contributions to Natural History," 361–75.

53. This is a growing focus in recent scholarship. For the best treatments of this face-to-face system of social interaction and value, see von Daacke, *Freedom Has a Face*; Thompson, *Exiles at Home*, chaps. 1 and 3; Ely, *Israel on the Appomattox*, chap. 3; and Winch, *Clamorgans*, chaps. 5 and 10.

54. See "Petición de aclaración de la partida de bautismo de Margarita Castañeda, colocados en los libros correspondientes de los de color quebrado siendo ella esagñola," in Castro, *Biblioteca de autores españoles*, 293; Carrera, *Imagining Identity in New Spain*, 3–11; and Bass, *Drama of the Portrait*, 101–5.

55. Dabney, "Captain Marryatt and His Diary," 263. Also see Wells, *Origins*, 86–87; and Goloboy, "Strangers in the South," 46–47.

56. See Patrick Johnson, free Negro v. Robert Battles, March 1807, Albemarle County Court Records, 1803–1810, mf #49–50, Library of Virginia, Richmond, Va. Also cited in von Daacke, *Freedom Has a Face*, 46–47; and Heinegg, *Free African Americans*, 132–33.

57. See CW v. Ferguson [sic], Prince Edward County Order book 16, #233, mf #16, Library of Virginia, Richmond, Va. Richard Foster later became an overseer outside of Farmville. In 1837, he was murdered by a slave named Tom, whose sentence of death was commuted due to Foster's reputation for "savagery" and "barbarous treatment." See Ely, *Israel on the Appomattox*, 248–49.

58. See *The Revised Code of the Laws of Virginia: Being a Collection of All Such Acts of the General Assembly* (Richmond, Va.: Thomas Ritchie, 1819), vol. 1, chap. 3, sec. 63; Wolf, *Race and Liberty*, 135–36; and John H. Russell, *Free Negro in Virginia*, 55–57.

59. See Edwards, *People and Their Peace*, 4–5.

60. Focused on the experiential and conceptual dichotomies created by local and state interpretations of justice and order, Laura Edwards provides the single best analysis of legal "belonging" in the early American republic. See Edwards, *People and Their Peace*, chaps. 1, 4, and 8. Quote from Ely, *Israel on the Appomattox*, 247.

61. See Sheperd, *Statutes at Large of Virginia*, 1:364–65; James Monroe to Thomas Jefferson, June 15, 1801, in Lowrie, *American State Papers*, 1:464; *Virginia Gazette and Gen-*

eral Advertiser, December 11, 1800; Wolf, *Race and Liberty*, 116; and Sidbury, *Ploughshares into Swords*, 130–31.

62. See Sen. W. Smith (S.C.), *Annals of Congress: The Debates and Proceedings in the Congress of the United States* (New York: D. Appleton, 1858), 6:668–69; and, for a similar view, Rankin v. Lydia (Kentucky, 1820), cited in Kettner, *Development of American Citizenship*, 319–20.

63. Many scholars have noted this outlook and accepted it as the quintessentially American continental purview, both in Louisiana and other places in what was at various times the West, especially at the beginning of the nineteenth century. See Bell, *Revolution, Romanticism*; Kastor, *Nation's Crucible*, chap. 2; Thompson, *Exiles at Home*, chap. 4; Aslakson, *Making Race in the Courtroom*, introduction and chap. 1; Logsdon and Bell, "Americanization of Black New Orleans"; Tregle, "Creoles and Americans"; and Tregle, "Early New Orleans Society," 30–35.

64. Benjamin Morgan to Chandler Price, August 7, 1803, in Clarence Edward Carter, *Territorial Papers*, 9:7. Also see Gross, *What Blood Won't Tell*, 27–28.

65. John Pintard to the Secretary of the Treasury, September 14, 1803, in Carter, *Territorial Papers*, 9:51.

66. On the difficulty of and questions surrounding the "incorporation" process, see Kastor, *Nation's Crucible*, chaps. 3 and 4; and Kukla, *Wilderness So Immense*, 307–11.

67. Mary Louise Christovich and Roulhac Toledano, "Banking and Commerce," in Christovich et. al, *New Orleans Architecture*, 2:65–67; and John G. Clark, *New Orleans*, 345–47.

68. "Bill of Sale," May 22, 1802, book 3, #390, Notary Narcisse Broutin, New Orleans Notarial Archives (hereafter NONA); "Bill of Sale," January 3, 1803, book 4, #91, Notary Narcisse Broutin, NONA; and John G. Clark, *New Orleans*, 344–52.

69. John G. Clark, *New Orleans*, 347–48; and Arthur and de Kernion, *Old Families of Louisiana*, 44–45.

70. See Conseil de Ville de la Nouvelle Orléans: Official Proceedings, February 6, 1804, book 3, #1, NOPL. Also cited, in different form, in Bradley, *Interim Appointment*, 289.

71. Lafon, *Annuaire louisianais*, 203.

72. There are countless examples of the French culture active in New Orleans at the time of the Purchase. Nearly every court document, even after the Purchase, was recorded in French. City directories, where they exist, were published in French. French served as the functional language of the city and the surrounding area, as well as of the Catholic church in the city. It was not until after the War of 1812 that New Orleans hosted a fully English newspaper, the *Louisiana Gazette*. Before then, the *Orleans Gazette*, as well as a smattering of other, shorter-lived periodicals, published in either French or equal parts English and French. See Historical Louisiana Newspapers Collection, series 1, box 1–2, Howard-Tilton Library, Tulane University.

73. *Annals of Congress*, 8th Congress, 1st session (1803–1804), 461–62, Library of Congress, Washington, D.C.

74. Ibid., 480–81.

75. See chap. 39 in Peters, *Public Statutes at Large*, 2:391–93. Also cited, in different form, in Kastor, *Nation's Crucible*, 86–87.

76. On Calvin's Case, see Kettner, *Development of American Citizenship*, 15–28; James Wilson, *Considerations on the Nature*, 2–24; and Scott, *Cases of International Law*, 141–42.

77. "Textual Transcription of the Louisiana Purchase," National Archives and Records Administration; also cited in Kastor, *Nation's Crucible*, 38–41.

78. We should recall that only North Carolina and Tennessee allowed free men of color the franchise in any form at any time in the early Republic.

79. Benjamin Morgan to Chandler Price, August 3, 1803, in Clarence Edward Carter, *Territorial Papers*, 9:7–8. For a brief but interesting discussion of Morgan's letter and the place of New Orleans free coloreds, also see Adam Rothman, *Slave Country*, 101–2.

80. Benjamin Morgan to Chandler Price, August 3, 1803, in Clarence Edward Carter, *Territorial Papers*, 9:7–8.

81. James Wilkinson to the Secretary of War, December 20, 1803, in Clarence Edward Carter, *Territorial Papers*, 9:139.

82. Governor William C. C. Claiborne to the President [Thomas Jefferson], September 29, 1803, in Clarence Edward Carter, *Territorial Papers*, 9:59.

83. Hening, *Statutes at Large*, 12:184. A number of scholars have misquoted this statute in a variety of ways. Some have claimed that it declared all people with a negro grandparent to be "Negroes" themselves. Others claim that it set the limit of "negro blood" at one-sixteenth, placing the hypodescendant marker at the generation of great-grandparents. See Zackodnik, "Fixing the Color Line," 433.

84. *Code of Virginia* (Richmond: William F. Ritchie, 1849), 747. Also cited in Schwarz, *Migrants against Slavery*, 104–5; Woodson, *Story of the Negro Retold*, 81–82; and DeRamus, *Forbidden Fruit*, 6–7.

85. On gradual emancipation and the emergence of antislavery activism in New York, see Gellman, *Emancipating New York*, chaps. 7 and 8; Leslie M. Harris, *In the Shadow of Slavery*, chaps. 2, 3, and 5; and Sinha, *Slave's Cause*, 171–74, 233–52.

86. "Ledger of Expences [sic]," box 21, folder 2, The House of Roberts and Colson Papers, Virginia State University Special Collections (hereafter VSU), Petersburg, Va.

87. Tredeger Iron Works Journal, Tredeger Iron Works Records, Virginia State Library and Archives, Richmond, Va.

88. Joseph Jenkins, "Joseph Jenkins Roberts: The Father of Liberia, Son of Petersburg," unpublished manuscript in Joseph Jenkins Papers, box 1, folder 8, VSU.

89. On this law, see von Daacke, *Freedom Has a Face*, 76–78; Wolf, *Race and Liberty*, 117–18; and Delaney and Rhodes, *Free Blacks of Lynchburg*, 20–22.

90. Von Daacke, *Freedom Has a Face*, 77.

91. One example of this is Robert Battles Jr., mentioned earlier in the chapter. The son of a veteran of the American Revolution and a highly respected landowner, Robert registered with the Albemarle County Court in 1821, twenty-two years after his birth and three years after he purchased his first plot of land. He did this in order to marry his fiancée, a union that required both parties to prove their free status in order make it official with the state. Needless to say, many free colored marriages went on without offi-

cial state recognition, as countless married men and women never registered at all. See "Albemarle County Personal Property Tax and Registration Lists, 1799–1813," mf #4–5, Library of Virginia, Richmond, Va. Battles does not show up in a single entry between these dates, which cover the time between his birth and his fourteenth birthday. For more specific details on Battles and his family and their registration practices, see Von Daacke, *Freedom Has a Face*, 60–61, 65–66.

92. Thirty-eight Virginians registered as "black" and 73 as "Negro." Some 43 out-of-state free coloreds registered as "yellow," while 78 registered as "mulatto" and/or "light brown." See "Register of Free Negroes & Mulattoes, 1794–1819," Petersburg, mf #47, VSU.

93. These estimates are based largely on highly inaccurate census data, and have come under scrutiny in recent years. See Berlin, *Slaves without Masters*, 177–78, table 12; Zack, *Race and Mixed Race*, 80–81; Schweninger, *Black Property Owners*, 72–74, 135–38, 160–61; and Phillips, *Freedom's Port*, 63–65.

94. See "Register of Free Negroes & Mulattoes, 1794–1819," Petersburg, mf #47, VSU; and "Petersburg Personal Property Tax List, 1800–1833," mf #360, VSU. The six "mulattoes" to appear in both were John Jones, no. 200, "very light coloured Mulatto"; Willis Bird, no. 214, "brown mulatto"; John Majeville Dutchfield, no. 221, "light brown Mulatto"; Henry Stewart, no. 239, "Bright Mulatto"; Berry Scott, no. 256, "light brown man"; and William Harris, no. 293, "brown Mulatto."

95. Similar to Robert Battles Jr., Joseph Jenkins Roberts, the eldest of James Roberts's sons, registered with the county in 1825 in order to marry his first wife, Lucinda. He left the United States for Liberia in 1829 following the deaths of both his father, James, and his wife. See Joseph Jenkins, no. 1362, "Registry of Free Negroes & Mulattoes, made & entered in the Clerk's office of the Hustings Court of the Town of Petersburg, 1819–1833," mf #73, VSU.

96. See "Roberts, James," pp. 137, 452, "Petersburg Personal Property Tax List, 1800–1833," mf #73, VSU.

97. Samuel D. Pennington to Amelia Roberts, his wife, May 10, 1827, in the personal collection of Patti Kennedy of Petersburg, Va.

98. See "Colson, William N.," pp. 396, 453, 947, "Petersburg Personal Property Tax List, 1800–1833," mf #73, VSU. Quote from Mr. Wm. Rails to Wm. Colson, March 2, 1817, Colson Family Papers, box 20, folder 10, VSU. For a brief but well-researched treatment of Colson and his partner Joseph Roberts, see Walker, *History of Black Business*, 1:154–55.

99. Edwards, *People and Their Peace*, 7–9, and chap. 3. For a related discussion centering on Louisiana's legal transition following the Purchase, see Fernandez, *From Chaos to Continuity*, chap. 2.

100. See Wingfield, "Creoles of Color," 36; and Flannery, *New Orleans in 1805*, 106.

101. William C. C. Claiborne to the President, August 24, 1803, in Clarence Edward Carter, *Territorial Papers*, 9:16.

102. Jefferson, *Notes on the State*, 151. On Jefferson's colonization scheme, see Onuf, *Jef-*

ferson's Empire, 147–88; Miller, *Wolf by the Ears*, 60–64; Freehling, *Road to Disunion*, 1:156–57; and Tyler-McGraw, *African Republic*, 28–30.

103. Burstein and Isenberg, *Madison and Jefferson*, 634.

104. See Wolf, *Race and Liberty*, 2–3, 117–18. On *octavóns* and albinos, see chap. 2 of this work; Mörner, *Race Mixture in the History*, 58–59; and Carrera, *Imagining Identity in New Spain*, 65–66.

105. Thomas Jefferson to Francis C. Gray, March 4, 1815, Thomas Jefferson Papers, series 1, General Correspondence, 1651–1827, Library of Congress Online, http://hdl.loc.gov/loc.mss/mtj.mtjbib021963. Also transcribed in Lewis and Onuf, *Sally Hemings and Thomas Jefferson*, 262–63.

106. Thomas Jefferson to Francis C. Gray, March 4, 1815, in Lewis and Onuf, *Sally Hemings and Thomas Jefferson*, 262.

107. Quotes from Burstein, *Jefferson's Secrets*, 147; and Foucault, *History of Sexuality*, 1:146.

108. Emily Clark, *Strange History*, 3; and Sollors, *Neither Black nor White*, 114–15.

109. Thomas Jefferson to Francis C. Gray, March 4, 1815, in Lewis and Onuf, *Sally Hemings and Thomas Jefferson*, 262–63.

110. Ibid.

111. Rush, *Sixteen Introductory Lectures to Courses*, 117. Also quoted, in slightly different form, in Boorstin, *Lost World of Thomas Jefferson*, 268n23.

112. Benjamin Morgan to Chandler Price, August 3, 1803, in Clarence Edward Carter, *Territorial Papers*, 9:7.

113. Louisiana Purchase Treaty (April 30, 1803), art. 3. Quoted in Kastor, *Nation's Crucible*, 43.

114. Kastor, *Nation's Crucible*, 45; and Spinner, *Boundaries of Citizenship*, 8–10.

115. Benjamin Morgan's letter to Chandler Price speaks to this. See Benjamin Morgan to Chandler Price, August 3, 1803, in Clarence Edward Carter, *Territorial Papers*, 9:7–8.

116. On sensibility and the Jeffersonian definition of nationhood, see Burstein, *Inner Jefferson*, 49–54; Valsania, *Limits of Optimism*, chaps. 1 and 3; Onuf, *Jefferson's Empire*, chaps. 1 and 2; and Burstein, *Jefferson's Secrets*, 39–41, 53–55.

117. For Enlightenment ideas on race contemporary to Thomas Jefferson, see Curran, *Anatomy of Blackness*, 78–125; Dain, *Hideous Monster of the Mind*, chap. 1; Dubos, *Réflexions critiques*, 2:14–15, 251–52, Historic New Orleans Collection, New Orleans, La.; Barrère, *Dissertation sur la cause physique*; Klaus, "History of the Science of Pigmentation," 7–19; and Leclerc, *Buffon's Natural History*, 6:320–30. For Jefferson's ideas on race, see Jefferson, *Notes on the State*, 145–48.

118. See "Act of May 4, 1805," *Acts Passed at the First Session of the First Legislature of the Territory of Orleans* (New Orleans: Bradford and Anderson, 1807), 67, NOPL; Bell, *Revolution, Romanticism*, 75; and Sterkx, *Free Negro in Ante-bellum Louisiana*, 160–61.

119. See "Act of June 7, 1806," *Acts Passed at the First Session of the First Legislature* , 138.

120. See "Act of March 31, 1808," *Acts Passed at the First Session of the Second Legislature of the Territory of Orleans* (New Orleans: Bradford and Anderson, 1808), 138–40.

Also cited in Sterkx, *Free Negro in Ante-bellum Louisiana*, 160. These designations usually took the forms of "f.m.c." and "f.w.c."

121. "Testimony of T. Lafon," n.d., Succession of François Lacroix, 1876, #9,804, Civil District Court, NOPL.

122. See "Testimony of F. Edgar Lacroix," n.d., ibid.; and "Death Certificate," April 15, 1876, ibid.

123. The massive influx of Saint Domingue refugees to New Orleans is a growing field in recent scholarship. See Dessens, *From Saint-Domingue to New Orleans*.

124. "Death Certificate," December 1, 1866, Succession of Pierre Casanave [*sic*] and Wife Rose Baraquin, December 5, 1865, #28,597 (misplaced at #25,597 in the collection), Second District Court, NOPL.

125. See Behtel v. Foucher [*sic*], 1809, #2,390, box 10, New Orleans City Court, NOPL (emphasis added).

126. Of the fifty-three signatories, fifty-two were members of either the first or second *pardo* regiments in 1801. One, Bazile Demazilière, appeared in the roll of the first *moreno* regiment. Along with a number of other signers, he also fought at the Battle of New Orleans. See 1801 Militia Rosters, May 1, 1801, folio 358, roll 160–A, PC-AGI, LSU-HM; and "Index to Compiled Service Records of Volunteer Soldiers Who Served during the War of 1812 in Organizations from Louisiana," National Archives, mf-M229, NOPL.

127. "Address from the Free People of Color," January 1804, in Clarence Edward Carter, *Territorial Papers*, 9:174.

128. Ibid., 9:174–75.

129. James Pitot to Governor William C. C. Claiborne, August 10, 1804, in Rowland, *Official Letter Books*, 2:302.

130. See "Act for Regulating and Governing the Militia of the Territory of Orleans," June 7, 1806, in *Acts Passed at the First Session of the First Legislature*, 146–48; and "Supplementary to 'An Act Regulating and Governing the Militia of the Territory of Orleans,'" April 29, 1811, in *Acts Passed at the First Session of the Second Legislature*, 148–64. Also cited in Bell, *Revolution, Romanticism*, 36–37; Emily Clark, *Strange History*, 87; and Aslakson, "Making Race," 178–80.

131. William C. C. Caliborne to James Madison, July 12, 1804, in Rowland, *Official Letter Books*, 2:245.

132. James Wilkinson to the Secretary of War, January 11, 1803 [1804], in Clarence Edward Carter, *Territorial Papers*, 9:160.

133. See Valsania, *Limits of Optimism*, 2, 33–34; and Louisiana Purchase Treaty, art. 3, quoted in Kastor, *Nation's Crucible*, 43.

134. Thomas Jefferson's phrase is "equivalent for all sensible purposes to the original blood," in Jefferson to Francis Gray, March 4, 1815, *The Papers of Thomas Jefferson*, Retirement Series, vol. 8, edited by J. Jefferson Looney (Princeton: Princeton University Press, 2011), 311.

135. On the increased nationalism following the War of 1812, see Watts, *Republic Re-*

born, esp. section 6; Hickey, *War of 1812*, 300–16; Wilentz, *Rise of American Democracy*, chap. 5; Waldstreicher, *In the Midst*, 269–348; and Burstein, *America's Jubilee*.

CHAPTER 4. A Fire of Color and Class

1. New Orleans *Daily Picayune*, June 13, 1861. The second incident, similar in nature to the first, occurred in 1871, five years before Lacroix's death. See "Report of Arrest," January 29, 1871, Succession of François Lacroix, #9,804, Orleans Parish Suit Records, New Orleans Public Library Special Collections (hereafter NOPL).

2. See *Daily Picayune*, June 13, 1861; and "Petition of Alcée Pierre Dumas," December 12, 1874, Second District Court, in Succession of François Lacroix, NOPL, for a secondhand account of the events.

3. The name "François Lacroix," or any variation of it, does not appear in any fashion in the 1861 Logbook of the New Orleans Municipal Guard, housed at NOPL.

4. "Bill of Sale," July 11, 1861, #1,020, vol. 40, Acts of Achille Chiapella, Notary, New Orleans Notarial Archives (hereafter NONA); and "Inventory," n.d., Succession of Julien Adolphe Lacroix, #32,561, Civil District Court, NOPL.

5. On the Native Guards, see chap. 5 and the epilogue of this work. For a detailed discussion of their experience in the Civil War under both the Confederate and Union armies, see Hollandsworth, *Louisiana Native Guards*.

6. On Lacroix's "eccentric" reputation, see Desdunes, *Our People and Our History*, 103; *Daily Picayune*, July 28, 1846; and "Petition of François Edgar Lacroix," May 23, 1876, and "Testimony of Mrs. Sarah Lacroix," n.d., Succession of François Lacroix, NOPL.

7. There are no extant descriptions or images of exactly how he dressed. The description given here is based on the inventory of his estate, taken on April 19, 1876, as well as sales records and advertisements for his clothing and tailoring shop at 123 St. Charles Street. See "Inventory of the Estate of François Lacroix," April 18, 1876, Acts of Christopher Morel, Notary, NONA; Shipment Records of Lacroix & Cordevielle, various dates, 1840–1842, Succession of François Lacroix, NOPL; and May 20, 1843, October 6, 1843, and February 10, 1845, in Soulié Family Ledgers, vol. 1, Historic New Orleans Collection, New Orleans, La. (hereafter HNOC). For an advertisement for Lacroix's shop, see "F. Lacroix, Fashionable Tailor," in *Crescent City Business Directory, 1858–1859* (n.p.; n.d.), 107.

8. See "Testimony of T. Lafon," July 1876, "Testimony of A. J. Villeré," July 24, 1876, and "Testimony of Theodule Drouet," July 25, 1876, all in Succession of François Lacroix, NOPL. Also see "Deposition of Ursule Péan Lacroix," May 14, 1868, Succession of Julien Adolphe Lacroix, NOPL.

9. Very little information exists on Lacroix's parents. Most historians have mistakenly concluded, often without citation, that his parents were the Frenchman Paul Lacroix and the free woman of color Elizabeth Norwood. See Gehman, "Visible Means of Support," 213; and Thompson, *Exiles at Home*, 144. There is no contemporary evidence of this, however. According to François's marriage certificate, dated December 6, 1832, he

was "*fils maj. d'âge de Jean Lacroix, et Anne Batecave.*" See "François Lacroix avec Cécile Édouary," no. 99, *Registre des mariages pour les personnes de couleur de la Paroisse de St. Louis*, in Succession of François Lacroix, NOPL.

10. See "Deposition of Sylvius DuBoys," May 15, 1869, Succession of Etienne Cordeviolle, 1868, #3,744, Civil District Court, NOPL; and "F. Lacroix, Fashionable Tailor," in *Crescent City Business Directory, 1858–1859* (n.p.; n.d.), 107.

11. See February 28, 1845, April 2, 1845, May 20, 1849, November 12, 1851, and October 17, 1857, in Soulié Family Ledgers, vols. 1 and 2, HNOC.

12. See "Testimony of Theodule Drouet"; "Felicie Dumaine, Lease," October 11, 1838; "F. A. Azreto, Lease," September 19, 1838; and "Testimony of François Métoyer," January 21, 1839, all in Succession of François Lacroix. For a list of his properties and debtors in the 1830s, see Soulié Family Ledgers, vol. 1, HNOC, and assorted leases established through Octave De Armas, Notary, found in vols. 20–23, Acts of Octave De Armas, Notary, NONA.

13. The four other largest colored landowners in Louisiana in the 1840s were the Soulié brothers (worth $500,000 and $125,000), Julien Lacroix ($200,000), August Dubuclet of Iberville Parish ($206,400), and Erasme Legoaster ($150,000). See 1850 Federal Census; "Inventory of François Lacroix," April 18, 1876, Acts of Christopher Morel, Notary, NONA; "New Orleans," R. G. Dun and Company Collection, Baker Library, Harvard Business School; and Walker, *History of Black Business*, 1:142, 200.

14. For the best treatment of this expulsion and the political turmoil surrounding it, see Dessens, *From Saint-Domingue to New Orleans*, chap. 1; Brasseaux and Conrad, *Road to Louisiana*, chaps. 2 and 3; and Lachance, "1809 Immigration of Saint-Domingue Refugees."

15. Jean Lacroix is an enigmatic figure. He appears in the 1810 Federal Census as a "free white male," but never appears in any extant record thereafter. Thus, we can only assume that he either died shortly after arriving in New Orleans or left his family. However, in François Lacroix's inventory, taken nearly seventy years later, there appears a small lot on St. Louis Street marked "*hérité de son père*"—"inherited from his father."

16. On the "Era of Good Feelings," see Howe, *What Hath God Wrought*, 91–124; Watts, *Republic Reborn*, section 6; Wilentz, *Rise of American Democracy*, chap. 5; and, for a cultural discussion, Burstein, *America's Jubilee*, to name a few.

17. The term "patriotic fire" comes from Groom, *Patriotic Fire*. On the pride of victory, see chap. 3 of this work; Kastor, *Nation's Crucible*, part 4; and Dargo, *Jefferson's Louisiana*, 70–88. Quote from *Louisiana Gazette*, May 6, 1815; also quoted in Kastor, *Nation's Crucible*, 194.

18. For valuable overviews on antebellum racial "science," see O'Brien, *Conjectures of Order*, vol. 1, book 2; Stanton, *Leopard's Spots*; and Stephens, *Science, Race, and Religion*, 78–100.

19. In 1841, the wealthy Philadelphia man of color Joseph Willson published an anonymous pamphlet titled *Sketches of the Higher Class of Colored Society in Philadelphia*. In the pamphlet, Willson described the skin color, approximate wealth, and social practices of all the "colored elites" of the town. Although outside the geographic scope of

this project, the pamphlet is enlightening to anyone interested in free colored society in antebellum America. See Winch, *Elite of Our People*, 79.

20. On the colored militia in Louisiana, see chap. 2 of this work; Hanger, *Bounded Lives, Bounded Places*, chap. 4; Bell, *Revolution, Romanticism*, chap. 2; and Spear, *Race, Sex, and Social Order*, 183–90. On colored troops outside of Louisiana, see Egerton, *Death or Liberty*, 55–81.

21. This idea is adapted largely from Burstein, *America's Jubilee*, and Waldstreicher, *In the Midst*.

22. This idea comes from Deal, "Middle-Class Benevolent Societies," 88.

23. See ibid., 93–97; Goloboy, "Strangers in the South," 40–48; Mushal, "Bonds of Marriage and Community," 62–74; and Wells, *Origins*, 67–68, chaps. 4 and 5. For the development of the Northern middle class, see the classic Wilentz, *Chants Democratic*, part 1 and chap. 3.

24. Scholarship on the relationship between free people of color as a wider community and middle- and upper-class whites across the United States is plentiful and decades old. Many early scholars of free people of color in the United States—universally identified in the aggregate as "free Negroes" and, later, "free blacks"—painted an image of a universally oppressed community of "slaves without masters" either mimicking the middle-class mores of white society or crushed beneath the weight thereof, unable to develop their own meaningful standards of wealth, class, and culture on the same terms as white society. Indeed, in the scholarship of the late 1960s to the mid-1980s, any free colored communities revealed to have established and maintained concepts of social class and even elitism were identified either as numerically unimportant outliers or veiled imitations of the real thing. These interpretations were not intentionally dismissive, of course. The apparent outliers or imitations simply complicated the macronarrative of "free Negro" history popular at the time. The same can generally be said of broader histories of the American Revolution, the early American Republic, and the antebellum era likewise popular in the three or four decades following the Second World War. Details, one could say, ought to be left for after the foundation is laid. And these studies indeed laid the foundation for more recent, much more nuanced, and thus much more representative, studies. See, most notably, Berlin, *Slaves without Masters*, particularly chap. 4; Letitia Woods Brown, *Free Negroes in the District*, introduction and chap. 1; Freehling, *Road to Disunion*, vol. 1, particularly chap. 11; MacLeod, *Slavery, Race*, chaps. 1 and 2; Boles, *Black Southerners*, chap. 5; Bracey, Meier, and Rudwick, *Free Blacks in America*, particularly chaps. 1, 2, and 11; and Curry, *Free Black in Urban America*, chap. 1 and appendix 1.

25. For Lacroix's net worth in 1861, see City of New Orleans v. François Lacroix, #637, Superior District Court, NOPL. The trial concerned the amount of delinquent taxes he owed to the city and, later, the state. The court decided that Lacroix owed a certain percentage of his total estate, as some of the properties upon which he owed taxes no longer belonged to him. The amount due to the city came to $9,893.70, some 3 percent of a total estate valued at $329,790. Several of Charleston's Brown Elite held estates approaching that of Lacroix. For example, the Holloway brothers held more than

$300,000 combined, as did the Westons. In Richmond, the wealth of the colored elite paled in comparison. On the Holloways and Westons, see Johnson and Roark, *Black Masters*, 242–44; Powers, *Black Charlestonians*, 40–43; and Drago, *Initiative, Paternalism, and Race Relations*, 23–28.

26. A number of studies have focused on the formation of a colored middle class in the antebellum North. However, none leave open even the possibility of a Southern counterpart. This scholarship also treats the formation of a colored middle class as a form of conscious social protest. See Rael, *Black Identity and Black Protest*, 3–7, chaps. 4 and 5; Ball, *To Live an Antislavery Life*, 2–8, chaps. 1 and 4; and Roberts, *Evangelism and the Politics*, chaps. 4 and 5.

27. On Haiti's successful revolution and subsequent civil war, see Dubois, *Avengers of the New World*; Dubois, *Haiti*, 15–89; and Frick, *Making of Haiti*, 183–212.

28. See Newton, *Children of Africa*, 225–60; and Heuman, *Between Black and White*, part 1.

29. See Esdaile, *Napoleon's Wars*; and Black, *George III*, chap. 18, 403–10.

30. Benjamin Russell, "Era of Good Feelings.". Portions of this article appear in numerous collections, most recently Dooley, *Early Republic*, 298.

31. Niles, "New Era."

32. See Burstein, *America's Jubilee*, 116–18, 142–44; Unger, *Last Founding Father*, 264–76; and Ammon, *James Monroe*, 382–90.

33. See Wilentz, *Chants Democratic*, 6–8; Halttunen, *Confidence Men and Painted Women*, 35–40; and Tregle, *Louisiana in the Age*, 42–46.

34. *Louisiana Gazette*, June 17, 1822. Also quoted, in slightly different form, in Tregle, *Louisiana in the Age*, 43.

35. Mordecai, *Virginia, Especially Richmond*, 58, 219–24.

36. Ibid., 45–46, 227. For more on antebellum Richmond from a cultural perspective, see Kimball, *American City, Southern Place*, 83–93.

37. For the best overview of Charleston's economic growth, see Walter J. Fraser Jr., *Charleston! Charleston!*, 187–98.

38. Charles Fraser, *Reminiscences of Charleston*, 23–27; and Walter J. Fraser Jr., *Charleston! Charleston!*, 194–95.

39. See Walsh, *Writings of Christopher Gadsden*, 237; Jaher, *Urban Establishment*, 337; and Goloboy, "Strangers in the South," 46.

40. Goloboy, "Strangers in the South," 44. In 1819, there were 429 landed merchants/professionals in Charleston. This amounted to 59 percent of the property-owning inhabitants of the city.

41. Goloboy, "Strangers in the South," 47–49, quote on 47. Also see Halttunen, *Confidence Men and Painted Women*, xv–xvii, 48–51; and Ball, *To Live an Antislavery Life*, 12–14.

42. The influx of Saint-Domingue refugees out of Cuba has received little academic study beyond New Orleans. On Cuba, see Dessens, *From Saint-Domingue to New Orleans*, chap. 1; Brasseaux and Conrad, *Road to Louisiana*, chaps. 2 and 3; and Lachance, "1809 Immigration of Saint-Domingue Refugees." On Saint-Domingue, see Hunt, *Haiti's Influence on Antebellum America*; and, more recently, Ashli White, *Encountering Revolution*.

43. On the migration that resulted from the long winter of 1816 in northern Europe, see Cohn, *Mass Migration under Sail*, 36–37.

44. Ibid., 32–34, 111–12. For Louisiana, see Merrill, *Germans of Louisiana*, chap. 1.

45. See Goloboy, "Strangers in the South," 43–53; Wells, *Origins*, 164–66; and Kaestle, *Pillars of the Republic*, 71–74.

46. See Cohn, *Mass Migration under Sail*, 30–48. On New Bern, see Bishir, *Crafting Lives*, 53–57.

47. There are commonalities between the North and South in this regard. Indeed, some scholars have argued that the South, perhaps unconsciously at first, then quite consciously, mimicked the process by which the Northern professional class found work. See Wells, *Origins*, 7–12. On this process in the North, see Wilentz, *Chants Democratic*.

48. The "middle-class" lifestyle and culture has become a popular focus of scholarship over the past decade or so. See Wells, *Origins*, 7–12; Mahoney, *Provincial Lives*, 83–113; Greenberg, *Manifest Manhood*, 9–14, 235–38; and Gitlin, *Bourgeois Frontier*, chap. 6.

49. On the struggle against "Americanization" in New Orleans, see Thompson, *Exiles at Home*, chaps. 1 and 2; Tregle , "Creoles and Americans"; and Lachance, "Foreign French." On the Irish and Germans, see Randall M. Miller, "Enemy Within"; and Gleeson, *Irish in the South*, chaps. 4 and 5.

50. Gleeson, *Irish in the South*, 63–66; and McInnis, *Politics of Taste*, 90–91, 104–8.

51. See Wells, *Origins*, 67–68.

52. One southerner described common schools as "pauper schools," claiming that they existed strictly for the benefit of "ignorant yeomen." See "Free School System of South Carolina," *Southern Quarterly Review* 2, no. 1 (November 1856): 127–28.

53. On antebellum private education, see Kaestle, *Pillars of the Republic*, 30–52; Wells, *Origins*, 142–50; Byrne, *Becoming Bourgeois*, 160–65; and Farnham, *Education of the Southern Belle*, chap. 3.

54. The original constitution of the Humane Association appeared in the *Daily Southern Argus*, December 5, 1848, when the association reorganized itself to fit a larger membership.

55. The *Richmond Daily Dispatch* published the Humane Association's charitable donations and some resolutions for most of the 1850s and early 1860s. The Norfolk *Daily Southern Argus* closely followed the association from the early 1840s to the beginning of the Civil War.

56. See George F. Anderson to [John Blair McPhail?], October 3, 1853, Carrington Family Papers, box 5, Virginia Historical Society (hereafter VHS), Richmond, Va. On the Dorcas Society, see Goldfield, *Urban Growth in the Age*, 161–63.

57. Charleston Library Society, *Catalogue of the Books*, ix–x.

58. For the history of the Charleston Library Society and a list of the officers from 1749 to 1826, see ibid., iii–vii, xii. The 375-page catalogue itself is separated into six divisions ranging from "The History of Man in Society" to "Metaphysics—Logic."

59. This idea relates almost exclusively to men. For middle- and even lower-class women, excessive fashion was seen by society as a provocatively sexual display. Flaunting new fashions and luxuries left women open to suggestions of promiscuity. See Isen-

berg, *Sex and Citizenship*, 48–51. My interpretation of male fashion is also heavily influenced by this work.

60. This was brought about largely, if not entirely, by the horrors of the Indian Removal Act of 1830 and Andrew Jackson's related policies. As a number of scholars have noted, although Louisiana was not one of the focal points of any specific removal policy, the sudden availability of newly federal lands in Mississippi and Alabama attracted many white speculators and yeoman farmers to move to the Louisiana side of the Mississippi Delta, where many found equally fertile land and cheap, readily available mortgages from salivating New Orleans banks. On this "Americanization," rather than that taking place in New Orleans, see Joshua Rothman, *Flush Times and Fever Dreams*, 209–13 and 266–73; Morris, *Big Muddy*, chap. 7; and Whayne, *Delta Empire*, 16–22.

61. The best treatment of Durnford is Whitten, *Andrew Durnford*, 8–9, 17–20. Durnford's father was Thomas Durnford. His mother was Rosaline Mercier.

62. Ibid., 18; and Everett, "Free Persons of Color," 216.

63. See Follett, *Sugar Masters*, 51; Schweninger, *Black Property Owners*, 119, 187–88; and "Inventory," April 27, 1867, Succession of Andrew Durnford, #252, Plaquemines Parish Probate Court, Earl K. Long Library, University of New Orleans (hereafter UNO). His estate, minus the slaves, was valued at $161,300.

64. Andrew Durnford to John McDonogh, June 10, 1835, John McDonogh Papers, Louisiana Research Center (hereafter LaRC), Tulane University, New Orleans, La. (emphasis added). Also see Whitten, "Slave Buying," 236.

65. Andrew Durnford to John McDonogh, July 6, 1835, John McDonogh Papers, LaRC; and Whitten, "Slave Buying," 240.

66. For more on the use of the terms "black" for slaves and "Negro" or "people of color" for freemen, see chap. 3 of this work.

67. Andrew Durnford to John McDonogh, July 6, 1835, John McDonogh Papers, LaRC. Quoted in part in Whitten, "Slave Buying," 240.

68. Andrew Durnford to John McDonogh, January 24, 1844, John McDonogh Papers, LaRC. Also cited in Whitten, *Andrew Durnford*, 119; and Berlin, *Slaves without Masters*, 276.

69. "Liabilities," n.d., and "Petitions," #95, 103, 141, Succession of Andrew Durnford, UNO.

70. See Andrew Durnford to John McDonogh, n.d., John McDonogh Papers, LaRC. Also see Berlin, *Slaves without Masters*, 274; Everett, "Free Persons of Color," 218n90; and Sterkx, *Free Negro in Ante-bellum Louisiana*, 227.

71. See "Cash Account," St. Rosalie Plantation Record Book, 1840–1868, St. Rosalie Plantation Records, LaRC, 50–51.

72. Baptism of Jean Baptiste François Boisdoré, May 9, 1837, St. Louis Cathedral, New Orleans, Baptisms, mf #136, Archives of the Archdiocese of New Orleans.

73. For examples of such shared "intimacies," see the successions of François Lacroix, François Boisdoré, Joseph Dolliole (#32,582, Second District Court), Jean Louis Dolliole (#17,714, Second District Court), Pouponne Adélaïde Beaulieu (#9,667, Second District Court), and Louis Découdreau (#19,481, Second District Court), all at NOPL.

74. See Soulié Family Ledgers, HNOC; "Testimony of Acquaintences [*sic*]," Succes-

sion of François Lacroix, NOPL; and "Deliberation of Family Meeting," February 19, 1861, Succession of Rose Gignac, Widow of Pierre Crockère, #17,513, Second District Court, NOPL.

75. This idea is informed by Cox, *Caste, Class, and Race*, 298–316.

76. For a brilliant treatment of the value of Revolutionary War service within the free colored community of Charlottesville, Va., see von Daacke, *Freedom Has a Face*, chaps. 1 and 2. Also see Egerton, *Death or Liberty*, chaps. 7 and 9. On Louisiana, see Hanger, *Bounded Lives, Bounded Places*, chap. 4; and McConnell, *Negro Troops of Antebellum Louisiana*, 18–28.

77. Although most colored militia units, especially those organized within the American colonies, did not fall under official musters and regulations, not one of the future Brown Elite in Charleston appears in the roll of Revolutionary War veterans. See Revolutionary War Rolls, 1775–1783 [online database], National Archives, Washington, D.C. Also see Wikramanayake, *World in Shadow*, 9–20.

78. *Rules and Regulations of the Brown Fellowship Society Established at Charleston, S.C., 1st November 1790* (Charleston, S.C.: J. B. Nixon, 1844), Addleston Library Special Collections, College of Charleston, Charleston, S.C. (hereafter ALSC); and *Negrin's Directory and Almanac for the Year 1806* (Charleston, S.C.: J. J. Negrin, 1806), 15.

79. For biographical information on these men, see *Negrin's Directory*, 43, 61; *Directory of the District of Charleston* (Charleston, S.C.: John Hoff, 1809), 6; *City-Gazette and Daily Advertiser* [Charleston, S.C.], January 9, 1797; Schweninger, "Black-Owned Businesses," 29; "Will of George Bedon," September 22, 1794, box 1, folder 6, Brown Fellowship Society Papers, Avery Research Center, Charleston, S.C. (hereafter ARC); and Holloway Family Scrapbook, pp. 1–4, ARC.

80. *Rules and Regulations of the Brown Fellowship Society*, 3, ALSC. The Brown Fellowship Society has received the most attention of any colored benevolent society of the antebellum era. See, for example, Wikramanayake, *World in Shadow*, 81–85; Powers, *Black Charlestonians*, 51–60; Johnson and Roark, *Black Masters*, 212–20; Lake, *Blue Veins and Kinky Hair*, 24–39; and Robert L. Harris Jr., "Charleston's Free Afro-American Elite."

81. *Rules and Regulations of the Brown Fellowship Society*, 8–9, ALSC; and "Certificate of Membership for J. H. Holloway," Holloway Family Scrapbook, ARC.

82. *Rules and Regulations of the Brown Fellowship Society*, 8–10, ALSC.

83. Ibid., 11. On apprenticeships in the early Republic and antebellum eras, see Zipf, *Labor of Innocents*, chap. 1; Mitchell, *Raising Freedom's Child*, 147–55; and Hasci, *Second Home*, 126–35.

84. *Rules and Regulations of the Brown Fellowship Society*, 10, ALSC.

85. See "W.P.A. Notes on the Brown Fellowship Society," Brown Fellowship Society Vertical File, Charleston County Public Library, Charleston, S.C.; and Brown Fellowship Society Minute Books, #9 and #10, box 2, folder 1, Organizational Materials, Brown Fellowship Society Papers, ARC.

86. *Rules and Regulations of the Brown Fellowship Society*, 12, ALSC.

87. There is some debate as to whether or not the increase in manumission following the American Revolution actually occurred due to an increase in virtue and humanitar-

ianism, or simple economic interests. For the former view, see MacLeod, *Slavery, Race*, 11–20; Nash, *Race and Revolution*, chap. 1; and Freehling, *Road to Disunion*, 1:126–33. For the latter, see Eslinger, "Liberation in a Rural Context," 365–71; and Wolf, *Race and Liberty*, chaps. 1–3.

88. The majority of the records of the Société d'Economie are in the possession of Fatima Shaik, a relative of one of its members. See Shaik, "Fatima Shaik."

89. Ibid.

90. *Prospectus de l'Institution Catholique des Orphelins Indigents* (New Orleans: Maître Desarzant, 1847), 3, LaRC. The records of the Société d'Economie are scattered and only partially available to the public. Of the ten *directeurs* of the Catholic Institution, François Éscoffier, S. Brulée, Martial Dupart, Nelson Fouché, Barthélémy Rey, Joseph Lanna, and Ludger Boguille were all members of the Société d'Economie before the Civil War. See "Judgment of P. H. Morgan, Second District Court," April 26, 1860, Succession of François Boisdoré, NOPL; "Testimony of Relations," n.d., Succession of Pierre Casenave and Wife Rose Baraquin, #28,597, Second District Court, NOPL; and Minute Book, #1, Société d'Economie et d'Assistance Mutuelle Collection, UNO.

91. *Prospectus de l'Institution Catholique*, 4, LaRC.

92. Ibid., 3; "Will of François Lacroix," Succession of François Lacroix, NOPL; and Bell, *Revolution, Romanticism*, 132–34.

93. See Bell, *Revolution, Romanticism*, 124–26; and Willey, "Education of the Colored Population," 247–48.

94. Very few rosters exist for the École des Orphelins. See *Prospectus de l'Institution Catholique*, 4–6, LaRC; Marcus A. Christian, "A Black History of Louisiana" (unpublished W.P.A. manuscript, 1936), chap. 19, accession #11, box 4, Marcus Christian Collection, UNO; "Note Cards," Marcus Christian Historical Source Material, box 11, Marcus Christian Collection, UNO; and "Reports," #3, #7, and #9, Records of the School for Free Women of Color, Sisters of Mount Carmel Archives, New Orleans, La.

95. *Rules and Regulations for the Government of a Society of the Free People of Color in the Town of Alexandria, to be called the "Mutual Relief and Friendly Society"* (Alexandria, Va.: Phenix Press, 1824), VHS.

96. Ibid., sections 3 and 5.

97. The roster of the Friendly Society is no longer extant, but the requirements for membership, as well as the monthly fees and fines, strongly suggest that its membership consisted of professional men with consistent and sufficient incomes. The only other scholar to mention the Mutual Relief and Friendly Society, although inexplicably in different form and language, is Stevenson, *Life in Black and White*, 316–17.

98. On the growth of urban America in the antebellum decades, see Goldfield, *Urban Growth in the Age*, chaps. 3 and 5; Doyle, *New Men, New Cities*, chap. 1; and Pflugrad-Jackisch, *Brothers of a Vow*, 11–20, 36–48

99. "Minutes," November 9, 1847, Proceedings of the Clionian Debating Society, 1847–1851, South Carolina Historical Society (hereafter SCHS), Charleston, S.C.

100. On the Dereefs as community leaders, see Johnson and Roark, *Black Masters*, 239; Powers, *Black Charlestonians*, 43, 65–66; and Wikramanayake, *World in Shadow*, 106–7.

101. On the guardianship law, see Koger, *Black Slaveowners*, 188. For the Dereefs as

guardians, see "Petition of Alexander G. Baxter," June 8, 1824; "Petition of William Lewis," August 1, 1839; and "Petition of John & Harriett Judah," March 1, 1853, Simons & Simons Miscellaneous Records, 1716–1874, SCHS.

102. See "Papers Concerning Free People of Color," Simons & Simons Miscellaneous Records, 1716–1874; "Report of Cases," 1840–1851, Stoney & Crossland Papers; and folder 1, Dereef Family History and Genealogical File, all at SCHS.

103. On the salons of Paris, see Kale, *French Salons*, chaps. 5 and 6. On intellectual life in early Victorian England, see Secord, *Victorian Sensation*, chap. 5.

104. "Minutes," November 9, 1847, and May 17, 1848, Proceedings of the Clionian Debating Society, SCHS.

105. "Minutes," January 1, 1849, Proceedings of the Clionian Debating Society, SCHS.

106. "Minutes," March 1, 1848, and February 7, 1849, ibid.

107. For the debate, see "Minutes," November 21, 1849; November 28, 1849; and December 5, 1849, Proceedings of the Clionian Debating Society, SCHS.

108. See Lévêque, "Revolutionary Crisis of 1848–1851," 91–100, 110–16.

109. Of the forty-one recorded members of the Clionian Debating Society, twenty-three owned at least one slave between 1820 and 1860. See 1840, 1850, and 1860 Manuscript Census Slave Schedules; *List of Tax Payers of the City of Charleston in 1859* (Charleston, S.C.: Walker, Evans, 1860); and Koger, *Black Slaveowners*.

110. "Minutes," August 1, 1849, and February 23, 1848, Proceedings of the Clionian Debating Society, SCHS.

111. "Minutes," March 21, 1849, ibid. On the two debaters, see 1850 Manuscript Census; Capitation Tax of Free People of Colour, Lower Ward, City of Charleston, 1852, SCHS; *List of Tax Payers of the City of Charleston*, SCHS; Free Blacks Vertical File, ARC; and Drago, *Initiative, Paternalism, and Race Relations*, 20.

112. "Minutes," April 12, 1848; July 17, 1850; and August 15, 1849, Proceedings of the Clionian Debating Society, SCHS.

113. The Société des Artisans has received scant and varied treatment from scholars and memoirists. See Desdunes, *Our People and Our History*, 29–30; McConnell, *Negro Troops of Antebellum Louisiana*, 105–6; Bell, *Revolution, Romanticism*, 90, 94–95; Brosman, *Louisiana Creole Literature*, 24; Clarana, "Colored Creoles of Louisiana," 193; and Blassingame, *Black New Orleans*, 156. For Lanusse's involvement with the Institution Catholique, see *Prospectus de l'Institution Catholique des Orphelins Indigents*, 3, LaRC.

114. Of the known members of the Société des Artisans, the majority owned slaves and practiced fine arts for a living. Of those who did neither, nearly all worked for their fathers as clerks or salesmen while producing literature or art in their spare time. See, generally, Records of Achille Chiapella, Notary, vols. 28–31, January 1, 1852–March 22, 1854, NONA; Succession of Michel Séligny, #29,793, Second District Court, NOPL; Soulié Family Ledgers, vol. 1, HNOC; Succession of Florville Foy, #70,093, Civil District Court, NOPL; Succession of Camille Thierry, #38,009, Second District Court, NOPL; and Succession of Paulin Bonseigneur, #32,932, Second District Court, NOPL.

115. See Succession of Michel Séligny, NOPL; and Desdunes, *Our People and Our History*, 28–30.

116. François Lacroix, along with his brother and mother, arrived in 1806. Pierre Case-

nave arrived in 1810. See Successions of "François Lacroix" and "Pierre Casanave [sic] and Wife Rose Baraquin," both at NOPL. On Louis Séjour, see Daley, "Victor Séjour," 6–7; and Perret, "Victor Séjour, Black French Playwright," 187–88.

117. See "Louis Séjour," note card, Historical Source Material, Marcus Christian Collection, UNO; "Inventory of Brig *Louisa*," November 14, 1823, New Orleans Passenger Lists, 1824, NOPL; and 1820 Manuscript Census. In the latter, he appears as a "free person of color" who is the head of a household and owner of six "black" slaves.

118. See Pierson, *Louisiana Soldiers in the War*, 12, 21, 22, 106, 108. Also see Succession of François Lacroix, François Boisdoré, and Jean Louis Dolliole, NOPL; and "Les Mémoriaux," in "Minute Book," 1876–1877, Société d'Economie et d'Assistance Mutuelle Collection, UNO.

119. Of the known members of both organizations, the vast majority either fought at the Battle of New Orleans or were descended directly from a veteran. See "Les Mémoriaux," in "Minute Book," 1876–1877, Société d'Economie et d'Assistance Mutuelle Collection, UNO; Pierson, *Louisiana Soldiers in the War*; Desdunes, *Our People and Our History*, 5, 28–30, 81; Bell, *Revolution, Romanticism*, 94–95; McConnell, *Negro Troops of Antebellum Louisiana*, 104–6; and Roussève, *Negro in Louisiana*, 65–72.

120. "Les Mémoriaux," in "Minute Book," 1876–1877, Société d'Economie et d'Assistance Mutuelle Collection, UNO; 1842 New Orleans City Directory, NOPL; 1850 Manuscript Census; and "October 5, 1844," Soulié Family Ledgers, HNOC.

121. *La Réforme*, April 12, 1846, Hill Memorial Library, Louisiana State University, Baton Rouge, La.; Roussève, *Negro in Louisiana*, 66; Tinker, *Les écrits de langue française*, 424–25; and Pratt, "Lyric Public of *Les cenelles*," 262.

122. The pages of the Soulié Family Ledgers, vols. 1 and 2, are full of exchanges, lines of credit, and notarized contracts between members of both societies. The ledgers are housed at HNOC. Also see vols. 20–33 of the Records of Achille Chiapella, Notary, NONA. Chiapella, for unknown reasons, seemed to be the favored notary of Creoles of color.

123. See Roussève, *Negro in Louisiana*, 82–84; McConnel, *Negro Troops of Antebellum Louisiana*, 105; Tinker, *Les écrits de langue française*, 428–30; and Séjour, *Les volontaires de 1815*. The play eventually made its debut in Paris at the Théâtre de la Porte-Saint-Martin on April 22, 1862. See original manuscript, and Peterson, *Early Black American Playwrights*, 175.

124. On Louis Séjour, see Daley, "Victor Séjour," 6–7; and Perrett, "Victor Séjour," 187–88. On Julien Lacroix, see "Death Certificate," March 19, 1868, Succession of Julien Adolphe Lacroix, #32,561, Civil District Court, NOPL. On Camille Thierry, see "Sale of Property," November 20, 1845; and "Petition of Florville Foy," August 23, 1875, Succession of Camille Thierry, NOPL.

125. As far as sources are extant, *L'album littéraire* ran from July 1843 to August 1844. Very few issues remain. The only known originals are held by the American Antiquarian Society and the University of Alabama's Hoole Library. A number of photocopies exist in the Charles B. Roussève Papers, folder 17, Amistad Research Center (hereafter Amistad), Tulane University, New Orleans, La. All the works that appeared in the journal are

too numerous to list here, but a few of the more notable pieces are Mitil-Ferdinand Lioteau's "Une impression"; Joanni Questy's "Prière" and "La nuit en pensant à toi"; Camille Thierry's "Idées"; Michel Saint-Pierre's "Duex ans après"; and Armand Lanusse's "Un mariage de conscience." See *L'album littéraire: Journal des jeunes gens, amateurs de littérature*.

126. Florville Foy signed "F. Foy" or "Florville" in the bottom right-hand corner of every headstone he made. His headstones and tombs still stand in every surviving cemetery in New Orleans, from St. Louis #1 to Greenwood to Lakelawn-Metairie Cemetery. He is buried in St. Louis Cemetery #3 in a self-made tomb signed "F. Foy."

127. *L'album littéraire*, August 1, 1843, 105, Amistad. For the only other treatment of *L'album littéraire*, as well as a detailed discussion of its Romantic voice, see Bell, *Revolution, Romanticism*, 106–14.

128. *L'album littéraire*, July 1, 1843, 50–51. Also cited, in slightly different form, in Bell, *Revolution, Romanticism*, 107.

129. See many transactions in Records of Achille Chiapella, Notary, vols. 19A–30, 1851–1854; Records of Octave De Armas, Notary, vols. 40–54, 1849–1855; Records of Henry Caire, Notary, vols. 3–5, 1851–1853; and Records of Alexandre Emile Bienvenue, Notary, vol. 19, 1861, all at NONA. Also see Succession of Camille Thierry, NOPL; and Soulié Family Ledgers, vol. 1, HNOC.

130. *L'union*, July 19, 1864. For an interesting exchange between Lanusse and a colleague about New Orleans politics and culture at the end of the Civil War, see Scott and Hébrard, *Freedom Papers*, 121–22.

131. Lanusse, *Les cenelles*, 1–2. In 1979, Régine Latortue and Gleason R. W. Adams translated and edited *Les Cenelles: A Collection of Poems of Creole Writers of the Early Nineteenth Century* (Boston: G. K. Hall, 1979) (see xxxviii–xxxix). Many recent scholars have challenged aspects of this translation as modern and unrepresentative of the context within which the originals were written. The translation of the passage from Lanusse's introduction was done by the author, based on the original French and that of Latortue and Adams.

132. See *Prospectus de l'Insitution Catholique*, 1–2, LaRC; *Les lois de l'association de la sainte famille* (New Orleans: Maitre Desarzant, 1847), 4, Archives of the Sisters of the Holy Family, New Orleans, La.; and Circular of the New Orleans Mutual Insurance Association, February 28, 1874, Succession of François Lacroix, NOPL.

133. New Orleans *Daily Picayune*, June 13, 1861.

CHAPTER 5. "A Call Back to the Original"

1. The political and legal debates surrounding colonization have received growing academic coverage over the past decade. For the oldest and possibly most influential treatment, see Staudenraus, *African Colonization Movement*. Among the more recent treatments, the most notable are Burin, *Slavery and the Peculiar Solution*; Clegg, *Price of Liberty*; Tyler-McGraw, *African Republic*; Tomek, *Colonization and Its Discontents*; and, most recently, Brandon Mills, *World Colonization Made*; and Murray, *Atlantic Passages*.

2. The number of terms used to describe free people of color and freedmen in state law is enormous. The most common term used was "free Negroes." Interestingly, as we have seen throughout this work, the term "blacks" rarely referred to free people of color, especially those born into freedom. See chap. 3 of this work for more on race-based citizenship law in the South and the legal language of race.

3. On the fear of free people of color, see Burin, *Slavery and the Peculiar Solution*, 7–10; Wolf, *Race and Liberty*, 115–20, 130–43; Berlin, *Slaves without Masters*, 79–198; and Sterkx, *Free Negro in Ante-bellum Louisiana*, 215–20, 285–93.

4. Jefferson, *Notes on the State*, 144–45. On Jefferson and colonization, see Onuf, *Jefferson's Empire*, chap. 5; Boles, *Jefferson*, chap. 12; and Guyatt, *Bind Us Apart*, 24–36, 250–59.

5. *National Intelligencer*, December 18, 1816. Also see Staudenraus, *African Colonization Movement*, 30–33; Tyler-McGraw, *African Republic*, 60–61; and Carey, *Letters on African Colonization*, 2–3, 17–18.

6. "The Meeting on the Colonization of Free Blacks," *Albany Register*, January 10, 1817.

7. The ACS existed from 1816 to 1964, when, all but forgotten, it disbanded and donated its voluminous papers to the Library of Congress. The most active years of the ACS were the 1820s and 1830s, as well as a resurgence in the 1850s through 1880s. Its West African colony, Liberia, founded in 1822, received more than thirteen thousand African Americans during those decades and remains an independent republic today. Scholarship on Liberia after its independence in 1847 is scanty. See Wegmann, "'Upon This Rock'"; and Ciment, *Another America*, chaps. 6–10.

8. It is important to note that the ACS did not entirely lack sustained support, particularly surrounding the slavery issue. Although its support remained relatively inconsistent—that is, few groups maintained their support throughout the entirety of the pre–Civil War decades—the ACS was particularly popular among conservative and religious white leaders in the urban North and moderate southern slaveholders like Henry Clay, James Monroe, and Thomas Hart Benton. As nearly all recent scholars have made clear, however, support for the ACS within the wider American population either did not exist or did not last very long. Most notably, as is the focus of several recent studies, African American leadership, with a few notable exceptions, largely rejected the ACS specifically, often identifying it as a pro-slavery ploy to rid the nation of a large native-born population that by nature challenged the primacy of slavery in the South. See, most recently, Power-Greene, *Against Wind and Tide*. Also see Egerton, "'Its Origin'"; Egerton, "Averting a Crisis"; and Everill, *Abolition and Empire*, 81–87.

9. Recently, an academic wave has pushed the ACS to the fringes of antebellum politics and society. See Tomek, *Colonization and Its Discontents*; Ciment, *Another America*, chaps. 1–4; Greenberg, *Manifest Manhood*, 45–50; Howe, *What Hath God Wrought*, 262–66; Horton and Horton, *In Hope of Liberty*, 177–202; Reynolds, *Waking Giant*, 22–29; and Lepore, *These Truths*, 179.

10. First quote from Massachusetts Colonization Society, *Sixth Annual Report*, 9–11. Second quote from Hinks, *David Walker's Appeal*, xxiii.

11. This was a phrase used by the ACS in nearly every publication they released. For a particularly interesting example, see "The Separation of the Two Races, Necessary to

Their Mutual Happiness," *Thirty-First Annual Report of the American Colonization Society* (Washington, D.C.: C. Alexander, 1848), 22–23.

12. Scholarship on Liberia, its origins, and its image in the minds of its African American founders, white colonizationists, and the larger African American community has thrived in recent years. The term "another America" comes from Ciment, *Another America*, the first serious, if flawed, popular treatment of Liberia's early history. For other, more scholarly studies of Liberia's founding and the people involved, see Clegg, *Price of Liberty*; Tyler-McGraw, *African Republic*; Everill, *Abolition and Empire*; Davis, *Problem of Slavery*, chaps. 3, 4, and 5; and Banton, *More Auspicious Shores*.

13. For the American "promise" of liberty, belonging, and citizenship, see the extended discussion in chap. 3 of this book as well as "To the Free Coloured Inhabitants of Louisiana," in Bassett, *Correspondence of Andrew Jackson*, 2:58–60.

14. See "Colonization," *Richmond Enquirer*, May 24, 1850.

15. *Journal of the Senate of the Commonwealth of Virginia* (Richmond: John Warrock, 1846), 13. Also quoted, in part, in Berlin, *Slaves without Masters*, 323.

16. See chap. 4 of this work for more on the standards of morality and respectability in antebellum American society, both white and colored. Also see Wells and Green, *Southern Middle Class*; Waldstreicher, *In the Midst*, chaps. 4 and 5; Wells, *Origins*; Wilentz, *Chants Democratic*, part 1 and chap. 3; and Halttunen, *Confidence Men and Painted Women*.

17. Edmund Pendleton, "Penitentiary," December 9, 1822, "Report of the Military Committee," in *Journal of the House of Delegates of the Commonwealth of Virginia* (Richmond: Thomas Ritchie, 1822), 18.

18. The first state to issue such a law was Virginia in 1793. The law required each "free Negro and Mulatto" living in a "town or city" to be "registered and numbered in a book to be kept . . . by the clerk of court." On this and other similar laws, see von Daacke, *Freedom Has a Face*, 76–78; Wolf, *Race and Liberty*, 117–18; Powers, *Black Charlestonians*, 61–62; Sterkx, *Negro in Ante-bellum Louisiana*, 103–6; and Berlin, *Slaves without Masters*, 319–20.

19. See *The Revised Code of the Laws of Virginia: Being a Collection of All Such Acts of the General Assembly* (Richmond, Va.: Thomas Ritchie, 1819), vol. 1, chap. 3, sec. 63; Wolf, *Race and Liberty*, 135–36; Berlin, *Slaves without Masters*, 316–20; Powers, *Black Charlestonians*, 55–61; John H. Russell, *Free Negro in Virginia*, 55–57; Franklin, *Free Negro in North Carolina*, 110–16; and Ford, *Deliver Us from Evil*, chap. 14.

20. "No. 105," March 4, 1852, in *Acts Passed by the Fourth Legislature of the State of Louisiana* (New Orleans: G. F. Weisse, 1852), 83 (emphasis added).

21. See "Third Municipality Guard Reports," Mayor's Records, vols. 7–9, New Orleans Public Library Special Collections (hereafter NOPL); and "Police Reports," Department of Police Records, vols. 1–3, NOPL.

22. "Petition of François Escoffier [*sic*], f.m. of c.," December 15, 1852, mss. 137, Louisiana & Lower Mississippi Valley Collections, Hill Memorial Library, Louisiana State University, Baton Rouge, La. This document is filed under the year 1840, although it is dated 1852 at both the top and bottom.

23. On the $80 fine, see ibid. On Escoffié's continued proprietorship, see New Orleans City Directories from 1852 to 1862, when directories stopped for two years. All are located at NOPL.

24. See "Historic Files," August 7, 1860, POL 1, Records of the Charleston Police Department, Charleston City Archives, Charleston County Public Library, Charleston, S.C. (CCPL); and *Charleston Courier*, August 9, 1860. This item is quite well known. Also see Powers, *Black Charlestonians*, 64; Johnson and Roark, *Black Masters*, 236–37; and Myers, *Forging Freedom*, 207–8.

25. See *Digest of the Ordinances of the City of Charleston* (Charleston, S.C.: Archibald E. Miller, 1818), 184–88; Johnson and Roark, *Black Masters*, 176; and Egerton, *He Shall Go Out Free*, 62–63.

26. Horsey, *Ordinances of the City*, 21–22.

27. Joseph Dereef owned twelve slaves and $25,000 in property in 1859, and was the son of a founding member of the Brown Fellowship Society. See "Dereef Family History and Genealogy File," South Carolina Historical Society, Charleston, S.C.; *List of the Tax Payers of the City of Charleston for 1859* (Charleston, S.C.: Walker, Evans, 1859), 41, Addleston Library Special Collections, College of Charleston, Charleston, S.C.; "Organizational Material," Brown Fellowship Society Papers, box 2, folder 1, Avery Research Center, Charleston, S.C. (hereafter ARC); and Holloway Family Scrapbook, pp. 1–4, ARC.

28. See *Charleston Courier*, August 9, 1860, and August 11, 1860; and "Historic Files," August 7, 1860, POL 1, Records of the Charleston Police Department, CCPL. The August 9, 1860, *Courier* article is also cited, in various forms, in Powers, *Black Charlestonians*, 64; Johnson and Roark, *Black Masters*, 376; and Koger, *Black Slaveholders*, 79.

29. On the Know-Nothings in general, see Link, *Roots of Secession*, chap. 4; Holt, *Rise and Fall*, chaps. 23 and 24; Sacher, *Perfect War of Politics*, chap. 6; and Soulé, *Know Nothing Party*.

30. See Holt, *Rise and Fall*, 853–78.

31. See John Slidell to James Robb, December 3, 1852, Robb Family Papers, Historic New Orleans Collection, New Orleans, La. (hereafter HNOC); and New Orleans *Bee*, December 20, 1852. Also cited in Sacher, *Perfect War of Politics*, 225.

32. On immigration, see Cohn, *Mass Migration under Sail*, chaps. 4 and 5; Greenberg, *Manifest Manhood*, 97–106; and Bergquist, *Daily Life in Immigrant America*, chaps. 1, 5, and 6.

33. *Judge Gayarré's Address to the Generals of the Know Nothing Party Held in Philadelphia in May 1854* (New Orleans: n.p., 1855), 17–18.

34. See Link, *Roots of Secession*, 123–27; Sacher, *Perfect War of Politics*, 243–50; and Soulé, *Know Nothing Party*, 102–10.

35. On the concept of archival imagery and the "image archive," see Peabody, "'Nation Born to Slavery,'" 113–16; and Spear, *Race, Sex, and Social Order*, 2–5. Also see chap. 1 of this work.

36. On the idea of Negro denizenship, see chap. 3 of this work; and, specifically relating to South Carolina, Wikramanayake, *World in Shadow*, chap. 3. Quote from New Orleans *Daily Picayune*, December 2, 1852.

37. On the efforts of European enlightenment thinkers to define and place racial mixture in the supposed "hierarchy of man," see chaps. 1 and 2 of this work; Curran, *Anatomy of Blackness*, primarily chaps. 2–4; and Kupperman, "Presentment of Civility." On humoral theory, see Vardi, *Physiocrats and the World*, 61–73; Wheeler, *Complexion of Race*, 15–40; and Dain, *Hideous Monster of the Mind*, chaps. 1 and 2.

38. On the growth and spread of abolitionism in the 1830s, see Howe, *What Hath God Wrought*, 425–32, 647–54; Newman, *Transformation of American Abolitionism*, 115–29; Harrold, *Abolitionists and the South*, 10–25; and O'Brien, *Conjectures of Order*, 1:32–46.

39. See, most specifically, Curran, *Anatomy of Blackness*, chap. 2; and O'Brien, *Conjectures of Order*, vol. 1, chap. 5.

40. Quote from Agassiz, "Diversity of Origin," 114. This article is covered in detail in Irmscher, *Louis Agassiz*, 236–39.

41. The American School of ethnography actually began in Charleston, South Carolina, with the ideas of John Bachman. But his and his colleagues' ideas, viewed as too "universalist," soon came under fire from within, and men like Nott, Gliddon, Morton, Agassiz, and even Philadelphia's Samuel Cartwright became the standard-bearers of the movement. On Bachman and his "Charleston Circle," see Stephens, *Science, Race, and Religion*. For more on the members of the American School, see Irmscher, *Louis Agassiz*, 228–64; Horsman, *Race and Manifest Destiny*, 125–40; Horsman, *Josiah Nott of Mobile*, chaps. 3 and 4; and Stanton, *Leopard's Spots*, 100–12, 184–91.

42. See Rosenthal, *Race Mixture*, chap. 2.

43. Bachman, *Doctrine of the Unity*, 290–98. Also cited in Irmscher, *Louis Agassiz*, 229. For more on Bachman, see Stephens, *Science, Race, and Religion*, 181–92.

44. Nott, "Examination of the Physical History," 100–101. Also cited, in different form, in Irmscher, *Louis Agassiz*, 230.

45. Polygenism suggests that the "varieties" of mankind had separate origins. Popular in the mid-eighteenth century, the theory quickly came under attack by Enlightenment thinkers and church members as heretical, as it fundamentally challenged the story of creation presented in the Bible. For a concise introduction to polygenism and its logical process, see Garrett, "Human Nature," 1:197–202.

46. See Agassiz, "Sketch of the Natural Provinces," lxxiv–lxxv (emphasis added).

47. Louis Agassiz to Samuel Howe, August 10, 1863, cited in Irmscher, *Louis Agassiz*, 247. Also see Stanton, *Leopard's Spots*, 190.

48. Louis Agassiz to Samuel Howe, August 9, 1863, cited in Stanton, *Leopard's Spots*, 191. For more on the origins of "hybrid theory," which was propounded initially by Josiah Nott, see Nott, "Mulatto a Hybrid-Probable Extermination"; and Nott, "Hybridity of Animals," 372–81.

49. See Nott, "Hybridity of Animals," 373–75; and Nott, "Mulatto a Hybrid-Probable Extermination," 253–54.

50. Nott, "Hybridity of Animals," 373–74.

51. Louis Agassiz to Samuel Howe, August 10, 1863, cited in Irmscher, *Louis Agassiz*, 247–48.

52. Louis Agassiz to Samuel Howe, August 9, 1863, cited in Sollors, *Neither Black nor White*, 298.

53. See Irmscher, *Louis Agassiz*, 245–46; Holder, *Louis Agassiz*, 114; Sanborn, *Dr. S. G. Howe*, 286–87; and "Comments by Dr. Louis Agassiz," in Nott, "Examination of the Physical History," 122–23.

54. On the sales and impact of Nott, Gliddon, Agassiz, and the American School, see Sussman, *Myth of Race*, 30–41; Rogers, *Delia's Tears*, chap. 10; Horsman, *Race and Manifest Destiny*, 134–42; and O'Brien, *Conjectures of Order*, 1:238–45. Also see Gobineau, *Moral and Intellectual Diversity*.

55. See "Messrs. Nott and Gliddon's Great Ethnological Work, 'Types of Mankind,'" *Daily Picayune*, April 16, 1854; and *Charleston Mercury*, January 10–17, 1856. The *Mercury*, oddly, published the same review for a full week a year and a half after its original publication. This quote is clearly lifted from the obituary of Samuel Morton published in the *Charleston Medical Journal* in 1851. For the quote, see Lurie, *Louis Agassiz and the Races*, 233.

56. Nott, "Mulatto a Hybrid-Probable Extermination," 253.

57. The independence of Liberia and the rhetoric and ideology that went into it will be discussed later in this chapter. Also see Shick, *Behold the Promised Land*, 102–4; Burrowes, "Black Christian Republicanism," 40–44; and Brandon Mills, "'United States of Africa.'"

58. See Nott, "Examination of the Physical History," 111, as well as Agassiz's commentary at the end, 123–27, for just two of many examples.

59. Nott, "Examination of the Physical History," 106.

60. Nott, "Hybridity of Animals," 373; and Nott, "Mulatto a Hybrid-Probable Extermination," 252–53.

61. See Agassiz, "Diversity of Origin," 113–15; Agassiz, "Sketch of the Natural Provinces," lxxiv–lxxv; and, for the quote, Nott, "Examination of the Physical History," 106. There is very little published information on Joseph Roberts. He will come under discussion later in this chapter, but also see chap. 4 of this work, as well as Tyler-McGraw, *African Republic*, 70–72; Shick, *Behold the Promised Land*, 45–49; and Wegmann, "'Upon This Rock,'" 64–70. For a fascinating look at depictions of mixed-race Liberian leadership in the 1850s, see Dinius, *Camera and the Press*, chap. 5.

62. Hodgkin, *Inquiry into the Merits*, 34–35.

63. "Address of Rev. Charles H. Read," in *Thirty-Sixth Annual Report of the American Colonization Society* (Washington: C. Alexander, 1853), 35.

64. *The Eleventh Annual Report of the American Society for the Colonization of Free People of Colour of the United States* (Georgetown, D.C.: James C. Dunn, 1828), 19–20; *Thirty-First Annual Report of the American Colonization Society* (Washington, D.C.: C. Alexander, 1848), 26–27; and Cheyne, *Relations*, 23–24.

65. See Nott, "Examination of the Physical History," 106; and Joseph Jenkins, "Joseph Jenkins Roberts: The Father of Liberia, Song of Petersburg," unpublished manuscript in Joseph Jenkins Papers, box 1, folder 8, Virginia State University Special Collections (hereafter VSU).

66. The best treatment of Colson remains Jackson, "Free Negroes of Petersburg, Virginia," 373–77. Also see Barnes, *Artisan Workers*, 135–36; and Walker, *History of Black Business*, 1:154–55.

67. "Ledger of Expences [sic]," 1827, box 21, folder 2, The House of Roberts and Colson Papers, VSU. The net profit split between the two partners was $9,801.84. Also see "Sales and Sundry Articles, Merchandise and Expences [sic] of Roberts, Colson, & Co.," December 19, 1828, box 21, folder 9, The House of Roberts and Colson Papers, VSU. For Colson's ownership of slaves, see "Colson, James and William," pp. 137, 452, "Petersburg Personal Property Tax List, 1800–1833," mf #73, VSU.

68. "Merchandise Held," January 8, 1829, box 21, folder 9, The House of Roberts and Colson Papers, VSU. For references and advertisements, see "Commercial," Charleston *City Gazette*, March 21, 1828; and "Daily Arrivals," *Providence (Rhode Island) Patriot, Columbian Phenix*, May 29, 1828.

69. See "Inventory and Appraisement of the Estate of James Roberts, free man of color," January 25, 1823, January Court, Petersburg City Court of Probates and Administration, Library of Virginia, Richmond, Va. (hereafter LoV). Joseph Roberts was the sole heir to his father's estate—an odd situation that requires further investigation. On Colson, see "Colson, James and William," pp. 137, 452, "Petersburg Personal Property Tax List, 1800–1833," mf #73, VSU.

70. See "Inventory of the Estate of William N. Colson," October 24, 1842, Husting's Court, City of Petersburg, LoV; "Inventory and Appraisement of the Estate of James Roberts, free man of color," January 25, 1823, January Court, Petersburg City Court of Probates and Administration, LoV; "Ledger of Expences [sic]," 1827, box 21, folder 2, The House of Roberts and Colson Papers, VSU; and City Directory of Petersburg, Virginia, 1826, 1827, 1829, and 1830, all held at VSU.

71. "Information Relative to the Operations of the United States Squadron on the West Coast of Africa," 28th Cong., 2d Sess., Sen. doc. 150, serial 458, Library of Congress, Washington, D.C. Also see Wegmann, "'Upon This Rock,'" 64–65; and Tyler-McGraw, *African Republic*, 70–71.

72. J. J. Roberts to Wm. N. Colson, January 2, 1829, "Correspondence," box 21, folder 13, The House of Roberts and Colson Papers, VSU.

73. 1820 Federal Census, Petersburg, Independent City, Virginia; and "Inventory and Appraisement of the Estate of James Roberts, free man of color," January 25, 1823, January Court, Petersburg City Court of Probates and Administration, LoV.

74. ACS rhetoric surrounding the Liberian colony consisted of repeated messages and advertisements of freedom, agricultural idealism (similar to Jefferson's yeoman idyll), and racial rebirth—very few of which sentiments ever appeared in the personal letters and actions of the first generation of settlers and leaders of the colony and later republic. See *The African Repository and Colonial Journal*, vols. 1–7 (Washington, D.C.: various printers for the American Colonization Society, 1826–1832).

75. "Beverly Page Yates," Biographical Material, J. Gus Liebenow Collection, box 2, folder 8, Liberian Collections, Indiana University, Bloomington, Indiana.

76. Payne & Yates was founded at least as early as 1831 by Francis Payne, a freeborn mulatto merchant from Richmond, and Beverly Page Yates. After Francis's death in 1843, the business passed on to his younger brother, James Spriggs Payne, himself a wealthy and powerful merchant and the future third president of the Republic of Liberia. The Paynes' father, David, a tobacconist in Richmond, was a client of Roberts, Col-

son, & Co. in the United States. See ibid.; J. J. Roberts to Wm. N. Colson, June 17, 1832, "Correspondence," box 21, folder 13, The House of Roberts and Colson Papers, VSU; and Crummell, *Future of Africa*, 135–36.

77. The House of Roberts and Colson Papers contain many letters sent back and forth between the two proprietors, as well as a few between Joseph Roberts and his brother Henry. On Joseph's travels to the United States on business, see Memorandum Book, 1833–1842, box 21, folder 12, The House of Roberts and Colson Papers, VSU.

78. On the positions held by freeborn Americo-Liberians—as the mixed-race settler elite called themselves, beginning in the 1830s—see Tyler-McGraw, *African Republic*, 159–64; Everill, *Abolition and Empire*, 57–60; Burrowes, *Power and Press Freedom*, 14–21, 50–52; and *Annual Report of the American Colonization Society*, vols. 19–32, 1836–1848. On the many positions held by Joseph Roberts before and after his presidencies—he was both the first and seventh president of Liberia—see "Obituary of The Hon. Joseph Jenkins Roberts," *African Repository* 53, no. 2 (April 1877): 34–35.

79. "President Roberts' Inaugural Address," *African Repository* 24, no. 4 (April 1848): 120–24 (emphasis added).

80. For the origin of the Liberian national motto, see *African Repository* 24, no. 7 (July 1848): 219–20.

81. For more on this idea and the prominence of American republicanism in the creation of the Liberian identity, see Burrowes, "Black Christian Republicanism," 40–44; Brandon Mills, "'United States of Africa,'" 81–90; Wegmann, "'Upon This Rock,'" 63–70; and Andrew N. Wegmann, "To Fashion Ourselves Citizens," 35–52.

82. Quote from *African Repository* 7, no. 9 (September 1831): 212. On the growth of middle-class America, see chap. 4 of this work, as well as Wilentz, *Chants Democratic*, chap. 5 and parts 5 and 6; Wells and Green, *Southern Middle Class*, chaps. 2, 3, 4, and 6; and Wells, *Origins*.

83. The term "Returned Africans" refers not to the settlers themselves, but to those slaves found in the holds of illicit slaving vessels off the coast of West Africa. Under the bylaws of the Slave Trade Act of 1819, Liberia was designated the location for the Africans' "return," giving them the name "Returned Africans."

84. On Benson's complexion, see U.S. Seamen's Protection Certification, #1670, October 19, 1841, Monrovia, Liberia, to New York City, Records Group 38, National Archives, Washington, D.C.

85. William Proby Young Jr., Diary, September 19–20, 1859, Virginia Historical Society, Richmond, Va. (emphases in original).

86. Nott, "Examination of the Physical History," 106.

87. On the recent surge in interest surrounding free African Americans and negative opinions of the ACS, see Power-Greene, *Against Wind and Tide*, chaps. 1 and 3; Tomek, *Colonization and Its Discontents*; Ciment, *Another America*, chaps. 1–4; Greenberg, *Manifest Manhood*, 45–50; Howe, *What Hath God Wrought*, 262–66; Horton and Horton, *In Hope of Liberty*, 177–202; Katherine J. Harris, "Colonization and Abolition in Connecticut"; and Matthews, *More American than Southern*, 60–63.

88. For more on *Les cenelles*, see chap. 4 of this work, and Bell, *Revolution, Romaticism*, 114–21; Desdunes, *Our People and Our History*, chap. 2; Thompson, *Exiles at Home*,

151–58; and Pratt, "Lyric Public of *Les cenelles.*" On L'Institution Catholique, see chap. 4 of this work, as well as Bell, *Revolution, Romanticism*, 124–28; Desdunes, *Our People and Our History*, 21–24; and Mitchell, *Raising Freedom's Child*, 17–20.

89. On Armand Lanusse, see Passenger List, Ship *Natchez*, Le Havre to New Orleans, March 7, 1836, Passenger List Quarterly Abstracts, mf #272, NOPL; Records of Achille Chiapella, Notary, vols. 19A-30, 1851–1854; Records of Octave De Armas, Notary, vols. 40–54, 1849–1855, New Orleans Notarial Archives; Soulié Family Ledgers, vol. 1, HNOC; Desdunes, *Our People and Our History*, chap. 2; and Fabre, *From Harlem to Paris*, 11–12.

90. On Édouard Tinchant, as well as some of the letters exchanged between Lanusse and Tinchant, see Scott and Hébrard, *Freedom Papers*, chap. 6 and 121–23.

91. "Explication," *L'union*, October 8, 1862. Translation by the author. Also cited in part in Scott and Hébrard, *Freedom Papers*, 121–22. Armand Lanusse was a founding member of the 1st Louisiana Native Guards, a company of mixed-race freemen who volunteered to fight in the Louisiana State Militia once the state seceded from the Union. The company lasted for about four months before New Orleans, the home of the majority of the company, fell to the Union. By the end of 1862, another Native Guards unit had formed under the command of the Union Army, but more than half of the original volunteers, Lanusse included, refused to join. For more on the Native Guards, see Hollandsworth, *Louisiana Native Guards*, chap. 1.

92. "Explication," *L'union*, October 8, 1862.

93. "Maximilien de Mexique," *L'union*, November 12, 1862.

94. François Lacroix to Etienne Cordeviolle, June 18, 1846, #3,744, Succession of Etienne Cordeviolle, Civil District Court, NOPL.

95. "Testimony of François Lacroix," October 2, 1847, Cordeviolle & Lacroix v. Evariste Wiltz, #9,804, Succession of François Lacroix, Civil District Court, NOPL.

96. See Succession of Joseph Dumas, 1880, #41,664, Second District Court; and Succession of Joseph Dumas, Wife, 1881, #41,812, Second District Court, both at NOPL.

97. See Succession of Julien Colvis, 1869, #32,714, Second District Court; Succession of Bernard Soulié, 1882, #8,029, Civil District Court, both at NOPL; Soulié Family Ledgers, vol. 2, HNOC; and, for more on Erasme Legoaster, an enigmatic figure, see Schweninger, *Black Property Owners*, 101–2.

98. See, for example, "J. Colvis," Le Havre to New Orleans, September 23, 1854, Passenger Lists of Vessels Arriving at New Orleans, Louisiana, 1820–1902, mf #40, series M256, NOPL

99. Lacroix and Cordeviolle continued in business together for nearly twenty years after the latter's departure. Cordeviolle still owned more than a dozen properties in New Orleans and served as the buying agent for the tailoring shop of Lacroix & Cordeviolle. See "Testimony of Léonard Commagère," January 6, 1876, Succession of Etienne Cordeviolle, #3,744, Civil District Court, NOPL.

100. On the French Revolution of 1848, see Sperber, *European Revolutions*, 91–125. On some of the French émigrés' interest in French Romantics, see Bell, *Revolution, Romanticism*, 98–103; and "Inventory of the Estate of Joseph Dumas," February 19, 1880, Succession of Joseph Dumas, #211, Civil District Court, NOPL. In his living room, Du-

mas had a portrait of Victor Hugo, as well as four volumes of Lamartine's work in his small library. Other volumes included the Bible, *Les cenelles*, Hugo's *Les orientales, Le roi s'amuse*, and *Napoléon le petit*, as well as two play scripts published by his friend and fellow New Orleans Creole, Victor Séjour. Also see Lanusse, *Les cenelles*, iv; and Lanusse, "La liberté." In both, Lanusse quotes the third stanza of Lamartine's poem "Épitre."

101. See "Testimony of Mrs. Sarah Lacroix," May 29, 1876; "Testimony of Elizabeth Garcia," n.d.; "Testimony of Julia Torregrossa," July 26, 1876, Succession of François Lacroix, #9,804, Civil District Court, NOPL. Lacroix had three sons with his wife, Cécile Édouary—Victor, François Edgar, and Joseph. Victor married a white woman named Sarah Brown, who claimed that she did not know that Victor was a man of color at the time of their marriage because his "complection [sic] was as fair as mine." See "Testimony of Mrs. Sarah Lacroix," May 29, 1876.

102. See "Petition of F. Edgar Lacroix," n.d., Succession of François Lacroix, NOPL.

103. François Lacroix to Etienne Cordevielle, February 12, 1862, Succession of Etienne Cordevielle, NOPL. The final line appears in the original as "Nous sommes tous bien. Nous sommes tous contentes." The repeated allusions to his emotional state are in response to Cordevielle's question, "How are things in New Orleans? We have heard the port no longer moves. I must admit I worry." See Etienne Cordevielle to François Lacroix, September 9, 1861, Succession of Etienne Cordevielle, NOPL.

104. On the short-lived Eureka colony, see *Documents relatif à la colonie d'Eureka dans l'état de Veracruz, République Mexicaine* (New Orleans: Imprimerie Mérider, 1857), Louisiana Research Center, Howard-Tilton Library Special Collections, Tulane University, New Orleans, Louisiana (hereafter LRC). The colony, and the movement that led to it, appear briefly in Desdunes, *Our People and Our History*, 86–87; Bell, *Revolution, Romanticism*, 85–86; and Sterkx, *Free Negro in Ante-bellum Louisiana*, 295–98.

105. "Communiqué," *L'union*, July 19, 1857. Also cited in Scott and Hébrard, *Freedom Papers*, 122.

106. *Documents relatif à la colonie d'Eureka*, 5, LRC.

107. "Immigration," *El siglo XIX*, July 15, 1857. Also cited, in slightly different form, in Lemelle, "'Circum-Caribbean' and the Continuity," 65.

108. "The Mulattoes," *El siglo XIX*, December 19, 1857.

109. Quote from "Communiqué," *L'union*, July 19, 1857.

110. The relationship between Haiti and New Orleans's Creoles of color has a long history, a small part of which is told in this book. That relationship, however, was not necessarily as reciprocal as may be expected. Indeed, even as Haitian leaders directly enjoined free people of color in the United States to remove themselves to the world's first black republic, noting specifically the Haitian origins and roots of many colored families in the Gulf Coast region, the island never attracted much interest, even from the francophone, Catholic Creoles of New Orleans. See Hunt, *Haiti's Influence on Antebellum America*, 58–75; Mitchell, *Raising Freedom's Child*, chap. 1; Emily Clark, *Luminous Brotherhood*, chap. 5; Desdunes, *Our People and Our History*, chap. 10; and Scott S. Ellis, *Faubourg Marigny of New Orleans*, chap. 9.

111. *Documents relatif à la colonie d'Eureka*, 4–5, 11, LRC.

112. Throughout the founding document, Fouché refers to his fellow settlers as *les*

étrangers nationaux, or "foreign nationals," implying that they considered themselves at least slightly American, or, if nothing else, Louisianan. Either way, this suggests that they never intended to give up their collective identity as Creoles or as natives of Louisiana or New Orleans. Rather, they simply looked to Mexico as a host for their entrepreneurial ventures into the aristocratic planter lifestyle. *Documents relatif à la colonie d'Eureka*, LRC.

113. Scholarly study of the Louisiana Colonization Society is almost nonexistent. Its papers no longer exist in any known archive, and its popularity never reached much further than a few zealous, albeit quite wealthy, donors—the most prominent being John McDonogh, who donated $50,000 to the organization in 1850 and sent all of his sixty-two slaves to Liberia. The only true studies of the society or movement in Louisiana focus on the religious affiliations of its leaders, which was primarily Methodist and Episcopalian. On this, see Reilly, "Louisiana Colonization Society"; and Poe, "Look at Louisiana Colonization."

114. Eleven separate newspapers were published in New Orleans during that time. ACS and LCS ads appeared in all of them, including the three French-language periodicals—*Courrier de la Louisiane*, *La gazette de l'état de la Louisiane*, and *L'union*, which ran for a combined period of eight years. Nearly every extant issue of these papers is housed at Howard-Tilton Library, Special Collections, Tulane University, and NOPL.

115. "Report of the American Colonization Society," *Niles' National Register*, June 30, 1849 (emphasis added).

116. The only New Orleans emigrant who owned property was Ely Gale, a fifty-eight-year-old mulatto brickmaker. He was also one of two literate emigrants. He owned one lot in the Second (American) Municipality worth a paltry $400. See "Gale, Ely," Square #3, Second Municipality, Early Assessment Records of New Orleans, 1841, vol. 5, NOPL; Shick, *Roll of Emigrants to Liberia*; and ACS Database in the possession of Eric Burin of the University of North Dakota. The eight emigrants likewise never show up in any business records, newspaper articles, successions, or personal correspondence. There is no evidence that they ever met, did business with, or knew the existence of men like François Lacroix, Jean Louis Dolliole, François Boisdoré, and Armand Lanusse.

117. "Testimony of François Lacroix," October 2, 1847, Cordevielle & Lacroix v. Evariste Wiltz, #9,804, Succession of François Lacroix, Civil District Court, NOPL.

118. For references to shipments, see J. Alfred Claiborne to Pierre Dufour, Marseille, France, December 16, 1856. For letters of advice, especially concerning inheritance, see Armand Grégoire to Armand Nicolas, Vicksburg, Miss., December 15, 1856; and M. L. Dupart to R. Barthélémy, Natchez, Miss., May 29, 1861, all in "L'Institution Catholique English Composition Copy-Book" (hereafter L'Institution Catholique Copy-Book), Archives of the Archdiocese of New Orleans (hereafter AANO).

119. The only other work to mention this is Mitchell, *Raising Freedom's Child*, chap. 1.

120. Armand Grégoire to Joni Beltier, New Orleans, La., November 28, 1857, L'Institution Catholique Copy-Book, AANO.

121. Armand Nicolas to William Green, Natchez, Miss., January 16, 1858, L'Institution Catholique Copy-Book, AANO.

122. Vasserot was listed as a "white" nine-year-old in the 1850 census, but was listed

as "mulatto" in 1860, as well as all other censuses thereafter. See 1850 Federal Census; 1860 Federal Census; and 1870 Federal Census, all New Orleans, Ward 3, Orleans Parish, Louisiana. Also see Henry Vasserot to Lucien Picou, New Orleans, La., March 16, 1858, L'Institution Catholique Copy-Book, AANO.

123. Ernest Brunet to M. Lombard, Saint Martinville, La., May 8, 1858, L'Institution Catholique Copy-Book, AANO. Also cited, in different form, in Mitchell, *Raising Freedom's Child*, 32.

124. Etienne Pérault to Léon Dupart, Cincinnati, Ohio, July 5, 1858, L'Institution Catholique Copy-Book, AANO.

125. Armand Nicolas to L. Posthel, Tlacotalpan, Mexico, June 12, 1858, L'Institution Catholique Copy-Book, AANO.

126. Eric Burin counts 10,939 emigrants to Liberia between 1820 and 1860. See Burin, *Slavery and the Peculiar Solution*, 170, chart 5.

127. More than two hundred people attended Boisdoré's funeral, including François Lacroix, Jean Louis Dolliole, Armand Lanusse, Myrtille Courcelle, Pierre Casenave, and Drauzin B. McCarty. See "Testimony of Jean Baptiste François Boisdoré," June 1, 1860, Succession of François Boisdoré, #16,146, Second District Court, NOPL.

128. "Inventory of the Heirs and the Estate," March 4, 1861, Succession of Jean Louis Dolliole, #17,714, Second District Court, NOPL; and 1860 and 1870 Federal Censuses, both New Orleans, Ward 8, Orleans Parish, Louisiana.

129. Lemelle, "'Circum-Caribbean' and the Continuity," 65; Sterkx, *Free Negro in Ante-bellum Louisiana*, 297–99; Brasseaux, Fontenot, and Oubre, *Creoles of Color*, 81–83; and "Passenger List," Brig *Augustine*, April 7, 1858; Brig *Hanover*, December 4, 1858; Ship *Dalia*, June 10, 1859; and Ship *Norcross*, January 26, 1860, all between New Orleans and Veracruz, Passenger List Quarterly Abstracts, mf #272, NOPL.

130. On Fouché, see Fouché, *Nouveau recueil de pensées*, vi–xii; New Orleans City Directory, 1861, 1866, 1870, 1872, and 1875; Thompson, *Exiles at Home*, 151; Desdunes, *Our People and Our History*, 133; and Tinker, *Les écrits de langue française*, 212–13.

BIBLIOGRAPHY

ARCHIVES AND SPECIAL COLLECTIONS

Addlestone Library, Special Collections, College of Charleston, Charleston, South Carolina
Amistad Research Center, Tulane University, New Orleans, Louisiana
Archives of the Archdiocese of New Orleans, New Orleans, Louisiana
Avery Research Institute, Charleston, South Carolina
Charleston County Public Library, Special Collections, Charleston, South Carolina
Charleston Historical Association, Charleston, South Carolina
Earl K. Long Library, Special Collections, University of New Orleans, New Orleans, Louisiana
Historic New Orleans Collection, New Orleans, Louisiana
Howard-Tilton Library Special Collections, Tulane University, New Orleans, Louisiana
Library of Congress, Manuscript Division, Washington, D.C.
Library of Virginia, Richmond, Virginia
Louisiana and Lower Mississippi River Valley Manuscript Collection, Hill Memorial Library, Louisiana State University, Baton Rouge, Louisiana
New Orleans Notarial Archives Research Center, New Orleans, Louisiana
New Orleans Public Library, City Archive and Louisiana Division, New Orleans, Louisiana
Troy H. Middleton Library, Special Collections, Louisiana State University, Baton Rouge, Louisiana
Virginia Historical Society, Richmond, Virginia
Virginia State University Special Collections, Petersburg, Virginia

ARTICLES, BOOKS, THESES, AND DISSERTATIONS

Adams, Thomas Jessen, and Matt Sakakeeny, eds. *Remaking New Orleans: Beyond Exceptionalism and Authenticity*. Durham, N.C.: Duke University Press, 2019.
Agassiz, Louis. "The Diversity of Origin of the Human Races." *Christian Examiner and Religious Miscellany* 49, no. 1 (July 1850): 110–45.

———. "Sketch of the Natural Provinces of the Animal World and Their Relation to the Different Types of Man." In Nott and Gliddon, *Types of Mankind*, lvii–lxxviii.
Aldridge, A. Owen. "Feijoo and the Problem of Ethiopian Color." In *Racism in the Eighteenth Century*, edited by Harold E. Pagliaro, 263–77. Cleveland: Press of Case Western Reserve University, 1973.
Alemán, Mateo. *The Rogue, or the Life of Guzman Alfarache*. Translated by James Mabbe. 2 vols. London: G. E. for E. Blunt, 1622.
Alencastro, Luiz Felipe de. "The Apprenticeship of Colonization." In *Slavery and the Rise of the Atlantic System*, edited by Barbara L. Solow, 151–76. New York: Cambridge University Press, 1991.
Alexander, Adele Logan. *Ambiguous Lives: Free Women of Color in Rural Georgia, 1789–1879*. Fayetteville: University of Arkansas Press, 1991.
Ammon, Harry. *James Monroe: The Quest for National Identity*. Charlottesville: University Press of Virginia, 1990.
Amos, Harriet E. *Cotton City: Urban Development in Antebellum Mobile*. Tuscaloosa: University of Alabama Press, 1985.
Anderson, Fred. *Crucible of War: The Seven Years' War and the Fate of Empire in British North America, 1754–1766*. New York: Vintage, 2000.
Andrien, Kenneth J. "The Coming of Enlightened Reform in Bourbon Peru: Secularization of the *Doctrinas de indios*, 1746–1773." In *Enlightened Reform in Southern Europe and its Atlantic Colonies, c. 1750–1830*, edited by Gabriel Paquette, 183–202. Burlington, Vt.: Ashgate, 2009.
Applebaum, Herbert. *The American Work Ethic and the Changing Work Force: An Historical Perspective*. Westport, Conn.: Greenwood, 1998.
Appleby, Joyce. *Inheriting the Revolution: The First Generation of Americans*. Cambridge, Mass.: Harvard University Press, 2000.
Arthur, Stanley Clisby, and George Campbell Huchet de Kernion. *Old Families of Louisiana*. New Orleans: Joseph S. W. Harmanson, 1931.
Asaka, Ikuko. *Tropical Freedom: Climate, Settler Colonialism, and Black Exclusion in the Age of Emancipation*. Durham, N.C.: Duke University Press, 2017.
Aslakson, Kenneth R. "Making Race: The Role of Free Blacks in the Development of New Orleans' Three-Caste Society, 1791–1812." PhD diss., University of Texas at Austin, 2007.
———. *Making Race in the Courtroom: The Legal Construction of Three Races in Early New Orleans*. New York: New York University Press, 2014.
———. "The 'Quadroon-Plaçage' Myth of Antebellum New Orleans: Anglo-American (Mis)interpretations of a French-Caribbean Phenomenon." *Journal of Social History* 45, no. 3 (Spring 2012): 709–34.
Aubert, Guillaume. "'The Blood of France': Race and Purity of Blood in the French Atlantic World." *William and Mary Quarterly* 61, no. 3 (July 2004): 439–78.
Augustine. *City of God*. Translated by Henry Bettenson. New York: Penguin Classics, 2003.
Baade, Hans W. "The Law of Slavery in Spanish *Luisiana*, 1769–1803." In *Louisiana's Le-

gal Heritage, edited by Edward F. Haas, 43–86. Pensacola, Fla.: Perdido Bay Press for the Louisiana State Museum, 1985.

Bachman, John. *Doctrine of the Unity of the Human Race Examined on the Principles of Science*. Charleston, S.C.: C. Canning, 1850.

Ball, Erica L. *To Live an Antislavery Life: Personal Politics and the Antebellum Black Middle Class*. Athens: University of Georgia Press, 2012.

Banton, Caree A. *More Auspicious Shores: Barbadian Migration to Liberia, Blackness, and the Making of an African Republic*. New York: Cambridge University Press, 2019.

Barnes, L. Diane. *Artisan Workers in the Upper South: Petersburg, Virginia, 1820–1865*. Baton Rouge: Louisiana State University Press, 2008.

Barrère, Pierre. *Dissertation sur la cause physique de la couleur des nègres*. Paris: Pierre-Guillaume Simon, 1741.

Bass, Laura R. *The Drama of the Portrait: Theater and Visual Culture in Early Modern Spain*. University Park: Pennsylvania State University Press, 2008.

Bassett, John Spencer, ed. *Correspondence of Andrew Jackson*. Vol. 2. Washington, D.C.: Carnegie Institution of Washington, 1927.

Bell, Caryn Cossé. *Revolution, Romanticism, and the Afro-Creole Protest Tradition in Louisiana, 1718–1868*. Baton Rouge: Louisiana State University Press, 1997.

Bennett, Herman L. *Colonial Blackness: A History of Afro-Mexico*. Bloomington: Indiana University Press, 2009.

Bergquist, James M. *Daily Life in Immigrant America, 1820–1870*. Westport, Conn.: Greenwood, 2008.

Berlin, Ira. *Many Thousands Gone: The First Two Centuries of Slavery in North America*. Cambridge, Mass.: Harvard University Press, 1998.

———. *Slaves without Masters: The Free Negro in the Antebellum South*. New York: Pantheon Books, 1974.

Berry, Daina Ramey. *The Price for Their Pound of Flesh: The Value of the Enslaved, from Womb to Grave, in the Building of a Nation*. Boston: Beacon Press, 2017.

Berry, Mary F. "Negro Troops in Blue and Gray: The Louisiana Native Guards, 1861–1863." *Louisiana History: Journal of the Louisiana Historical Association* 8, no. 2 (Spring 1967): 165–90.

Bethel, Elizabeth Rauh. *The Roots of African-American Identity: Memory and History in Antebellum Free Communities*. New York: St. Martin's Press, 1997.

Bishir, Catherine W. *Crafting Lives: African American Artisans in New Bern, North Carolina, 1770–1900*. Chapel Hill: University of North Carolina Press, 2013.

Black, Jeremy. *George III: America's Last King*. New Haven, Conn.: Yale University Press, 2006.

Blassingame, John W. *Black New Orleans, 1860–1880*. Chicago: University of Chicago Press, 1973.

Blumenbach, Johann Friedrich. "Contributions to Natural History, Part II." In *The Anthropological Treatises of Johann Friedrich Blumenbach*, edited and translated by Thomas Bendyshe, 361–75. London: Longman, Green, Longman, Roberts, and Green, 1865.

Bodenhorn, Howard. "The Mulatto Advantage: The Biological Consequences of Complexion in Rural Antebellum Virginia." *Journal of Interdisciplinary History* 33, no. 1 (Summer 2002): 21–46.

Bodenhorn, Howard, and Christopher S. Ruebeck. "Colorism and African-American Wealth: Evidence from the Nineteenth-Century South." National Bureau of Economic Research Working Paper Series, no. 11732, November 2005.

Boelhower, William, ed. *New Orleans in the Atlantic World: Between Land and Sea*. New York: Routledge, 2010.

Bogger, Tommy L. *Free Blacks in Norfolk, Virginia, 1790–1860: The Darker Side of Freedom*. Charlottesville: University Press of Virginia, 1997.

Boles, John B. *Black Southerners, 1619–1869*. Lexington: University Press of Kentucky, 1984.

———. *Jefferson: Architect of American Liberty*. New York: Basic Books, 2017.

Bond, Bradley G., ed. *French Colonial Louisiana and the Atlantic World*. Baton Rouge: Louisiana State University Press, 2005.

Boorstin, Daniel J. *The Lost World of Thomas Jefferson*. Chicago: University of Chicago Press, 1981.

Bracey, John H., August Meier, and Elliott Rudwick, eds. *Free Blacks in America, 1800–1860*. Belmont, Calif.: Wadsworth, 1971.

Bradburn, Douglas. *The Citizenship Revolution: Politics and the Creation of the American Union, 1774–1804*. Charlottesville: University of Virginia Press, 2009.

Brading, D. A. *The First America: The Spanish Monarchy, Creole Patriots, and the Liberal State, 1492–1867*. New York: Cambridge University Press, 1991.

Bradley, Jared Williams, ed. and comp. *Interim Appointment: W. C. C. Claiborne Letter Book, 1804–1805*. Baton Rouge: Louisiana State University Press, 2002.

Brady, Patricia. "Black Artists in Antebellum New Orleans." *Louisiana History: Journal of the Louisiana Historical Association* 32, no. 1 (Winter 1991): 5–28.

———. "Florville Foy, F.M.C.: Master Marble Cutter and Tomb Builder." *Southern Quarterly* 31, no. 2 (Winter 1993): 8–20.

Branche, Jerome C. *Colonialism and Race in Luso-Hispanic Literature*. Columbia: University of Missouri Press, 2006.

Brasseaux, Carl A. *French, Cajun, Creole, Houma: A Primer on Francophone Louisiana*. Baton Rouge: Louisiana State University Press, 2005.

Brasseaux, Carl A., and Glenn R. Conrad, eds. *The Road to Louisiana: The Saint-Domingue Refugees, 1792–1809*. Lafayette: University of Southwestern Louisiana Press, 1992.

Brasseaux, Carl A., Keith P. Fontenot, and Claude F. Oubre. *Creoles of Color in the Bayou Country*. Jackson: University Press of Mississippi, 1994.

Brewer, Holly. *By Birth or Consent: Children, Law, and the Anglo-American Revolution in Authority*. Chapel Hill: University of North Carolina Press, 2005.

Bristol, Douglas Walter, Jr. *Knights of the Razor: Black Barbers in Slavery and Freedom*. Baltimore: Johns Hopkins University Press, 2009.

Brooks, George E. *Eurafricans in Western Africa: Commerce, Social Status, Gender, and Religious Observance from the Sixteenth to the Eighteenth Century*. Athens: Ohio University Press, 2003.

Brosman, Catharine Savage. *Louisiana Creole Literature: A Historical Study.* Jackson: University Press of Mississippi, 2013.
Brown, Letitia Woods. *Free Negroes in the District of Columbia, 1790–1846.* New York: Oxford University Press, 1972.
Brown, Tamara L., Gregory S. Parks, and Clarenda M. Phillips, eds. *African American Fraternities and Sororities: The Legacy and the Vision.* Lexington: University Press of Kentucky, 2005.
Brown, William. "Mask of the Colonizer: French Men, Native Passions, and the Culture of Diplomacy in New France." In Englebert and Wegmann, *French Connections,* 35–72.
Browning, James B. "The Beginnings of Insurance Enterprise among Negroes." *Journal of Negro History* 22, no. 4 (October 1937): 417–32.
Burin, Eric. *Slavery and the Peculiar Solution: A History of the American Colonization Society.* Gainesville: University Press of Florida, 2005.
Burnard, Trevor. *Creole Gentlemen: The Maryland Elite, 1691–1776.* New York: Routledge, 2002.
Burnard, Trevor, and Emma Hart. "Kingston, Jamaica, and Charleston, South Carolina: A New Look at Comparative Urbanization in Plantation Colonial British America." *Journal of Urban History* 39, no. 2 (2013): 214–34.
Burns, Sarah. "Black Quadroon Gypsy Women in the Art of George Fuller." *Massachusetts Review* 26, no. 2/3 (Summer–Autumn 1985): 405–24.
Burrowes, Carl Patrick. "Black Christian Republicanism: A Southern Ideology in Early Liberia, 1822 to 1847." *Journal of Negro History* 86, no. 1 (Winter 2001): 30–44.
———. *Power and Press Freedom in Liberia, 1830–1970: The Impact of Globalization and Civil Society on Media-Government Relations.* Trenton, N.J.: Africa World Press, 2004.
Burstein, Andrew. *America's Jubilee: How in 1826 a Generation Remembered Fifty Years of Independence.* New York: Alfred A. Knopf, 2001.
———. *The Inner Jefferson: Portrait of a Grieving Optimist.* Charlottesville: University Press of Virginia, 1995.
———. *Jefferson's Secrets: Death and Desire at Monticello.* New York: Basic Books, 2005.
———. *Sentimental Democracy: The Evolution of America's Romantic Self-Image.* New York: Hill and Wang, 1999.
Burstein, Andrew, and Nancy Isenberg. *Madison and Jefferson.* New York: Random House, 2010.
Burton, Richard D. E. *Afro-Creole: Power, Opposition, and Play in the Caribbean.* Ithaca, N.Y.: Cornell University Press, 1997.
Buscaglia-Salgado, José F. *Undoing Empire: Race and Nation in the Mulatto Caribbean.* Minneapolis: University of Minnesota Press, 2003.
Byrne, Frank J. *Becoming Bourgeois: Merchant Culture in the South, 1820–1865.* Lexington: University Press of Kentucky, 2006.
Cable, George Washington. *The Grandissimes.* 1888. Reprint, Gretna, La.: Pelican, 2001.
Cañizares-Esguerra, Jorge. *Nature, Empire, and Nation: Explorations of the History of Science in the Iberian World.* Stanford, Calif.: Stanford University Press, 2006.

Carey, Mathew. *Letters on African Colonization, with a View of its Probable Results*. Philadelphia: Young, 1832.
Carrera, Magali M. *Imagining Identity in New Spain: Race, Lineage, and the Colonial Body in Portraiture and Casta Paintings*. Austin: University of Texas Press, 2003.
Carroll, Patrick J. *Blacks of Colonial Veracruz: Race, Ethnicity, and Regional Development*. Austin: University of Texas Press, 2001.
Carson, James Taylor. "Sacred Circles and Dangerous People: Native American Cosmology and the French Settlement of Louisiana." In Bond, *French Colonial Louisiana and the Atlantic World*, 65–82.
Carter, Clarence Edward, ed. *The Territorial Papers of the United States*. Vol. 9. *The Territory of Orleans, 1803–1812*. Washington, D.C.: United States Government Printing Office, 1940.
Carter, Greg. *The United States of the United Races: A Utopian History of Racial Mixing*. New York: New York University Press, 2013.
Castro, Adolfo de, ed. *Biblioteca de autores españoles desde la formación del lenguaje hasta nuestros días*. Madrid: M. Rivadeneyra, 1855.
Chandler, Allen D., ed. and comp. *The Colonial Records of the State of Georgia*. Vol. 19. Atlanta: Chas. P. Byrd, 1911.
Charleston Library Society. *Catalogue of the Books Belonging to the Charleston Library Society*. Charleston: A. E. Miller, 1826.
Charlevoix, Pierre-François-Xavier de. *Journal d'un voyage fait par ordre du roi dans l'Amérique septentrionale: Adressé à madame la duchesse de Lesdiguières*. Paris: Rolin Fils, 1744.
Chase, John. *Frenchmen, Desire, Good Children . . . And Other Streets of New Orleans*. 1960. Reprint, Gretna, La.: Pelican, 2010.
Cheyne, Thomas Kelly. *The Relations between Civilized and Uncivilized Races*. Oxford, UK: T. and G. Shrimpton, 1864.
Christovich, Mary Louise, Roulhac Toledano, Betsy Swanson, and Pat Holden. *New Orleans Architecture*. Vol. 2, *The American Sector*. Gretna, La.: Pelican, 1972.
Ciment, James. *Another America: The Story of Liberia and the Former Slaves Who Ruled It*. New York: Hill and Wang, 2012.
Clarana, José. "The Colored Creoles of Louisiana." *Crisis* 11, no. 4 (February 1916): 192–93.
Clark, Emily. *Masterless Mistresses: The New Orleans Ursulines and the Development of a New World Society, 1727–1834*. Chapel Hill: University of North Carolina Press, 2007.
———. *The Strange History of the American Quadroon: Free Women of Color in the Revolutionary Atlantic World*. Chapel Hill: University of North Carolina Press, 2013.
———, ed. *Voices from an Early American Convent: Marie Madeleine Hachard and the New Orleans Ursulines, 1727–1760*. Baton Rouge: Louisiana State University Press, 2007.
Clark, Emily, and Virginia Meachem Gould. "The Feminine Face of Afro-Catholicism in New Orleans, 1727–1852." *William and Mary Quarterly* 59, no. 2 (April 2002): 409–48.
Clark, Emily, Cécile Vidal, and Ibrahima Thioub, eds. *New Orleans, Louisiana, and*

Saint-Louis, Senegal: Mirror Cities in the Atlantic World, 1659–2000s. Baton Rouge: Louisiana State University Press, 2019.
Clark, Emily Suzanne. *A Luminous Brotherhood: Afro-Creole Spiritualism in Nineteenth-Century New Orleans*. Chapel Hill: University of North Carolina Press, 2016.
Clark, John G. *New Orleans, 1718–1812: An Economic History*. Baton Rouge: Louisiana State University Press, 1970.
Clegg, Claude A., III. *The Price of Liberty: African Americans and the Making of Liberia*. Chapel Hill: University of North Carolina Press, 2004.
Cohen, William B. *The French Encounter with Africans: White Response to Blacks, 1530–1880*. Bloomington: Indiana University Press, 1980.
Cohn, Raymond L. *Mass Migration under Sail: European Immigration to the Antebellum United States*. New York: Cambridge University Press, 2009.
Cole, Gibril R. *The Krio of West Africa: Islam, Culture, Creolization, and Colonialism in the Nineteenth Century*. Athens: Ohio University Press, 2013.
Conroy-Krutz, Emily. *Christian Imperialism: Converting the World in the Early American Republic*. Ithaca, N.Y.: Cornell University Press, 2015.
Cooper, Thomas, ed. *The Statutes at Large of South Carolina*. Vols. 1–3. Columbia, S.C.: A. S. Johnston, 1836–38.
Cope, R. Douglas. *The Limits of Racial Domination: Plebeian Society in Colonial Mexico City, 1660–1720*. Madison: University of Wisconsin Press, 1994.
Cox, Oliver Cromwell. *Caste, Class, and Race: A Study in Social Dynamics*. Garden City, N.Y.: Doubleday, 1948.
Cromwell, Adelaide M. *The Other Brahmins: Boston's Black Upper Class, 1750–1950*. Fayetteville: University of Arkansas Press, 1994.
Crummell, Alexander. *The Future of Africa: Being Addresses, Sermons, etc., etc., Delivered in the Republic of Liberia*. New York: Charles Scribner, 1862.
Curran, Andrew S. *The Anatomy of Blackness: Science and Slavery in an Age of Enlightenment*. Baltimore: Johns Hopkins University Press, 2011.
Curry, Leonard P. *The Free Black in Urban America, 1800–1850: The Shadow of the Dream*. Chicago: University of Chicago Press, 1981.
Curtis, Christopher Michael. *Jefferson's Freeholders and the Politics of Ownership in the Old Dominion*. New York: Cambridge University Press, 2012.
Dabney, John Blair. "Captain Marryatt and His Diary." *Southern Literary Messenger*, no. 7 (April 1841).
Daggett, Melissa. "Henry Louis Rey, Spiritualism, and Creoles of Color in Nineteenth-Century New Orleans." Master's thesis, University of New Orleans, 2009.
Dain, Bruce. *A Hideous Monster of the Mind: American Race Theory in the Early Republic*. Cambridge, Mass.: Harvard University Press, 2002.
Daley, T. A. "Victor Séjour." *Phylon* 4, no. 1 (1st Quarter 1943): 2, 5–16.
Dargo, George. *Jefferson's Louisiana: Politics and the Clash of Legal Traditions*. Cambridge, Mass.: Harvard University Press, 1975.
d'Auberteuil, Hilliard. *Considerations sur l'état present de la colonie française de St. Domingue*. 2 vols. Paris: N.p., 1776–77.

Davis, David Brion. *The Problem of Slavery in the Age of Emancipation*. New York: Alfred A. Knopf, 2014.
Dawdy, Shannon Lee. *Building the Devil's Empire: French Colonial New Orleans*. Chicago: University of Chicago Press, 2008.
Deal, John G. "Middle-Class Benevolent Societies in Antebellum Norfolk, Virginia." In Wells and Green, *Southern Middle Class*, 84–104.
de Faria y Sousa, Manuel. *Lusiadas de Luís de Camoens . . . Comentadas por Manuel de Faria i Sousa . . . Contienen lo más de lo principal de la historia i geografía del mundo, i singularmente de España*. Madrid: Ivan Sanchez, 1639.
Deggs, Sister Mary Bernard, *No Cross, No Crown: Black Nuns in Nineteenth-Century New Orleans*. Edited by Virginia Meacham Gould and Charles E. Nolan. Bloomington: Indiana University Press, 2001.
De la Fuente, Alejandro, and Ariela J. Gross. *Becoming Free, Becoming Black: Race, Freedom, and Law in Cuba, Virginia, and Louisiana*. New York: Cambridge University Press, 2020.
Delaney, Ted, and Philip Wayne Rhodes. *Free Blacks of Lynchburg, Virginia, 1805–1865*. Lynchburg, Va.: Warwick House, 2001.
de Pauw, Cornelius. *Recherches philosophiques sur les Américains, ou Mémoires intérressants pour servir à l'histoire de l'espèce humaine*. Vol. 1. Berlin: G. J. Decker, 1768.
DeRamus, Betty. *Forbidden Fruit: Love Stories from the Underground Railroad*. New York: Atria Books, 2005.
Desdunes, Rodolphe Lucien. *Our People and Our History: Fifty Creole Portraits*. Translated by Sister Dorothea Olga McCants. 1973. Reprint, Baton Rouge: Louisiana State University Press, 2001.
Dessens, Nathalie. *From Saint-Domingue to New Orleans: Migration and Influences*. Gainesville: University Press of Florida, 2007.
Diemer, Andrew K. *The Politics of Black Citizenship: Free African Americans in the Mid-Atlantic Borderland, 1817–1863*. Athens: University of Georgia Press, 2019.
Din, Gilbert C. *Spaniards, Planters, and Slaves: The Spanish Regulation of Slavery in Louisiana, 1763–1803*. College Station: Texas A&M University Press, 1999.
Dinius, Marcy J. *The Camera and the Press: American Visual and Print Culture in the Age of the Daguerreotype*. Philadelphia: University of Pennsylvania Press, 2012.
Domínguez, Virginia R. *White by Definition: Social Classification in Creole Louisiana*. New Brunswick, N.J.: Rutgers University Press, 1986.
Dooley, Patricia L., ed. *The Early Republic: Primary Documents on Events from 1799 to 1820*. Westport, Conn.: Greenwood, 2004.
Dormon, James H., ed. *Creoles of Color of the Gulf South*. Knoxville: University of Tennessee Press, 1996.
Douglas, Kelly Brown. *Stand Your Ground: Black Bodies and the Justice of God*. Maryknoll, N.Y.: Orbis Books, 2015.
Doyle, Don H. *New Men, New Cities, New South: Atlanta, Nashville, Charleston, Mobile, 1860–1910*. Chapel Hill: University of North Carolina Press, 1990.

Drago, Edmund L. *Initiative, Paternalism, and Race Relations: Charleston's Avery Normal Institute*. Athens: University of Georgia Press, 1990.

Dubois, Laurent. *Avengers of the New World: The Story of the Haitian Revolution*. Cambridge, Mass.: Harvard University Press, 2004.

———. *Haiti: The Aftershocks of History*. New York: Picador, 2012.

Dubos, Jean-Baptiste. *Réflexions critiques sur la poésie et sur la peinture*. Vol. 2. Paris: Pierre-Jean Mariette, 1733.

Dugatkin, Lee Alan. *Mr. Jefferson and the Giant Moose: Natural History in Early America*. Chicago: University of Chicago Press, 2009.

Dunbar-Nelson, Alice Moore. "People of Color in Louisiana." In Kein, *Creole*, 3–41.

Eastman, Scott. *Preaching Spanish Nationalism across the Hispanic Atlantic, 1759–1823*. Baton Rouge: Louisiana State University Press, 2012.

Edwards, Laura F. *The People and Their Peace: Legal Culture and the Transformation of Inequality in the Post-Revolutionary South*. Chapel Hill: University of North Carolina Press, 2009.

Egerton, Douglas. "Averting a Crisis: The Proslavery Critique of the American Colonization Society." *Civil War History* 43, no. 2 (June 1997): 142–56.

———. *Death or Liberty: African Americans and Revolutionary America*. New York: Oxford University Press, 2009.

———. *He Shall Go Out Free: The Lives of Denmark Vesey*. Lanham, Md.: Rowman and Littlefield, 2004.

———. "'Its Origin Is Not a Little Curious': A New Look at the American Colonization Society." *Journal of the Early Republic* 5, no. 4 (Winter 1985): 463–80.

Ellis, Elizabeth. "Petite Nation with Powerful Networks: The Tunicas in the Eighteenth Century." *Louisiana History* 58, no. 2 (Spring 2017): 133–78.

Ellis, Scott S. *The Faubourg Marigny of New Orleans: A History*. Baton Rouge: Louisiana State University Press, 2019.

Eltis, David. *The Rise of African Slavery in the Americas*. New York: Cambridge University Press, 2000.

Ely, Melvin Patrick. *Israel on the Appomattox: A Southern Experiment in Black Freedom from the 1790s through the Civil War*. New York: Alfred A. Knopf, 2004.

Englebert, Robert. "Making Indians in the American Backcountry: *Récits de voyage*, Cultural Mobility, and Imagining Empire in the Age of Revolutions." in Englebert and Wegmann, *French Connections*, 193–220.

Englebert, Robert, and Andrew N. Wegmann, eds. *French Connections: Cultural Mobility in North America and the Atlantic World, 1600–1875*. Baton Rouge: Louisiana State University Press, 2020.

Epstein, Linda S. "Pierre André Destrac Cazenave: Judah Touro's 'Pet' or a Man of Means?" *Louisiana History: Journal of the Louisiana Historical Association* 53, no. 1 (Winter 2012): 5–29.

Esdaile, Charles. *Napoleon's Wars: An International History, 1803–1815*. New York: Viking, 2007.

Eslinger, Ellen. "Liberation in a Rural Context: The Valley of Virginia, 1800–1860." In *Paths to Freedom: Manumission in the Atlantic World*, edited by Rosemary Brana-Shute and Randy J. Sparks, 363–79. Columbia: University of South Carolina Press, 2009.
Evans, Freddi Williams. *Congo Square: African Roots in New Orleans*. Lafayette: University of Louisiana at Lafayette Press, 2011.
Everett, Donald E. "Emigres and Militiamen: Free Persons of Color in New Orleans, 1803–1815." *Journal of Negro History* 38, no. 4 (October 1953): 377–402.
———. "Free Persons of Color in New Orleans, 1803–1865." PhD diss., Tulane University, 1952.
Everill, Bronwen. *Abolition and Empire in Sierra Leone and Liberia*. New York: Palgrave Macmillan, 2013.
Faber, Eberhard L. *Building the Land of Dreams: New Orleans and the Transformation of Early America*. Princeton, N.J.: Princeton University Press, 2016.
Faber, Michel. "New Orleans Creole Expatriates in France: Romance and Reality." In Kein, *Creole*, 179–95.
Fabian, Ann. *The Skull Collectors: Race, Science, and America's Unburied Dead*. Chicago: University of Chicago Press, 2010.
Fabre, Michel. *From Harlem to Paris: Black American Writers in France, 1840–1980*. Urbana: University of Illinois Press, 1991.
Fanon, Frantz. *Black Skin, White Masks*. Translated by Richard Philcox. 1952. Reprint, New York: Grove, 2008.
———. *The Wretched of the Earth*. Translated by Richard Philcox. New York: Grove, 2004.
Farnham, Christie Anne. *The Education of the Southern Belle: Higher Education and Student Socialization in the Antebellum South*. New York: New York University Press, 1994.
Feijoo y Montenegro, Benito Jerónimo. *Obras escogidas del padre fray Benito Jerónimo Feijoo y Montenegro*. Madrid: M. Rivadeneyra, 1863.
Fernandez, Mark F. *From Chaos to Continuity: The Evolution of Louisiana's Judicial System, 1712–1862*. Baton Rouge: Louisiana State University Press, 2001.
Flannery, Matthew, comp. *New Orleans in 1805: A Directory and a Census, Together with Resolutions Authorizing Same, Now Printed for the First Time from the Original Manuscript*. Facsimile. New Orleans, La.: Pelican Gallery, 1936.
Follett, Richard. *The Sugar Masters: Planters and Slaves in Louisiana's Cane World, 1820–1860*. Baton Rouge: Louisiana State University Press, 2005.
Foner, Eric. *The Fiery Trial: Abraham Lincoln and American Slavery*. New York: W. W. Norton, 2010.
———. *Free Soil, Free Labor, Free Men: The Ideology of the Republican Party before the Civil War*. New York: Oxford University Press, 1970.
Foner, Laura. "The Free People of Color in Louisiana and St. Domingue: A Comparative Portrait of Two Three-Caste Slave Societies." *Journal of Social History* 3, no. 4 (Summer 1970): 406–30.
Fontenelle, Bernard de. "Observations de physique générale." In *Histoire de l'Académie royale des sciences*. Paris: Imprimerie royale, 1734, 15–17.

Forbes, Ella. "African-American Resistance to Colonization." *Journal of Black Studies* 21, no. 2 (December 1990): 210–33.

Forbes, Jack D. *Africans and Native Americans: The Language of Race and the Evolution of Red-Black Peoples.* Urbana: University of Illinois Press, 1993.

Ford, Lacy K. *Deliver Us from Evil: The Slavery Question in the Old South.* New York: Oxford University Press, 2009.

Foucault, Michel. *The History of Sexuality.* Vol. 1, *An Introduction.* New York: Vintage, 1990.

Fouché, Louis Nelson. *Nouveau recueil de pensées, opinions, sentences et maximes de différents écrivains, philosophes et orateurs, anciens, modernes et contemporains.* New Orleans: M. Capo, 1882.

Franklin, John Hope. *The Free Negro in North Carolina, 1790–1860.* Chapel Hill: University of North Carolina Press, 1943.

Franklin, John Hope, and Loren Schweninger. *In Search of the Promised Land: A Slave Family in the Old South.* New York: Oxford University Press, 2006.

Fraser, Charles. *Reminiscences of Charleston.* Charleston, S.C.: John Russell, 1854.

Fraser, Walter J., Jr. *Charleston! Charleston!: The History of a Southern City.* Columbia: University of South Carolina Press, 1989.

Freehling, William W. *The Road to Disunion.* Vol. 1, *Secessionists at Bay, 1776–1854.* New York: Oxford University Press, 1990.

Freeman, A. C., ed. and comp. *The American Decisions: Cases of General Value and Authority Decided in the Courts of the Several States.* Vol. 17. San Francisco: Bancroft-Whitney, 1910.

French, Benjamin Franklin, ed. *Historical Collections of Louisiana, Embracing Many Rare and Valuable Documents Relating to the Natural, Civil and Political History of that State.* Vol. 5, *Historical Memoirs of Louisiana.* New York: Lamport, Blakeman and Law, 1853.

Frick, Carolyn E. *The Making of Haiti: The Saint Domingue Revolution from Below.* Knoxville: University of Tennessee Press, 1990.

Fuchs, Barbara. *Passing for Spain: Cervantes and the Fictions of Identity.* Urbana: University of Illinois Press, 2003.

Gage, Thomas. *A New Survey of the West Indies, or The English American, his Travels by Sea and Land.* London: A. Clark, 1677.

Garrett, Aaron. "Human Nature." In *The Cambridge History of Eighteenth-Century Philosophy*, vol. 1, edited by Knud Haakonssen, 160–233. New York: Cambridge University Press, 2006.

Garrigus, John D. *Before Haiti: Race and Citizenship in French Saint-Domingue.* New York: Palgrave Macmillan, 2006.

———. "Colour, Class, and Identity on the Eve of the Haitian Revolution: Saint-Domingue's Free Coloured Elite as *colons américains.*" In *Against the Odds: Free Blacks in the Slave Societies of the Americas*, edited by Jane G. Landers, 20–43. London: Frank Cass, 1996.

Gatewood, Willard B. *Aristocrats of Color: The Black Elite, 1880–1920.* Bloomington: Indiana University Press, 1990.

Gayarré, Charles. *Louisiana: Its Colonial History and Romance*. New York: Harper and Brothers, 1851.

Gehman, Mary. *The Free People of Color of New Orleans: An Introduction*. New Orleans: Margaret Media, 1994.

———. "The Mexico-Louisiana Creole Connection." *Louisiana Cultural Vistas* 11, no. 4 (Winter 2001–2002): 68–76.

———. "Visible Means of Support: Businesses, Professions, and Trades of Free People of Color." In Kein, *Creole*, 208–22.

Gellman, David N. *Emancipating New York: The Politics of Slavery and Freedom, 1777–1827*. Baton Rouge: Louisiana State University Press, 2006.

Gill, James. *Lords of Misrule: Mardi Gras and the Politics of Race in New Orleans*. Jackson: University Press of Mississippi, 1997.

Giraud, Marcel. *A History of French Louisiana*. Vol. 5: *The Company of the Indies, 1723–1731*. Translated by Brian Pearce. Baton Rouge: Louisiana State University Press, 1991.

Gitlin, Jay. *The Bourgeois Frontier: French Towns, French Traders, and American Expansion*. New Haven, Conn.: Yale University Press, 2010.

Gleeson, David T. *The Irish in the South, 1815–1877*. Chapel Hill: University of North Carolina Press, 2001.

Glover, Kathryn. *The Fugitive's Gibraltar: Escaping Slaves and Abolitionism in New Bedford, Massachusetts*. Amherst: University of Massachusetts Press, 2001.

Gobineau, Arthur de. *The Moral and Intellectual Diversity of Races*. Edited and translated by Henry Hotz. Philadelphia: J. B. Lippincott, 1856.

Goldfield, David R. *Urban Growth in the Age of Sectionalism: Virginia, 1847–1861*. Baton Rouge: Louisiana State University Press, 1977.

Goloboy, Jennifer L. "Strangers in the South: Charleston's Merchants and Middle-Class Values in the Early Republic." In Wells and Green, *Southern Middle Class*, 40–61.

Gomez, Michael A. *Exchanging Our Country Marks: The Transformation of African Identities in the Colonial and Antebellum South*. Chapel Hill: University of North Carolina Press, 1997.

Gonzalez, Aston. *Visualizing Equality: African American Rights and Visual Culture in the Nineteenth Century*. Chapel Hill: University of North Carolina Press, 2020.

Gossett, Thomas F. *Race: The History of an Idea in America*. New York: Oxford University Press, 1963.

Gotanda, Neil. "A Critique of 'Our Constitution Is Color-Blind.'" In *Critical Race Theory: The Key Writings That Formed the Movement*, edited by Kimberlé Crenshaw, Neil Gotanda, Gary Peller, and Kendall Thomas, 257–75. New York: New Press, 1995.

Gould, Virginia Meacham. "The Free Creoles of Color of the Antebellum Gulf Ports of Mobile and Pensacola: A Struggle for the Middle Ground." In Dormon, *Creoles of Color*, 28–50.

———. "The Parish Identities of Free Creoles of Color in Pensacola and Mobile, 1698–1860." *U.S. Catholic Historian* 14, no. 3 (Summer 1996): 1–10.

Graham, Lawrence Otis. *Our Kind of People: Inside America's Black Upper Class*. New York: HarperCollins, 1999.

———. *The Senator and the Socialite: The True Story of America's First Black Dynasty.* New York: HarperCollins, 2006.
Grant, Benjamin, ed. and comp. *Reports of Cases Argued and Adjudged in the Supreme Court of Pennsylvania.* Vol. 1. Philadelphia: H. P. and R. H. Small, 1859.
Gravier, Henri. *La colonisation de la Louisiane à l'époque de Law, octobre 1717–janvier 1721.* Paris: Masson, 1904.
Greenberg, Amy S. *Manifest Manhood and the Antebellum American Empire.* New York: Cambridge University Press, 2005.
———. *A Wicked War: Polk, Clay, Lincoln, and the 1846 U.S. Invasion of Mexico.* New York: Alfred A. Knopf, 2012.
Groom, Winston. *Patriotic Fire: Andrew Jackson and Jean Lafitte at the Battle of New Orleans.* New York: Alfred A. Knopf, 2006.
Gross, Ariela. *What Blood Won't Tell: A History of Race on Trial in America.* Cambridge, Mass.: Harvard University Press, 2008.
Gudmestad, Robert H. *A Troublesome Commerce: The Transformation of the Interstate Slave Trade.* Baton Rouge: Louisiana State University Press, 2003.
Gutiérrez, Ramòn A. "New Mexico, Mestizaje, and the Transnations of North America." In *Mexico and Mexicans in the Making of the United States,* edited by John Tutino, 257–284. Austin: University of Texas Press, 2012.
Guyatt, Nicholas. *Bind Us Apart: How Enlightened Americans Invented Racial Segregation.* New York: Basic Books, 2016.
———. *Providence and the Invention of the United States, 1607–1876.* New York: Cambridge University Press, 2007.
Haddox, Thomas F. "The 'Nous' of Southern Catholic Quadroons: Racial, Ethnic, and Religious Identity in *Les cenelles.*" *American Literature* 73, no. 4 (December 2001): 757–78.
Hall, Benjamin F., ed. and comp. *Official Opinions of the Attorneys General of the United States.* Vol. 1. Washington, D.C.: United States Government Printing Office, 1852.
Hall, Gwendolyn Midlo. *Africans in Colonial Louisiana: The Development of Afro-Creole Culture in the Eighteenth Century.* Baton Rouge: Louisiana State University Press, 1992.
———, ed. *Databases for the Study of Afro-Louisiana History and Genealogy: Computerized Information from Original Manuscript Sources.* CD-ROM. Baton Rouge: Louisiana State University Press, 2000.
———. "Saint Domingue." In Cohen and Greene, *Neither Slave nor Free: The Freedmen of African Descent in the Slave Societies of the New World,* edited by David W. Cohen and Jack J. Greene, 172–92. Baltimore: Johns Hopkins University Press, 1972.
Hall, Stephen G. *A Faithful Account of the Race: African American Historical Writing in Nineteenth-Century America.* Chapel Hill: University of North Carolina Press, 2009.
Halttunen, Karen. *Confidence Men and Painted Women: A Study of Middle-Class Culture in America, 1830–1870.* New Haven, Conn.: Yale University Press, 1982.
Hanger, Kimberly S. *Bounded Lives, Bounded Places: Free Black Society in Colonial New Orleans, 1769–1803.* Durham, N.C.: Duke University Press, 1997.

———. "Origins of New Orleans's Free Creoles of Color." In Dormon, *Creoles of Color*, 1–27.

———. "Patronage, Property and Persistence: The Emergence of a Free Black Elite in Spanish New Orleans." *Slavery & Abolition: A Journal of Slave and Post-Slave Studies* 17, no. 1 (April 1996): 44–64.

Harris, Katherine J. "Colonization and Abolition in Connecticut." In *African American Connecticut Explored*, edited by Elizabeth J. Normen, 64–68. Middletown, Conn.: Wesleyan University Press, 2013.

Harris, Leslie M. *In the Shadow of Slavery: African Americans in New York City, 1626–1863*. Chicago: University of Chicago Press, 2003.

Harris, Robert L., Jr. "Charleston's Free Afro-American Elite: The Brown Fellowship Society and the Humane Brotherhood." *South Carolina Historical Magazine* 82, no. 4 (October 1981): 289–310.

Harrold, Stanley. *Abolitionists and the South, 1831–1861*. Lexington: University Press of Kentucky, 1995.

Hasci, Timothy A. *Second Home: Orphan Asylums and Poor Families in America*. Cambridge, Mass.: Harvard University Press, 1997.

Havard, Gilles. *L'Amérique fantôme: Les aventuriers francophones du Nouveau Monde*. Paris: Flammarion, 2019.

———. *Empire et métissages: Indiens et français dans le Pays d'en Haut, 1660–1715*. Paris: Presses de l'Université Paris-Sorbonne, 2003.

———. "'Protection' and 'Unequal Alliance': The French Conception of Sovereignty over Indians in New France." In *French and Indians in the Heart of North America, 1630–1815*, edited by Robert Englebert and Guillaume Teasdale, 13–38. East Lansing: Michigan State University Press, 2013.

Havard, Gilles, and Cécile Vidal. *Histoire de l'Amérique française*. Paris: Flammarion, 2003.

Heinegg, Paul, ed. and comp. *Free African Americans of North Carolina, Virginia, and South Carolina: From the Colonial Period to About 1820*. Baltimore: Genealogical Publishing, 2005.

Hening, William W., ed. *The Statutes at Large: Being a Collection of All the Laws of Virginia*. Vols. 10–12. Richmond, Va.: Printed for the editor by George Cochran, 1822–23.

Herzog, Tamar. *Defining Nations: Immigrants and Citizens in Early Modern Spain and Spanish America*. New Haven, Conn.: Yale University Press, 2003.

Heuman, Gad J. *Between Black and White: Race, Politics, and the Free Coloreds in Jamaica, 1792–1865*. Westport, Conn.: Greenwood, 1981.

Hickey, Donald R. *The War of 1812: A Forgotten Conflict*. Urbana: University of Illinois Press, 1989.

Hill, Ruth. *Hierarchy, Commerce, and Fraud in Bourbon Spanish America: A Postal Inspector's Exposé*. Nashville, Tenn.: Vanderbilt University Press, 2005.

Hinks, Peter, ed. *David Walker's Appeal to the Coloured Citizens of the World*. University Park: Pennsylvania State University Press, 2000.

Hirsch, Arnold R., and Joseph Logsdon, eds. *Creole New Orleans: Race and Americanization*. Baton Rouge: Louisiana State University Press, 1992.

Hobbs, Allyson. *A Chosen Exile: A History of Racial Passing in American Life*. Cambridge, Mass.: Harvard University Press, 2014.

Hodes, Martha. *White Women, Black Men: Illicit Sex in the Nineteenth-Century South*. New Haven, Conn.: Yale University Press, 1997.

Hodgkin, Thomas. *An Inquiry into the Merits of the American Colonization Society and a Reply to the Charges Brought against It*. London: R. Watts, 1833.

Hofstadter, Richard. *The Age of Reform*. New York: Vintage, 1955.

Holder, Charles Frederick. *Louis Agassiz: His Life and Work*. New York: G. P. Putnam and Sons, 1893.

Hollandsworth, James G., Jr. *The Louisiana Native Guards: The Black Military Experience during the Civil War*. Baton Rouge: Louisiana State University Press, 1995.

Holly, Nathaniel. "From Itsa'ti to Charlestown: The Urban Lives of Cherokees in Early America." PhD diss., William and Mary, 2019.

Holt, Michael F. *The Rise and Fall of the American Whig Party: Jacksonian Politics and the Onset of the Civil War*. New York: Oxford University Press, 1999.

Hood, Robert E. *Begrimed and Black: Christian Traditions on Blacks and Blackness*. Minneapolis, Minn.: Augsburg Fortress Press, 1994.

Hopkins, A. G. *American Empire: A Global History*. Princeton, N.J.: Princeton University Press, 2018.

Horsey, John R., ed. and comp. *Ordinances of the City of Charleston from the 14th of September 1854 to the 1st of December 1859*. Charleston, S.C.: Walker, Evans, 1859.

Horsman, Reginald. *Josiah Nott of Mobile: Southerner, Physician, and Racial Theorist*. Baton Rouge: Louisiana State University Press, 1987.

———. *Race and Manifest Destiny: The Origins of American Racial Anglo-Saxonism*. Cambridge, Mass.: Harvard University Press, 1981.

Horton, James Oliver, and Lois E. Horton. *In Hope of Liberty: Culture, Community, and Protest among Northern Free Blacks, 1700–1860*. New York: Oxford University Press, 1997.

Howe, Daniel Walker. *What Hath God Wrought: The Transformation of America, 1815–1848*. New York: Oxford University Press, 2007.

Hunt, Alfred N. *Haiti's Influence on Antebellum America: Slumbering Volcano in the Caribbean*. Baton Rouge: Louisiana State University Press, 1988.

Hunter, Tera W. *Bound in Wedlock: Slave and Free Black Marriage in the Nineteenth Century*. Cambridge, Mass.: Belknap Press of Harvard University Press, 2017.

Ingersoll, Thomas N. "Free Blacks in a Slave Society: New Orleans, 1718–1812." *William and Mary Quarterly*, 3rd. ser., 48, no. 2 (April 1991): 173–200.

———. *Mammon and Manon in Early New Orleans: The First Slave Society in the Deep South, 1718–1819*. Knoxville: University of Tennessee Press, 1999.

———. "The Slave Trade and the Ethnic Diversity of Louisiana's Slave Community." *Louisiana History* 37, no. 2 (Spring 1996): 133–61.

Irmscher, Christoph. *Louis Agassiz: Creator of American Science*. New York: Houghton Mifflin Harcourt, 2013.

Isenberg, Nancy. *Sex and Citizenship in Antebellum America*. Chapel Hill: University of North Carolina Press, 1997.

———. *White Trash: The 400-Year Untold History of Class in America*. New York: Random House, 2016.

Isenberg, Nancy, and Andrew Burstein. *The Problem of Democracy: The Presidents Adams Confront the Cult of Personality*. New York: Random House, 2019.

Israel, Jonathan. *The Expanding Blaze: How the American Revolution Ignited the World, 1775–1848*. Princeton, N.J.: Princeton University Press, 2017.

Jackson, Luther P. "Free Negroes of Petersburg, Virginia." *Journal of Negro History* 12, no. 3 (July 1927): 365–88.

Jaher, Frederic Cople. *The Urban Establishment: Upper Strata Boston, New York, Charleston, and Los Angeles*. Champaign: University of Illinois Press, 1982.

Jefferson, Thomas. *Notes on the State of Virginia*. Edited by Frank Shuffelton. 1785. Reprint, New York: Penguin Classics, 1999.

Johnson, Jerah. *Congo Square in New Orleans*. New Orleans: Louisiana Landmarks Society, 1995.

Johnson, Michael P., and James L. Roark. *Black Masters: A Free Family of Color in the Old South*. New York: W. W. Norton, 1984.

———, eds. *No Chariot Let Down: Charleston's Free People of Color on the Eve of the Civil War*. Chapel Hill: University of North Carolina Press, 1984.

Johnson, Walter. *Soul by Soul: Life Inside the Antebellum Slave Market*. Cambridge, Mass.: Harvard University Press, 1999.

Johnson, Whittington B. *Black Savannah, 1788–1864*. Fayetteville: University of Arkansas Press, 1996.

Johnston, James Hugo. *Race Relations in Virginia and Miscegenation in the South, 1776–1860*. Amherst: University of Massachusetts Press, 1970.

Jones, Bernie D. *Fathers of Conscience: Mixed-Race Inheritance in the Antebellum South*. Athens: University of Georgia Press, 2009.

Jones, Hilary. *The Métis of Senegal: Urban Life and Politics in French West Africa*. Bloomington: Indiana University Press, 2013.

Jones, Martha S. *Birthright Citizens: A History of Race and Rights in Antebellum America*. New York: Cambridge University Press, 2018.

Jordan, Winthrop D. "American Chiaroscuro: The Status and Definition of Mulattoes in the British Colonies," *William and Mary Quarterly* 19, no. 2 (April 1962): 183–200.

———. *White over Black: American Attitudes toward the Negro, 1550–1812*. Chapel Hill: University of North Carolina Press, 1968.

Kaestle, Carl F. *Pillars of the Republic: Common Schools and American Society, 1780–1860*. New York: Hill and Wang, 1983.

Kale, Steven. *French Salons: High Society and Political Sociability from the Old Regime to the Revolution of 1848*. Baltimore: Johns Hopkins University Press, 2004.

Kastor, Peter J. *The Nation's Crucible: The Louisiana Purchase and the Creation of America*. New Haven, Conn.: Yale University Press, 2004.

———. "'They Are All Frenchmen': Background and Nation in an Age of Transformation." In Kastor and Weil, *Empires of the Imagination: Transatlantic Histories of the Louisiana Purchase*, edited by Peter J. Kastor and François Weil, 239–67. Charlottesville: University of Virginia Press, 2009.

Katzew, Ilona. *Casta Painting: Images of Race in Eighteenth-Century Mexico*. New Haven, Conn.: Yale University Press, 2004.

Kein, Sybil, ed. *Creole: The History and Legacy of Louisiana's Free People of Color*. Baton Rouge: Louisiana State University Press, 2000.

Kerr, Audrey Elisa. "The Paper Bag Principle: Of the Myth and the Motion of Colorism." *Journal of American Folklore* 118, no. 469 (Summer 2005): 271–89.

Kettner, James H. *The Development of American Citizenship, 1608–1870*. Chapel Hill: University of North Carolina Press, 1978.

Kimball, Gregg D. *American City, Southern Place: A Cultural History of Antebellum Richmond*. Athens: University of Georgia Press, 2000.

King, Grace. *New Orleans: The Place and the People*. New York: MacMillan, 1895.

King, Nicole. *C. L. R. James and Creolization: Circles of Influence*. Jackson: University Press of Mississippi, 2001.

King, Stewart R. *Blue Coat or Powdered Wig: Free People of Color in Pre- revolutionary Saint Domingue*. Athens: University of Georgia Press, 2001.

Kingstone, Peter. *The Political Economy of Latin America: Reflections of Neoliberalism and Development*. New York: Routledge, 2011.

Kinnaird, Lawrence. *Spain in the Mississippi Valley, 1765–1792*. Vol. 2. Washington, D.C.: Government Printing Office for American Historical Association, 1946.

Kinsbruner, Jay. *The Colonial Spanish-American City: Urban Life in the Age of Atlantic Capitalism*. Austin: University of Texas Press, 2012.

Kinshasa, Kwando M. *Emigration vs. Assimilation: The Debate in the African American Press, 1827–1861*. Jefferson, N.C.: McFarland, 1988.

Klaus, Sidney N. "A History of the Science of Pigmentation." In *The Pigmentary System: Physiology and Pathophysiology*, edited by James L. Nordlund, 1–10. New York: Oxford University Press, 1998.

Knight, Alan. *Mexico: The Colonial Era*. New York: Cambridge University Press, 2002.

Koger, Larry. *Black Slaveowners: Free Black Slave Masters in South Carolina, 1790–1860*. Jefferson, N.C.: McFarland, 1985.

Konetzke, Richard, ed. *Colección de documentos para la formación social de Hispanoamerica*. 3 vols. Madrid: Consejo Superior de Investigaciones Cientificas, 1953–58.

Kukla, Jon. *A Wilderness So Immense: The Louisiana Purchase and the Destiny of America*. New York: Alfred A. Knopf, 2003.

Kupperman, Karen Ordahl. "Presentment of Civility: English Reading of American Self-Presentation in the Early Years of Colonization." *William and Mary Quarterly* 54, no. 1 (January 1997): 193–228.

Kuznesof, Elizabeth Anne. "Ethnic and Gender Influences on 'Spanish' Creole Society in Colonial Spanish America." *Colonial Latin American Review* 4, no. 1 (1995): 153–76.

Lachance, Paul F. "The 1809 Immigration of Saint-Domingue Refugees to New Orleans: Reception, Integration, and Impact." *Louisiana History* 29, no. 2 (Spring 1988): 109–41.

———. "The Foreign French." In Hirsch and Logsdon, *Creole New Orleans*, 101–30.

———. "The Formation of a Three-Caste Society: Evidence from Wills in Antebellum New Orleans." *Social Science History* 18, no. 2 (Summer 1994): 211–42.

———. "The Growth of the Free and Slave Populations of French Colonial Louisiana." In Bond, *French Colonial Louisiana and the Atlantic World*, 204–43.

———. "The Limits of Privilege: Where Free Persons of Colour Stood in the Hierarchy of Wealth in Antebellum New Orleans." *Slavery & Abolition: A Journal of Slave and Post-Slave Studies* 17, no. 1 (April 1996): 65–84.

———. "The Politics of Fear: French Louisianans and the Slave Trade, 1786–1809." *Plantation Society in the Americas* 1 (June 1979): 162–97.

———. "Repercussions of the Haitian Revolution in Louisiana." In *The Impact of the Haitian Revolution in the Atlantic World*, edited by David P. Geggus, 209–30. Columbia: University of South Carolina Press, 2001.

Lafaye, Jacques. *Quetzalcóatl and Guadalupe: The Formation of Mexican National Consciousness, 1531–1813*. Chicago: University of Chicago Press, 1976.

Lafon, B[arthélémy]. *Annuaire louisianais*. New Orleans: printed by the author, 1808.

Lake, Obiagele. *Blue Veins and Kinky Hair: Naming and Color Consciousness in African America*. Westport, Conn.: Praeger, 2003.

Landers, Jane G. *Atlantic Creoles in the Age of Revolutions*. Cambridge, Mass.: Harvard University Press, 2010.

Langlois, Gilles-Antoine. *Des villes pour la Louisiane française: Théorie et pratique de l'urbanistique coloniale au 18e siècle*. Paris: L'Harmattan, 2003.

Lanusse, Armand. *Les cenelles: Choix des poésies indigènes*. New Orleans: H. Lauvre, 1845.

———. "La liberté." *L'union*, October 18, 1862.

Latimer, Jon. *1812: War with America*. Cambridge, Mass.: Belknap Press of Harvard University Press, 2009.

Lebsock, Suzanne. *The Free Women of Petersburg: Status and Culture in a Southern Town, 1784–1860*. New York: W. W. Norton, 1985.

Le Cat, Claude-Nicolas. *Traité de la couleur de la peau humaine en général, de celle des nègres en particulier, et de la métamorphose d'une de ces couleurs en l'autre, soit de naissance, soit accidentellement*. Amsterdam, 1765.

Leclerc, Georges-Louis. *Buffon's Natural History*. Translated by J. S. Barr. 9 vols. London: H. D. Symons, 1797.

———. *Histoire naturelle, générale et particulière*. Paris: Imprimerie Royale, 1749–88.

———. "A Natural History, General and Particular." In *Race and the Enlightenment: A Reader*, edited by Emmanuel Chukwudi Eze, 15. –29. Malden, Mass.: Blackwell, 1997.

Lemelle, Sidney J. "The 'Circum-Caribbean' and the Continuity of Cultures: The Donato Colony in Mexico, 1830–1860." *Journal of Pan African Studies* 6, no. 1 (July 2013): 57–75.

Lemire, Elise. *"Miscegenation": Making Race in America*. Philadelphia: University of Pennsylvania Press, 2002.

Le Page du Pratz, Antoine-Simon. *The History of Louisiana*. Edited by Joseph G. Tregle Jr. Baton Rouge: Louisiana State University Press for the Louisiana American Revolution Bicentennial Commission, 1975.
Lepore, Jill. *These Truths: A History of the United States*. New York: W. W. Norton, 2019.
Leroy-Beaulieu, Paul. *De la colonisation chez les peuples modernes*. 6th ed. 2 vols. Paris: Libraire Félix Alcan et Guillaumin Réunies, 1908.
Lévêque, Pierre. "The Revolutionary Crisis of 1848–1851 in France: Origins and Course of Events." In *Europe in 1848: Revolution and Reform*, edited by Dieter Dowe, Heinz-Gerhard Haupt, Dieter Langewiesche, and Jonathan Sperber. New York: Berghahn Books, 2001.
Lewis, Jan Ellen, and Peter S. Onuf, eds. *Sally Hemings and Thomas Jefferson: History, Memory, and Civic Culture*. Charlottesville: University of Virginia Press, 1999.
Link, William A. *Roots of Secession: Slavery and Politics in Antebellum Virginia*. Chapel Hill: University of North Carolina Press, 2003.
Lislet, L. Moreau, and Henry Carleton, eds. and trans. *The Laws of Las Siete Partidas, Which Are Still in Force in the State of Louisiana*. Vol. 1. New Orleans: James McKaraher, 1820.
Logsdon, Joseph, and Caryn Cossé Bell. "The Americanization of Black New Orleans, 1850–1900." In Hirsch and Logsdon, *Creole New Orleans*, 201–61.
Long, Carolyn Morrow. "The Macarty Family of Orleans Parish." *New Orleans Genesis* (April 2013): 101–7.
———. *Madame Lalaurie: Mistress of the Haunted House*. Gainesville: University Press of Florida, 2012.
Lovato, Frank Joseph. "Households and Neighborhoods among Free People of Color in New Orleans: A View from the Census, 1850–1860." Master's thesis, University of New Orleans, 2010.
Lovett, Bobby L. *The African-American History of Nashville, Tennessee, 1780–1930: Elites and Dilemmas*. Fayetteville: University of Arkansas Press, 1999.
Lowrie, Walter, ed. and comp. *American State Papers: Documents, Legislative and Executive, of the Congress of the United States*. Vol. 1. Washington: Gales and Seaton, 1834.
Lowther, Kevin G. *The African American Odyssey of John Kizell: A South Carolina Slave Returns to Fight the Slave Trade in His African Homeland*. Columbia: University of South Carolina Press, 2011.
Lurie, Edward. *Louis Agassiz and the Races of Man*. Boston: Massachusetts Institute of Technology Press, 1954.
Macdonald, Robert R., John R. Kemp, and Edward F. Haas, eds. *Louisiana's Black Heritage*. New Orleans: Louisiana State Museum, 1979.
MacLeod, Duncan J. *Slavery, Race and the American Revolution*. New York: Cambridge University Press, 1974.
Mahoney, Timothy R. *Provincial Lives: Middle-Class Experience in the Antebellum Middle West*. New York: Cambridge University Press, 1999.
Mannhard, Marilyn. "The Free People of Color in Antebellum Mobile County, Alabama." Master's thesis, University of South Alabama, 1982.

Maris-Wolf, Ted. *Family Bonds: Free Blacks and Re-enslavement Law in Antebellum Virginia*. Chapel Hill: University of North Carolina Press, 2015.

Mark, Peter A. *"Portuguese" Style and Luso-African Identity: Precolonial Senegambia, Sixteenth–Nineteenth Centuries*. Bloomington: Indiana University Press, 2002.

Marks, John Garrison. *Black Freedom in the Age of Slavery: Race, Status, and Identity in the Urban Americas*. Columbia: University of South Carolina Press, 2020.

Martin, Charles D. *The White African American Body: A Cultural and Literary Exploration*. New Brunswick, N.J.: Rutgers University Press, 2002.

Mascou, Margot. *New Orleans' Free-Men-of-Color: Cabinetmakers in the New Orleans Furniture Trade*. New Orleans: Xavier Review Press, 2008.

Mason, Matthew. *Slavery and Politics in the Early Republic*. Chapel Hill: University of North Carolina Press, 2006.

Massachusetts Colonization Society. *Sixth Annual Report of the Board of Managers of the Massachusetts Colonization Society*. Boston: Press of T. R. Marvin, 1847.

Matthews, Gary. *More American Than Southern: Kentucky, Slavery, and the War for an American Ideology, 1828–1861*. Knoxville: University of Tennessee Press, 2014.

Maxcy, Virgil, ed. and comp. *The Laws of Maryland*. Baltimore: Philip H. Nicklin, 1811.

McAlister, L. N. "Social Structure and Social Change in New Spain." *Hispanic American Historical Review* 43, no. 3 (August 1963): 349–70.

McBride, Spencer W. *Pulpit and Nation: Clergymen and the Politics of Revolutionary America*. Charlottesville: University of Virginia Press, 2016.

McCaa, Robert. "*Calidad, Clase*, and Marriage in Colonial Mexico: The Case of Parral, 1788–90." *Hispanic American Historical Review* 64, no. 3 (August 1984): 477–501.

McConnell, Roland C. "Louisiana's Black Military History, 1729–1865." In Macdonald, Kemp, and Haas, *Louisiana's Black Heritage*, 32–62.

———. *Negro Troops of Antebellum Louisiana: A History of the Battalion of Free Men of Color*. Baton Rouge: Louisiana State University Press, 1968.

McCullugh, Erin Elizabeth. "'Heaven's Last, Worst Gift to White Men': The Quadroons of Antebellum New Orleans." Master's thesis, Portland State University, 2010.

McDonald, Robert M. S. *Confounding Father: Thomas Jefferson's Image in His Own Time*. Charlottesville: University of Virginia Press, 2016.

McInnis, Maurie Dee. *The Politics of Taste in Antebellum Charleston*. Chapel Hill: University of North Carolina Press, 2005.

Meckel, Johann Friedrich. "Recherches anatomiques, sur la nature de l'épiderme, et du réseau, qu'on appelle Malpighien." In *Mémoires de l'Académie royale des sciences et des belles letters de Berlin*, 79–113. Berlin: Ambroise Haude, 1755.

Merrill, Ellen C. *Germans of Louisiana*. Gretna, La.: Pelican, 2005.

Miceli, Mary Veronica. "The Influence of the Roman Catholic Church on Slavery in Colonial Louisiana under French Dominion, 1719–1763." PhD diss., Tulane University, 1979.

Miller, John Chester. *The Wolf by the Ears: Thomas Jefferson and Slavery*. Charlottesville: University Press of Virginia, 1991.

Miller, Monica L. *Slaves to Fashion: Black Dandyism and the Styling of Black Diasporic Identity*. Durham, N.C.: Duke University Press, 2009.

Miller, Randall M. "The Enemy Within: Some Effects of Foreign Immigrants on Antebellum Southern Cities." In *The Making of Urban America*, edited by Raymond A. Mohl, 52–67. 2nd ed. Lanham, Md.: SR Books, 1997.

Mills, Brandon. "'The United States of Africa': Liberian Independence and the Contested Meaning of a Black Republic." *Journal of the Early Republic* 34, no. 1 (Spring 2014): 79–107.

———. *The World Colonization Made: The Racial Geography of Early American Empire.* Philadelphia: University of Pennsylvania Press, 2020.

Mills, Gary B. *The Forgotten People: Cane River's Creoles of Color.* Baton Rouge: Louisiana State University Press, 1977.

———. "Miscegenation and the Free Negro in Antebellum 'Anglo' Alabama: A Reexamination of Southern Race Relations." *Journal of American History* 68, no. 1 (June 1981): 16–34.

Mills, Kenneth, William B. Taylor, and Sandra Lauderdale Graham, eds. *Colonial Latin America: A Documentary History.* Lanham, Md.: SR Books, 2002.

Mitchell, Mary Niall. "'A Good and Delicious Country': Free Children of Color and How They Learned to Imagine the Atlantic World in Nineteenth-Century Louisiana." *History of Education Quarterly* 40, no. 2 (Summer 2000): 123–44.

———. *Raising Freedom's Child: Black Children and Visions of the Future after Slavery.* New York: New York University Press, 2008.

Moitt, Bernard. *Women and Slavery in the French Antilles, 1635–1848.* Bloomington: Indiana University Press, 2001.

Mordecai, Samuel. *Virginia, Especially Richmond, in By-Gone Days.* Richmond, Va.: West and Johnson, 1860.

Moreau de Maupertuis, Pierre Louis. *Venus physique: Première partie, contenant une dissertation sur l'origine des hommes et des animaux.* Lyon: Jean-Marie Bruyset, 1756.

Moreau de Saint-Méry, Médéric Louis Élie. *Description topographique, physique, civile, politique et historique de la partie française de l'isle Saint Domingue.* Edited by Blanche Maurel and Etienne Taillemite. 1797. Reprint, Philadelphia: Société de l'Histoire des Colonies Françaises, 1984.

———. *Loix et constitutions des colonies françaises de l'Amérique sous le Vent.* 6 vols. Paris, 1784–90.

Morgan, Kenneth. *Slavery and the British Empire: From Africa to America.* New York: Oxford University Press, 2007.

Morgan, Ronald J. *Spanish American Saints and the Rhetoric of Identity, 1600–1810.* Tempe: University of Arizona Press, 2003.

Mörner, Magnus. *Race Mixture in the History of Latin America.* Boston: Little, Brown, 1967.

Morris, Christopher. *The Big Muddy: An Environmental History of the Mississippi and Its People.* New York: Oxford University Press, 2012.

Morrisson, Christian, and Wayne Snyder. "The Income Inequality of France in Historical Perspective." *European Review of Economic History* 4, no. 1 (2000): 59–83.

Morton, Patricia. "From Invisible Man to 'New People': The Recent Discovery of American Mulattoes." *Phylon* 46, no. 2 (2nd Quarter 1985): 106–22.

Murray, Robert. *Atlantic Passages: Race, Mobility, and Liberian Colonization.* Gainesville: University Press of Florida, 2021.

Mushal, Amanda Reece. "Bonds of Marriage and Community: Social Networks and the Development of a Commercial Middle Class in Antebellum South Carolina." In Wells and Green, *Southern Middle Class*, 62–83.

Myers, Amrita Chakrabarti. *Forging Freedom: Black Women and the Pursuit of Liberty in Antebellum Charleston.* Chapel Hill: University of North Carolina Press, 2011.

Nash, Gary B. "The Hidden History of Mestizo America." In *Sex, Love, Race: Crossing Boundaries in North American History*, edited by Martha Hodes, 10–32. New York: New York University Press.

―――. *Race and Revolution.* Madison, Wis.: Madison House, 1990.

Nelson, William J. "The Free Negro in the Ante Bellum New Orleans Press." PhD diss., Duke University, 1977.

Newman, Richard S. *The Transformation of American Abolitionism: Fighting Slavery in the Early Republic.* Chapel Hill: University of North Carolina Press, 2002.

Newton, Melanie J. *The Children of Africa in the Colonies: Free People of Color in Barbados in the Age of Emancipation.* Baton Rouge: Louisiana State University Press, 2008.

Nieto-Phillips, John M. *The Language of Blood: The Making of Spanish-American Identity in New Mexico, 1880s–1930s.* Albuquerque: University of New Mexico Press, 2004.

Niles, John Milton. "A New Era." *Harford (Conn.) Times*, September 23, 1817.

Nordmann, Christopher Andrew. "Free Negroes in Mobile County, Alabama." PhD diss., University of Alabama, 1990.

Nott, J[osiah] C. "An Examination of the Physical History of the Jews, in Its Bearings on the Question of the Unity of Races." In *Proceedings of the American Association for the Advancement of Science: Third Meeting, Held at Charleston, S.C., 1850.* Charleston, S.C.: Walker and James, 1850.

―――. "Hybridity of Animals, Viewed in Connection with the Natural History of Mankind." In Nott and Gliddon, *Types of Mankind*, 372–410.

―――. "The Mulatto a Hybrid-Probable Extermination of the Two Races If the Whites and Blacks Are Allowed to Intermarry." *American Journal of the Medical Sciences* 6, no. 11 (July 1843): 252–56.

Nott, J[osiah] C., and Geo. R. Gliddon. *Types of Mankind: Ethnological Researches Based upon Ancient Monuments, Paintings, Sculptures, and Crania of Races.* 7th ed. Philadelphia: Lippincott, Grambo, 1855.

O'Brien, Michael. *Conjectures of Order: Intellectual Life and the American South, 1810–1860.* 2 vols. Chapel Hill: University of North Carolina Press, 2004.

Ochs, Stephen J. *A Black Patriot and a White Priest: André Cailloux and Claude Paschal Maistre in Civil War New Orleans.* Baton Rouge: Louisiana State University Press, 2000.

O'Crouley, Pedro Alonso. *A Description of the Kingdom of New Spain.* Translated by Seán Galvin. 1774. San Francisco, Calif.: John Howell Books, 1972.

Olmsted, Frederick Law. *Cotton Kingdom: A Traveller's Observations on Cotton and Slavery in the American Slave States, Based upon Three Former Volumes of Journeys and Investigations.* 2 vols. New York: Mason Brothers, 1861.

Olwell, Robert. *Masters, Slaves, and Subjects: The Culture of Power in the South Carolina Low Country, 1740–1790.* Ithaca, N.Y.: Cornell University Press, 1998.

O'Neill, Charles Edwards. "Fine Arts and Literature: Nineteenth Century Louisiana Black Artists and Authors." In Macdonald, Kemp, and Haas, *Louisiana's Black Heritage,* 63–84.

Onuf, Peter S. *Jefferson and the Virginians: Democracy, Constitutions, and Empire.* Baton Rouge: Louisiana State University Press, 2018.

———. *Jefferson's Empire: The Language of American Nationhood.* Charlottesville: University Press of Virginia, 2000.

Painter, Nell Irvin. *The History of White People.* New York: W. W. Norton, 2010.

Palmer, Jennifer L. *Intimate Bonds: Family and Slavery in the French Atlantic.* Philadelphia: University of Pennsylvania Press, 2016.

Parham, Angel Adams. *American Routes: Racial Palimpsests and the Transformation of Race.* New York: Oxford University Press, 2017.

Park, Benjamin E. *American Nationalisms: Imagining Union in the Age of Revolutions, 1783–1833.* New York: Cambridge University Press, 2018.

Parry, John H. *The Spanish Seaborne Empire.* Berkeley: University of California Press, 1990.

Patch, Robert. *Maya Revolt and Revolution in the Eighteenth Century.* New York: M. E. Sharpe, 2002.

Payne, Daniel Alexander. *Recollections of Seventy Years.* 1888. Reprint, New York: Arno, 1968.

Peabody, Sue. "'A Nation Born to Slavery': Missionaries and Racial Discourse in Seventeenth-Century French Antilles." *Journal of Social History* 38, no. 1 (Autumn 2004): 113–26.

———. *"There Are No Slaves in France": The Political Culture of Race and Slavery in the Ancien Régime.* New York: Oxford University Press, 1996.

Perkins, A. E., ed. *Who's Who in Colored Louisiana.* Baton Rouge, La.: Douglas Loan Company, 1930.

Perret, J. John. "Victor Séjour, Black French Playwright from Louisiana." *French Review* 57, no. 2 (December 1983): 187–93.

Peters, Richard, ed. *The Public Statutes at Large of the United States of America.* Vol. 2. Boston: Charles C. Little and James Brown, 1845.

Peterson, Bernard L., Jr. *Early Black American Playwrights and Dramatic Writers: A Biographical Directory and Catalog of Plays, Films, and Broadcasting Scripts.* Westport, Conn.: Greenwood, 1990.

Petit, Emilien. *Traité sur le gouvernement des esclaves.* 2 vols. Paris: Knapen, 1777.

Peytraud, Lucien Pierre. *L'esclavage aux Antilles françaises avant 1789.* Paris: Hachette, 1897.

Pflugrad-Jackisch, Ami. *Brothers of a Vow: Secret Fraternal Orders and the Transformation of White Male Culture in Antebellum Virginia.* Athens: University of Georgia Press, 2010.

Phillips, Christopher. *Freedom's Port: The African American Community of Baltimore, 1790–1860.* Urbana: University of Illinois Press, 1997.

Pierson, Marion John Bennett, ed. *Louisiana Soldiers in the War of 1812.* Baton Rouge: Louisiana Genealogical and Historical Society, 1963.

Poblete, JoAnna. "Multitasking Mediators: Intracolonial Leadership in Filipino and Puerto Rican Communities in Hawai'i, 1900–1928." In *Transnational Crossroads: Remapping the Americas and the Pacific*, edited by Camilla Fojas and Rudy P. Guevarra Jr., 291–312. Lincoln: University of Nebraska Press, 2012.

Poe, William A. "A Look at Louisiana Colonization in Its African Setting." *Louisiana Studies* 11, no. 2 (Summer 1972): 111–24.

Powell, Lawrence N. *The Accidental City: Improvising New Orleans*. Cambridge, Mass.: Harvard University Press, 2012.

Power-Greene, Ousmane K. *Against Wind and Tide: The African American Struggle against the Colonization Movement*. New York: New York University Press, 2014.

Powers, Bernard E., Jr. *Black Charlestonians: A Social History, 1822–1885*. Fayetteville: University of Arkansas Press, 1994.

Pratt, Adam J. *Toward Cherokee Removal: Land, Violance, and the White Man's Chance*. Athens: University of Georgia Press, 2020.

Pratt, Lloyd. "The Lyric Public of *Les Cenelles*." In *Early African American Print Culture*, edited by Lara Langer Cohen and Jordan Alexander Stein, 253–74. Philadelphia: University of Pennsylvania Press, 2012.

Pritchard, James. "Population in French America, 1670–1730: The Demographic Context of Colonial Louisiana." In Bond, *French Colonial Louisiana and the Atlantic World*, 175–203.

Pryor, Elizabeth Stordeur. *Colored Travelers: Mobility and the Fight for Citizenship before the Civil War*. Chapel Hill: University of North Carolina Press, 2016.

Quarles, Benjamin. "Antebellum Free Blacks and the 'Spirit of '76.'" *Journal of Negro History* 61, no. 3 (July 1976): 229–42.

Rael, Patrick. *Black Identity and Black Protest in the Antebellum North*. Chapel Hill: University of North Carolina Press, 2002.

Rankin, David Connell. "The Forgotten People: Free People of Color in New Orleans, 1850–1870." PhD diss., Johns Hopkins University, 1976.

———. "The Politics of Caste: Free Colored Leadership in New Orleans during the Civil War." In Macdonald, Kemp, and Haas, *Louisiana's Black Heritage*, 107–46.

Reddick, Lawrence Dunbar. "The Negro in the New Orleans Press, 1850–1860: A Study in Attitudes and Propaganda." PhD diss., University of Chicago, 1939.

Reid-Vasquez, Michele. *The Year of the Lash: Free People of Color in Cuba and the Nineteenth-Century Atlantic World*. Athens: University of Georgia Press, 2011.

Reilly, Timothy F. "The Louisiana Colonization Society and the Protestant Missionary, 1830–1860." *Louisiana History: Journal of the Louisiana Historical Association* 43, no. 4 (Autumn 2002): 433–77.

Reinders, Robert C. "The Decline of the New Orleans Free Negro in the Decade before the Civil War." *Journal of Mississippi History* 25, no. 2 (April 1962): 88–99.

———. "The Free Negro in the New Orleans Economy, 1850–1860." *Louisiana History: Journal of the Louisiana Historical Association* 6, no. 3 (Summer 1965): 273–85.

Reynolds, David S. *Waking Giant: America in the Age of Jackson*. New York: Harper Perennial, 2008.

Rieder, Milton P., Jr., and Norma Gaudet Rieder, eds. *The Crew and Passenger Registration Lists of the Seven Acadian Expeditions of 1785: A Listing by Family Groups of the Refugee Acadians Who Migrated from France to Spanish Louisiana in 1785*. Metairie, La.: printed by the authors, 1965.

Roberts, Rita. *Evangelism and the Politics of Reform in Northern Black Thought, 1778–1863*. Baton Rouge: Louisiana State University Press, 2010.

Robertson, Ritchie. *The Enlightenment: The Pursuit of Happiness, 1680–1790*. New York: Harper, 2021.

Rogers, Molly. *Delia's Tears: Race, Science, and Photography in Nineteenth-Century America*. New Haven, Conn.: Yale University Press, 2010.

Rosenthal, Debra J. *Race Mixture in Nineteenth Century U.S. and Spanish American Fictions: Gender, Culture, and Nation Building*. Chapel Hill: University of North Carolina Press, 2004.

Rothman, Adam. *Slave Country: American Expansion and the Origins of the Deep South*. Cambridge, Mass.: Harvard University Press, 2005.

Rothman, Joshua D. *Flush Times and Fever Dreams: A Story of Capitalism and Slavery in the Age of Jackson*. Athens: University of Georgia Press, 2012.

Roussève, Charles Barthelemy. *The Negro in Louisiana: Aspects of His History and His Literature*. New Orleans: Xavier University Press, 1937.

Rout, Leslie B., Jr. *The African Experience in Spanish America: 1502 to the Present Day*. New York: Cambridge University Press, 1976.

Rowland, Dunbar, ed. *The Official Letter Books of W. C. C. Claiborne, 1801–1816*. 6 vols. Jackson, Miss.: State Department of Archives and History, 1917.

Royster, Charles. *A Revolutionary People at War: The Continental Army and American Character, 1775–1783*. Chapel Hill: University of North Carolina Press, 1980.

Rush, Benjamin. *Sixteen Introductory Lectures, to Courses of Lectures upon the Institutes and Practices of Medicine*. Philadelphia: Bradford and Innskeep, 1811.

Rushforth, Brett. *Bonds of Alliance: Indigenous and Atlantic Slaveries in New France*. Chapel Hill: University of North Carolina Press for the Omohundro Institute of Early American History and Culture, 2012.

Russell, Benjamin. "Era of Good Feelings," *Boston Columbian Centinel*, July 12, 1817.

Russell, John H. *The Free Negro in Virginia, 1619–1865*. Baltimore: Johns Hopkins University Press, 1913.

Sacher, John M. *A Perfect War of Politics: Parties, Politicians, and Democracy in Louisiana, 1824–1861*. Baton Rouge: Louisiana State University Press, 2003.

Saether, Steinar A. "Bourbon Absolutism and Marriage Reform in Late Colonial Spanish America." *Americas* 59, no. 4 (April 2003): 475–509.

Sala-Molins, Louis. *Le code noir, ou le calvaire de Canaan*. Paris: Presses Universitaires de France, 1987.

Sanborn, Franklin Benjamin. *Dr. S. G. Howe, the Philanthropist*. New York: Funk and Wagnalls, 1891.

Schafer, Judith Kelleher. *Becoming Free, Remaining Free: Manumission and Enslavement in New Orleans, 1846–1862*. Baton Rouge: Louisiana State University Press, 2003.

Schwarz, Philip J. *Migrants against Slavery: Virginians and the Nation.* Charlottesville: University Press of Virginia, 2001.
Schweninger, Loren. "Antebellum Free Persons of Color in Postbellum Louisiana." *Louisiana History: Journal of the Louisiana Historical Association* 30, no. 4 (Autumn 1989): 345–64.
———. "Black-Owned Businesses in the South, 1790–1880." *Business History Review* 63, no. 1 (Spring 1989).
———. *Black Property Owners in the South, 1790–1915.* Urbana: University of Illinois Press, 1990.
———, ed. *From Tennessee Slave to St. Louis Entrepreneur: The Autobiography of James Thomas.* Columbia: University of Missouri Press, 1984.
———. "A Negro Sojourner in Antebellum New Orleans." *Louisiana History: Journal of the Louisiana Historical Association* 20, no. 3 (Summer 1979): 305–14.
———. "Prosperous Blacks in the South, 1790–1880." *American Historical Review* 95, no. 1 (February 1990): 31–56.
———. "Socioeconomic Dynamics among the Gulf Creole Populations: The Antebellum and Civil War Years." In Dormon, *Creoles of Color*, 51–66.
Scott, James Brown, ed., *Cases of International Law.* St. Paul, Minn.: West Publishing Company, 1922.
Scott, Rebecca J. *Degrees of Freedom: Louisiana and Cuba after Slavery.* Cambridge, Mass.: Harvard University Press, 2005.
Scott, Rebecca J., and Jean M. Hébrard. *Freedom Papers: An Atlantic Odyssey in the Age of Emancipation.* Cambridge, Mass.: Harvard University Press, 2012.
Scott, Sterling C. "Aspects of the Liberian Colonization Movement in Louisiana." Master's thesis, Tulane University, 1952.
Secord, James A. *Victorian Sensation: The Extraordinary Publication, Reception, and Secret Authorship of "Vestiges of the Natural History of Creation."* Chicago: University of Chicago Press, 2000.
Seed, Patricia. *American Pentimento: The Invention of Indians and the Pursuit of Riches.* Minneapolis: University of Minnesota Press, 2001.
Séjour, Victor. *Les volontaires de 1815; drame en cinq actes et quatorze tableaux.* Paris: Michel Lévy et Frères, 1862.
Sens, Angelie. "Dutch Debates on Overseas Man and his World, 1770–1820." In *Colonial Empires Compared: Britain and the Netherlands, 1750–1850*, edited by Bob Moore and Henk van Nierop, 77–93. Burlington, Vt.: Ashgate, 2003.
Shaik, Fatima. "Fatima Shaik: Translation, Semantics, and Race." *PEN America*, February 6, 2012. www.pen.org/fatima-shaik-translation-semantics-and-race.
Sharfstein, Daniel J. *The Invisible Line: Three American Families and the Secret Journey from Black to White.* New York: Penguin, 2011.
Sheperd, Samuel, ed. *Statutes at Large of Virginia.* Vol. 1. Richmond, Va.: Samuel Sheperd, 1836.
Shick, Tom W. *Behold the Promised Land: A History of Afro-American Settler Society in Nineteenth-Century Liberia.* Baltimore: Johns Hopkins University Press, 1980.

———, comp. and ed. *Roll of Emigrants to Liberia, 1820–1843*. Online database. https://www.disc.wisc.edu/archive/Liberia/liberia_pubs.html.

Shuffelton, Frank, ed. *A Mixed Race: Ethnicity in Early America*. New York: Oxford University Press, 1993.

Sidbury, James. *Ploughshares into Swords: Race Relations, Rebellion, and Identity in Gabriel's Virginia, 1730–1810*. New York: Cambridge University Press, 1997.

Singh, Joshua A., and Gayle Y. Iwamasa. "Biracial." In *Encyclopedia of Multicultural Psychology*, edited by Yo Jackson, 72–76. Thousand Oaks, Calif.: Sage, 2006.

Sinha, Manisha. *The Slave's Cause: A History of Abolition*. New Haven, Conn.: Yale University Press, 2016.

Smith, Rogers M. *Civic Ideals: Conflicting Visions of Citizenship in U.S. History*. New Haven, Conn.: Yale University Press, 1997.

Sollors, Werner. *Beyond Ethnicity: Consent and Descent in American Culture*. New York: Oxford University Press, 1986.

———. *Neither Black nor White Yet Both: Thematic Explorations of Interracial Literature*. Cambridge, Mass.: Harvard University Press, 1997.

Soulé, Leon Cyprian. *The Know Nothing Party in New Orleans: A Reappraisal*. Baton Rouge: Louisiana Historical Association, 1961.

Sparks, Randy J. *Africans in the Old South: Mapping Exceptional Lives across the Atlantic World*. Cambridge, Mass.: Harvard University Press, 2016.

Spear, Jennifer M. *Race, Sex, and Social Order in Early New Orleans*. Baltimore: Johns Hopkins University Press, 2009.

Spencer, C. A. "Black Benevolent Societies and the Development of Black Insurance Companies in Nineteenth Century Alabama." *Phylon* 46, no. 3 (3rd Quarter 1985): 251–61.

Sperber, Jonathan. *The European Revolutions, 1848–1851*. New York: Cambridge University Press, 1994.

Spinner, Jeff. *The Boundaries of Citizenship: Race, Ethnicity, and Nationality in the Liberal State*. Baltimore: Johns Hopkins University Press, 1994.

Spooner, Matthew. "Freedom, Reenslavement, and Movement in the Revolutionary South." In Stewart and Marks, *Race and Nation in the Age of Emancipations*, 13–34.

Stanton, William. *The Leopard's Spots: Scientific Attitudes toward Race in America, 1815–59*. Chicago: University of Chicago Press, 1960.

Staudenraus, P. J. *The African Colonization Movement, 1816–1865*. New York: Columbia University Press, 1961.

Stephens, Lester D. *Science, Race, and Religion in the American South: John Bachman and the Charleston Circle of Naturalists, 1815–1895*. Chapel Hill: University of North Carolina Press, 2000.

Sterkx, H. E. *The Free Negro in Ante-bellum Louisiana*. Rutherford, N.J.: Fairleigh Dickinson University Press, 1972.

Stevenson, Brenda E. *Life in Black and White: Family Community in the Slave South*. New York: Oxford University Press, 1997.

Stewart, Whitney Nell, and John Garrison Marks, eds. *Race and Nation in the Age of Emancipations*. Athens: University of Georgia Press, 2018.

Sublette, Ned. *The World That Made New Orleans: From Spanish Silver to Congo Square.* Chicago: Lawrence Hill Books, 2008.

Sumpter, Amy R. "Segregation of the Free People of Color and the Construction of Race in Antebellum New Orleans." *Southern Geographer* 48, no. 1 (May 2008): 19–37.

Sussman, Robert Wald. *The Myth of Race: The Troubling Persistence of an Unscientific Idea.* Cambridge, Mass.: Harvard University Press, 2014.

Sweet, John Wood. *Bodies Politic: Negotiating Race in the American North, 1730–1830.* Philadelphia: University of Pennsylvania Press, 2003.

Syrett, Harold C. ed. *The Papers of Alexander Hamilton.* Vol. 1, *1768–1778.* New York: Columbia University Press, 1961.

Takaki, Ronald. *Iron Cages: Race and Culture in 19th-Century America.* New York: Oxford University Press, 1990.

Tansey, Richard. "Out-of-State Free Blacks in Late Antebellum New Orleans." *Louisiana History: Journal of the Louisiana Historical Association* 22, no. 4 (Autumn 1981): 369–86.

Taylor, Alan. *American Colonies.* New York: Viking, 2001.

———. *The Civil War of 1812: American Citizens, British Subjects, Irish Rebels, and Indian Allies.* New York: Alfred A. Knopf, 2010.

Terrell, Mary. *The Man Who Flattened the Earth: Maupertuis and the Sciences in the Enlightenment.* Chicago: University of Chicago Press, 2002.

Thompson, Shirley Elizabeth. *Exiles at Home: The Struggle to Become American in Creole New Orleans.* Cambridge, Mass.: Harvard University Press, 2009.

Thorpe, Francis Newton, ed. and comp. *The Federal and State Constitutions[,] Colonial Charters, and Other Organic Laws of the States, Territories, and Colonies Now and Heretofore Forming the United States of America.* Vol. 5. Washington: United States Government Printing Office, 1909.

Tinker, Edward Larocque. *Les écrits de langue française en Louisiane au XIX siècle: Essais biographiques et bibliographiques.* Paris: Librairie Ancienne Honoré Champion, 1932.

Toledano, Roulhac. *The National Trust Guide to New Orleans: The Definitive Guide to Architectural and Cultural Treasures.* New York: John Wiley and Sons, 1996.

Toledano, Roulhac, Mary Louise Christovich, Samuel Wilson Jr., and Sally K. Evans. *New Orleans Architecture.* Vol. 4, *The Creole Faubourgs.* Gretna, La.: Pelican, 1974.

Toledano, Roulhac, and Mary Louise Christovich. *New Orleans Architecture.* Vol. 6, *Faubourg Tremé and the Bayou Road.* Gretna, La.: Pelican, 1980.

Tomek, Beverly C. *Colonization and Its Discontents: Emancipation, Emigration, and Antislavery in Antebellum Pennsylvania.* New York: New York University Press, 2011.

Toplin, Robert Brent. "Between Black and White: Attitudes toward Southern Mulattoes, 1830–1861." *Journal of Southern History* 45, no. 2 (May 1979): 185–200.

Tregle, Joseph, Jr. "Creoles and Americans." In Hirsch and Logsdon, *Creole New Orleans,* 131–85.

———. "Early New Orleans Society: A Reappraisal." *Journal of Southern History* 18, no. 1 (February 1952): 20–36.

———. *Louisiana in the Age of Jackson: A Clash of Cultures and Personalities*. Baton Rouge: Louisiana State University Press, 1999.
Twinam, Ann. *Public Lives, Private Secrets: Gender, Honor, Sexuality, and Illegitimacy in Colonial Spanish America*. Stanford, Calif.: Stanford University Press, 1999.
Tyler-McGraw, Marie. *An African Republic: Black and White Virginians in the Making of Liberia*. Chapel Hill: University of North Carolina Press, 2007.
Unger, Harlow Giles. *The Last Founding Father: James Monroe and a Nation's Call to Greatness*. Philadelphia: Da Capo, 2009.
Usner, Daniel H., Jr. *American Indians in Early New Orleans: From Calumet to Raquette*. Baton Rouge: Louisiana State University Press, 2018.
———. "'The Facility Offered by the Country': The Creolization of Agriculture in the Lower Mississippi Valley." In *Creolization in the Americas*, edited by David Buisseret and Steven G. Reinhardt, 35–62. Austin: University of Texas Press, 2000.
———. "From African Captivity to American Slavery: The Introduction of Black Laborers to Colonial Louisiana." *Louisiana History* 20, no. 1 (Winter 1979): 25–48.
———. *Indians, Settlers, and Slaves in a Frontier Exchange Economy: The Lower Mississippi Valley before 1785*. Chapel Hill: University of North Carolina Press, 1992.
Valdés, Dennis Nodin. "The Decline of the *Sociedad de Castas* in Mexico City." PhD diss., University of Michigan–Anne Arbor, 1976.
Valsania, Maurizio. *The Limits of Optimism: Thomas Jefferson's Dualistic Enlightenment*. Charlottesville: University of Virginia Press, 2011.
Van Ravensway, Charles. *Saint Louis: An Informal History of the City and its People, 1764–1865*. St. Louis: Missouri Historical Society Press, 1991.
Van Ruymbeke, Bertrand. *Histoire des États-Unis: De 1492 à nos jours*. Paris: Tallandier, 2018.
Vardi, Liana. *The Physiocrats and the World of the Enlightenment*. New York: Cambridge University Press, 2012.
Vento, Arnoldo C. *Mestizo: The History, Culture and Politics of the Mexican and the Chicano*. Lanham, Md.: University Press of America, 1998.
Vernet, Julien. *Strangers on Their Native Soil: Opposition to United States' Governance in Louisiana's Orleans Territory, 1803–1809*. Jackson: University Press of Mississippi, 2013.
Vidal, Cécile. *Caribbean New Orleans: Empire, Race, and the Making of a Slave Society*. Chapel Hill: University of North Carolina Press for the Omohundro Institute of Early American History and Culture, 2019.
———, ed. *Louisiana: Crossroads of the Atlantic World*. Philadelphia: University of Pennsylvania Press, 2014.
Von Daacke, Kirt. *Freedom Has a Face: Race, Identity, and Community in Jefferson's Virginia*. Charlottesville: University of Virginia Press, 2012.
Voss, Barbara L. *The Archaeology of Ethnogenesis: Race and Sexuality in Colonial San Francisco*. Berkeley: University of California Press, 2008.
Waldstreicher, David. *In the Midst of Perpetual Fetes: The Making of American Nationalism, 1790–1820*. Chapel Hill: University of Chapel Hill Press, 1997.

Walker, Juliet E. K. *The History of Black Business in America: Capitalism, Race, Entrepreneurship*. 2 vols. Chapel Hill: University of North Carolina Press, 2009.

Walsh, Richard, ed. *The Writings of Christopher Gadsden*. Columbia: University of South Carolina Press, 1966.

Watts, Steven. *The Republic Reborn: War and the Making of Liberal America, 1790–1820*. Baltimore: Johns Hopkins University Press, 1987.

Weddle, Robert S. *The French Thorn: Rival Explorers in the Spanish Sea, 1682–1762*. College Station: Texas A&M University Press, 1991.

Wegmann, Andrew N. "Christian Community and the Development of an Americo-Liberian Identity, 1824–1878." Master's thesis, Louisiana State University, 2010.

———. "To Fashion Ourselves Citizens: Colonization, Belonging, and the Problem of Nationhood in the Atlantic South, 1829–1859." In Stewart and Marks, *Race and Nation in the Age of Emancipations*, 35–52.

———. "'Upon This Rock We Shall Build Our Homes': The Development of the Americo-Liberian Community, 1822–1980." In *Back to Africa*. Vol. 2, *The Ideology and Practice of the African Returnee Phenomenon from the Caribbean and North-America to Africa*, edited by Kwesi Kwaa Prah, 60–77. Cape Town: Centre for Advanced Studies of African Society, 2012.

———. "The Vitriolic Blood of a Negro: The Development of Racial Identity and Creole Elitism in New Spain and Spanish Louisiana, 1763–1803." *Journal of Transatlantic Studies* 13, no. 2 (Autumn 2015): 204–25.

Welch, Kimberly M. *Black Litigants in the Antebellum American South*. Chapel Hill: University of North Carolina Press, 2018.

Wells, Jonathan Daniel. *The Origins of the Southern Middle Class, 1800–1861*. Chapel Hill: University of North Carolina Press, 2004.

Wells, Jonathan Daniel, and Jennifer R. Green, eds. *The Southern Middle Class in the Long Nineteenth Century*. Baton Rouge: Louisiana State University Press, 2011.

West, Emily. *Family or Freedom: People of Color in the Antebellum South*. Lexington: University Press of Kentucky, 2012.

Whayne, Jeannie. *Delta Empire: Lee Wilson and the Transformation of Agriculture in the New South*. Baton Rouge: Louisiana State University Press, 2011.

Wheeler, Roxann. *The Complexion of Race: Categories of Difference in Eighteenth-Century British Culture*. Philadelphia: University of Pennsylvania Press, 2000.

White, Ashli. *Encountering Revolution: Haiti and the Making of the Early Republic*. Baltimore: Johns Hopkins University Press, 2010.

White, Richard. *The Middle Ground: Indians, Empires, and Republics in the Great Lakes Region, 1650–1815*. New York: Cambridge University Press, 1991.

White, Sophie. *Wild Frenchmen and Frenchified Indians: Material Culture and Race in Colonial Louisiana*. Philadelphia: University of Pennsylvania Press, 2012.

Whitten, David O. *Andrew Durnford: A Black Sugar Planter in the Antebellum South*. New Brunswick, N.J.: Transaction, 1995.

———. "Slave Buying in 1835 Virginia as Revealed by Letters of a Louisiana Negro Sugar Planter." *Louisiana History* 11, no. 3 (Summer 1971).

Wikramanayake, Marina. *A World in Shadow: The Free Black in Antebellum South Carolina*. Columbia: University of South Carolina Press, 1973.

Wilentz, Sean. *Chants Democratic: New York City and the Rise of the American Working Class, 1788–1850*. New York: Oxford University Press, 1984.

———. *The Rise of American Democracy: Jefferson to Lincoln*. New York: W. W. Norton, 2005.

Willey, Nathan. "Education of the Colored Population of Louisiana." *Harper's New Monthly Magazine*, vol. 33 (July 1866): 244–50.

Williamson, Joel. *New People: Miscegenation and Mulattoes in the United States*. Baton Rouge: Louisiana State University Press, 1995.

Willoughby, Urmi Engineer. *Yellow Fever, Race, and Ecology in Nineteenth-Century New Orleans*. Baton Rouge: Louisiana State University Press, 2017.

Wilson, Carol. *The Two Lives of Sally Miller: A Case of Mistaken Racial Identity in Antebellum New Orleans*. New Brunswick, N.J.: Rutgers University Press, 2007.

Wilson, James. *Considerations on the Nature and Extent of Legislative Authority of the British Parliament*. Philadelphia: W. and T. Bradford, 1774.

Wilson, Judith. "Optical Illusions: Images of Miscegenation in Nineteenth- and Twentieth-Century American Art." *American Art* 5, no. 3 (Summer 1991): 88–107.

Winch, Julie. *The Clamorgans: One Family's History of Race in America*. New York: Hill and Wang, 2011.

———, ed. *The Colored Aristocracy of St. Louis by Cyprian Clamorgan*. Columbia: University of Missouri Press, 1999.

———, ed. *The Elite of Our People: Joseph Willson's Sketches of Black Upper-Class Life in Antebellum Philadelphia*. University Park: Pennsylvania State University Press, 2000.

———. *Philadelphia's Black Elite: Activism, Accommodation, and the Struggle for Autonomy, 1787–1848*. Philadelphia: Temple University Press, 1988.

Wingfield, Roland. "The Creoles of Color: A Study of a New Orleans Subculture." Master's thesis, Louisiana State University, 1961.

Wokler, Robert. "Ideology and the Origins of Social Science," In *The Cambridge History of Eighteenth-Century Political Thought*, edited by Mark Goldie and Robert Wokler, 688–710. New York: Cambridge University Press, 2006.

Wolf, Eva Sheppard. *Almost Free: A Story about Family and Race in Antebellum Virginia*. Athens: University of Georgia Press, 2012.

———. *Race and Liberty in the New Nation: Emancipation in Virginia from the Revolution to Nat Turner's Rebellion*. Baton Rouge: Louisiana State University Press, 2006.

Wood, Gordon S. *The Radicalism of the American Revolution*. New York: Vintage, 1991.

Woodson, Carter G. *The Story of the Negro Retold*. 4th ed. Washington, D.C.: Associated Publishers, 1959.

Wright, Ben. *Bonds of Salvation: How Christianity Inspired and Limited American Abolitionism*. Baton Rouge: Louisiana State University Press, 2020.

Wyse, Akintola J. G. *The Krio of Sierra Leone: An Interpretive History*. Washington, D.C.: Howard University Press, 1991.

Zack, Naomi. *Race and Mixed Race*. Philadelphia: Temple University Press, 1993.
Zackodnik, Teresa C. "Fixing the Color Line: The Mulatto, Southern Courts, and Racial Identity." *American Quarterly* 53, no. 3 (September 2001): 420–51.
———. *The Mulatta and the Politics of Race*. Jackson: University Press of Mississippi, 2004.
Zipf, Karen L. *Labor of Innocents: Forced Apprenticeships in North Carolina, 1715–1919*. Baton Rouge: Louisiana State University Press, 2005.

INDEX

abolitionism, 127, 136
Adams, John, 94
Affranchis, 24, 27–28, 29
Agassiz, Louis, 127, 128–130, 193n41
amalgamation, 8, 127–128, 129–131
American Colonization Society (ACS), 119–120, 121–122, 130–131, 132, 133–134, 135–136, 137, 139, 144; and Louisiana Colonization Society, 140–141, 199n114
American Revolution, 69, 85, 92, 94, 103, 105, 121, 171n29, 175n91
American School of Ethnography. *See* ethnography
Americanos, 55; revolt of, 37–39, 55, 159n25; in Sistema de Castas, 35–39
Anderson, Joseph, 77
Anglo-Saxons, 127–128; in American national identity, 118–119, 125
Aubri, Pierre, 56
Aurélie, Marie Françoise, 56
Azémare, Geneviève. *See* Dolliole, Geneviève
Azémare, Louis, 52

Bachman, John, 128, 193n41
Bampfield, George, 103
Barrère, Pierre, 17, 21, 36
Batecave, Anne, 89
Battle of New Orleans, 60, 87, 90–91, 112–113, 114, 121, 137, 143
Battles, Robert, 70, 71, 73, 175n91
Beaird, Enoch G., 110
Beauregard, Martin Barthelemy Toutant, 53
Beauregard, P. G. T., 53
Bedon, George, 103
Beltier, Joni, 141
Benson, Stephen Allen, 135–136
Berlin, Ira, 3–4

"blacks," xvi, 3–5, 19, 104, 107, 120, 129, 135–136; in Enlightenment racial science, 19–20; in ethnology, 130–131; in law, 22–25; in New Orleans, 75–76, 100, 145; as slaves, 9, 24, 26, 64–65, 79, 100–101; in United States, 64–65, 75–76, 78–79, 100, 117
Blanc, Luis Antoine, 52
Blandin, Jean, 1–3, 4, 9
Blumenbach, Johann Friedrich, 69
Boisdoré, François, 8, 63, 64, 86; as businessman, 61–62, 84, 102; as Creole, 61–62, 72, 90, 113; militia membership, 60–62, 143; reputation, 60–61, 83, 86, 126, 137; social network, 102, 113
Boisdoré, Isabel, 57
Boisdoré, Julia, 57
Boré, Don Alexander, 51
Boré, Joseph, 51
Brown Elite, 91, 93, 103–105
Brown Fellowship Society, 91, 103–105, 106, 108, 109, 111, 116, 125
Brown, Sarah, 89, 198n101
Brunet, Ernest, 142
Buffon, Georges-Louis Leclerc, Comte de, 23, 36, 151n41

Cabildo, 33, 46–47, 49
Camps, Julia, 53
Cardozo, Henry, 111, 117
Carrière, Marie Thérèze, 57
Carrière, Noël, 57, 58, 165n110
Casenave, Joseph, 51
Casenave, Pierre, 61, 84, 102, 112, 168n5
Catalina, Juana, 47
Catholic Church, 14, 48, 49, 97, 105–107, 174n72
Catholicism, 140; Creoles of color and, 90–91, 96–97, 121, 140–143, 144; as identity, 49, 54, 90–91, 96–97, 121, 125, 138, 140–143, 144

Cattle, William, 103
Cazelar, Adelaïde, 55
Cazelar, Isabelle, 55
Chalmette. *See* Battle of New Orleans
Charles I, King (Spain), 5, 36
Charles III, King (Spain), 48
Charleston, S.C., 7, 87, 91–92, 93, 95–97, 98, 130, 132; free people of color in, 103–105, 108, 109–111, 115; racial legislation, 124–125
Charleston Library Society, 98
Charlevoix, Pierre-François-Xavier de, 19, 21
Cheval, Luison, 53
Cheval, Maria Theresa, 52
Cheval, Marie Adelaïde, 55
Cheval, Murville, 84
Cheval, Paul, 52
Cheval, Prudence, 52
citizenship: Calvin's Case and, 74, 171n36; in colonial France, 13, 65; in colonial Spain, 36, 65–66; debate over, in Louisiana Territory, 61–62, 73–74, 75, 82–87, 90–91; denizenship and, 63, 65, 71–72, 126, 144; in individual U.S. states, 66–68, 69, 73, 75; in Liberia, 134–135, 137; in New Orleans, 75–76, 79, 82–87, 121, 137–138; reputation and, 106, 110, 126; in United States, 9–10, 60–72, 75, 82, 100, 118, 121, 122, 137; virtue as requirement of, 68–69, 72–73, 97, 111–112, 134; whiteness and, 9–10, 65, 75, 79, 110, 126
Civil War, 1–2, 3, 91, 96, 99, 118, 122, 125, 139, 143, 144
Claiborne, William C. C., 64, 76, 79, 84–87
Clark, Emily, 80
class, 3, 15–16, 19, 141–142; Creoles of color and, 84–87, 105–108, 112–116, 118; as identity, 72–75, 84–85, 91–93, 95–99, 130, 132; as performance, 95–99, 102–108, 109–116; race and, 3, 8, 12–13, 40–41, 52, 84, 91–93, 102–108, 118, 122–127, 129–130, 135–136; Sistema de Castas and, 40–41, 52, 55
Clay, Henry, 119
Clionian Debating Society (Charleston, S.C.), 109–112
coartación, 35, 46–47, 51–52
Code Noir of 1685, 22
Code Noir of 1724, 10, 19, 21–24, 25–29, 45–46; Article 6 of, 23–24, 26–27
colonization, 118–122, 130–131, 132, 133–134, 136, 139–141, 144

Colson, William N., 76–77, 78, 79, 132–133
Colvis, Julien, 138
Confederate States of America, 1, 2, 53, 88, 142
Congo Square, 47
Cordevoille, Etienne, 89, 107, 137–138, 139
Creole, 1–2, 3, 4, 30–31; definition of, 2–3
Creoles of color, 4, 8–9, 32–35, 83–87, 89–91, 99, 101, 105–107, 112–117, 120–122, 124; as American, 1–3, 121–122, 143–145; citizenship and, 60–64, 84–86, 90–91, 106, 118, 121–122, 137–138; emigration and, 137–141, 143–144; identity of, 1–3, 30–31, 48–49, 141–142; New Orleans as "home," 1–2, 6–7, 32–33, 137–143, 144–145; under Spanish, 50–58; women's role in community, 12–13, 30–31
Cromwell, Oliver, 111
Cuba, 47, 84, 90, 93, 114
Curse of Ham, 20–21

D'Aquin, Louis, 113
Daunoy, Louis, 113
Dawdy, Shannon, 28
De Gobineau, Arthur, 130
De Pauw, Cornelius, 22–23, 27
Dearborn, Henry, 75–76
Dereef, Joseph, 109, 117, 125, 130
Dereef, Richard, 109
Destrehan, Jean-Baptiste, 47
Dolliole, François, 53
Dolliole, Geneviève, 10–13, 31, 33, 52–53, 72
Dolliole, Jean Louis, 8, 10, 50, 52, 64; militia membership, 32–34, 58, 86; social network and reputation, 83–89 passim, 91, 102, 113, 126, 137, 143
Dolliole, Jean-François, 10
Dolliole, Joseph, 10, 33–34, 52, 102, 137
Dolliole, Louis, 10–13, 33
Dolliole, Marie Françoise, 10, 11
Dolliole, Rosette (alias Madeleine), 10, 11
Domínguez, Virginia, 29
Donato, Lucien, 139, 140, 143
Dorcas Society, 98
Dorville, François, 33, 57–58
Dubos, Abbé Jean-Baptiste, 20
Ducasse, Adolphe-Joseph, 223
Duhart, Louis, 142
Dumanoir, Jean-Baptiste Faucon, 17–18
Dumas, Joseph, 138
Durnford, Andrew, 99–102, 117

INDEX   235

Éduary, Cécile (Lacroix), 102
Edwards, Laura, 71, 79
emancipation, 22, 28, 47, 77, 78, 119, 126
engagés, 18–19
Erskine, William, 101
Escoffié, François, 107, 124, 130, 137
ethnography, 3, 9, 127–131, 135–136
Eureka Colony, 139–142, 143, 144; creole students' perception of, 141–142

fashion, 89, 92, 102, 114, 116, 132, 141
Faubourg Marigny, 11, 89
Feijoo, Benito, 42–43
Ferdinand IV, King (Spain), 44
Forgason, Charles, 8, 70, 71, 73, 79, 126
Fortier, Michel, 73, 74, 106
Fouché, Joseph, 84
Fouché, Louis Nelson, 107, 121–122; Eureka Colony and, 139–141, 142, 143
Foy, Florville, 114
free people of color: in colonial France, 5, 23; in colonial Spain, 5–6, 46, 56; elite, 99–101, 131, 134, 142; as "free black"/"free Negro" in historiography, 3–5; in French Louisiana, 5, 23–28, 29, 30; Jefferson on, 79, 81–82, 87, 118–119; law and, 23, 76–78, 82–83, 109, 118, 122–125, 129–130, 137; in Louisiana, 140–141; in Louisiana Territory, 6, 63–65, 73–76, 79–80, 82–87, 90; middle-class, 2–3, 8–9, 102–108, 109–117, 120–122, 124–125, 137, 140, 141; militia/military service and, 29–30, 60–63, 69–70, 76, 84–87, 90–91, 103, 137; in New Orleans, Louisiana, 7, 105–108, 121–122, 124, 136–137, 143–145; public perceptions of, 23, 71, 75, 78, 83, 108, 118–119, 120–122, 124–127; in Spanish Louisiana, 5, 30, 50–53, 54, 56; in United States, 2, 69–71, 76–77, 78, 87, 90–91, 103, 121–122, 129–130
Freetown, Sierra Leone, 133

Gage, Thomas, 41–42
Gayarré, Charles, 15, 126, 144
gens de couleur libre, 50–51. *See also* Creoles of color
George III, King (Britain), 93
Gliddon, George, 127; *Types of Mankind*, 130
Gravier, Henri, 15
Grégoire, Armand, 141
Grima, Félix, 89

Haiti, 83, 84, 90, 93, 112–113, 114, 122, 140
Hamilton, Alexander, 68
Harriet (ship), 100–101, 132
Holloway, Richard, 109, 126
Hugo, Victor, 138
hybridity (theory), 128–130

immigrants, 6, 95–97, 105, 125–126
Institution Catholique des Orphelins Indigent, 106–107, 136, 141

Jackson, Andrew, 60–65, 86, 87, 90, 121, 137
Jefferson, Thomas, 64, 66, 72, 74–75, 87, 118–119; race and, 8, 27, 79–82, 100, 126–127
Jeffersonianism, 68, 87, 142

King, John, 124
Know-Nothing Party, 125–126

Lacroix, Cécile, 102
Lacroix, François, 88–91, 102, 116–117, 137–139; as businessman, 89, 107, 137; as Creole, 89–90, 116, 137–138; reputation, 83–84, 88–89, 113, 116, 138–139, 140, 141; thoughts on emigration, 121–122, 137–138; wealth, 89–90, 93, 137
Lacroix, François Edgar, 139
Lacroix, Jean, 89
Lacroix, Julien, 88, 90, 114
Lafayette, Marquis de, 137
Lafon, Barthélémy, 73, 75, 106
Lafon, Thomy, 73, 83–84, 89
Lamartine, Alphonse de, 138
Lanusse, Armand, 112, 117; as artisan and poet, 114–116, 136–137; on colonization and emigration, 121–122, 136–138, 139–141, 142, 143, 144; reputation and social standing, 140–141, 142
Le Cat, Claude-Nicolas, 22–23, 27
Le Page du Pratz, Antoine-Simon, 19
Le Porche, Vincent, 28–29
Legare, Jacob, 111
Legoaster, Erasme, 138
Les cenelles, 115, 136
Leveillé, Joseph, 57
Liberia, 77, 101, 120, 122, 132–136, 137–138, 139, 141; Americo-Liberians in, 136, 144, 196n78; mulattoes in, 130–131, 135–136, 140, 144
Líma, Peru, 41
Lincoln, Abraham, 1–2, 118

Livingston, Edward, 73
Livingston, Robert, 82
Louisiana Colonization Society (LCS), 140–141, 199nn113–114
Louisiana Native Guards, 88, 142, 197n91
Louisiana Purchase, 5–6, 61, 63–64, 65–66, 67, 72, 74–75; Treaty of 1803, 82–83, 90–91

Madison, James, 64, 82, 86
Magdalena (slave), 51
Malpighi, Marcello, 17
manumission, 5, 28–29
Marie Louise (slave), 28–29
Marigny, Bernard, 89
Mazange, Léonard, 53, 166n119
McDonogh, John, 73, 100, 101; friendship with Durnford, 100–102; support of Louisiana Colonization Society, 199n113
Meckel, Johann, 17, 22–23, 36
Mercer, Charles Fenton, 119
métis(se), 28
Mexico: as destination for emigration, 122, 139–140; Eureka Colony in, 139–142; interracial marriage in, 40; Sistema de Castas in, 36–38, 43–44, 46, 49, 55–56
middle class, 132, 135, 137, 141; as public character and identity, 98–99, 102–105, 108–117; white urban, 92–97, 105–107. *See also* Creoles of color; free people of color: middle-class
miscegenation, 127–128, 129–130
Mitchell, James, 103
Mitchill, Samuel Latham, 73–74
Monroe, James, 82, 93–94
Monrovia, Liberia, 133, 135
Mordecai, Samuel, 94–95
Moreau, Manuel, 60, 62–63, 64, 83
morenos: freedmen, 51–52, 59; marriage and, 56–57; militia in Spanish New Orleans, 34, 57, 58, 84 171n29; in Sistema de Castas, 30–31, 35, 43–44, 45, 57, 59; slaves, 35
Morgan, Benjamin, 72–73, 75–76, 79
Morton, Samuel, 127, 129, 130
mulattoes: in Enlightenment racial science, 21–23; ethnography and, 3, 128–131, 135–136; under French (*mulâtres*), 3, 8, 10, 22, 26–30, 33–34, 45, 48, 54, 58–59; Jefferson on, 80–82, 126–127; in law, 26–27, 79, 121–122, 123; as leaders, 131, 132, 135–136, 140; in Louisiana Territory, 75–76, 79, 86; in Mexico, 139–140; in New Orleans, Louisiana, 7–9, 75–76, 78–79, 126–127, 140, 141, 144–145; under Sistema de Castas (*mulatos*), 8–9, 41–44, 48, 55–56, 58–59; as targets for colonization, 135–136, 140–141, 144; in United States, 3, 8–9, 76–77, 78–79, 80, 81, 122, 126–127, 128–130, 136, 144
Mutual Relief and Friendly Society (Alexandria, Va.), 108

Napoleon Bonaparte, 111, 114
nationalism: in Liberia, 134–135, 139; in United States, 93–95, 102, 125–126, 134
negroes: in British North America, 26; in Enlightenment racial science, 17, 21–22, 27, 43–44, 91; in ethnography, 128, 130–131; under French (*nègres*), 4–5, 12, 17–18, 19–20, 22–23, 25–27, 29–30, 34, 44, 45; Jefferson on, 27, 80–82, 100, 118–119; in Liberia, 135–136; in New Orleans, 3, 25–27, 29, 76, 81, 87, 91, 116–117, 122, 145; public perception of, 91–92, 103–106, 108, 115–116, 119–121, 122–127, 129–130; in Saint Domingue, 53–54; under Sistema de Castas (*negros*), 5–6, 35, 41, 43–44, 57; as slaves, 14, 22; in state law (U.S.), 121–125, 129–130; in United States, 3, 64–65, 69–70, 76–80, 91, 118–120, 126–127, 135–136, 144, 145. *See also* free people of color
New Orleans, 2–3, 94, 95–96, 99, 120; in historiography, 4–8; as "home" of Creoles of color, 1–2, 8–9, 137–143, 144–145; as part of "circum-Caribbean," 4–5. *See also* Creoles of color; free people of color; mulattoes; negroes
Nicolas, Armand, 142
Niles, John Milton, 94
Norfolk Humane Association (Va.), 97–98, 117
Nott, Josiah, 127, 128–131, 132, 136

O'Crouley, Alonso, 43
O'Reilly, Alexander, 5–6

Pantalon, Marguerite, 53
Papaloapan River, 143
pardos: freedmen, 51–52; as identity, 33–35, 52, 53; marriage and, 53, 57–58; militia in Spanish New Orleans, 11, 32–34, 35, 56, 58; in Sistema de Castas, 8, 30, 43–44, 45, 49–50, 57. *See also* Creoles of color; free people of color; Sistema de Castas

Paris, France, 23, 89, 137, 138–139
Payne, James Spriggs, 133, 135, 136, 139
Pendleton, Edmund, 122
Pérault, Etienne, 142
personalism, 3, 38–39, 69–70, 73, 86–87, 122, 124, 144
Petersburg, Va., 76–77, 87, 120, 132, 133; free people of color in, 7, 77–79, 87, 120, 132
Picou, Lucien, 142
Pintard, John, 72
Planter elite, 99, 101
Prieto, Juan, 53
Protestantism, 125

quadroons, 8; under French (*quartéron[ne]s*), 10–11, 33, 45, 55, 58–59; Jefferson on, 80–81; in New Orleans, 7, 73–76, 79, 82, 84, 143; under Sistema de Castas (*cuarteróns*), 44–45, 48, 49, 51, 53, 55–56, 57; in United States, 3, 7, 8, 76, 80–81. *See also* Creoles of color; free people of color
Questy, Joanni, 114

race: class and, 2–3, 8, 12–13, 40–41, 84, 92–97, 108–117, 122–127, 129–131, 135–138, 141–142; identity and, 1–3, 30–31, 48–49, 54–56, 108–117, 137–140, 141–142, 144–145
racial science: Enlightenment and, 3, 17, 21–23, 27, 43–44, 91, 127; United States and, 3, 75–76, 91–92, 126–131, 135–136
Randolph, John, 119
Raphael (*nègre libre*), 17–18
respectability, 104–105
Rey, Barthélémy, 107
Rey, Henry Louis, 113
Richmond, Va., 7, 94–95, 96–97, 100, 120, 133
Rillieux, Norbert, 101–102
Roberts, Amelia Jenkins, 78, 132, 133
Roberts, Elizabeth (Yates), 132, 133
Roberts, Henry, 132, 133
Roberts, James, 77, 78
Roberts, John, 132, 133
Roberts, Joseph Jenkins, 8, 77, 78, 79, 121, 131, 132–136, 137, 139, 143, 144
Roberts, William, 132, 133
Rousseau, Jean, 113
Rousseau, Joseph Colastin, 113
Rush, Benjamin, 81–82
Russell, Benjamin, 93–94

Saint Domingue, 8, 84, 87, 90, 93; refugees from, 6, 90–93, 95–97. *See also* Haiti
Saint-Pierre, Michel, 114
Saltus, Samuel, 103
Second Great Awakening, 125
Séjour, Louis, 112–113
Séjour, Victor, 112, 114
Seven Years' War, 29
Sistema de Castas, 5–6; in colonial New Orleans, 37, 45–46, 48–50; inclusion of African blood, 41–42, 43–44; across Spanish American colonies, 41–43; structure and language of, 37–41
Slave Trade Act of 1819, 120
slavery, 110–111
social organizations, 91–92, 97–99, 103–108, 109–117, 119, 132
social standing, reputation as measurement of, 38–39, 69–73, 77–79, 84–87, 98–99, 102–106, 108–117, 120–122, 124–126, 135–138, 141–142. *See also* personalism
Société d'Economie et d'Assistance Mutuelle, 105–106, 107, 108, 113, 116, 141
Société des Artisans, 112–116
Soulié, Albin, 89
Soulié, Bernard, 102, 138
Soulié, Lucien, 89
Soulié, Norbert, 89
Soulié, Pierre, 113
Smilie, John, 74
St. Augustine, 20
St. Louis Cathedral (New Orleans), 26, 32, 55

Tampico, Mexico. *See* Eureka Colony
Thierry, Bazile, 113
Thierry, Camille, 113, 114
Toutant, Hortense, 56
Types of Mankind (Gliddon), 130

Ursuline nuns, 16

Valcour, Pierre, 141
Vasserot, Henry, 1, 142
Veracruz, Mexico. *See* Eureka Colony
Vidal, Cécile, 7, 29
Villanausa, Lucas, 28
virtue, 53–54, 63, 68, 69, 72–75, 82, 94, 105, 111, 134
Vivant, Charles, 53

War of 1812, 93, 101
Washington, Bushrod, 119
Washington, George, 111
Weston, Anthony, 93, 109
Whig Party, 125
Whitman, Walt, 127
Wilkinson, James, 86

Willson, Joseph, 91
Winch, Julie, 92

Yates, Beverly, 8, 133, 135, 136, 139, 143
Yates, Elizabeth, 132, 133
Young, William Proby, Jr., 135–136

RACE IN THE ATLANTIC WORLD, 1700–1900

The Hanging of Angélique: The Untold Story of Canadian Slavery and the Burning of Old Montréal
BY AFUA COOPER

Christian Ritual and the Creation of British Slave Societies, 1650–1780
BY NICHOLAS M. BEASLEY

African American Life in the Georgia Lowcountry: The Atlantic World and the Gullah Geechee
EDITED BY PHILIP MORGAN

The Horrible Gift of Freedom: Atlantic Slavery and the Representation of Emancipation
BY MARCUS WOOD

The Life and Letters of Philip Quaque, the First African Anglican Missionary
EDITED BY VINCENT CARRETTA AND TY M. REESE

In Search of Brightest Africa: Reimagining the Dark Continent in American Culture, 1884–1936
BY JEANNETTE EILEEN JONES

Contentious Liberties: American Abolitionists in Post-emancipation Jamaica, 1834–1866
BY GALE L. KENNY

We Are the Revolutionists: German-Speaking Immigrants and American Abolitionists after 1848
BY MISCHA HONECK

The American Dreams of John B. Prentis, Slave Trader
BY KARI J. WINTER

Missing Links: The African and American Worlds of R. L. Garner, Primate Collector
BY JEREMY RICH

Almost Free: A Story about Family and Race in Antebellum Virginia
BY EVA SHEPPARD WOLF

To Live an Antislavery Life: Personal Politics and the Antebellum Black Middle Class
BY ERICA L. BALL

Flush Times and Fever Dreams: A Story of Capitalism and Slavery in the Age of Jackson
BY JOSHUA D. ROTHMAN

Diplomacy in Black and White: John Adams, Toussaint Louverture, and Their Atlantic World Alliance
BY RONALD ANGELO JOHNSON

Enterprising Women: Gender, Race, and Power in the Revolutionary Atlantic
BY KIT CANDLIN AND CASSANDRA PYBUS

Eighty-Eight Years: The Long Death of Slavery in the United States, 1777–1865
BY PATRICK RAEL

Finding Charity's Folk: Enslaved and Free Black Women in Maryland
BY JESSICA MILLWARD

The Mulatta Concubine: Terror, Intimacy, Freedom, and Desire in the Black Transatlantic
BY LISA ZE WINTERS

The Politics of Black Citizenship: Free African Americans in the Mid-Atlantic Borderland, 1817–1863
BY ANDREW K. DIEMER

Punishing the Black Body: Marking Social and Racial Structures in Barbados and Jamaica
BY DAWN P. HARRIS

Race and Nation in the Age of Emancipations
EDITED BY WHITNEY NELL STEWART AND JOHN GARRISON MARKS

Vénus Noire: Black Women and Colonial Fantasies in Nineteenth-Century France
BY ROBIN MITCHELL

City of Refuge: Slavery and Petit Marronage in the Great Dismal Swamp, 1763–1856
BY MARCUS P. NEVIUS

An American Color: Race and Identity in New Orleans and the Atlantic World
BY ANDREW N. WEGMANN

www.ingramcontent.com/pod-product-compliance
Lightning Source LLC
Chambersburg PA
CBHW032213230426
43672CB00011B/2536